THE OFFICE OF GOVERNOR IN THE UNITED STATES

THE OFFICE OF GOVERNOR IN THE UNITED STATES

By COLEMAN B. RANSONE, Jr.
University of Alabama

1956
University of Alabama Press
UNIVERSITY, ALABAMA

DRAWER 2877
UNIVERSITY, ALABAMA

LIBRARY OF CONGRESS CATALOG
CARD NUMBER 56-7220

PRINTED AND BOUND
BY BIRMINGHAM PRINTING COMPANY

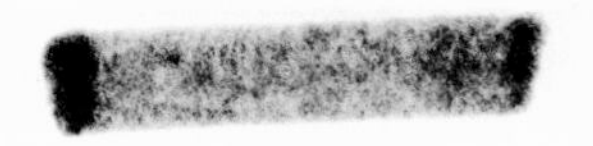

To

KATHERINE M. RANSONE

PREFACE

ONE OF THE CENTRAL problems of democratic government is to devise a system by which there can be strong leadership combined with real accountability to the electorate. We must have responsible government if we are to have democratic government, but we must also have government capable of decisive action if our democracy is to survive in a world of antagonistic and competitive governmental philosophies.

This problem is applicable to all three branches of government in our democracy, and it is applicable at all three levels—federal, state and local. In this book we are concerned with the executive branch at the state level and more especially with an analysis of the actual operations of the office of governor. The primary purpose of the study is to present a clearer picture of the governor's role in the day-to-day conduct of the business of state government. For this reason, the study concentrates on the functions of the governor as they are carried out in daily operations and on the staff which the governor needs for effective performance of his duties.

The chief executive of a state, however, does not operate in a vacuum, and the political setting in which he finds himself has an intimate and frequently a controlling influence upon the performance of his functions. This political setting is examined in the first section of the book as a background to the central discussion of the gubernatorial functions.

In addition, the final section of the book considers the important question of the governor's accountability to the electorate, the legislature and the courts. The American answer to the problem of strong leadership combined with real accountability is to provide for a popularly elected chief executive with broad political and administrative powers. This office has become the focus of leadership in our governments. The development of the Presidency is the most striking example of the application of this theory, but it is well illustrated also by the development of the office of governor in many of our states. An examination of the governorship should be useful in determining just how successfully this theory has worked out in practice when applied at the state level.

Because the study attempts to deal with the office of governor as it now exists, much of the data on which it is based was collected by the author in interviews with governors, members of the staff in the governors' offices, legislators, state officials, politicians, and newsmen in some 25 states. The interview method has its limitations. Perhaps the most obvious one is the possibility that the interviewer, because of lack of time or inability to grasp the subtleties of the local situation, may get only a partial picture of the political situation and the mode of gubernatorial operations in a given state.

The author had neither the time nor the funds to visit personally all of the 48 states. The states visited were chosen, however, with an eye to such factors as their political complexion, size, population, economic base, and geographical location. Consequently, the sample selected should prove adequate.

Most of the actual interviewing was done in the summers of 1948-51 and many of the governors interviewed are no longer in office. The views they expressed, however, probably represent a cross section of gubernatorial opinion adequate for an examination of the office at mid-century.

Although the author must take the responsibility for the accuracy of the interviewing and for the interpretation of results, sincere thanks are due to the considerable number of state officials, legislators, newsmen, and others interviewed. A particular note of gratitude should go also to the governors themselves. If this study proves anything at all about the role of the governor, it shows that he is a very busy individual. The fact that the governors were willing to take time from their crowded schedules to discuss their concept of the office with the author added considerably to his understanding of the governorship.

Funds supplied by the Research Committee of the University of Alabama made possible the travel necessary in the interviewing for a major part of the study and the writer wishes to express his sincere thanks to the Committee for its support. Thanks are due also to the Southern Regional Training Program in Public Administration for an advanced fellowship which enabled the writer to collect the material on the southern states during the summers of 1948 and 1949.

Several of my professional colleagues have reviewed various sections of the manuscript and given me the benefit of their critical evaluation. I wish to thank especially, Charles D. Farris, Robert B. Highsaw, and York Willbern of the Department of Political Science of the University of Alabama and V. O. Key of Harvard University. I am also indebted to Professor Key for suggesting many of the techniques of political analysis used in the book. The writer is responsible, however, for the application of these methods to the data used and for the interpretation of the results obtained.

I wish to acknowledge also the assistance of John L. Sanders, a graduate student of the University of Alabama, who did the initial work on the indexing for the volume. My wife, Katherine M. Ransone, not only typed the manuscript but also provided unfailing encouragement and understanding during its preparation.

COLEMAN B. RANSONE, JR.

University, Alabama
July, 1956

ACKNOWLEDGMENTS

SINCE THE FORM of the footnotes does not provide for a citation of the publishers of the works used, the author wishes to take this opportunity to express his appreciation to all those publishers who allowed him to quote from their publications.

In particular he would like to thank the following publishers for permission to quote from the works listed: The University of California Press, *California Government* and *State and Local Government in California;* Alfred A. Knopf Inc., *Southern Politics* and *Politics in the Empire State;* The Tax Foundation, *The Tax Review* for a quotation from the article "Fiscal Relations in a Working Federalism" by Governor Alfred E. Driscoll; the Thomas Y. Crowell Company, *Politics, Parties and Pressure Groups;* the B. C. Forbes & Sons Publishing Co., Inc., *The Political Almanac;* The Council of State Governments, *State Government* and *The Proceedings of the Governors' Conference;* The American Society for Public Administration, *Public Administration Review;* The Wisconsin State Historical Society, *Wisconsin Magazine of History;* the New Hampshire Taxpayers Federation, the *New Hampshire Taxpayer;* the National Municipal League, *National Municipal Review,* and the *Alabama Magazine.*

CONTENTS

PART III

THE GOVERNOR AND DEMOCRATIC CONTROL

TABLES AND CHARTS

TABLES

CHARTS

PART ONE

THE CHARACTER OF GUBERNATORIAL POLITICS

1. PARTIES, POLITICS AND THE GOVERNOR

DURING THE LAST FIFTY YEARS the American governor has emerged as a policy leader of no mean proportions. He also is emerging gradually as a leader in terms of more recently gained powers in the field of state management. His office has become the primary center of public attention at the state level and his actions and speeches have considerable influence in molding public opinion. This tendency toward a strong governor is discussed in some detail in the later chapters of this book. If this thesis is accepted for the moment without further proof, it means that the office has assumed a greatly increased importance and that the governor of most states is now one of the key men in the fascinating game of political chess. It is now of crucial importance to the state party to elect their candidate as governor and of considerable importance to the national party as well. Furthermore, the citizens of the state have an important stake in the governorship because with the governor's increased power and importance comes the ability to take action which can affect the lives of the state's citizens.

The American state has not been displaced as a unit of government. Its role has been somewhat altered by increasing federal participation in fields formerly thought to be reserved for the states, but the status of the states has actually grown rather than been diminished by the programs of co-operative federalism as they are carried out in practice. While it is undeniable that the federal government has assumed new powers and functions, this is also true of the states. The governor, as the chief figure on the state political scene, has assumed increased importance as a result of these federally-financed, state-administered programs.

The major thesis of this book is a description and analysis of the functions of the American governor. This analysis is presented in summary form in Chapter 6 and is developed in detail in the succeeding chapters of the book. However, in order to understand the functions of the governor it is first necessary to understand the political process, informal as well as formal, by which the governor is selected. This process not only determines who runs and who is elected but it also determines with whom the governor must deal in the legislature and with whom he must contend as elected department heads. His major functions of policy formation, public relations and management are all intimately connected with how he was selected, the groups to which he is beholden for that election and the influence, or lack of influence, of the party on his election.

Because the governorship is a political office in both meanings of the term, the first five chapters of this book deal in a very broad way with the character of gubernatorial politics. In these chapters the process by which the governor is nominated and elected receives the most emphasis as the most significant part of the political processes surrounding the governor. In later chapters in the book the significance of this process in terms of the governor's relation with the legislature and with his department heads is examined.

From a surface point of view, the general pattern for the selection of the governor is not particularly complex. In most states, the standard pattern of nomination by convention or primary is followed by a general election in which the candidate with a plurality of the popular vote is elected.[1] The difficulty in describing this process comes partly in the variety of patterns which have developed in the primary but more especially in the party processes which lie behind the legal pattern and which actually determine who is selected as the gubernatorial candidate of a given party.

[1] In Georgia, Maine, Mississippi, and Vermont the candidate must receive a majority of the popular vote. If no candidate receives a majority, the governor is selected by the legislature. In Mississippi the winning candidate must receive a majority of both the popular and the county electoral vote.

Even the question of the proper type of nominating system to be used in the selection of gubernatorial candidates has been the subject of a great deal of discussion. Each of the various methods now in use has its supporters both among those who practice the art of politics and those who profess to teach it. Those who favor the convention system point with pride to the records of governors nominated by that process in New York and other states still retaining the convention. Those who favor the primary point to equally outstanding governors chosen by that system. Within the group favoring the primary there is a considerable division between those who favor the closed as opposed to the open primary, or the cross-filing system as opposed to the single filing system. More recently there have come forward advocates of the pre-primary nominating convention who feel that this system combines the best features of both the primary and the convention. There have been many prophets and many panaceas. As yet the political chaos predicted by some when the convention system was abandoned does not seem to have developed. On the other hand, the millennium prophesied by the proponents of the direct primary does not yet seem to have been fully realized.

The analysis which was made of the nominating systems of the respective states in the course of this study did not reveal that any one of the systems described in the following sections is an ideal system which can be applied with equal success in all states. Even if one of the systems is selected as superior to the others, there is some doubt as to whether or not it can be transplanted in its entirety to any given state. This is true primarily because the fabric of the nominating process is composed partly of the legally established system and partly of the informal party system which has grown up over the years. This party nominating process may in practice closely follow the legal process or it may operate in such a way as to modify substantially or even nullify the formally established procedure. The whole nominating process is a part of the ecology of government in a given state and is not susceptible of uprooting and transplanting, at least in its informal aspects, to another state.

It is these party processes which lie behind the formal nominating procedures which determine who shall be the gubernatorial candidate of the major parties in most states. Because each party process is unique and not repeated in whole in any two states, it is extremely difficult to classify these processes or even describe them without describing 48 different sets of circumstances. Nevertheless, if we are to seek to understand the process by which our governors are nominated and elected, some attempt must be made to find the similarities in these procedures and to classify the states into reasonable groupings on the basis of the nature of gubernatorial politics in each state.

The classifications which are suggested in this chapter are admittedly rough groupings of the states on the basis of the over-all party pattern which seems to have prevailed in gubernatorial politics over the last twenty years. Such classifications conceal the wide range which exists in the informal nominating procedures within the states in each group. In order to suggest this range without describing each state individually, a fairly detailed description is presented of the informal party processes in the states which seem to stand at the extremes in each group, or which have some peculiarity that distinguishes them from other states in the group. In this fashion one may proceed from the general to the particular without attempting to dissect the party structure of every state since such an endeavor would result in a sizable volume and lead into fields beyond the scope of this study.

Any attempt to consider the nature of gubernatorial politics as a separate entity is complicated by the fact that the state political parties do not operate in a vacuum but are affected by the ebb and flow of the tides of success of the national parties with which they are connected. In some of the states there appears to be a demonstrable connection between the fortunes of a party's candidate for governor and the fortunes of its presidential or congressional candidates. In other states, however, the voters seem impervious to national political trends and continue to elect gubernatorial candidates of a particular party without much regard to the presidential race and frequently elect a governor of one party, while voting for the presidential candidate of another. In a fairly sizable group of states there is a close correlation between the fate of candidates of the same party for the governorship and United States House of Representatives but much less correlation between the governorship and presidential or senatorial races.

The variety of these relationships and the difficulty of isolating the factors affecting the races for the governorship from those which affect the races for national offices which fall at the same elections certainly complicates the task of the student of state politics. Perhaps the best way to show something both of the interrelation of gubernatorial and national politics and of the need for the separation of the two is to illustrate the effects of a key presidential race on the governorship. This relationship emerges most clearly in those presidential races which involve a shift in party control but even here is not as clear as might be imagined from a simple enumeration of the states which voted for both the gubernatorial and presidential candidates of the same party. For example, in 1932 when Roosevelt led the Democratic Party to victory after a long period of Republican control, an analysis of the election returns shows that of the 33 states which held gubernatorial elections in that year Roosevelt carried 28. In 25 of these 28 states the voters also elected Democratic governors. The three exceptions were Minnesota where Floyd B. Olson, the incumbent, was re-elected as a Farmer-Labor candidate, North Dakota, where William Langer was elected as a Republican although later disqualified, and Kansas, where Alfred M. Landon was elected to his first term.

On the surface it would appear that Roosevelt's tremendous vote getting ability carried over for his party to the race for governor and that some 25 governors came in "on his coattails." This does not seem to be the entire explanation of the 1932 situation, however. If the Democratic victories were a product of the Roosevelt sweep in 1932, then one would expect to find that the Democrats not only carried the governorship but that the Democratic victory represented a shift from Republican to Democratic control at the state level as well as at the national level. This was not the case in most of the states in 1932.

In the South in 1928 Hoover carried Florida, North Carolina, Texas, and Tennessee in the Democratic split over Al Smith. He did not, however, carry Louisiana or Arkansas. Furthermore, his victory did not result in the election of a Republican governor in any of these states nor did any of them elect a Republican governor in the off-year election of 1930. Consequently, all these states went into the 1932 presidential election with Democratic governors and emerged with Democratic governors. The election of Democratic governors in these states can hardly be said to be the result of a Roosevelt sweep, since they all had Democratic governors in 1932 and also had been in the habit of electing Democrats since the turn of the century.

In addition to the six southern states there were ten states outside the South which were carried by Roosevelt and which had also elected a Democratic governor either in 1928 or in the off-year election of 1930. In Arizona, Colorado, Idaho, Massachusetts, New Mexico, New York, Nebraska, and Ohio a Democratic governor was elected in 1930, while in Utah and Montana the voters had elected a Democrat for a four-year term in the dark days of 1928. Hence, all ten of these states had a Democratic governor going into the 1932 Presidential election, and the election of a Democrat in those states cannot be entirely credited to the Roosevelt sweep, although his victory certainly materially increased the chances of the Democratic candidate in several of the notoriously changeable states in this group.

The revised score on the presidential election of 1932 in terms of its effect on the governorship probably should read somewhat as follows: no positive correlation between the Roosevelt sweep and gubernatorial races in Vermont, New Hampshire, and Delaware, which failed to go for Roosevelt or elect a Democratic governor; no positive relationship in Kansas, which went for FDR but elected Alf Landon as governor, North Dakota, which elected a Republican, or Minnesota, which elected a Farmer-Laborite; no actual correlation between the Roosevelt victory in 1932 and the victory of the Democratic candidates in the six southern states involved, since to judge from their past performance they probably would have elected Democratic governors even if Hoover had won again; a stronger assist in the ten states outside the South which had Democratic governors going into the 1932 Presidential election; considerable credit for the Democratic victories in South Dakota, Iowa, Wisconsin, Missouri, Rhode Island, West Virginia, Idaho, Illinois, Indiana, Michigan, and Washington. All of these states except Rhode Island had gone Republican in 1928 and all had elected Republican governors except South Dakota. In the 1930 election South Dakota elected a Republican, as did Iowa, Michigan, Rhode Island, and Wisconsin. Since Missouri, West Virginia, Illinois, Indiana, and Washington had previously elected Republicans in 1928, all eleven of these states went into the 1932 election with Republican governors. Since they emerged from the election with Democratic governors and since this represented a change in party control from the previous election, it would seem that the Roosevelt sweep had a more direct connection in these eleven states than in the remainder of the group.

This cursory analysis of the 1932 election reveals that the "coat-tails" theory of the interrelation between gubernatorial and presidential politics, while it appears to be valid in at least eleven of the states discussed, still leaves us with a doubtful explanation for the behavior of ten states and no solid grounds for explaining the action of the southern states or such states as Maine, Minnesota, or Connecticut, in which the voters split their tickets.

The discrepancies between the vote of the states for president and their vote for governor is even more marked in the elections which came after 1932. For example, of the 32 states which held a regular election for governor in 1948 there were twelve states which elected Republican governors despite the Democratic victory in the presidential race and five of these twelve elected Republican governors while voting for the Democratic candidate for president. In 1952 in the face of the Eisenhower landslide, there were eleven states which elected Democratic governors out of 31 states holding a regular gubernatorial election, and seven of these eleven elected a Democrat as governor, while voting for the Republican presidential candidate.[2]

Because of the tendency of certain states to present a picture in gubernatorial politics contrary to that in presidential politics there seems to be some justification for basing our analysis of the character of gubernatorial politics primarily on the party pattern at the state level. Viewed from this perspective the states seem to fall into three categories in gubernatorial politics. The first of these groups is made up of those states in which one party has consistently elected its candidate for governor over the period 1930 through 1950. This group includes the eleven southern states plus

[2] The apparent discrepancy in the number of states holding regular gubernatorial elections in 1948 and in 1952 is explained by the fact that Connecticut, which held a gubernatorial election in 1948, shifted from a two to a four-year term in 1950 and therefore did not hold a gubernatorial election in 1952.

Oklahoma, which are sure states for the Democratic Party, and Vermont and New Hampshire, which are sure states for the Republican Party.[3] The second category is made up of states in which the minority party has apparently been very weak over this period. These states are also generally sure for the dominant party but the minority party occasionally captures the governorship and frequently polls a fairly substantial vote in the general election. For the lack of a better term, these states may be designated as normally Democratic or Republican states. This group includes Arizona, New Mexico, West Virginia, Kentucky, Utah, Rhode Island, Nevada, Missouri, and Maryland on the Democratic side and California, Pennsylvania, Maine, South Dakota, Kansas, Iowa, Wisconsin, Oregon, North Dakota, Minnesota, and Nebraska on the Republican side. The remaining fourteen states fall into a category in which party competition for the governorship had apparently been the keenest over the period 1930 through 1950. These states, therefore, follow more nearly the pattern which is usually considered to be characteristic of a two-party state.

Classifications, of course, are the children of criteria, and the grouping of the several states into the categories suggested above is dependent upon the basis for these groupings. In general the states are placed in one of these three categories on the basis of their relative ranking in regard to two criteria. The first of these is the number of elections which have been won by one or the other of the major parties in the period 1930 through 1950, and the second is the strength shown by each party in terms of the percentage of the major party vote for the party's candidate in the gubernatorial elections over the same period. In certain cases the rankings of the states on the basis of these two criteria are not followed exactly as will be explained when the classifications are discussed in more detail. Such departures are based on information collected in interviews in these states which indicates that the state is, for example, "more Republican" than the figures suggest. In the main, however, the impressions gained in interviews are supported by the data presented in Tables I, IV, and V in the next three chapters. In these tables the states are grouped on the

[3] In this analysis the South includes Virginia, North Carolina, South Carolina, Georgia, Florida, Tennessee, Alabama, Louisiana, Mississippi, Arkansas, and Texas (the eleven Confederate states).

basis of party control and party strength. Both criteria have been reduced to percentage figures for ease in comparison. Accompanying each table is a brief explanation of the reasons why these particular states were chosen for inclusion in a given group and some analysis of the effects which the party structure of each group of states seems to have on the selection process in those states.

Political classifications are very tenuous and change under the impact of local or national pressures. Consequently, it should be emphasized that the classifications in the chapters which follow are made in retrospect over the period 1930 to 1950. Some of the classifications probably will not apply with equal force to the situation existing when this book is released, since it appears that some of the states are even now in the process of change. The classifications certainly should not be taken as a prediction of future gubernatorial trends. The purpose of these classifications and the discussion of the process of gubernatorial nominations and elections in the states in each group is to form a background for the later discussion of the functions of the governor.

2. THE ONE-PARTY STATES

THE TERM "ONE-PARTY STATES" which is used in the title of this chapter has a limited denotation in that it is used to refer to those states which have consistently elected a Democratic or Republican governor in the period 1930 through 1950. The use of the term does not imply that these states are one-party in other respects in their politics as, for example, in their presidential politics, although all of these states tend to one-party politics at that level also.

The states which make up this one-party group are shown in Table I. In this table the state's attachment to one of the two major parties from 1930 through 1950 is indicated by a figure representing the per cent of gubernatorial elections won by the dominant party and by a figure representing the average per cent of the vote for the dominant party in the elections for governor.

If the number of elections won by the major party is taken as the sole criterion of a state's attachment to a given party, there seems to be little doubt that the eleven southern states and Oklahoma should be classified as sure states for the Democratic Party. In each of these states during the entire period the Democratic candidate has either defeated his Republican opponent or has been unopposed in the general election. In both Georgia and Mississippi the Republicans have been unable or unwilling to place a candidate for governor in the field, with the result that the Democratic candidate has been unopposed except by an occasional independent in the general election in these states throughout the entire period. The situation is much the same in South Carolina and Louisiana, except that the Republicans did have a candidate in South Carolina in 1938 and in Louisiana in 1928 and 1940. In the remainder of the states the Republicans

TABLE I

Party Control and the Governorship: States in Which One Party Consistently Elected Its Candidate for Governor 1930-1950

DEMOCRATIC STATES	*Per Cent of Elections Won by Democratic Party*	*Average Per Cent Democratic of Major Party Vote for Governor*	REPUBLICAN STATES	*Per Cent of Elections Won by Republican Party*	*Average Per Cent Republican of Major Party Vote for Governor*
Georgia	100.0	100.0	Vermont	100.0	68.5
Mississippi	100.0	100.0	New Hampshire	100.0	58.6
South Carolina	100.0	99.9			
Louisiana	100.0	99.2			
Alabama	100.0	90.6			
Texas	100.0	89.0			
Arkansas	100.0	88.6			
Florida	100.0	78.5			
Virginia	100.0	74.0			
Tennessee	100.0	73.8			
North Carolina	100.0	68.5			
Oklahoma	100.0	57.7			

at least had a candidate in the general election except in Alabama in 1930, in Arkansas in 1942, in Florida in 1940, and in Tennessee in 1934 and 1936. Republican opposition in these states has been completely ineffective, however, and the result of the election is never in doubt. The formalities of the general election are carried out on the appointed day but the results actually have been known since the victor in the Democratic primary was announced some months previously. In the South the primary *is* the election. In the 134 gubernatorial elections held in the period 1919-1952, the Democratic candidate was victorious in 133 instances. The one exception was in 1920, when Alfred A. Taylor, a Republican, was elected in Tennessee, probably as a result of Harding's sweep of the state in the presidential election of that year. It is interesting to note, however, that although Hoover carried Texas, Tennessee, Virginia, Florida, and North Carolina in 1928, his victory did not result in the election of a Republican governor in these states, although all of them except Virginia held gubernatorial elections in that year. The same can be said of the Republican breakthrough in 1952 when Eisenhower carried Tennessee, Virginia, Florida, and Texas. Although three of these four states held a gubernatorial election in 1952, the Republican sweep at the presidential level did not result in the election of a single Republican governor in the South. The situation in the gubernatorial race in Texas was somewhat confused since the incumbent governor, Allan Shivers, ran as a Republican-Democrat and was unopposed in his race. Since he had previously been elected in 1950 as a Democrat, however, it seems fair to say that his re-election still left the Democratic domination of the state at the gubernatorial level unimpaired.

While there is little ground to distinguish between the Democratic states simply on the basis of elections won, a somewhat different pattern begins to emerge if the per cent of the vote polled by the Democratic Party in each state is considered. Obviously, we might expect to find some difference in the party pattern in a state like Mississippi, where the Democratic candidate was unopposed and hence where the Party may be credited with 100 per cent of the vote, and a state like Oklahoma, where the Democratic candidate polled an average of only 57.7 per cent of the vote. There, indeed, seems to be considerable difference between these two states and there is some indication of a possible change in the party pattern in Oklahoma which may further emphasize this difference.

If the Republicans are showing any signs of increasing strength in Mississippi in recent years, it is not reflected in the gubernatorial politics of the state during this period. On the other hand, there is some indication of increasing Republican strength in Oklahoma. The average vote of 57.7 per cent for the Democratic candidate during this period conceals the fact that in recent elections the Republicans have shown an increase in strength as revealed in their ability to increase their percentage of the two-party vote. The Republican vote has not increased steadily from election to election, but it has increased over the last three elections of the period as opposed to the first three elections in the period. From 1930 to 1942 the Republican average was around 36.8 per cent of the total major party vote, while from 1942 to 1950 it was around 47.8 per cent. The best showing of the Republicans was in 1950 when the Republican candidate polled 48.7 per cent of the major party vote. Just what this portends for the future in Oklahoma the writer certainly would not care to predict, but it does point to a wide difference in party competition among the sure Democratic states themselves. This point will be discussed in more detail later in the section, but it is well to emphasize at the very beginning of this discussion that while it seems legitimate to put into one group all those states which have consistently elected a Democratic governor for the last twenty odd years, it should also be kept in mind that such a governor may have been elected with no Republican opposition or in a situation where there is some significant second party opposition. This is of some importance both in the election process itself and in the governor's later relations with the legislature.

If the single criterion of elections won is applied to the Republican states, Vermont and New Hampshire emerge as the leading contenders for the Republican crown for party regularity. In Vermont, although the Democrats at least had a standard bearer in each election, the Republican candidate won in all eleven elections from 1930 through 1950 and, as expected, was again successful in 1952. Vermont's 68.5 per cent Republican of the major party vote also places it at the top of the Republican roster in that category. However, it should be noted that this most Republican of states rates above only one sure Democratic state, Oklahoma, and is on a par with North Carolina, which is the least "solid" of the southern states. While Vermont, therefore, certainly should be classified as a sure Republican state in gubernatorial politics, even the Green Mountain State does not approach for the Republicans the apparent solidarity of at least ten of its Democratic counterparts.

New Hampshire is another state which has so far been sure for the Republicans, having religiously elected Republican governors in all eleven elections in the period covered and in 1952. However, the Republican empire in New Hampshire apparently is based on a less solid foundation than that in Vermont, since the average per cent of the two-party vote for the Republican candidate is 58.6, some ten percentage points below that of its neighbor.

It is obvious with the wide range in party strength within the one-party group that it would not be logical to expect to find the same brand of gubernatorial politics in each of the states which make up the group. On the other hand, if such a grouping has any practical significance, there should be some features of the group as a whole which set it apart from the other groups of states.

One feature sets these states apart from most of the other states in the nation. In all of these states during the period covered the candidate of the dominant party invariably won in the ensuing general election. Thus, as a practical matter the primary of the dominant party assumed the importance that is reserved for the general election in most of the other states.

Since the primary is the election, it would seem logical to suppose that the voters in the one-party states might be expected to show an unusual interest in the primary. This is indeed the case in all of the southern states except North Carolina. In North Carolina the governor is elected only in presidential years and this tends to bring the voters to the polls in large numbers for the general election, and, hence, exaggerates the interest of the voters of that state in the general election. In addition to North Carolina, the voters of Oklahoma, Vermont, and New Hampshire also show relatively little interest in the primary. New Hampshire in particular shows a surprisingly small turnout in the Republican primary as compared to the general election. In Table II the states in the one-party group are ranked in accordance with primary interest. The figure for primary interest was determined by comparing the number of persons voting in the primary with the number voting in the general election. For the Democratic states the comparison was made between the first Democratic primary for governor and the general election. For the Republican states the comparison was between the turnout in the Republican primary and the general election. In each election primary interest was calculated on the basis of the turnout in the primary as a percentage of the turnout in the general election for the period 1930 to 1950. The average of these percentages is shown in Table II as the figure for primary interest. Also shown in Table II is a recapitulation of the percentages of the major party vote polled by the dominant party in each state over this period.

As can be seen from an examination of the figures on primary

TABLE II

Total Participation in the Gubernatorial Primary of the Dominant Party as a Percentage of Total Participation in the General Election for Governor in the One-Party States 1930-1950

DEMOCRATIC STATES	Primary Interest	Average Per Cent Democratic of Major Party Vote	REPUBLICAN STATES	Primary Interest	Average Per Cent Republican of Major Party Vote
South Carolina	1009.1	99.9	Vermont	56.0	68.5
Mississippi	550.1	100.0	New Hampshire	33.5	58.6
Louisiana	511.1	99.2			
Georgia	315.8	100.0			
Alabama	211.1	90.6			
Texas	194.8	89.0			
Arkansas	139.4	88.6			
Florida	111.4	78.5			
Tennessee	108.2	73.8			
Virginia	101.5	74.0			
Oklahoma	88.9	57.7			
North Carolina	54.4	68.5			

interest in Table II, there is a wide range of interest among the one-party states. In the Democratic group all of the states except Oklahoma and North Carolina show more interest in the primary than in the general election. However, even in those states in which there is more interest in the primary than in the general election, there is still a rather wide range of intensity in that interest. In South Carolina the ratio of persons voting in the primary to persons voting in the general election is more than ten to one in favor of the primary. At the other end of the scale, in Virginia interest in the primary and general election is almost even, with a very slight edge in favor of the primary.

Perhaps it is somewhat easier to see these comparisons if an example of the actual turnout in these two states over this period is examined in more detail. In South Carolina the election of 1946 falls closest to the average, since the figure for primary interest in that year was 1090.5 per cent. In actual figures this breaks down to a turnout of 289,214 in the primary as compared to 26,520 in the general election—a ratio of more than ten to one. In all elections in this period the voters in South Carolina flocked to the polls in the primary in such numbers that the primary always outdrew the general election by over six to one. The general election in South Carolina is nothing more than a mere formality, since the Democratic candidate generally runs unopposed. In the period under consideration, the Democratic candidate had Republican opposition in only one election.

In Virginia, on the other hand, the general election is something more than a formality. The outcome is never in doubt, but there are enough Republicans in the Old Dominion to encourage the Democratic voters to turn out in the general elections as well as in the primary. In two of the six elections during this period the general election actually outdrew the primary, a circumstance which would be without parallel in South Carolina. Because there are some years in which the general election outdraws the primary and others in which the reverse is the case, it is difficult to pick a typical year with which to illustrate the Virginia pattern. However, the last two elections of the period are fairly representative of the two kinds of situations which existed during the period under consideration. In 1945 the general election attracted more voters than the primary, the figures being roughly 168,000 for the general election to 139,000 for the primary. In 1949 the reverse was true, with the primary attracting more voters than the general election. In that year the primary drew approximately 316,000 voters, while the general election drew only 262,000.

The clue to the disparity of interest among the various southern states in the general election as compared to the primary seems to lie primarily in the presence or absence of Republican opposition in those states. The seven southern states which show the least interest in the primary as revealed by the figures in Table II are also those states in which there is the most Republican opposition. If the figures of the Democratic percentage of the major party vote in Table II are compared with the figures on primary interest, it will be noted that in most instances as the percentage polled by the Democratic gubernatorial candidates decreases, the interest in the primary also decreases. To put the and that the warm bi-partisan contests in the western counties of North Carolina and in some of the southwestern counties in Virginia bring the voters to the polls and help swell the general election total. This is not the case in Tennessee, however, since local elections are not held at the same time as gubernatorial contests.

The interest in the general election shown by North Carolina and Florida is probably not as strong as their relative ranking in Table II would indicate, since these states elect their governor only in presidential years. While the pull of the presidential election in the South is not as great as in other parts of the country, it does offer a relatively strong attraction to the voter to appear at the polls. Hence, these voters, who also generally vote for the governor, add to the gubernatorial totals and make it appear that there is relatively more interest in the gubernatorial election in these states than is actually the case. This factor also operates to some extent in Tennessee, Texas, Arkansas, and Georgia, where every other gubernatorial election was held in a presidential year.[1] In these states the presidential years show a peak of interest in the general election, while there is a definite drop in general election interest in off years. The remainder of the southern states do not elect their governor in presidential years, and this helps to explain the low turnout in such states in gubernatorial elections.

The effect of the presidential election in acting as a stimulus to voters to participate in the election of not only the president but also the governor is clearly revealed if the participation in the primary as opposed to the general election is compiled separately for presidential and for non-presidential years. The two sets of figures for those states with a two-year term in the Democratic group which elect every other governor in presidential years would be as follows:

	Presidential Years	*Off Years*
Georgia	131.8	426.1
Arkansas	114.2	160.5
Texas	104.6	270.0
Tennessee	67.2	142.4

[1] In Georgia alternate gubernatorial elections fell in presidential years up to 1942, when the state switched to a four-year term.

In all of these states except Tennessee the primary still attracts more voters than the general election even in presidential years. However, in each case the number of persons who voted in the general election is much larger proportionately in presidential years than the number who voted in the general election in off years. Consequently, the figures on primary interest show a sharp drop in presidential years as compared to those elections in which the governorship alone was at stake. In Tennessee, where interest in the general election is at a much higher peak than in most southern states because of the presence of active Republican competition, the combined effects of the election of a presidential candidate, the governor, and other state and local officials brings the electorate out in considerable numbers for the general election, and the totals in presidential years for the general election are actually higher than for the primary.

In off years the interest in the primary exceeds that of the general election in all of these states. The figures for the off years, if used as a basis for comparison with those states which elect the governor entirely in non-presidential years, would leave Georgia in its same relative position as the fourth state in primary interest but would place Texas above Alabama and Tennessee above Florida. This sort of reshuffling might be a valid one except perhaps for Florida and North Carolina. Since these two states elect their governor only in presidential years, there would be no way of taking this factor into account. From the evidence in the other states as set out above it seems quite clear that the interest of these two states in the general election is undoubtedly exaggerated because of the influence of the presidential election.

The other state in the Democratic group, Oklahoma, seems to follow the pattern established by its southern counterparts. Since Oklahoma is the least sure of the Democratic states, it could be expected to exhibit more interest in the general election than do the southern states. With the exception of North Carolina, Oklahoma shows the least interest in the primary and, hence, the most interest in the general election of any state in the Democratic group. In four out of the six elections during this period more voters in Oklahoma went to the polls in the general election than in the Democratic primary. The Republican Party in addition to polling some 42.3 per cent of the vote in the gubernatorial elections also showed enough interest in the gubernatorial race to hold a Republican primary in each of the election years covered by this analysis. Turnout in the primary was relatively light, with an average of less than 30 per cent of those voting for the Republican candidate in the general election bothering to turn out for the Republican primary. However, the fact that the Republicans did hold a primary in Oklahoma is of some significance, since the Republicans in the southern states rarely bother to go through the procedure of holding a formal primary. Technically speaking, the Republicans must hold a primary in Florida, Louisiana, Mississippi, North Carolina, and Tennessee, since it is a mandatory device for nomination. Actually, the Republicans seldom hold a primary in these states. They generally nominate a candidate for the governorship by caucus or convention and he is able to run unopposed in the Republican primary, thus eliminating the need for actually holding the primary. However, the Republicans actually held gubernatorial primaries in Florida in 1944 and 1948, in Tennessee in 1948, and in North Carolina in 1940.

In the southern states where the primary is not mandatory the Republicans also generally nominate by caucus or convention, but occasionally a primary is held, as in Texas in 1930 and 1934. Such unusual interest in the selection of a gubernatorial candidate is exceptional for the Republicans in the South where it is frequently difficult to get anyone to agree to run for governor, much less stir up any competition over the nomination. Hence, it is worthy of note that the G. O. P. in Oklahoma is apparently active enough to actually have at least three candidates for the Republican gubernatorial nomination in each of the primaries held during this period and is eager enough to hold the primary.

One of the distinguishing features of the southern group of Democratic one-party states is the unusual interest evidenced by the voters in these states in the primary. Except for North Carolina, all of the southern states show more interest in the primary than in the general election, although in Virginia and Tennessee the balance is almost even. Since the primary is the election in these states, in all of them except Virginia and Tennessee it has taken on an altered form in keeping with its importance and is of the double variety, a form almost unknown outside its natural habitat. Only three of the twelve states which have at any time vote receives *all* of its unit votes. Thus, in Georgia the gubernatorial primary evolves as a series of separate plurality nominations in each of the state's 159 counties. A majority of the unit votes rather than the popular vote is required for the candidate's nomination. In the event that no candidate receives a majority of the unit votes a run-over, as the Georgians call the second primary, is held. This is not the same as a run-off in the other states, for it is possible to win the gubernatorial election without having a majority of the popular vote. This would not generally be the case in the other states, although it could happen if the second highest candidate waived his right to a run-off, as he can do in some of the states. In the gubernatorial primary of July 17, 1946, Eugene Talmadge won the nomination without polling a majority of the popular vote. A breakdown of the vote shows how this rather neat trick was accomplished.[4]

Candidate	*Popular Vote*	*Unit Vote*	*Counties Carried*
James V. Carmichael	313,389	146	44
Hoke O'Kelly	11,758	0	0
E. D. Rivers	68,489	22	10
Eugene Talmadge	297,245	242	105

Eugene Talmadge won the gubernatorial nomination in 1946 with a minority of the popular vote because he was able to pile up enough of the unit votes in the rural counties to overbalance the vote of the most populous counties. Since the latter are underrepresented in the legislature they also have a reduced share of the county unit votes in proportion to their population. Thus, the cards are stacked in the gubernatorial primary in favor of the candidate who has the greatest appeal to the rural voters. In Georgia during the period under consideration this has generally meant one of the Talmadges or a member of their faction.[5]

The Republican one-party states differ from their counterparts in the deep South both in the form of the primary and in primary interest. In Vermont and New Hampshire the standard single

[4] Based on figures taken from the *Georgia Official and Statistical Register 1945-50,* p. 486.

[5] See Key, pp. 117-28 and 419 for a more detailed discussion of this system and its effects in gubernatorial nominations.

primary with a plurality nomination is used.[6] While in some elections the vote in the primary has been very close, there does not seem to be any sentiment for a shift to a double primary system.

In primary interest both Vermont and New Hampshire rank well below the states in the Democratic group with the exception of North Carolina. Since North Carolina and Vermont have the same index of party strength, it seems logical to suppose that the Democratic voters in North Carolina would have about the same interest in the Democratic primary as would the voters in Vermont in the Republican primary. Such, however, is not the case, as may be seen from a comparison of the two states on the basis of primary interest as follows:

1932		1940		1948	
North Carolina	53.4	North Carolina	42.3	North Carolina	54.2
Vermont	57.6	Vermont	30.0	Vermont	60.2
1936		1944			
North Carolina	63.6	Vermont	42.8		
Vermont	40.8	North Carolina	58.4		

The elections shown are only those held in presidential years, since North Carolina elects its governor only in those years. The comparison, therefore, somewhat inflates the interest of Vermonters in the general election, as may be seen by a comparison of the figures on Vermont shown above with the figures on primary interest in non-presidential years. The same figures for Vermont for both presidential and off years would be as follows:

Presidential Years	*Off Years*
57.6	82.3
40.8	47.2
42.8	42.7
30.0	51.4
60.2	78.3
	82.1

The average of these percentages shows that primary interest in Vermont in off years is approximately 64.0 per cent, which is considerably greater than the average in presidential years of only

6 The single primary is also used in Virginia and Tennessee and in Oklahoma. In Vermont and New Hampshire, of course, Democratic and Republican primaries are held at the same time as is the case in Oklahoma. However, in Virginia and Tennessee only the Democratic primary is held in a normal election year.

46.3 per cent. This is the same pattern which we saw in Tennessee, Arkansas, Georgia, and Texas in the South and is a pattern which is also followed by New Hampshire. The intensity of primary interest is, of course, much greater in the southern states and is even weaker in New Hampshire than in Vermont. Nevertheless, in all these states there is the same cyclical fluctuation in primary interest with the peaks in the off years and the low points in the presidential years. Conversely, the pattern for the general election in each case shows the high points in the presidential years and the valleys in the off years. It would appear, therefore, that the real interest of Vermont in the primary is probably closer to 60 per cent than to 56 per cent. In either case, however, it would be greater than North Carolina, even though the states have the same figure for party strength. The real explanation of the Vermont interest in the primary in comparison to North Carolina, however, probably lies not so much in the actual interest of Vermont but in the reduction of the primary interest figure in North Carolina due to the fact that the North Carolina gubernatorial elections are held only in presidential years. Note, for example, that the Vermont figure on primary interest is well below that of Oklahoma, which is a less sure state for the Democrats than is North Carolina. Oklahoma's figure on primary interest is probably more accurate than is that for North Carolina, because in Oklahoma the governor is not elected in presidential years and the turnout in the primary and general election is governed primarily by the interest of the voters in state elections alone. Vermont is also well below the primary interest figure for Virginia, which is probably the southern state it most closely resembles. Virginia shows about five percentage points greater strength for the Democrats than does Vermont for the Republicans, but the minority parties in both states are probably about at the same level of activity, with a possible edge for the Democratic Party in Vermont in spite of the slight edge in the vote held by the Republicans in Virginia. Aside from the rather unusual case of North Carolina, primary interest in Vermont is considerably below that of its southern counterparts. The Republican primary is the election in Vermont as surely as the Democratic primary is the election in Virginia, but the voters in Vermont continue to come out for each general election in greater numbers than they do for the primary, while in Virginia, although on a few occasions the general election vote exceeds that of the primary, the reverse is much more likely to be true.

To judge from their turnout in the general election, the voters in New Hampshire apparently consider their state to fall in the two-party category in spite of the fact that they regularly elected a Republican as governor. New Hampshire shows even less interest in the primary than does Vermont and far less interest than Oklahoma, which is the state most comparable to it in terms of party strength in the Democratic group. Since the winner of the Republican primary in New Hampshire was also the winner in the subsequent general election in all elections during this period, it might be expected that voters in New Hampshire would show a greater interest in the primary than is apparently the case. This lack of emphasis on the primary and the corresponding emphasis on the general election seem to best be explained in terms of party competition. The Republican voters in New Hampshire apparently see in each general election a possible Democratic threat to the long Republican domination of the state. If the voters do have such a view, they seem to have sound grounds for such concern, for a quick survey of recent gubernatorial elections shows that Styles Bridges won his first race for governor in 1934 by only 50.7 per cent of the major party vote and that Robert O. Blood was victorious in his first race by the same percentage in 1940. As recently as 1948, Sherman Adams won by only 52.5 per cent of the major party vote.[7]

This summary of primary versus general election interest reveals that within the one-party group there is a wide range in primary

[7] These figures seem to bear out the analysis of the New Hampshire political situation suggested to the writer by Governor Sherman Adams in an interview on August 3, 1951. Governor Adams pointed out that while New Hampshire was a traditionally Republican state, the one-party pattern was not the same as that in the writer's home state of Alabama. The Governor felt that the writer would be "wrongly advised" to consider New Hampshire a solidly Republican state in gubernatorial politics and suggested that a check of recent gubernatorial elections would show that the vote in the general election has been close in several instances, with governors being elected with as little as a 3,000 vote majority. Governor Adams felt that this was a distinct contrast to the situation in most of the southern states where the primary is the election and the general election is not close. The general analysis of this section certainly seems to support the Governor's observations.

interest. On the basis of the figures presented in Table II it would seem that there is a rough correlation between the strength of the dominant party in a given state and interest in the primary. Those states in which the dominant party is extremely strong show an unusual interest in the primary and those in which the party is relatively weak show correspondingly less interest. To be sure, the first four states in the southern bloc do not fall in the same order in both party strength and primary interest. It must be remembered, however, that only .8 of 1 per cent separates these states in party strength and this is hardly a significant difference. The correlation between the two indices in all other states except North Carolina and New Hampshire is close enough so that it does not seem too much to say that, for this group of states at any rate, interest in the primary seems to vary with party strength. In those states where the opposition party is extremely weak the voters do not turn out for the formality of the general election but confine their efforts to voting in the primary where the real choice is made. In those states in which the opposition party shows even a modicum of strength we find an increasing interest in the general election. This interest increases as opposition grows until in such states as North Carolina and Oklahoma on the Democratic side and Vermont and New Hampshire on the Republican side the point is reached where more voters turn out for the general election than the primary.

Thus, within the one-party group there are to be found different party patterns which are concealed by the generalized description of the group as a whole. Nevertheless, in comparison to the other states this group stands out as one in which the dominant party has controlled the governorship over the last 22 years and where it has polled a fairly impressive proportion of the major party vote. This has resulted in the primary becoming the election in these states, which in turn has placed a premium on an aspiring gubernatorial candidate's securing the nomination of the dominant party. The real battle for the governorship in these states takes place in the primary of the dominant party, although the general election is far from unimportant in such states as Oklahoma or New Hampshire where the swing of a few thousand votes might well spell a break in one-party domination, at least for a given election. However, it is important to remember that for most of these states the generally held notions as to the nature of a political party and the nature of party competition may have to be revised if the process which actually takes place in the selection of a governor is to be seen in its proper light.

The dominant party in the one-party states is actually a holding company for various factions within its ranks. In the South the major function of the Democratic Party in the gubernatorial selection process is to act as a non-partisan agency in holding the Democratic primary where the real choice for governor is made. It is not considered good form for the Democratic state committee to intervene in behalf of any particular candidate in the primary, although there are occasional charges that this is done. Once the Democratic candidate has been selected the Party gives him only token support in the general election because it realizes full well that Republican opposition, if any, is not a really serious threat to its candidate.

The same situation seems to prevail to a considerable extent in Vermont, where the Republican state organization does not seem to make a really serious effort to rally the state's voters behind its candidate in the general election. On the other hand, the Democratic state organization in Oklahoma and the Republican state organization in New Hampshire seem to make a bona fide effort in the general election, although the amount of actual campaigning done seems to be left pretty largely to the discretion of the individual candidate for governor.

Since the primary is the election in the one-party states, it is necessary to look behind the formal nominating process in order to see how gubernatorial candidates are actually chosen. In most of these states it is relatively easy to get on the primary ballot, which generally requires only the personal declaration of the would-be candidate and a small filing fee. The question of obtaining enough support to be a really serious contender in the primary is another matter and how a would-be candidate actually becomes a serious contender varies considerably from state to state.[8] In general there is a good deal of jockeying back and forth between

[8] V. O. Key suggests that a "serious" contender might be defined as a candidate who polls at least 5 per cent of the vote in the first or only gubernatorial primary. See *Southern Politics,* p. 411.

aspiring candidates, the usual conferences in smoke-filled rooms, and trips around the state to check on possible support or to drum up supporters. By the time the date set for filing in the primary of the dominant party rolls around, the would-be candidates have a pretty good idea of their chances and the field has actually been narrowed down to a fairly small number of real contenders.

The number of candidates who actually appear in the primaries of some of the southern states would astound the voters in a two-party state in which a more orderly selection process usually narrows down the number of candidates appearing in the primaries of the two major parties. For example, in Florida in 1936 some fourteen candidates, serious and otherwise, appeared in the first gubernatorial primary, while in Texas the same figure was reached in the first gubernatorial primary in 1946. Oklahoma, however, takes the prize for the largest number of candidates to appear in any primary during this period when in 1934 it had a peak of fifteen candidates in the first primary. On the other hand, there are states like Tennessee and Virginia in which more than two candidates seldom appear in the primary and the situation more nearly resembles that in a primary in one of the two-party states.

In those southern states in which a large number of candidates do appear in the primary, the actual choice is not as great as it would appear because many of these are not really serious candidates. However, even if the less serious candidates are eliminated from consideration, the southern voter is still faced with a choice from two to six candidates in the primary. Thus, while the primary in the South resembles the general election in other states in many respects, it seems to resemble a general election under a multi-party system rather than a general election under a two-party system. Using the figure of 5 per cent of the total vote cast in the primary as a rough measure of whether or not a candidate can be considered as a serious contender, the states would rank in the order set out in Table III. The median number of candidates ranges from two in Vermont, New Hampshire, and Tennessee to six in Florida, and the number of serious contenders who appeared in the primary ranges from one in Vermont, where in two primaries there was an unopposed candidate, to nine in Florida, where the would-be candidates can always be sure of plenty of competition.

The number of serious candidates which appear in the primary

TABLE III*

Number of Candidates Receiving 5 Per Cent or More of Total Vote Cast in the First or Only Gubernatorial Primary in the One-Party States, 1930-1950

	Median Number	*Low Number*	*High Number*
Vermont	2	1	3
New Hampshire	2	2	3
Tennessee	2	2	3
Virginia	2.5	2	4
Georgia	3	2	4
North Carolina	3	2	5
Mississippi	3	3	4
Louisiana	3.5	2	5
Alabama	3.5	3	5
Oklahoma	4	3	6
Arkansas**	4	2	4
Texas	4	2	7
South Carolina	5	2	6
Florida	6	5	9

*Table III is based on a concept presented by V. O. Key in *Southern Politics,* p. 411. In a similar table Key presents an analysis of the eleven southern states for the period 1919-48. The ranking of the states over this longer period is slightly different from that shown above. The three states at the extremes of the southern group remain essentially the same, but the states in the center shift their positions somewhat.

**The figures for Arkansas are based only on those primaries in which the incumbent was not a candidate for re-nomination.

of the dominant party in a one-party state serves as a rough index to the factional nature of party politics in the state. In general in those states with fairly well defined dual-factional groups, the number of candidates which appear in the primary is limited, with normally only two contenders in the race. One of these has been informally nominated by one of the factions of the party and the other is put up by the opposing faction. On the other hand, in those states in which there are not two well defined factions the primary becomes a more wide-open affair and a large number of self-nominated candidates appear.

Of the states in the one-party group, Virginia and Vermont seem to have the most clearly defined dual-factional structure. In Virginia the Byrd and anti-Byrd forces give the Democratic Party two fairly definite wings and the same is true in Vermont where the Proctor and anti-Proctor forces make up two wings of the Republican Party. At the other end of the scale is Florida, which has no discernible factions of a continuing nature. Hence in Florida it is pretty much every man for himself in the primary, and it tends to be a state of free-for-all politics and self-nominated candidates.

In Virginia, and to some extent in Vermont, there is a careful sifting process by which the "organization" candidate in the gubernatorial primary is chosen. In these states an aspiring gubernatorial candidate works his way up through the organization with a series of minor elected posts such as local political offices, the state legislature, or the lieutenant governorship. When he is judged to have reached enough political maturity to take on the governorship, he is given the organization approval to run in the primary. Customarily, he is not opposed by any other organization candidate, with the result that he is usually able to win handily over the anti-organization candidate.

The opposition in Virginia and Vermont did not seem to be able to agree on a candidate in several of the primaries during this period and this, of course, considerably weakened its position. In both Vermont and Virginia there is no second primary as there is in most of the southern states. Hence, it is vital for the opposition to concentrate their support behind one candidate if they are to win in the primary.

In Virginia, the opposition apparently was able to agree upon a candidate in three of the six primaries during the period but was successful in only one primary. In 1937 James H. Price, an insurgent ex-Byrd organization member, was nominated, but on the other two occasions when only two contenders appeared in the primary the Byrd candidate was victorious. In two of the other three races the opposition votes were split between two candidates, while in 1949 disorganization reached a high for Virginia when three anti-organization candidates appeared in the primary. The combined vote of the three candidates not endorsed by the Byrd organization was some 45,000 votes more than the winning total of the Byrd candidate. However, the winning candidate, John Stewart Battle, polled some 23,000 votes more than Francis P. Miller, a long-time Byrd opponent and the leading spirit of the opposition, who was the second highest candidate in the primary.

In Virginia, with its very limited electorate, a small number of sure votes can pay large dividends, especially if the opposition is divided.

In Vermont, the opposition has fared somewhat better and has been able to concentrate its fire more effectively. This appears to be largely due to the efforts of Ernest W. Gibson, who acted as the leader of the opposition in the middle part of the period under consideration. In 1946 and 1948, Gibson was a candidate for the gubernatorial nomination and successfully defeated the younger Proctor in both primaries. Since Gibson's appointment as a Federal judge, the opposition has been without a leader of the same stature. In the 1950 election there were two anti-Proctor candidates who together polled more than the Proctor candidate, but the division of the vote enabled the Proctor candidate to win by a fairly respectable margin. The factional situation in Vermont has not been as definite as that in Virginia, or perhaps one should say that the Proctor faction has not been as well organized as the Byrd faction in Virginia. It has, however, been successful in securing the nomination of a candidate acceptable to it in all but two of the primary elections during the period under consideration. In two other primaries, those of 1940 and 1942, William H. Wills was unopposed in the primary. As far as the writer can determine, this was not due to the breakdown of either faction but to an agreement to a cessation of hostilities on a temporary basis and the nomination of a candidate acceptable to both factions.

The orderly process of pre-primary nominations which takes place in Virginia and Vermont is quite different from that in Florida. In the Peninsula State no well-oiled, state-wide machine exists to which aspiring young politicians attach themselves with the hope of rising through the ranks to the governorship. Pre-primary nominations in Florida are very much a rough and tumble fight, no holds barred, with every man for himself. Aspiring candidates take a pre-primary swing through the state contacting local political leaders and labor, fraternal, business, and professional associations with the hope of gaining enough commitments in the way of political and financial support to enable them to run a respectable race. After preliminary investigation, many are discouraged and withdraw, and those that remain, sometimes as many as nine candidates, square off for the primary fight. Occasionally, a candidate appears whose program is definite enough to be labeled as being far right or far left, and the voters eliminate such rash extremists. Generally, however, there is not much choice of program among the numerous competitors and, therefore, the first primary generally resembles a state-wide lottery. Out of this mélange two strong men emerge who compete in the run-off primary for the Democratic nomination, with the successful candidate regularly being elected in the succeeding general election.

In terms of the pre-primary selection process the other states in the one-party group seem to fall somewhere between the rather definite sifting process that occurs in Virginia and Vermont and the free-for-all that takes place in Florida. While New Hampshire ranks at the top of the list of the one-party states in terms of the small number of candidates which appeared in the primary, the dual-factionalism in that state does not appear to be as definite as that in Vermont. The Republican Party in New Hampshire is divided into two wings on a roughly conservative-liberal basis in most of the primaries of this period. However, as one of the elected officials interviewed put it, these are "relative New Hampshire terms" and none of the would-be gubernatorial nominees is very far to the left in the political spectrum. It seems to be primarily a question of the degree of conservatism exhibited by the members of the two groups, not the degree of liberalism. The two factions in New Hampshire have not had the same continuing leadership under a recognized head as has been provided by Senator Byrd in Virginia or the Proctor family in Vermont. The leadership for the two wings has generally been provided by the governor if his group is in power or by the ex-governor if his group is in a period of temporary eclipse. Since 1936 New Hampshire has had only four governors, each of whom has served for two terms. Of these four, Francis P. Murphy (1936-40) and Charles M. Dale (1944-48) seem to be roughly of the same wing of the party, while Robert O. Blood (1940-44) and Sherman Adams (1948-52) seem to be of the other wing. The pattern in New Hampshire, however, does not reveal the presence of an organization in the sense applicable to Virginia and Vermont.

Tennessee, which appears as the third state in Table III, also has a dual-factional character in gubernatorial politics, although of a somewhat different nature than Virginia's. The Crump machine in Tennessee, although beaten in the 1948 and 1950 elections, is still a potent force. During the period in question the factional division in Tennessee in the Democratic Party was largely along pro and anti-Crump lines. The careful sifting process present in Virginia is largely absent from the Tennessee picture, however. Mr. Crump was a power unto himself in his organization and generally personally selected a candidate for governor who would run in the Democratic primary. Crump also generally endorsed candidates for the United States Senate and for the railroad and public utilities commission. The Crump-endorsed candidates for these three state-wide offices usually, although not always, conducted a coalition campaign from a joint headquarters.[9] Thus, the pre-primary selection process in Tennessee is not as "democratic" as that in Virginia, where aspiring candidates within the organization compete on a more or less even basis and can expect orderly promotions if they prove to be effective in minor posts.

Georgia with pro and anti-Talmadge factions, Louisiana with Long and anti-Long factions, and North Carolina with its Shelby County Dynasty all have dual-factional gubernatorial politics. None of these states, however, has a single faction which is as well organized as the Byrd or Crump factions in Virginia and Tennessee. While the opposition all seems to have at least a common aversion to the leader of the factions mentioned, this does not seem to be enough to force them to work together for a single candidate. Two or more opposition candidates are quite common in these states, with the result that a divided vote generally favors the political powers that be. North Carolina differs from Louisiana and Georgia in that the so-called Shelby County Dynasty has not been founded on a personal following as was the Long machine in Louisiana or the Talmadge machine in Georgia. The principal power in the pre-primary selection process in North Carolina is a coalition of state officials who frequently are able to agree on a candidate and work for his nomination in the primary. Sometimes, however, these officials are split in their loyalties and a candidate not acceptable to the machine is nominated.

[9] See Key, p. 414ff. for a discussion of the Tennessee factional division and for a more detailed discussion of the factionalism in the other southern states.

Mississippi, although ranking above Louisiana in Table III, is not primarily a dual-factional state. Like Alabama, Oklahoma, and Arkansas it tends to be a state of self-nominated candidates. Texas and South Carolina also lean toward the Florida wide open version, with numerous candidates competing in the initial primary. Such sifting as is done in these states is done by the voters in the first primary and not through any pre-primary selection process.

Oklahoma presents a picture in its primary politics which seems to be a bit puzzling in view of the Republican opposition in that state. It might be supposed since Oklahoma has the strongest Republican party of any state in the group, to judge by its ability to attract a substantial vote for its candidate in the general election, that Oklahoma Democrats might be forced into some sort of dual-factionalism. This does not seem to be true, however, for a substantial number of individuals appear in the primary in that state and it appears to be a state with definite multi-factional characteristics.

This brief description of the factional situation at the two extremes of the two-party group is far from a complete analysis of the variety of situations in the states in this group, but it does indicate the fact that the states do vary considerably in their factional structure as they do in their over-all party pattern.

Even with all these variations, however, the states in the one-party group do present a picture somewhat different from the rest of the states in the nation. In the one-party states the primary is the election, and while the voters in all of the states do not turn out in greater numbers for the primary than for the general election, this emphasis on the primary is a matter of considerable importance in practical political terms. The aspiring gubernatorial candidate in the one-party state must win the primary election of the dominant party if he is to be the next governor of the state. While party competition in the general election varies greatly from state to state, in the main it is not the intense rivalry found in a real two-party situation. Consequently, those who aspire to the state's highest office are well advised to run under the banner of the dominant party no matter what their actual politics may be. This results in a wide variety of "Democratic" or "Republican" governors whose party label may have little meaning in national political terms. The really meaningful label so far as state politics is concerned is that of the factional group to which the governor belongs. This is important not only in the process of nomination and election but also in terms of dealing with the legislature. The governor in all of these states will be faced with a legislature which is almost entirely made up of members of his party. The significant question, however, is not to what party the legislators belong but what faction, if any, of the dominant party they support. The governor in a one-party state is in the apparently enviable position of having been elected with a sizable majority and having an overwhelming proportion of the legislature made up of members of his party. As the foregoing analysis has revealed, this is a largely illusory situation and the governor at best will be dealing with two or more factions of his own party and at worst with a legislature which forms and reforms into factions on every major issue or on every conflict of personality that arises. This matter will be discussed in more detail in a later chapter, but is an important by-product of the kind of politics which prevails in the one-party states.

3. THE NORMALLY DEMOCRATIC OR REPUBLICIAN STATES

BETWEEN THE ONE-PARTY STATES on one hand and the two-party states on the other lies a group of states which are exceedingly hard to categorize in a meaningful phrase. In these states one party has not dominated gubernatorial politics to the same extent as in the one-party states, but one of the two major parties has seemed unusually strong and has captured what might be considered more than its fair share of the gubernatorial elections. However, to say that this is a group of states in which the dominant party has showed unusual strength or conversely to say that the minority party appears to have been relatively weak does not distinguish them from the one-party group for which both of these statements are also true. Even the phrase used in the heading of Table IV is somewhat ambiguous, for while the dominant party has "generally" elected its candidate as governor over the period 1930-1950 in these states, it is also true that the dominant party has generally elected its governor in the one-party states. To say that these states are generally sure for one of the two major parties in gubernatorial politics also does not resolve the dilemma, since the one-party states are also sure for one of the major parties. Faced with these difficulties in description, the writer has turned to the short hand phrase "normally" Republican or Democratic states to refer to this group. While this phraseology leaves much to be desired, it does attempt to convey the idea that the normal pattern in gubernatorial elections in these states over the last twenty years has been that one of the two major parties has captured the governorship with such regularity that for the minority party to elect a governor is regarded as a departure from the norm. This distinguishes these states roughly from the one-party group in which the minority party has never captured the governorship during this period and also distinguishes them from the states in the two-party group where it is not a departure from the norm for either party to capture the governorship. This category is perhaps the most difficult of the three to distinguish and to describe in meaningful terms, for by the virtue of its middle position it shades off into the one-party group on one hand and the two-party group on the other. However, it is important for a better understanding of gubernatorial politics to recognize the existence of such a group and to recognize that it includes a fairly substantial number of states. If the twenty states in this group are added to the fourteen one-party states, the two groups together make up some 34 states which are relatively sure for one party or the other in gubernatorial politics. If this analysis is correct, then there appear to be far fewer real two-party states than might be imagined from some descriptions of the nature of the two-party system in the United States. At the state level, at any rate, there seems to be some doubt whether there is a real two-party system in most states or if there is such a system whether it actually functions in the manner in which it is sometimes pictured with really active competition between two relatively equal parties.

The states which seem to fall in the normally Democratic or Republican group are listed in Table IV. In this table, as in Table I, the states are ranked in accordance with the per cent of elections won by the dominant party. Included also is the average per cent of the major party vote for the dominant party.

In terms of party control of the governorship the states range from Arizona and New Mexico with 90.9 per cent each to Nebraska with only 54.5 per cent. In terms of the average per cent of the major party vote polled by the dominant party they range from Arizona with 64.1 per cent to Wisconsin with 47.2 per cent. With the exception of Nebraska, which is a special case as will be explained later, the general range in terms of party control is from 60 per cent to 90 per cent. The level of party control is perhaps more easily visualized when we remember that the figure 60 per cent means that in a state with a two-year term the dominant party elected its candidate in seven out of the eleven elections

TABLE IV

Party Control and the Governorship: States in Which the Dominant Party Generally Elected Its Candidate for Governor 1930-1950

DEMOCRATIC STATES			REPUBLICAN STATES		
	Per Cent of Elections Won by Democratic Party	*Average Per Cent Democratic of Major Party Vote for Governor*		*Per Cent of Elections Won by Republican Party*	*Average Per Cent Republican of Major Party Vote for Governor*
Arizona	90.9	64.1	California	83.3	66.7
New Mexico	90.9	53.3	Pennsylvania	83.3	53.1
West Virginia	83.3	54.6	Maine	81.8	59.0
Kentucky	83.3	54.5	South Dakota	81.8	55.9
Utah	83.3	53.6	Kansas	81.8	54.5
Rhode Island	81.8	55.4	Iowa	72.7	55.2
Nevada	66.6	55.5	Wisconsin	72.7	47.2*
Missouri	66.6	54.0	Oregon	66.6	59.4
Maryland	66.6	52.0	North Dakota	63.6	56.3
			Minnesota	63.6	49.8*
			Nebraska	54.5	50.1

*Republican per cent of the three-party vote. See the accompanying text for an explanation of this division.

in the period, or that in states with a four-year term the dominant party elected its candidate in four out of the six elections in the period. The range of the average per cent of the major party vote is not as great, generally running from 66.7 per cent to 52.0 per cent of the total. The exceptions are Wisconsin, Minnesota, and Nebraska, where a special situation in each case seems to warrant their inclusion in this group in spite of the relatively low per cent of the vote captured by the dominant party.

It is somewhat surprising at first glance to see the apparent discrepancy between the figure for party control and the figure for party strength. In many of the states in this group, however, the percentage of the two-party vote polled by the minority party while fairly consistent runs along just below 50 per cent and only occasionally pushes over into the above 50 per cent level which is necessary to win the election. A typical example of this pattern is found in Maryland. In the Old Line State the Democratic Party controlled the governorship for 66.6 per cent of the period with only 52.0 per cent of the major party vote. The Republican vote, however, was fairly consistent, as is shown by the Republican percentages in the gubernatorial elections during this period which were as follows:

Year	Per cent	Year	Per cent
1930	43.3	1942	47.4
1934	50.6	1946	45.3
1938	44.0	1950	57.3

The Republican candidates in Maryland in those years in which they did not win the election were never more than about 7 percentage points away from the mythical 50.1 per cent which was necessary to swing the election. When the minority party polls a consistent vote which is not quite high enough to swing the election, as was the case in Maryland and a good many other states in this group, the majority party is able to ensure its domination of the gubernatorial election with a relatively small percentage of the major party vote in favor of its candidate.

The over-all averages in the two-party vote conceal many variations, of course, for the average of the vote over a period of time gives us no indication whether the minority party in the other states follows the Maryland pattern, where every election was reasonably close, or follows a pattern like that in Nebraska, where the Democratic Party dominated the state for the first half of the period and ran up most of its total vote in some rather close elections during this period but dropped from the winning column in 1940 and since 1940 has polled over 40 per cent of the vote in only one election. In the paragraphs which follow some attempt is made to explain several patterns which seem to emerge from an analysis of party control and party strength in these states and to comment on exceptional cases, like Nebraska, where there appears to have been a distinct shift in party dominance during the period.

The states which make up the normally Democratic group range in terms of party control from Arizona and New Mexico, which show a very impressive 90.9 per cent, to Missouri and Maryland which show 66.6 per cent Democratic control. In average per cent of the major party vote, the highest ranking state is Arizona, with 64.1 per cent, and the lowest ranking state is Maryland, with 52.0 per cent of the major party total.

Three of the states in this group, Arizona, New Mexico and Utah, reflect much the same pattern of party control, for the dominance of the Democratic Party in gubernatorial politics was not successfully challenged until a very recent date. In Arizona the Democratic Party consistently elected its candidate for governor from 1930 until 1950, when Howard Pyle was elected as the first Republican governor of the period. Prior to 1950 Republican strength in Arizona fluctuated considerably. In the early part of the period, with some ups and downs, it dropped gradually from 48.6 per cent in 1930 to a low of 21.4 per cent in 1944. From 1944 to 1952 Republican strength increased, with a sharp rise in 1946 to 39.9 per cent, followed by a slight increase in 1948 to 40.4 per cent and by a more important rise in 1950 to 50.8 per cent. Howard Pyle was re-elected to the governorship in 1952 with a fairly substantial 60.7 per cent of the major party vote, which is a high for the Republicans in Arizona since 1930.

The Republican victories in 1950 and 1952 may presage a shift in party control in Arizona, but it seems too early to make any predictions on that score. For the period covered from 1930 to 1950 Arizona was a strongly Democratic state, in which the candidates of the Democratic Party won ten out of the eleven elections covered. This fact added to the rather healthy Democratic average of 64.1 per cent of the major party vote seems to classify Arizona as a normally Democratic state for the period in question.

The pattern of party control in New Mexico is, on the surface, very much like that in Arizona. The Democratic candidate was successful in all of the elections during the period covered until 1950, when Edwin L. Mechem was elected as the first Republican governor of the period. The Republican vote in New Mexico, however, was much more consistent than that in Arizona, running around 45 per cent of the total during most of the period with the low in Republican strength coming in 1936 when the Republican candidate polled 42.5 per cent of the major party vote and the high, prior to 1950, coming in 1944 when the Republican candidate polled 48.2 per cent of the major party vote. In the 1950 election Governor Mechem polled 53.7 per cent in winning the election, while in his race for re-election in 1952 he polled 53.8 per cent, not an impressive increase in view of the Republican sweep nationally.

As in Arizona, the Republican challenge in New Mexico came at the end of the period under consideration. However, in New Mexico the core of Republican strength apparently has been more solid than in Arizona. Throughout the period the Republicans in New Mexico, like the Republicans in Maryland, have polled a respectable percentage of the major party vote but have not had quite enough strength to swing the election. In 1950 apparently either enough new voters rallied to the Republican cause to provide the necessary margin of victory or enough disgruntled Democrats swung over to make the difference. Both explanations were advanced in the interviews conducted in New Mexico. One source close to the present administration suggested that enough new voters had come into the state in the last few years to swing the balance. This gentleman believed that most of these voters were professional people who had come into the state in connection with the activities of the Federal government, particularly those activities concerned with the development of atomic weapons. These new voters, according to this source, were probably either Republicans in their home states and continued to vote the Republican ticket or as professional people they were better educated and more interested in "efficient" government and, hence, voted for Mechem as a reform candidate. Other political observers discounted the possible influx of new voters and credited the Republican victory to some rather bitter infighting within the Democratic Party between the Chavez and anti-Chavez factions and to the disgruntlement of some Democrats with both the previous Democratic administration in New Mexico and the Democratic administration in Washington. Some of those interviewed in New Mexico in 1951 suggested that the New Mexico gubernatorial election of 1950 was largely a reaction to the Democratic administration in Washington rather than any real dissatisfaction with the previous Democratic administration in New Mexico and, hence, was a feather in the wind as to the Presidential race in 1952. These prophets proved to be correct in their analysis, for in the 1952 presidential election New Mexico did go Republican and the 59.7 per cent of the major party vote polled by Eisenhower was greater than the 53.8 per cent polled by Mechem in his race for governor.

Whatever the real reasons for the shift, in 1950 enough voters cast their ballot for the Republican gubernatorial candidate to give the Party the needed margin of victory. It is significant that in New Mexico, however, the number of additional voters needed to make up this margin was not as great as in some of the other states in the group, for there was already a fairly consistent bloc of Republican votes in New Mexico on which to build the necessary winning margin.

The pattern of party control in Utah is very similar to that in Arizona and New Mexico, but the shift to the Republican Party came in the 1948 election rather than in 1950. In 1948 J. Bracken Lee was elected the first Republican governor of Utah for the period, polling 55.0 per cent of the major party vote. Governor Lee was re-elected in 1952 with 55.1 per cent of the major party vote. Thus, in Utah, as in Arizona and New Mexico, the successful Republican challenge to a long series of Democratic victories came at the end of the period which we have been using as the basis for our classifications.

Again, it is difficult to determine whether this change represents only a temporary situation, the beginning of a real shift to the Republican camp, or a shift to a more competitive party situation. Without the benefit of a crystal ball, however, we must rely on past experience for our classifications. On this basis Utah seems to warrant classification as a normally Democratic state, for the Republicans won only one election during the period in question, even though they repeated their victory in 1952.

In Rhode Island and West Virginia the pattern of party control tends to be the reverse of that found in Arizona, New Mexico, and Utah in so far as the timing of the Republican upsurge is concerned. In these two states the Republican's successful challenge to Democratic rule came at the beginning rather than at the end of the period under consideration. In West Virginia, the Republicans, who had held sway since the turn of the century, elected William G. Conley in 1928 but failed to elect their candidate in any of the five elections in the period since that date. Democratic control has continued up to the time of this writing, since in the 1952 gubernatorial election West Virginia elected a Democrat, William C. Marland, as governor and was one of the faithful states which cast its electoral vote for Stevenson in spite of the Eisenhower landslide. It seems clear, therefore, that there are sound grounds for the classification of West Virginia as a "normally" Democratic state for the period covered. This view is also supported by an analysis of the trend of the vote in the state. The Republicans, while polling a fairly consistent vote, have averaged only about 44.6 per cent of the two-party total in the five elections from 1932 to 1950. They have not increased their vote substantially in recent elections, although they did make some inroads in the 1952 election, as might be expected, and polled 48.6 per cent of the major party vote, for their best showing since 1928.

The over-all pattern of party control in Rhode Island has been much like that in West Virginia except that the Republicans not only elected a governor in 1930 but also elected their candidate in 1938. The 1938 election of William H. Vanderbilt seems to be largely attributable to a factional fight in the Democratic Party which caused some defections to the Republican candidate in that election. In the three elections just prior to the Vanderbilt race, the Republicans polled an average vote of 44.4 per cent of the vote, while in the six elections following the 1938 election they polled an average of only 41.7 per cent of the major party total. Thus, Democratic control in Rhode Island seems to be based on fairly solid ground. The fact that the Democrats have elected their candidate in nine out of the eleven elections during this period and that the state has been consistently Democratic in gubernatorial politics since 1938 both seem sound grounds for classifying it as a normally Democratic state. Republican opposition, while fairly consistent, has been at a relatively low level and was not sufficient to keep the Democrats from electing a Democratic governor in 1952, although Eisenhower carried the state by a narrow margin for the Republicans.

Maryland and Nevada seem to be somewhat akin to Arizona, New Mexico, and Utah in their patterns of party control since they both elected Republican governors in 1950. However, these states differ in that they also elected a Republican governor in the early part of the period, Maryland having elected a Republican in 1934 and Nevada in 1930. Thus, these states have not been as consistently Democratic as the states thus far discussed in this group. Nevertheless, the Democrats have won four of the six elections in both of these states and their gubernatorial politics seem to have been largely dominated by the Democratic Party.

In Maryland, the Republicans have polled a very respectable proportion of the major party vote. As has already been pointed out, the Republicans in Maryland have generally been quite consistent in the support of their candidate and in those elections in which they did not win have generally polled an average of 45 per cent of the vote and, therefore, needed only a shift of five plus percentage points to win the election. This certainly indicates two-party competition of a sort, but since the Democrats have generally been successful in spite of their relatively small margin of strength, it does not seem to be the same kind of party competition which is found in a state where the shift of a few percentage points not only can mean the election but every two or three elections actually does mean the difference.

In Nevada, as the average percentage of the vote for the Democratic Party reveals, the party has been even stronger than in Maryland. While the Republicans captured the governorship in 1930 and in 1950, in the elections between these two the Democrats held sway and polled just over 60 per cent of the major party vote. The Republican vote in Nevada in those years in which they did not win the election has been even more consistent than that in Maryland. There has been a spread of only 4.5 percentage points between the highest and lowest vote in any of the elections which the party did not win in this period. If those elections in which the Republican candidate won are included, the range is much greater since there is a spread of 25.8 percentage points between the 57.6 per cent of the major party vote polled by Charles H. Russell in 1950 and the low of 31.8 per cent polled by the party's unsuccessful candidate for the governorship in 1938. Even so, the hard core of Republican strength in Nevada seems to be fairly consistent, although at a lower level than that in Maryland. Here again is a state in which the minority party has made a consistent showing with around 40 per cent of the vote in most elections and twice has gone over the line to capture the governorship. However, this kind of two-party competition in which the minority party rarely wins the election seems to distinguish Nevada from the states in the third category in which party competition is such that the minority party not only can but actually does capture the governorship at fairly frequent intervals.

Missouri and Kentucky do not fall readily into either of the two patterns discussed above. Kentucky elected Simeon S. Willis, its one Republican governor of the period, in 1943. The race was extremely close, with Willis polling only 50.8 per cent of the major party vote. Republican opposition in Kentucky is rather consistent, running 45 per cent plus in 1931, 1935, and 1951, 43.4 per cent in 1939 and 42.6 per cent in 1947. While gubernatorial races in Kentucky are sometimes in doubt, as a matter of practice its politics show considerable kinship to that of its one-party neighbors in the South.

The pattern of party competition in Missouri is such that the state is not as sure for the Democrats in gubernatorial elections as is Kentucky. This is reflected in the fact that Missouri has twice during the period under consideration elected Republican governors for a four-year term. The first Republican governor of the period was elected in the Republican sweep of 1928, when it seemed to be established practice to elect Republican governors. The second, however, came in 1940 and, hence, cannot be credited to any Republican presidential influence, since Missouri went for Roosevelt in that election. Forrest C. Donnell was elected with only 50.1 per cent of the vote, which is a close election in almost any terms. Except for this election and that of 1928, however, the Democrats have been victorious and have polled a fairly substantial proportion of the vote. In 1932, 1936, and 1948 the Democratic candidate received 57 per cent or better of the major party vote, but in 1944 he was able to poll only 51.0 per cent. Missouri is one of those states which seem to be subject to definite political divisions along geographic lines with some areas of the state regularly electing Democrats to Congress and others just as regularly electing Republicans. In gubernatorial politics, however, it was predominantly Democratic during this period, although it did shift to the Republican camp on two occasions. In 1952 Phil M. Donnelly was elected to the governorship. Donnelly, a Democrat, had previously been elected in 1944 but was succeeded by Forrest Smith in 1948.

It is interesting to compare the voters' behavior in these states in gubernatorial elections with their behavior in presidential elections. Just before the period under consideration most of the normally Democratic states had a distinctly Republican flavor to their politics. In 1928 all of these states except Rhode Island had voted for Hoover and all six of the states which elected governors in 1928 except Utah also elected a Republican governor. With the 1932 election came the familiar reversal of pattern since all of the normally Democratic states went for Roosevelt and all six of those holding elections for governor also elected Democratic candidates to that office. In 1940 all of this group again went for Roosevelt and five of the six holding gubernatorial elections elected a Democratic governor. The one exception was Missouri, where Republican Forrest C. Donnell was elected with the slim 50.1 per cent of the major party vote. The 1944 election saw Roosevelt again carrying all of these states and found the Democratic candidate for governor victorious in all six of the elections held in that year. In 1948 Truman failed to carry Maryland; and Utah, while giving Truman 54.0 per cent of the major party vote, elected a Republican, J. Bracken Lee, to his first term as governor with 55.0 per cent of the major party vote. The other eight states in the group remained faithful to the Democratic Party in the presidential race and all of those which held gubernatorial elections, except Utah, also elected Democratic governors.

In the off-year elections up to this point the states with two-year terms had all been consistently electing Democratic governors. In 1950, however, there was a change in that both Arizona and New Mexico elected their first Republican governor since 1926. In the same year both Maryland and Nevada, which do not elect in presidential years, elected a Republican governor. These four states and Utah, therefore, all had Republican incumbents going into the 1952 presidential election.

In 1952 Eisenhower carried all of the normally Democratic states except West Virginia and Kentucky. The six governorships which were at stake in 1952 were evenly divided. Arizona, New Mexico, and Utah re-elected the incumbent Republican governors, while Missouri, Rhode Island, and West Virginia elected Democrats. Phil M. Donnelly of Missouri had served as governor previously, having been elected in 1944 for a four-year term. The successful candidate in Rhode Island was the Democratic incumbent, Dennis J. Roberts, while William C. Marland of West Virginia had not previously served as governor of that state.

As was suggested earlier in this section, it is difficult to determine just how meaningful is the shift of Arizona, New Mexico, Utah, Maryland, and Nevada to the Republican camp in gubernatorial elections, since the shift is of such recent origin. The election of three Republican governors in this group in 1952, however, cannot be attributed entirely to the pull of the Eisenhower name, since all three of these governors had previously been elected in their own right.

The normally Democratic states are just beginning what may be a long battle if the Republicans continue to win the presidency. In the first skirmish in 1952 three governors fell and three remained standing. This is somewhat better than the Republican record of five down and two standing after the Roosevelt sweep in 1932. The Republicans may argue, however, that the 1950 skirmish should be counted, which would give them two additional states to make the score five to four as of 1952. In any event, it will be interesting to note whether or not the states which were classified as normally Democratic on the basis of their record over the period 1930-1950 will continue that status or change to competitive or even normally Republican states.

The over-all pattern of control by the Republican Party in the normally Republican states is more uniform than in the Democratic states, although there are some significant state-to-state variations, as will be brought out in this section. The general pattern which emerges in these states is that the successful challenge to the Republican domination in gubernatorial politics was made very early in the period. This stands out clearly when the elections are laid out in the form of a simple bar chart such as that depicted in Figure 1.

In seven of the eleven normally Republican states shown in Figure 1 the non-Republican governors of the period were all elected prior to 1938. The exceptions are Wisconsin, which elected a Democratic governor in 1932, and three Progressive governors in 1934, 1936, and 1942; North Dakota, which elected a Democratic governor in 1934, 1938, 1940, and 1942; California, which elected its only Democratic governor of the period in 1938; and Nebraska, which elected five Democratic governors, beginning with the election of 1930 and ending with the election of 1938.

Except for these four states, which will be discussed in more detail later in the section, the pattern of party control in the

FIGURE 1

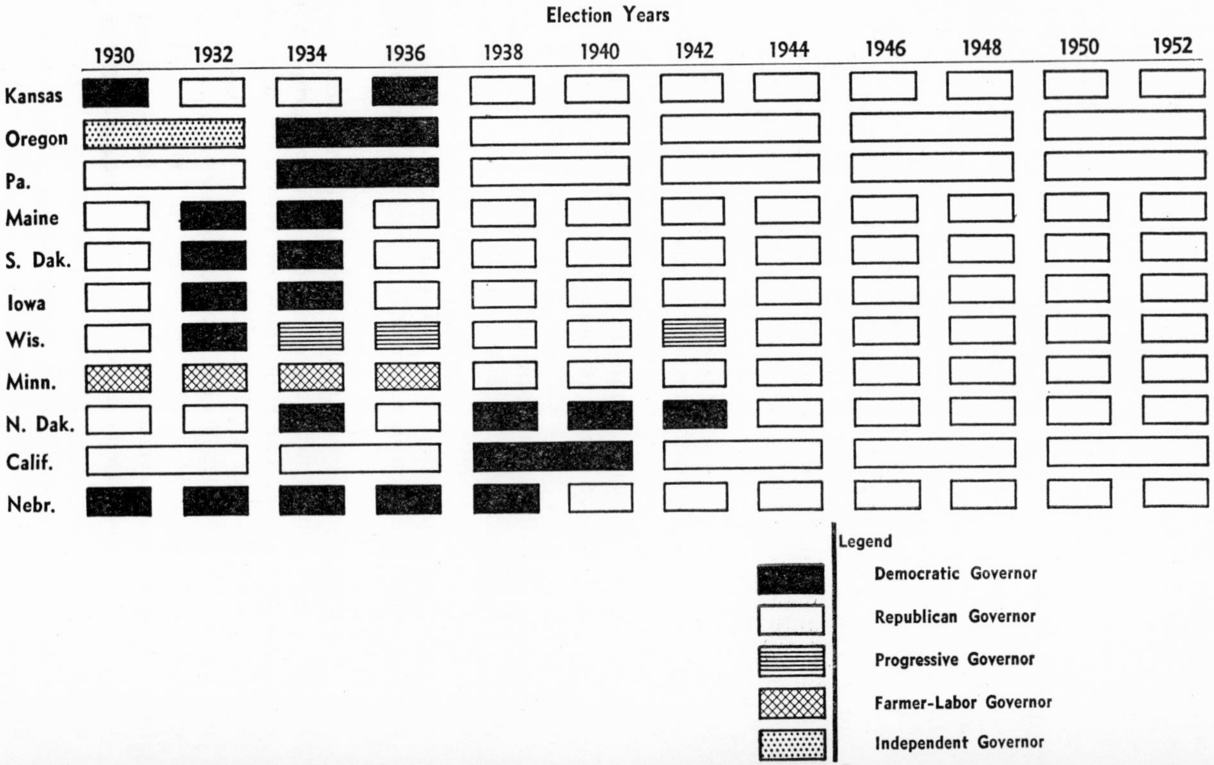

Years in Which the Opposition Party Elected Its Candidate for Governor in the "Normally" Republican States 1930-1950

normally Republican states shows remarkable similarities. Maine, South Dakota, and Iowa all elected two Democratic governors during the period, and these victories came in the 1932 and 1934 elections in all three states. While local factors probably influenced the elections in these states, it seems likely that the Democratic victories in these traditionally Republican states during the depression period can be largely credited to the economic state of the country and to national political trends. The same factors which influenced the voters of both South Dakota and Iowa to vote for Franklin Roosevelt in 1932 probably influenced their voting in the 1932 gubernatorial race. The same parallel does not exist in Maine, since the state was carried by Hoover. However, his margin of victory was only 37,724 votes, which is not an impressive victory in such a traditionally Republican state. It seems probable, therefore, that the force of the depression and the desire for a change also were contributing factors in the Maine gubernatorial election of 1932. The 1934 election was, of course, a mid-year election in presidential terms, but the effects of the F. E. R. A. and other Federal programs to combat the depression had begun to be felt at the state level and may have had some effect in predisposing the voters to a more sympathetic view toward a Democratic gubernatorial candidate than is usual in these states.

Much the same pattern is found in Kansas, Pennsylvania, and Oregon. In Kansas the first Democratic victory came in 1930 in a three-way race for the governorship, in which an independent candidate polled some 29 per cent of the total vote. Harry H. Woodring, running as a Democrat, managed to nose out both the Republican and independent candidates to give the Democrats their first election of the period. This election came too early to be called a part of the Roosevelt sweep in 1932, but it did not come too early for the voters to be influenced by the "depression philosophy" which may have been a contributing factor in the Democratic victory. If this is true, however, it is difficult to explain the behavior of the Kansas voters in the subsequent gubernatorial election in 1932. In that year Roosevelt carried the state with 54.8 per cent of the major party total, but the Democratic candidate for governor was able to poll only 49.5 per cent of the major party vote for that office and, hence, lost the election. One explanation, which seems to have some merit, lies in the fact that the Republican candidate in that year was Alfred M. Landon, who supposedly proved his vote-getting ability with his victory in 1932 and his re-election in 1934. In 1936 Roosevelt carried the state again with 53.9 per cent of the major party total despite the fact that his opponent was the same Alfred M. Landon who had just been Governor of the state for two terms. However, even with Mr. Landon safely out of the gubernatorial picture and helped by the Roosevelt drawing power, the Democratic candidate for governor in 1936, Walter A. Huxman, just managed to ease past the Republican candidate with 51.3 per cent of the two-party total.

In Pennsylvania there was only one Democratic governor during this period. In 1934 George H. Earle was elected with a rather slim 51.1 per cent of the major party total, but since he was elected for a four-year term this reduces the Republican control figure in Pennsylvania to 83.3 per cent. Both before and after the Earle election, Pennsylvania was rather solidly Republican, although as the 53.1 per cent average of the major party total indicates, the Democrats polled a fairly respectable share of the vote, running from 41.0 per cent to 48.8 per cent of the total. The pattern is not very consistent, however, since these two figures representing the high and low points in the period came in successive elections in 1946 and 1950.

In Oregon there is a relatively unique situation, where Julius L. Meier won the election in 1930 as an independent candidate. The three-way division of the vote resulted in Meier's polling about 55 per cent of the vote, while the Democratic candidate received 26 per cent, and the Republican candidate received 19 per cent of the total. As far as the writer can determine, this is the only case during the period in which an independent candidate actually won the election, although independent candidates of one kind or another frequently turn up in gubernatorial races throughout the United States.[1] The number of independent candidates seems to be greater in the West than in other parts of the country, and these candidates generally seem to make a better showing in this section than elsewhere.

Of the eleven independent candidates for governor who polled more than 10 per cent of the total vote in any election during

[1] A possible exception is William Langer's victory in North Dakota in 1936, which is discussed in the next paragraph.

this period, eight were from states west of the Mississippi, while three were from states in the South. In addition to Meier's victory in the 1930 election in Oregon, an independent candidate also polled 32 per cent of the vote in Oregon in 1934 to give it two independent candidates over the 10 per cent minimum. Kansas also had two independent candidates who polled a respectable vote. In the 1930 election an independent polled 29 per cent of the total vote, while in 1932 an independent candidate secured 30 per cent of the total. North Dakota also had two independent candidates in this period, if the candidacy of William Langer as an Independent-Republican is counted in the tabulation. Langer won the election of 1936 in a three-way split with 36 per cent of the total vote. His regular Republican rival polled 35 per cent, and the Democratic candidate polled 29 per cent of the total. Since Langer had previously been elected to the governorship as a Republican in 1932, there is some doubt of the authenticity of his "independent" status. In this study the Republicans have been credited with control of the governorship during this period, although admittedly it was not control by the established powers in the party. Following the Langer victory in 1936, an independent candidate polled 19 per cent of the total vote in North Dakota in 1944.

In addition to these three states, all of which had two independent candidates over the 10 per cent mark, there were two additional states in the West which had one independent candidate in this category. These were Nebraska, where an independent collected 15 per cent of the total vote in 1938 and Nevada, where an independent polled 30 per cent of the total in 1934.

In the South there were independent candidates in both Alabama and Tennessee who made very respectable showings during this period. In Alabama the independent candidate was Hugh A. Locke, who had previously been a Democrat but who was excluded from the Democratic gubernatorial primary in 1930 because he had supported Hoover in the 1928 presidential race. Since Locke could not compete in the primary, he ran as an independent in the general election. Thus, a rather unique situation developed in which the "regular" Democratic candidate was opposed by an "independent" of some stature. This contest aroused considerable interest in the state, and the general election pulled some 250,000 voters to the polls. This is a record high for the entire period of 1930 to 1950 and also was some 54,000 more voters than had participated in the Democratic primary. A situation in which the general election draws more voters than the primary is exceptional in Alabama, where the primary normally outdraws the general election by a little better than two to one. Locke did not win the election but he did poll some 30 per cent of the vote, which is an unusual showing in a state where the Democratic candidate generally wins by a very wide margin.

In Tennessee an independent featured in two races in the 1930's. In 1932 there were six candidates in the Democratic primary, including Hill McAlister and Lewis S. Pope. McAlister won the primary by almost a 10,000 vote margin over Pope, with the remaining votes split among the four other candidates, none of whom was a real threat. Pope, however, ran in the general election as an independent and was opposed by McAlister as the regular Democratic candidate and by the Republican nominee. In the ensuing election McAlister was elected with 42.3 per cent of the vote to 30.6 per cent for his Republican opponent and 27.1 per cent for Pope.

In 1934 McAlister and Pope were the only two candidates in the Democratic primary, and McAlister again defeated Pope, this time by a 54,000 vote margin. Pope, however, again ran in the general election as an independent and was again defeated by McAlister, who ran up a 75,000 vote margin.[2]

[2] In addition to the independent candidates mentioned above, there were several elections in which minor party candidates polled over 10 per cent of the total vote. In California in the 1934 election the combined minor party vote totaled 15 per cent of the entire vote. In Connecticut a Socialist candidate received 26 per cent of the vote in 1938, while in New York the American Labor Party candidate for governor received 10 per cent of the total vote in 1942. Several independents and minor party candidates polled a combined total of 12 per cent of the vote in the gubernatorial election in Utah in 1936.

However, during the entire period from 1930 to 1950 there were only fifteen elections in which the vote for the two major parties did not comprise 90 per cent or more of the total vote. For this reason the figures for party strength used in this chapter are based on the average per cent of the major party vote. *The Political Almanac* (New York, 1952), pp. 96-316 gives the per cent Democratic of the major party vote in the gubernatorial elections from 1928 through 1950. It also has a series of footnotes following the data for each state which give the percentages for independent candidates and for minor parties. The

It is extremely difficult to determine the degree of "independence" of these independent candidates and, on the whole, they must be accepted at face value. Except in the case of Oregon and North Dakota, they have not been an important factor in gubernatorial politics in their own right, but the split in the voting caused by some of their candidacies sometimes was significant. In some instances this split may have favored the minority party, since the independent was frequently a dissatisfied member of the dominant party and may have carried some of the party's voters with him in his withdrawal from the party. The situation varies so much from state to state and from election to election that no valid generalizations seem possible on the evidence available. It seems fair to say, however, that except in Wisconsin and Minnesota, third party candidates have not been a major factor in gubernatorial politics and, except in the instances cited above, independent candidates also do not seem to have been a factor of real importance in the struggle for the control of the governorship.[3]

In Wisconsin and Minnesota the challenge to the Republican Party also came in the 1930's, but it was primarily a challenge of a third party in each instance rather than a challenge by the Democratic Party. The situation is confused by a shifting of some of the major protagonists from party to party as is evidenced by the fact that Philip F. La Follette won the governorship in Wisconsin in 1930 as a Republican with 69.8 per cent of the vote as opposed to 30.2 per cent for his Democratic opponent, while in 1934 he won the governorship as a Progressive with 41.2 per cent of the three-party vote, the Republican candidate polling 19.1 per cent and the Democratic candidate polling 39.7 per cent in a three-way split. In the intervening election in 1932 Albert G.

---

percentages of the major party vote used in this chapter are taken from this source in most instances.

[3] The third party situation in New York might be considered an exception to this statement. In New York third parties are a factor in gubernatorial politics because until very recently they have been able to endorse as their candidate the nominee of one of the two major parties. The third party vote has been of importance in one or two elections but the third parties have not been able to elect a gubernatorial candidate in their own right. It is for this reason that the writer does not consider the third parties in New York a major factor in gubernatorial politics in the same sense that they have been a major factor in Wisconsin and Minnesota.

Schmedeman was elected as a Democrat with 55.6 per cent of the two-party total, but there was no Progressive candidate in the field in that election. The three-way fight continued in the elections of 1936 through 1944, with the Republicans winning all the elections except that of 1936, when Philip F. La Follette was elected as a Progressive, and the election of 1942, when Orland S. Loomis was elected as a Progressive. La Follette won in 1936 with only 47.5 per cent of the three-way total, and Loomis won in 1942 with 50.5 per cent of the total. To further complicate the situation Loomis died before the oath of office was administered and was succeeded by Walter S. Goodland, a Republican. Thus while the Progressives won the election, they lost the governorship and this term is figured in Table IV as a Republican election even though technically it was not. In the 1944 election the Progressives polled only 5.8 per cent of the three-party vote and dropped from the picture in succeeding elections during the period. The fight for the governorship after 1942 was really a two-way battle between the Democrats and the Republicans, with the Republicans victorious.

As this brief survey reveals, the presence of three parties and the shifting of major political figures from party to party makes it very difficult to characterize Wisconsin politics during this period. A good case can probably be made for placing Wisconsin and Minnesota in a special three-party category, since these are the only states where a third party has been enough of a factor in gubernatorial politics during this period to have actually elected a candidate. However, during this entire period the Republicans have polled a respectable percentage of the two or three-party vote, as the case might be, and after all, did succeed in electing seven of their candidates to office in the eleven elections covered. An eighth Republican, Walter S. Goodland, was elected lieutenant governor but actually served the full term as governor. Consequently, the Republican figure for party control may be logically set at 72.7 per cent for the period under consideration. From 1944 to the end of the period, the Republicans dominated the state scene, with their gubernatorial candidates polling an average vote of 55.6 per cent. In 1952 the Republican incumbent, Walter J. Kohler, Jr., was re-elected with 62.0 per cent of the two-party total.

The classification of Wisconsin as a normally Republican state, therefore, rests on Republican victories in seven of the eleven elections in the period and the substantial percentage of the Republican vote since the reversion of the state to two-party competition. Admittedly, however, it is also based on the impressions gained in interviews in the state which indicated that it is somewhat more Republican than the figures reveal.

In Minnesota an even more complex picture of party competition emerges, since during the period in question there were four different parties in the field in gubernatorial elections at one time or another. From 1930 to 1942 there was a three-way fight in each election except that of 1936, when there was no Democratic candidate. In the other four elections the Republican, Democratic, and Farmer-Labor parties all had candidates in each election. In addition, the field usually included an independent and sometimes a Communist or an Industrial Government candidate.

The two major parties in the early part of the period were the Republican and the Farmer-Labor groups. In the seven elections during the period 1930 to 1942 the Republican candidates polled an average of 45.4 per cent of the three-party vote, while the Farmer-Labor candidates averaged 46.5 per cent. During this same period the Democratic candidates polled only 10.6 per cent of the three-party vote in the six elections in which there was a Democratic candidate. In 1930 the Farmer-Labor candidate, Floyd B. Olson, was elected with 59.8 per cent of the three-party total and in 1932 he was re-elected with 50.9 per cent of the total. In 1934 there was a more even division of the vote, with Olson getting 45.0 per cent to 38.0 per cent for his Republican opponent and 17.0 per cent for his Democratic rival. In 1936 the Democrats did not have a separate candidate and the field was left to the Republicans and Farmer-Laborites. The latter won the election with Elmer Benson, who polled 61.2 per cent of the two-party total. From this point on the Farmer-Labor percentage of the vote declined and the Republicans succeeded in electing their candidates in 1940 and 1942. In the 1944 election the Democratic and Farmer-Labor parties combined to form the Democratic-Farmer-Labor Party. This coalition has not had very marked success, however, since its candidates have polled an average vote of only 40.7 per cent in the four elections since its formation.

The box score for the Republicans during the entire period from 1930 to 1950 shows seven victories against four losses to a rather mixed opposition. Only the Farmer-Labor Party has been effective against the Republicans and then only in the first four elections of the period. Since 1938 the Republicans have won the governorship in each election and have polled an average vote of 57.4 per cent of the two or three-party total. This rather impressive period of Republican control and the increasing Republican percentage of the vote in recent years seems to warrant the classification of Minnesota in the group of normally Republican states in spite of the unusual three-party situation which prevailed over the first part of the period under consideration.

North Dakota shows the same figure for Republican control as does Minnesota: the Republicans were victorious in seven out of the eleven elections in North Dakota, as in Minnesota. However, in North Dakota the opposition has come from the Democratic Party and has been of a more recent date than in Minnesota. The Democrats elected their candidate for governor in 1934 but failed to repeat in 1936 when the victor was the Independent-Republican William Langer. In 1938, 1940, and 1942, however, the Democrats returned to power under the leadership of John Moses. Governor Moses seems to represent a good example of a political phenomenon which sometimes occurs when a personally popular candidate of a minority party is able to win elections in spite of his party connections.

North Dakota is probably legitimately classified as hostile territory as far as the Democratic Party is concerned. In the two elections prior to 1934 the Democrats had polled the not too impressive totals of 25.1 per cent and 45.0 per cent of the major party vote. In 1934 they came up to 53.2 per cent for their first victory of the period, and in 1936 against Langer they polled 29.0 per cent to 35.0 per cent for the regular Republican candidate and 36.0 per cent for Langer. John Moses in his three victories in 1938, 1940, and 1942 polled an average vote of 57.7 per cent of the major party total. However, following Moses' last victory in 1942, the Democratic percentage dropped to 35.7 per cent and averaged only 34.6 per cent in the last four elections of the period. In 1952 Norman Brunsdale, running for re-election, beat his Democratic opponent, Ole S. Johnson, by 146,000 votes, to bring the Democratic percentage of the major party vote to a new low of only 21.3 per cent.

It would seem, therefore, that prior to Governor Moses' advent on the scene North Dakota was a rather sure state for the Republicans in gubernatorial terms and that after his three terms it reverted to this status. In spite of this Republicanism, however, the fact remains that Democrat John Moses was three times elected governor of the traditionally Republican State of North Dakota and that, consequently, in terms of party control North Dakota must rate below its neighbor, South Dakota, although such a rating would probably be disputed by some North Dakota party leaders.

North Dakota has had its share of dissension in the ranks of the Republican Party. The Republican Organizing Committee and the Non-Partisan League each generally sponsors candidates in the Republican primary, and the in-fighting is frequently bitter. Such intra-party controversies have produced an Independent-Republican who could win the governorship and sharp fights in the Republican primaries. Nevertheless, the G. O. P. has come up with winners in seven of the eleven elections of the period and has polled a healthy average per cent of the major party vote. Consequently, in terms of party control and party strength it seems reasonable to classify North Dakota as a normally Republican state.

On the surface there appears at least as good a case for the classification of California as a normally Republican state as any of the other states in the Republican group. In the period 1930-1950 the Republican candidates were successful in five of the six elections and the Republican average per cent of the vote is a healthy 66.7 per cent, the highest of any state in this group. Yet, there are some aspects of politics in California which make placing it in the suggested category a risky business. In particular, the cross-filing system formerly used in California primary nominations made it extremely difficult to say in some instances whether the winning candidate was actually a Republican or a Democrat or was some sort of peculiar California product called a Republican-Democrat.[4]

[4] This aspect of California gubernatorial politics is discussed at more length later in this chapter.

To the writer's way of thinking this feature of California politics made seeming party control somewhat illusory, particularly in connection with the legislature, where many legislators were elected after winning the primaries of both major parties. In gubernatorial politics, the situation is less confused, for although both candidates usually cross-filed in the primaries of both major parties it was unusual for a candidate to win both of these primaries. This feat was actually accomplished in 1946 by Earl Warren, who thus became the candidate of both major parties. There is, of course, little doubt that Governor Warren was a Republican, for he had been active in the affairs of his party at both the state and national levels and was the Republican candidate for vice-president in 1948. However, the real allegiance of the members of the state legislature who were elected after having won both primaries is not clear.

In terms of the governorship California normally has been a Republican state, since the only Democratic governor of the period was Culbert L. Olson, who was elected in 1938. Olson was succeeded by Earl Warren who was twice re-elected for four-year terms. Thus, Governor Warren and Thomas E. Dewey of New York share the distinction of being the Republican governors with the longest consecutive service since both served three terms of four years. This record is also unmatched by any of the Democratic governors of this period, although this comparison is hardly a fair one in some instances, because many of the states have a provision which prevents a governor from succeeding himself.

On the basis of the record, therefore, California seems to be a logical candidate for the normally Republican group at the gubernatorial level. It certainly cannot claim this appellation in national politics, however, since it cast its vote for the Democratic candidate for the Presidency from 1932 to 1948. In the latter year it had the "distinction" of going for Truman, although its own governor, Earl Warren, was the Republican vice-presidential candidate.

The party pattern in Nebraska is unique among the states in the normally Democratic or Republican group and is unique among the states as a whole with the exception of an almost parallel situation in New York.[5] In Nebraska there is an almost

[5] In spite of this parallel, New York is classified in this study as a state with active party competition for reasons which are explained in the next chapter.

even division of party control with the Democratic Party in control of the governorship for the first half of the period and the Republican Party in control during the second half. The Democrats captured the governorship from the Republicans in 1930 with Charles W. Bryan as the successful Democratic candidate. Bryan was re-elected in 1932 and was succeeded in 1934 by R. L. Cochran, also a Democrat. Cochran in turn was twice re-elected, thus serving a total of three terms. In 1940 the balance changed and a Republican, Dwight Griswold, was elected and served for three terms, being twice re-elected to office. Griswold was succeeded by Val Peterson, who also served three terms, ending his stay in office in 1952, at the end of the period under consideration. Thus, in Nebraska there have been only two Democratic and two Republican governors over the entire period, although Nebraska is a state with only a two-year term. Apparently the no-third-term tradition has not made much headway in the Corn Husker State.

Party control in the state shows a slight edge for the Republicans, since their two governors served a total of twelve years, while the two Democratic governors served a total of only ten years. This would hardly justify the classification of Nebraska as a normally Republican state, however, for on this basis the Republicans would have an index of only 54.5 per cent of elections won during this period, which would not place it in the 60 per cent or above category which marks the lower limit for most of this group. The primary reason for placing Nebraska in this category is not the number of years that the governorship was controlled by the Republicans but the fact that this control covered the entire latter half of the period under consideration and was accompanied by a marked falling off in the Democratic vote. This leads to the conclusion that since 1940 there has probably not been a competitive party situation in Nebraska. Some support for this thesis is found in an analysis of the major party vote in Nebraska before and after the 1940 election which marked the resurgence of the Republican Party. In 1928, which was the election just prior to the beginning of the period under consideration, the Republicans polled 57.2 per cent of the major party vote. In 1930 there was a shift, and the Democratic candidate was able to take the election with 50.7 per cent of the vote. In 1932 the incumbent was re-elected with a slight increase in the major party percentage, polling 53.2 per cent of the vote. In 1934 the election was again very close, with R. L. Cochran carrying the election for the Democrats with 51.6 per cent of the total. The 1936 election represented the high point for the Democrats, with Cochran running ahead of his Republican rival by 56.4 per cent of the total. In his third race, however, Cochran dropped to 52.0 per cent and this election proved to be the last Democratic victory of the period. All of these elections, except 1936, would generally be considered as close elections, since the Democratic candidate won by an average of only 1.9 per cent of the total major party vote.

The situation since 1940 has been quite different, for the Republicans have won all six elections with an average of 64.5 per cent of the major party total. In only one election, that of 1950, have the Democrats polled over 40 per cent of the vote, and the 1950 figure was only 45.1 per cent. This is a distinct contrast to the picture presented when the Republicans were the minority party before 1940, since the Republicans during the ten-year period prior to that date averaged 47.2 per cent of the major party vote.

On the basis of this analysis, it seems reasonable to conclude that there has been a considerable shift in the party pattern since 1940. Prior to that date there was a competitive party situation in Nebraska, although the Democrats did manage to carry each election by a very small margin. Since 1940 the Republicans seem to have dominated the gubernatorial elections by a much more substantial margin. This fact, coupled with the fact that this domination has come in the latter part of the period, seems to be some justification for classifying Nebraska as a normally Republican state. It is not literally true that the Republicans generally elected a governor during the entire period in question, so that the inclusion of Nebraska in Table IV does not entirely fit the statement at the head of the table. In Nebraska, however, the presence of what appears to be a definite shift in the party pattern must be taken into consideration in spite of the fact that it does some violence to the general criteria established for the classification of the states in this group. It may be that the last two elections in Arizona, New Mexico, and Utah mark the beginning of such a shift in those states. However, this can be but speculation, since it will take several more elections before we can say that a trend has been established. In Nebraska, however, the fact that Republican domination has extended over six elections in the latter part of the period and continued with the election of Robert B. Crosby by the Republicans in 1950 seems to indicate that the shift in this state has already taken place and that, hence, there are reasonable grounds for classifying Nebraska as a normally Republican state.

The relationship between presidential and gubernatorial politics in the states in the normally Republican group is more easily seen than in the case of the Democratic states. The normally Republican states were faced with winning Democratic presidential candidates in all the elections after 1928 until the Eisenhower victory of 1952. Therefore, the persistence of these states in electing Republican governors stands in marked contrast to the national presidential trend and even to their own actions in several of the presidential elections.

Of the eleven normally Republican states there are eight which have a two-year term for governor and, hence, hold every other gubernatorial election in a presidential year. The other three states in the group elect their governors in off-years and, hence, are not considered in this comparison.

In 1928 all of the eight states which held both gubernatorial and presidential elections voted for Hoover for President and all but South Dakota also elected Republican governors. In 1932 came the now familiar switch, with all of the group except Maine winding up in the Democratic column in the presidential race and five of the eight electing Democratic governors. Maine, while failing to go for Roosevelt, elected a Democrat as governor in 1932, while Kansas and North Dakota, which did go for Roosevelt, nevertheless, elected a Republican governor, and Minnesota came up with the second of four Farmer-Labor gubernatorial victories. In 1936 all the states except Maine again voted for Roosevelt but only two, Kansas and Nebraska, elected Democratic governors. The Republicans carried all the remaining governorships except in Minnesota and Wisconsin. In the former state a Farmer-Labor candidate was again elected, while in the latter a Progressive was elected. The 1940 election saw a "return to normalcy" when all the states except Minnesota deserted the Democratic presidential camp, and all but North Dakota elected a Republican governor. The same presidential pattern was repeated in 1944, but in this election

North Dakota rejoined the Grand Old Party to make the gubernatorial sweep for the Republicans complete. In 1948 Truman carried Iowa, Minnesota, and Wisconsin, but the Republicans again swept the gubernatorial races. In 1952 all eight of the states went to Eisenhower and, as might be expected, all eight returned Republicans to the governors' chairs.

While the switch to the Democratic camp both presidentially and gubernatorially among these states in 1932 was striking, it seems equally important to notice how quickly the effects of this election wore off at the state level. In 1932 the score read five Democratic governors, three Republican governors, and one Farmer-Labor governor. In 1936 it read two Democratic governors, four Republican governors, one Farmer-Labor governor, and one Progressive governor. But by 1940 it read seven Republicans and one Democrat, while in 1944, and 1948 the score was eight to zero in favor of the G. O. P. Such resistance to national trends, while it does not match the record of Vermont and New Hampshire in the one-party Republican group or the states in the solid South for the Democrats, is, nevertheless, a noteworthy accomplishment.

The formal selection process in the majority of the normally Democratic or Republican states follows the same general pattern as in the states as a whole. The primary, in some form, is used as the method of nominating the governor in all of the states except Rhode Island, where the convention is still used. Non-partisan primaries are used for the selection of state legislators in both Minnesota and Nebraska, but in both states the gubernatorial nomination is still on a partisan basis. This presents some interesting problems in the relationship between a non-partisan legislature and a partisan governor which will be discussed at more length in a subsequent chapter.

As in the one-party states, the gubernatorial primary has developed some interesting aberrations in the normally Democratic or Republican states. Two of the most striking of these innovations might be briefly described, since they seem to have had some effect on the character of gubernatorial politics in the states in which they were used.

In California a system of cross-filing in the gubernatorial primary was used widely during the period under consideration.[6] Under the cross-filing provisions of the California law an individual could file as a candidate in as many party primaries as he wished. However, he had to win the nomination of his own party in order to compete in the general election. If a candidate failed to win the nomination of his own party, he was also prohibited from competing in the general election as an independent candidate. There is only one instance in recent California history of a gubernatorial candidate winning the nomination in the primary of the opposing party while failing to carry his own party, although this frequently happened in races for the state legislature. The one example in gubernatorial politics occurred in 1918 when James Rolph, Jr. won the Democratic nomination for governor but was not permitted to accept because he lost that of his own party.

The political career of Earl Warren, the recent Governor of California, may be cited as an example of the operation of this system. Warren cross-filed in all three of his races for the governorship. In 1942, he won the Republican nomination but lost the Democratic nomination. He was, however, elected in the ensuing general election. In 1946 he became the first gubernatorial candidate in California history to win both the Democratic and Republican nominations. The 1946 general election, therefore, was largely a formality. In 1950 both Warren and his Democratic opponent, James Roosevelt, cross-filed in both primaries. Roosevelt defeated Warren in the Democratic primary to become the Democratic candidate, while Warren defeated Roosevelt in the Republican primary to become the Republican candidate. The vote in the two primaries gave a fair indication of the candidates' strength. In the Republican primary, Warren received 1,101,411

[6] The California system was abolished by a constitutional amendment in 1953. However, for the period we are considering it was a factor of considerable importance in gubernatorial politics.

Cross-filing in gubernatorial primaries is permitted in Maine, Massachusetts, and Vermont. However, in these states it does not seem to have been a factor of real importance in gubernatorial elections. For a discussion of the former California system as compared to other primary systems see Arthur Harris and Carl Uhr, *Direct Primary Elections* (Bureau of Public Administration, University of California, Berkeley, 1941).

votes and Roosevelt 120,328, a margin of 981,083 votes for Warren. In the Democratic primary Warren received 719,468 votes, while Roosevelt received 969,433 votes, a margin of only 249,965 votes for Roosevelt. In the general election Warren, running as a Republican, defeated Roosevelt, running as a Democrat, by 1,127,898 votes.

It is difficult to evaluate the effects of this system on the governorship in California, but there are three interesting results which are worth noticing. In the first place, the presence of the cross-filing system together with the non-partisan character of local elections tended to give California wide open politics which in many ways resembled the free-for-all in a one-party state like Florida. The reasons for the open nature of Florida politics stem from the complete domination of the state by the Democratic Party. The open nature of California politics stemmed from the lack of domination of the state by any party.[7] The results are somewhat similar, however, in that a gubernatorial aspirant must build his own organization and conduct his campaign, at least in the primary, without party support. The type of candidate these two systems frequently produce is also somewhat similar. Because of the personal nature of politics in states in which there is no strong party organization the candidate must have a program or campaign techniques which verge on the spectacular in order to be successful. This, of course, is not always the case, as is well illustrated by the career of the recent Governor of California. Governor Warren did not use helicopters, hill-billy bands, or "fifty dollars every month" as part of his campaign techniques and slogans. He does, however, have a folksy approach and a genial personality which was particularly effective in a state where personalities are as important as parties. Warren, moreover, could not be regarded as a typical California politician and there are numerous examples of candidates in California whose antics are just as flamboyant as those of their southern counterpart. One result of the cross-filing system in California seemed to be that personal politics was the general rule and that the political parties in

[7] In spite of the fact that California was classified as a normally Republican state because that party has been dominant in control of the governorship and party strength, the cross-filing system so destroyed party solidarity that this classification is probably not actually in accord with the political facts of life.

California during this period were probably weaker than in other normally Republican states.

A second result of the cross-filing system was to increase the importance of the primary in the process of selecting the governor. Californians showed considerable interest in the primary and while primary interest in California does not rank with states like those in the Democratic one-party group, it, nevertheless, seems relatively high. For example, in the 1950 gubernatorial election only 10 per cent more voters participated in the general election than in the primary. The general election in California is important but its open primary system actually resulted in the "election" in the primary of many state legislators, sometimes a member of the United States House of Representatives and occasionally a United States senator or a governor. If a candidate won the nomination of both major parties, there was little chance that he would be defeated in the general election. This tended to focus interest on the primary in somewhat the same fashion that interest is concentrated on the primary in the South.

A third result of the cross-filing system was to place the governor in a somewhat anomalous position in regard to the legislature. When the governor is elected with strong bi-partisan support and a great many members of the legislature are elected in the same fashion, it is not unreasonable to expect that party lines will not be sharply drawn and that the governor must seek support from both parties. This is exactly what seems to have happened in Governor Warren's case since he built up his legislative support from what may be called roughly the liberal wings of both parties.

In New Mexico, Utah, and Nebraska a pre-primary nominating convention is used in conjunction with the primary.[8] New Mexico is the most recent state to have changed to this system, having adopted it in 1949. The plan established by the New Mexico statute calls for conventions by all major political parties prior to the primary. Delegates to the state convention are chosen by county conventions. The purpose of the state convention is to nominate candidates who will run in the primary. Only one ballot is taken for each office unless no candidate receives as much as

[8] Colorado also uses the pre-primary nominating convention, and it has been tried but abandoned in Massachusetts, Minnesota, and South Dakota.

20 per cent of the vote of the convention. Since only 20 per cent of the vote is required to place the candidates' names in nomination, it is probable that two or three candidates will be nominated since no one candidate is likely to have sufficient strength to dominate the convention. The names of the candidates thus selected are placed on the primary ballot of their party under the rubric "candidates designated by convention." Other individuals who wish to run in the primary may have their names placed on the ballot by a petition process. These candidates are listed in a second group designated as "candidates nominated by petition."[9]

The system has been in operation for only two elections in New Mexico and it is too early to judge the results. On the basis of the experience with the system in other states, however, it seems probable that it will result in stronger party organizations than the cross-filing system. Candidates who wish to have party support will have to take some cognizance of the political powers-that-be in lining up the vote in the convention, since those who attend the convention are selected by county conventions, largely controlled by the local political machines. While independents can be nominated by petition, the label "nominated by convention" has considerable value, and the control of this label will give the party organization an important bargaining position. This system seems to give greater emphasis to party regularity and to provide greater party control than either the cross-filing system or the usual direct primary in which all the candidates are nominated by petition. Whether it actually results in the nomination of better candidates or makes for more democratic government is a question which still seems to be unresolved.[10]

[9] For a discussion of the present law and the struggle between the advocates of the primary and convention see three articles by Dorothy I. Cline in *National Municipal Review:* "New Mexico Makes Changes in Pre-primary Convention Law," XL (September, 1951), 423; "New Mexico Retains Pre-primary Convention," XL (January, 1951), 42; and "New Mexico Retains Primary," XXXIX (May, 1950), 233.

[10] The pre-primary nominating convention discussed in this section is not to be confused with the post-primary convention which is used in Iowa and South Dakota. In these states if no candidate receives more than 35 per cent of the total vote in the primary, the nomination is made by a state party convention. This provision is intended to insure the nomination of a candidate who represents the majority of the party voters. See Harris and Uhr, p. 33.

In Chapter 2 it was suggested that one of the distinguishing features of gubernatorial politics in the one-party states is the cardinal importance of the primary in the process of selecting the governor. In this group of states the primary *is* the election and the ensuing general election only a ratification of the choice made by the voters in the primary of the dominant party. In the case of the one-party states, interest in the primary seems roughly to parallel party strength. This is revealed in the correlation between the average per cent which the gubernatorial candidate for the dominant party polled over the elections during the period in question and voter turnout in the primary. The interest in the primary was much greater in the one-party Democratic states in the South than in the rest of the one-party group, although all of these states seemed to show considerable interest in the primary except New Hampshire. In that state voters showed remarkably little interest in the primary even if the comparatively low percentage of the major party vote polled by the Republican candidate over the period in question is taken into consideration.

The primary of the dominant party also seems to be the key to the selection process in the normally Democratic or Republican group, but the writer certainly cannot bring forward any very convincing evidence to show that the voters of these states agree with this analysis. The voters in some of the normally Democratic and Republican states evince considerable interest in the primary as compared to the general election, while in other states the voters show remarkably little interest. The writer has not been able to complete an analysis of the primary versus general election interest for the states as a whole over the entire period in question.[11] However, two complete analyses were made of the primary versus the general election interest in those states which held gubernatorial elections in 1942 and 1950. These two analyses do not

[11] The data on primary elections is available in the blue books or other official publications of some states, but in others it is available only from the Secretary of State or corresponding official. In still others the data which are compiled by these officials is incomplete. Thus, the compilation of the figures on primary elections is a rather considerable task which was beyond the financial and physical capabilities of a one-man research team. Fortunately, the data on the southern states is available in *Southern Primaries and Elections, 1920-1949,* a very useful volume by Alexander Heard and Donald Strong (University, Alabama, 1950). A similar volume on the states as a whole would be a most useful tool in studies of state politics.

reveal that there is any uniform pattern of higher than average interest in the primary in the states in the normally Democratic or Republican groups. Consequently, on the basis of the data available on voter interest, it cannot be said that the voters in the normally Democratic or Republican states show an unusual interest in the primary.

This lack of interest in the primary does not square with the fact that the primary in these states actually forms a most important part of the selection process. In more than one-half of the states in this group past experience shows that the odds are better than four to one that the next governor will actually be chosen in the primary of the dominant party. In the remaining states the odds are somewhat less but still rather impressive. Hence, the primary is practically of great importance since the general election will confirm the choice of the voters in the primary of the dominant party in most instances. Thus, in these states the primary, while not assuming the importance that it has in the one-party states, is actually the key to the process of selecting the governor.

As has been indicated by the foregoing analysis of the party patterns in the normally Democratic or Republican states and by the sketchy summary of nominating procedures in these states, it is apparent that there is an even wider variety of party patterns and nominating procedures within this group than there is among the one-party states. However, the groups do have some features in common and the states within each party category also seem to reveal something of a pattern. In all these states one of the two major parties has dominated the gubernatorial selection process effectively enough to have its candidate win the election for governor at least 60 per cent of the time, except in the unique case of Nebraska, which was previously explained. The dominant party was also able to poll a fairly respectable percentage of the major party vote, although the vote actually polled varied considerably, and in several states party domination was continued election after election with a rather slim but secure margin over the minority party.

The Democratic states in this group do not present an entirely uniform pattern of party control, but in most of them the successful Republican challenge came late in the period under consideration, generally in the 1948 or 1950 election. This leaves open the question of whether or not such states as Arizona, New Mexico, Utah, Maryland, and Nevada are in the process of a shift in party alignment to the Republican Party, a shift to a more active two-party pattern, or simply have shifted temporarily into the Republican camp. On the other hand, in those states like West Virginia and Rhode Island, where the Republican challenge came very early in the period and then subsided, leaving the Democrats in possession of the office for the remainder of the period, the probability of a shift does not seem as likely.

In spite of these conflicting patterns in the Democratic group, during the period in question the Democratic Party did dominate gubernatorial politics in these states and the nature of the party struggle was rather unequal in its character. Party competition for the governorship certainly did take place in the states in this group but as a relative matter does not seem to have been as sharp or to have been crowned with the same degree of success as in the real two-party states in the nation.

On the Republican side the pattern is more uniform, since in all but three of these states the successful challenge to the Republicans came before 1938 and then apparently subsided, leaving the Republicans in undisputed control. In the three states where the Democrats elected a governor after 1938 the Democratic upswing receded rapidly, so that by 1942 the Republicans were once again in control in all of these states.

The degree of party competition which actually exists in a state is very difficult to determine and certainly is not always revealed by an examination of the vote in a given election or series of elections. The writer was able to visit only about one-half of the states in the normally Republican or Democratic group. The general consensus among those interviewed was that the pattern of party competition is somewhat different in these states than in either the one-party states or the two-party states. While most of those interviewed did not speak in comparative terms, the burden of their discussion was to the effect that in spite of the fact that there was two-party competition in the states, in actual practice this competition was not extremely sharp and that one party actually dominated state politics to a large extent. This domination gave rise to factions in the major party which were much like the factions in the one-party states and this factionalism frequently extended even to the minority party. Certainly one cannot discuss state politics with many different persons around most state capitols without being told that to understand the local political scene you must know the two or more factions which make up one or both parties. These may be fairly permanent affairs which follow a roughly conservative-liberal split in the party, or they may be simply affairs of the moment based on some incident in a recent bitterly fought primary. Or they may be simply a division on a pro and anti-governor basis. This factionalism is generally conceded to be a part of the pattern in the one-party states but is perhaps more widespread than is generally thought to be the case. It is certainly also a feature of gubernatorial politics in the normally Democratic and Republican states and in many of the so-called two-party states as well.

4. THE "TWO-PARTY" STATES

THE WORD "TWO-PARTY" appears in quotes in this chapter heading and is used throughout this book as if it appeared in quotes because the writer is not exactly sure just what constitutes a "two-party" state. In Table V these states are listed under the heading "states in which there appeared to be the sharpest party competition." This title is perhaps more descriptive than the term two-party, for there are two parties of some description in all the states and the difference between the three groups of states as characterized in these three chapters is not based on the presence or absence of two parties in the literal meaning of the term but on the degree of competition which seems to exist between these two parties.

As was explained in Chapter 2 the term one-party is used to denote a group of states in which one party has consistently elected its candidate for governor over the entire period 1930-1950 and where party competition appears to be non-existent or relatively weak. In this chapter we are concerned with those states which appear to be at the other end of the scale from the one-party states in terms of party competition. This is suggested partly by the fact that in a majority of these states no one party has been able to capture the governorship for a very substantial part of the period under consideration. In those states where one party did make a relatively good showing, such as Indiana, Montana, and Delaware, the margin of victory was very narrow. In most of the states there was a fairly even division both in gubernatorial control and also in the vote over the period in question. Therefore, on the same basis that the states in the first group were called one-party states, the states in this third group probably qualify for the title of two-party states. In between these two groups came that group of states which was characterized by the title "normally Democratic or Republican" states. In these states there was also two-party competition and in two of them three-party competition. In practice, however, it appears that one or the other of the major parties actually dominated gubernatorial politics so that the opposing party played the part of a permanent minority except under rather unusual circumstances.

The states which appear to fall in the two-party category are shown in Table V. It is extremely difficult to determine just which states to include in this group and the point at which this classification becomes most difficult is the division between the most competitive of the normally Democratic or Republican states and the least competitive of the two-party group. For example, Maryland is classified as a normally Democratic state. This classification was made primarily on the grounds that the Republicans, while polling about 45.0 per cent of the vote in the elections which they did not win, had taken the governorship in only two elections during the period, and one of these had come in 1950 at the very end of the period. The Republicans in Maryland during the period 1930 to 1950 were in most elections a faithful but ineffective minority party. The Democratic Party appeared actually to dominate gubernatorial politics even though its victories were based on a rather slim margin.

On the other hand, Indiana has been classified as a two-party state, although the Republicans also won two elections during the period in question and the average per cent of the Democratic vote of 52.2 is slightly above the 52.0 per cent in Maryland. In two cases, which are apparently so similar, it is difficult to give valid reasons within the framework of the two simple criteria suggested for this diverse classification. In such cases, the writer admittedly has not based these distinctions simply on the data shown in the tables but has gone outside the tables in an attempt to reach a valid conclusion. While it is difficult to pin down a judgment on what might be called the general state of politics in a given state, it is possible to get some clues from elections other than gubernatorial contests. For example, the general political situation of these two states in 1950, at the close of the period under consideration, might be summarized somewhat as

TABLE V

Party Control and the Governorship: States in Which There Appeared to be the Sharpest Party Competition 1930-1950

STATES IN WHICH THE DEMOCRATIC PARTY WON A MAJORITY OF THE GUBERNATORIAL ELECTIONS			STATES IN WHICH THE REPUBLICAN PARTY WON A MAJORITY OF THE GUBERNATORIAL ELECTIONS		
	Democratic Per Cent of Elections Won	*Democratic Per Cent of Vote*		*Republican Per Cent of Elections Won*	*Republican Per Cent of Vote*
Indiana	66.6	52.2	Delaware	66.6	51.8
Montana	66.6	51.6	New Jersey	62.5	51.1
Massachusetts	63.6	51.4	Michigan	54.5	51.6
Ohio	63.6	50.1			
Colorado	54.5	52.8			
New York	54.5	52.8			
Idaho	54.5	51.8			
Connecticut	54.5	49.8			

STATES WITH AN EVEN DIVISION OF PARTY CONTROL

	Per Cent of Elections Won by Two Major Parties		*Average Per Cent of Major Party Vote*	
	Dem.	Rep.	Dem.	Rep.
Washington	50.0	50.0	54.5	45.5
Illinois	50.0	50.0	51.7	48.3
Wyoming	50.0	50.0	49.7	50.3

follows. In 1948 both Indiana and Maryland went for Dewey by narrow margins, the Republicans polling 50.7 per cent of the major party vote in Indiana and 51.6 per cent in Maryland. In 1946 Indiana elected a Republican to the United States Senate, while Maryland elected a Democrat. In 1950, however, both elected Republicans. In the 1950 election for the United States House of Representatives, Indiana elected nine Republicans and two Democrats, while Maryland elected three Republicans and three Democrats. In 1950, the State Legislature in Indiana was composed of 29 Republicans and 22 Democrats in the Senate and 69 Republicans and 31 Democrats in the House. In Maryland the comparable figures were eleven Republicans to eighteen Democrats in the Senate and 35 Republicans to 88 Democrats in the House.

These figures on the presidency and Congress do not have direct application to the governorship, but the figures on the legislature certainly have considerable significance in gubernatorial relations with that body. On the other hand, all of these elections give something of the political atmosphere in the two states which seems to the writer to be just a little more Democratic in Maryland than in Indiana. Maryland is located next door to the southern one-party states and tends to take on something of the same complexion in spite of the fact that the Republican Party is a going concern at present in Maryland.

The decision to place Indiana and perhaps Montana in the two-party category is, of course, a matter of judgment, as are really all the other classifications in this chapter. The writer has attempted to give his reasons for such classifications and it is hoped that most of them are based on sound grounds.

The remaining states in the two-party group all seem to fall logically into the two-party category in terms of gubernatorial control, with the possible exception of Delaware. From the turn of the century until 1936 Delaware had a succession of Republican governors and the Democrats made little headway in the gubernatorial race. However, in 1936 the Democrats elected Richard C. McMullen with a fairly respectable 55.3 per cent of the major party vote and in 1948 elected Elbert N. Carvel with 53.7 per cent of the major party total. On the other hand, the Republicans, although victorious in four of the six elections during the period 1928 to 1952, have elected their candidates with a steadily declining percentage of the major party vote. This percentage has dropped in each succeeding election, falling from 60.9 per cent in 1928 to 50.7 per cent in 1944. As was indicated above, the Democrats won in 1944, with the Republicans polling 46.3 per cent of the major party total. In 1952 the national Republican sweep proved strong enough to assist James Caleb Boggs, the former Republican Representative-at-Large from Delaware, to unseat the incumbent, Elbert N. Carvel, by a rather narrow margin, the vote for the Republican being 52.1 per cent of the major party total. In spite of Delaware's long Republican gubernatorial history, it would seem that active party competition has existed in the state during the period 1928 to 1952 and that it can be legitimately classified as a two-party state.

It should not be assumed, however, that the pattern of party control in the two-party states is the same or that all of them would fit some definitions of what actually constitutes a two-party state. It is primarily because these patterns do vary that the writer uses the term "two-party" as explicitly defined on page 73. Is New York, for example, a two-party state? It has been so classified in this study, and it is probably generally so regarded.[1] In New York, while the pattern has been one of real party competition in most elections, the efforts of the Democrats were crowned with success under Al Smith, Franklin D. Roosevelt, and Herbert Lehman for a continuous period of some twenty years followed by a Republican period under Thomas E. Dewey which continued for twelve years. If two-party competition is taken to mean that the opposition party not only puts up a fight but that this fight is successful at least every two or three elections, then New York does not qualify as a real two-party state. However, the writer feels that there has been active two-party competition in New York in spite of the recent dominance of the Republicans in both gubernatorial and legislative politics. In fact, the gubernatorial race in recent years has taken on something of the flavor of a multi-party contest. The formation of the American Labor Party in 1936 and the entry of the Liberal Party on the political scene in 1944 has given New York not one but two additional parties. Until recently these parties have been able to endorse as their candidate for governor one of the candidates of the two major parties. In this role they have had some influence in the gubernatorial picture but neither of them as an individual party has come anywhere near showing enough strength to elect a candidate of its own. In 1942 when the American Labor Party had a candidate of its own in the gubernatorial race, he polled only about 11 per cent of the total vote. Thus, the third-party picture in New York differs from that of the 1930's in Minnesota and Wisconsin because the Farmer-Labor and Progressive Parties in those states assumed the status of a major party in the early part of the period from 1930 to 1950, while in New York the new parties have played only the role of minority parties during this period.

[1] See Warren Moscow, *Politics in the Empire State* (New York, 1948), Chapter I, and V. O. Key, *Politics, Parties and Pressure Groups*, 3rd. ed. (New York, 1952), p. 324; Professor Key says in part " . . . competition for the New York governorship takes on quite as much a two-party form as does competition for the Presidency."

In addition to the party pattern which has emerged in New York where the two major parties have shared the governorship, each ruling for a fairly long uninterrupted period, there are several other two-party patterns which are to be found in this group of states. Two of these might be mentioned briefly to show some of the variety of party patterns which seems to be one of the outstanding characteristics of this group.

If the reader prefers a two-party pattern which features more frequent shifts in the governorship and gubernatorial races won by an eyelash, then he should be happy with the pattern presented by Connecticut. In Connecticut inter-party competition, if judged primarily on narrow margins of victory, is probably as keen as in any state in the two-party group. In the six elections won by the Democratic Party the winning candidate polled over 51.0 per cent of the vote in only *one* election. The exception came in 1936 when Wilbur Cross, in his fourth successful bid for the governorship during the period 1930 to 1950, polled 57.4 per cent of the major party vote. On the Republican side the victories of the G. O. P. were a trifle more secure, but only in relative Connecticut terms, since the average vote in the five Republican victories was only 52.5 per cent. The high point for the Republicans was the 1946 election, in which the winning candidate polled 57.4 per cent of the major party total, exactly the same vote polled by Cross for the Democrats in 1936.

The Connecticut pattern is, therefore, one of extremely close elections and fairly frequent shifts in party control, with a final score of six elections to five in favor of the Democrats during the period 1930 to 1950. However, it should be pointed out that even in such a highly competitive state the Democrats controlled the governorship for four consecutive elections from 1930 to 1938, while the Republicans controlled for three consecutive elections, from 1942 to 1948. Thus, even in Connecticut we find a pattern where one party controlled the governorship for roughly half of the period and the other party controlled it for the other half. The Democratic control of the first half of the period from 1930 to 1942 was broken only by a Republican victory in 1940, while the Republican control of the second half of the period from 1942 to 1950 was broken only by the election of Chester Bowles for the Democrats in 1948. Republican control is still in the ascendency with the election of John D. Lodge in 1950 for the first of the new four-year terms.

In order to find a state which not only furnishes fairly close elections but also rather frequent shifts in party control one must go to the West Coast to the State of Washington. While the pattern is not perfect, the party shifts in Washington come closer than those of any other state in this group to furnishing an example of a change in control of the governorship in every election. In Washington the Republicans elected a governor in 1928, 1940, and 1948, while the Democrats elected a governor in 1932, 1936, and 1944. Thus, the only period in which one party controlled the governorship for two consecutive elections was from 1932 to 1940 when there were two Democratic governors in succession. In those elections which the Democrats won they polled an average of 61.9 per cent of the major party vote, while the Republican average for their winning candidates was only 53.0 per cent. However, the last several elections of the period were extremely close and illustrate something of the nature of two-party politics as practiced in this particular state.

The State of Washington is roughly divided on an east-west basis between the Republicans and the Democrats. The Democratic strongholds mainly lie to the west of the Cascades, while the Republicans are generally stronger in the territory east of the mountains. The vote in the last three elections seems to have roughly paralleled this division, with the Republican victories coming in those elections in which they were able to hold the more rural east and cut into the Democratic vote in the cities in the western half of the state. The Democrats usually win when they hold their own in the Republican east and pile up a majority in the normally Democratic cities of the west. In the 1944 election, for example, both parties increased their vote in their respective sections of the state over the 1940 figures. The Democrats, however, were able to increase their vote in the cities in the normally Democratic western half of the state, and since this section has a greater concentration of population than the east, this was enough to elect Monrad C. Wallgren over Arthur B. Langlie in a close race in which Wallgren polled only 51.7 per cent of the major party total. On the other hand, in 1948 with the same two candidates running, while the Democrats were able to just about hold on to their 1948 percentages in the Republican east, the Republicans made sufficient inroads into the Democratic strongholds of the west to elect Arthur B. Langlie by the same 51.7 per cent of the vote with which Wallgren was elected in 1944. In 1952 Langlie was again a candidate for the Republicans but was faced by Hugh B. Mitchell for the Democrats. The race was not as close, but for a presidential year in which the Republicans swept the country and carried Washington, the figure of 52.6 per cent for the winner still makes it a decidedly two-party contest.

As was previously noted, one of the outstanding characteristics of the two-party group is the diversity of party patterns which the states in this group exhibit while still remaining in the over-all framework of what appears to be a very competitive two-party pattern. The discussion of New York, Connecticut, and Washington showed that while all of these states had a competitive party situation the pattern of party control differed in each state. The contrast between New York and Washington in the matter of shifts in party control of the governorship during the period under consideration was rather striking. In New York party control had shifted in only one of the eight elections during this period, while in Washington control of the governorship had shifted at every election except one. If the other states in the two-party group are examined with a view to determining the shifts in party control, it will be found that most of them actually had a change in party control in 50 per cent or less of the elections during the period 1930-1950.

Since all of these states do not have the same gubernatorial terms and since some of them changed the length of the governor's term during the period, it is difficult to compare all of them simply on the basis of the number of times the governorship changed hands. Six of the states in the two-party group had a four-year term for governor during the entire period and, therefore, had six elections during the period. Four other states had a two-year term throughout the period and, therefore, held eleven elections in the period, since the 1950 election is counted in these calculations. New York held only eight elections during the period, since it changed to a four-year term in 1942, while Idaho held ten elections rather than the normal eleven contests since it shifted to the four-year term in 1946. New Jersey had a three-year term until 1949 and, therefore, held a total of eight elections in the period.

In order to compare the changes in party control of the governorship in states with varying terms and a varying number of elections, the number of changes as compared to the total number of elections may be expressed as a percentage of change for each state. For example, six elections were held in Washington during the period and the governorship changed hands in four elections, so that the per cent of change for Washington would be 66.6. In Massachusetts, the governorship also changed hands four times, but Massachusetts held eleven elections during this period so that the per cent of change for Massachusetts would be only 34.6. If the per cent of change for each state is calculated on this basis, the comparison between the fourteen states in this group may be expressed as follows:

Washington	66.6	Idaho	50.0
Michigan	63.6	Connecticut	45.5
Delaware	50.0	Massachusetts	36.4
Illinois	50.0	Ohio	36.4
Indiana	50.0	Montana	33.3
Wyoming	50.0	Colorado	27.3
New Jersey	50.0	New York	12.5

As may be seen from this list, Washington and Michigan stand at one extreme as examples of states in which the governorship has changed hands frequently, while New York and Colorado stand at the other extreme as states which have had very infrequent shifts in party control. The most significant point which emerges from the figures on shifts in party control is the fact that these shifts are not as frequent as might be expected in a two-party situation. Twelve of the fourteen states fall in the 50 per cent or below category and six of these show the governorship changing hands less than 50 per cent of the time. This means that the normal pattern of party control in the majority of the two-party states is for one of the major parties to hold control of the governorship for two or three terms and then for the opposing party to take over the governorship for a similar period.

Of the two major parties, the Democrats have been slightly more successful in holding the governorship for longer consecutive periods of time than the Republicans. On the other hand the

Republicans usually manage to maintain control of one or both houses of the legislature. These bodies, in most of these states, have had their districts so arranged by skillful Republican gerrymandering that a Republican majority is generally assured in one or both houses. The Republicans when out of power in the executive branch frequently retreat to their legislative stronghold to await a turn of the political tide which will once again place them in power in both branches.

When a Democratic governor comes into office, he is quite likely to discover that several of his department heads, sometimes a majority of them, are Republicans. In many of these states there are some department heads who are elected. These may have terms which coincide with the governor's or they may have longer terms. In either case they will not necessarily be of the same party, for in a close election it is not unusual for one party to capture the governorship and the opposing party to capture one or more of the other high elected offices. Furthermore, the governor will probably be faced by several holdover officials who have been appointed by the out-going Republican governor. Since these officials may have terms longer than the governor who appointed them, they will continue through a part, and sometimes all, of the next governor's term.

Thus, an incoming Democratic governor is quitely likely to find himself faced by a rather unsympathetic group of colleagues in the executive branch. If the governor stays in power for only one term, he will probably end that term with a number of these officials still in office. If he can continue for two or more terms, however, the Republican officials can gradually be weeded out as their term of office expires or as they are pressured into resigning. Given our present system of elected department heads or appointed department heads who have terms that do not coincide with that of the governor, it is probably fortunate that a given party tends to stay in power for more than one term. If this were not the case, each incoming governor would find himself in the unenviable position of being forced to work with department heads who are not only not individuals of his choice but are not even individuals of his own party. This is already the case in many states when a shift in parties occurs, but would be more frequently the case if there were a shift at every election.

As will be stressed in later chapters in this book, the implications of the pattern of gubernatorial politics in a given state are felt throughout the exercise of the governor's many and varied functions. The effect of the party pattern on the governor's relations with his department heads is but one example of this influence. The retreat of the Republicans into their legislative fortress is another which has very important connotations for the governor's function as a legislative policy leader. Other effects of equal importance, which will be explained later in the book, flow from the basic facts of political life which form a continuing conditioning force in all the governor's activities.

The influence of presidential elections on gubernatorial politics has been briefly summarized in connection with both the one-party states and the normally Democratic or Republican states. In the case of the one-party group the presidential election seems to have no discernible effect on the gubernatorial race. In the normally Democratic or Republican group there seems to be a more direct connection, particularly in the latter group. In the Roosevelt sweep of 1932 several of the normally Republican states elected Democratic governors. The effects of the presidential victory for the Democrats soon wore off, however, and the normally Republican states went back to their old habit of electing Republican governors. In the two-party group the connection seems to be more direct and slightly more lasting. In a two-party state in a close gubernatorial race the pull of a strong presidential candidate is sometimes enough to swing the vote for his party in the gubernatorial race as well. It is, of course, difficult to estimate just how important the influence of the presidential race really is in the gubernatorial races in these states. One has only to stop and think a moment to remember that in the Eisenhower presidential sweep of 1952 both Governor Frank J. Lausche of Ohio and "Soapy" Williams of Michigan were re-elected against impressive opposition in spite of the fact that both Ohio and Michigan went to Eisenhower. The pull of the presidential race can be exaggerated even in the two-party states and there is some evidence to show that occasionally it is the governor who pulls the president through in a doubtful state rather than vice versa. On the whole, however, the presidential race seems to be a fairly important factor in gubernatorial politics in the two-party states and the gubernatorial and presidential races tend to go the same way in a given election if there is a major change in national party control.

Of the fourteen states in the two-party group there are four states which elect their governor for a two-year term in even years. Thus, in these states the voters cast their ballots for both governor and for president in every other gubernatorial election year. Two additional states may be included in this group for the purpose of calculation, since Idaho had gubernatorial elections every two years up to 1946 when it switched to a four-year term, and Connecticut had gubernatorial elections every two years until 1950 when it also changed to a four-year term. There are also five additional states which elect their governor for a four-year term in presidential years, which makes comparison in these states exceptionally easy.

There are three states in the group, however, which cannot be readily compared as to their gubernatorial and presidential politics. New York changed from a two-year to a four-year term in 1938, so could be compared for only two elections and, hence, has been excluded from these calculations. Wyoming has a four-year term but elects only in off years and, consequently, is not exactly comparable to the other states in the group. The same is true of New Jersey, which until 1949 had a three-year term, so that only the gubernatorial election of 1928 coincided with a presidential election.[2]

If these three states are excluded from this analysis, there remain eleven states in which the gubernatorial elections and presidential elections were held in the same years over the period 1928 to 1952. Normally, there would be seven elections over this period in each state for a total of 77 elections. However, since Idaho did not hold a gubernatorial election in 1948 and 1952 and Connecticut did not in 1952 because of a change to the four-year term, the total is cut to 74 elections.

[2] This does not mean, of course, that the presidential election has no effect in these states. However, it is rather tricky at best to compare presidential and gubernatorial politics even in years in which the elections coincide. The additional factors which come into the picture in an election just before or just after a presidential election make it extremely difficult to judge the influence of the presidential race which is pending or has just been completed.

Of the 74 elections held in which the voters expressed a choice for both governor and president they elected a Democratic governor and cast their vote for the Democratic presidential candidate in thirty elections, while in twenty others they elected a Republican governor, while casting their vote for the Republican candidate for president. In twelve elections, however, they elected a Democratic governor but cast their vote for the Republican presidential candidate, while in twelve others they elected a Republican governor, while voting for the Democratic presidential candidate. Thus, in fifty of the 74 elections, or about 67 per cent of the time, the vote for both the gubernatorial and presidential candidates went to the same party, while in 24 elections or about 32 per cent of the time the voters split their ticket and elected a governor of one party and presidential electors of another.

The pattern of voting in terms of the Democratic vote for the comparable states in this group is shown in Figure 2. The voting for the presidential and gubernatorial candidates of the Democratic Party follows roughly the same pattern, with the greatest difference in voting behavior being found in the elections of 1940, 1944 and 1948. The year of greatest divergence was 1944 when only four states elected a Democratic governor, while eight states voted for the Democratic presidential nominee. The point of greatest correlation is in 1936. Here the two columns are of equal height since in this election all eleven states voted for Franklin D. Roosevelt and also elected a Democratic governor.

The pattern revealed by Figure 2 and the accompanying comments suggest that there is a discernible relationship between the vote of these states for president and their vote for governor. However, since only the Democratic vote is presented in Figure 2, the vote of the Republican states which were consistent in their allegiance to that party is not clearly evident. Figure 3 shows the combined totals for both the Republican and Democratic states which were consistent in their voting and also the combined totals for the states which split their vote. This gives a better picture of the correlation which exists between presidential and gubernatorial voting and also points up more sharply those elections in which the presidential and gubernatorial voting was not the same.

In 1928 all of the eleven two-party states under consideration

FIGURE 2

The Presidency and the Governorship—The Number of Two-Party States Voting for the Democratic Candidate for the Presidency Compared to the Number of Two-Party States Electing Democratic Governors 1928-1952

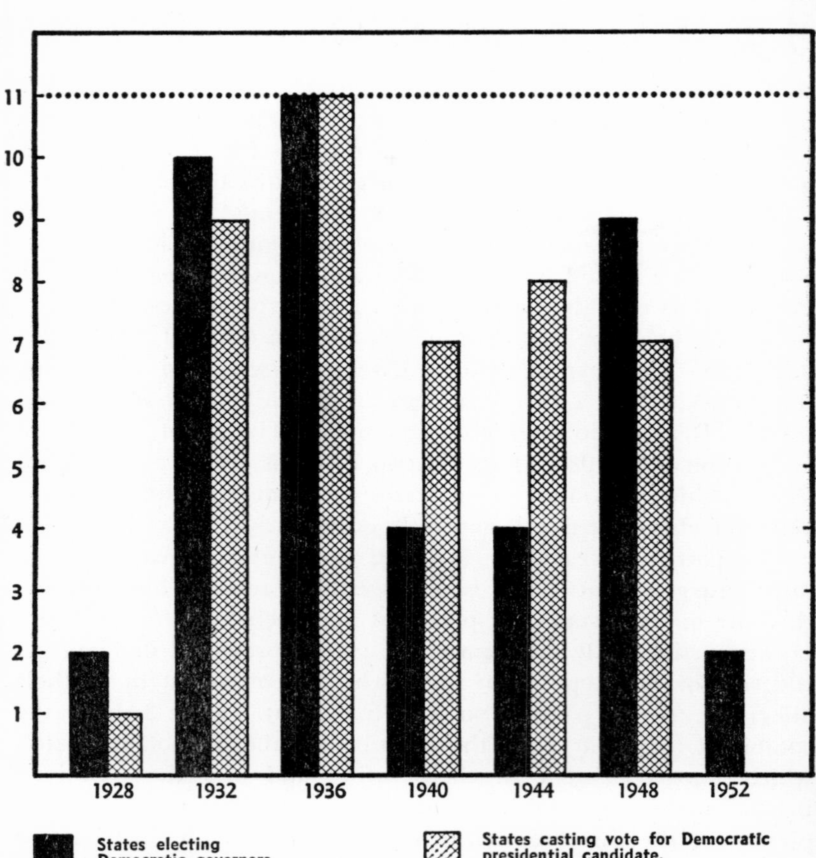

FIGURE 3

The Presidency and the Governorship—The Number of States in the Two-Party Group Which Voted for the Candidates of the Same Party for Both Governor and President Compared to the Number of States in the Two-Party Group Which Split Their Vote for Governor and President 1928-1952

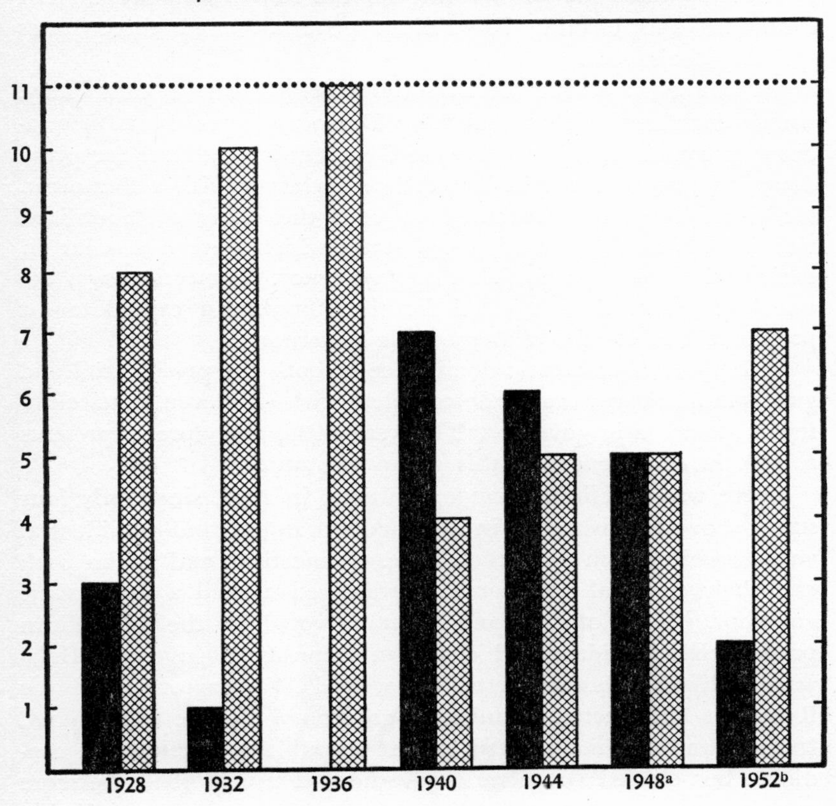

States voting for gubernatorial candidate of one party and presidential candidate of another party.

States voting for gubernatorial and presidential candidates of the same party.

a Idaho did not hold a gubernatorial election in 1948 due to change in governor's term from two to four years.

b Idaho and Connecticut did not hold gubernatorial elections due to previous changes in governors' terms.

voted for Hoover in the presidential race except Massachusetts, which voted for the Democratic presidential nominee. Massachusetts, however, elected a Republican governor. On the other hand, Colorado and Montana voted for Hoover but elected Democratic governors. Consequently, the score in 1928 in terms of consistency was eight states voting for the Republican presidential candidate and electing Republican governors and three states splitting their vote.

In 1932 eight of the eleven states switched parties completely, voting for Roosevelt and electing Democratic governors. Massachusetts continued to vote for the Democratic candidate for president and also replaced its Republican governor with a Democrat. However, Delaware continued to vote the straight Republican ticket. This made a total of ten states which were consistent in their voting for both president and governor. Connecticut was the one holdout in that it voted for the Republican candidate for president but elected a Democratic governor.

In 1936 the Democratic dominance of both the presidential and gubernatorial races was made complete with all eleven states electing a Democratic governor. The year 1936, therefore, represents a peak in consistency for this group of states.

There was a definite change, however, in 1940, since only four states showed consistency in their gubernatorial and presidential voting, while seven split their vote. Connecticut and Idaho both cast their electoral vote for Roosevelt and elected a Democratic governor, while Colorado and Montana voted for the Republican presidential candidate and elected a Republican governor. Delaware, Illinois, Massachusetts, Ohio, and Washington voted for Roosevelt but elected Republican governors. On the other hand, Indiana and Michigan voted for the Republican presidential candidate but elected Democratic governors. Thus, in 1940 the score was four states with consistent voting and seven states splitting their vote.

In 1944 the pattern was much the same. Colorado and Indiana voted for the Republican candidate in both races, while Idaho, Washington, and Massachusetts voted for the Democratic candidate in both races. All of the remaining six states voted for Roosevelt but elected Republican governors, except Ohio, which reversed the process by voting for Thomas E. Dewey for president, while electing Frank J. Lausche, a Democrat, to his first term as governor. The score in 1944, therefore, was five states showing consistent voting and six states splitting their vote.

In 1948 Illinois, Massachusetts, Montana, and Ohio all voted for Truman and elected Democratic governors. These four states were joined by Colorado, which switched parties but remained consistent by voting for both the presidential and gubernatorial candidates of the Democratic Party. Washington voted for Truman but elected a Republican governor, while Connecticut, Delaware, Indiana, and Michigan voted for Dewey but elected Democratic governors. Idaho voted for Truman but did not elect a governor in 1948, since it had shifted to a four-year term at the 1946 election. In 1948, therefore, five states voted for Truman and elected Democratic governors, while five additional states split their votes and one, Idaho, did not hold a gubernatorial election.

The 1952 election saw an almost complete repetition of the 1932 pattern except that the parties were reversed. All eleven states voted for Eisenhower and all nine which held gubernatorial elections except Michigan and Ohio also elected Republican governors. In Michigan "Soapy" Williams was elected to his second term by such a narrow margin that the election was not decided until after a recount. In Ohio Frank J. Lausche, one of the most durable of the Democratic governors, was elected to his third consecutive term by 55.8 per cent of the vote to achieve what was probably the most outstanding Democratic victory of the year. Two states, Idaho and Connecticut, did not hold gubernatorial elections in 1952 because of a previous shift to a four-year term. Thus, the score in 1952 was seven states which featured consistent voting as opposed to two which split their vote. This may be compared with the score in 1932 when ten states were consistent and one state split its vote.

This analysis covers too short a period of time to serve as the basis for any valid generalizations concerning the nature of the relationship between presidential and gubernatorial voting in the two party states. An examination of the data for this period, however, tends to make the writer rather cautious in ascribing very much weight to the pull of the presidential election. While the hypothesis that the governors in the two-party states tend to ride into office on the presidential coattails seems to have some validity for elections in which there is a national sweep by one of the major parties, it does not seem to be as valid for those elections which fall in between such major party shifts.

The previous analyses of the effects of the presidential race on the states in the one-party group showed that these states paid little attention to presidential sweeps or even to their own vote in the presidential election. The Democratic states continued to elect Democratic governors even in those rare instances such as in 1928 and 1952 when several of them voted for the Republican presidential candidate, and the Republican states continued to elect Republican governors even though New Hampshire did go for Roosevelt in three elections.

In the normally Democratic or Republican group the influence of the presidential race was more marked but still hardly a determining factor in gubernatorial politics. In 1932 Roosevelt managed to carry all of the normally Republican states except Maine and five of the eight elected Democratic governors. Maine, while failing to go for Roosevelt, also elected a Democratic governor so that if the coattails theory is accepted, Roosevelt might be credited with a total of six Democratic governors in these states. The effects of this shift soon wore off, however, for in 1936, while all of the states except Maine again voted for Roosevelt, only two elected Democratic governors.

In the normally Democratic group there is little chance to judge the effects of the pull of presidential races except in 1952, since this was the first Republican victory of the period which represented a change in party control. In the 1952 election three of the six states which went for Eisenhower elected Republican governors and three elected Democrats. Eisenhower, however, cannot be entirely credited with these three governorships, since Utah, New Mexico, and Arizona, which are the three states in question, all went into the 1952 presidential election with Republican governors.

Taking the evidence on all of these groups over the period 1928-1952, it would seem that the coattails theory has some application in years in which there is a change in the presidency from one major party to the other. In the interval between such changes the presidential race does not seem to be a decisive factor in gubernatorial politics in most states. Of the three groups of states suggested in this study, the group which seems to be most affected by the pull of presidential elections is the two-party group. The presidential race has apparently no effect on the governorship in the one-party states and only a fleeting effect on the normally Republican group. In the two-party states the effects of the Roosevelt sweep in 1932 apparently lasted for two elections, since 1936 was a high point in the correlation between the two races. From 1940 to 1952, however, the correlation was negative, while in 1952 the shift to the Republicans in both the presidential and gubernatorial races gives some support to the coattails theory. It would seem, therefore, that even in these states this hypothesis should be applied with caution. Taking the states as a whole, the writer does not feel that the pull of the presidential election is generally a decisive factor in gubernatorial politics.

In the majority of two-party states the primary is in both theory and practice a device for the nomination of gubernatorial candidates. Primaries are normally held by both major parties, although in some states this is optional with the party. The primaries vary somewhat from state to state but generally follow the standard patterns for either the open or closed variety.

Perhaps the most interesting deviation from the normal nominating process is to be found in Connecticut, Indiana, and New York. In these states the governor is still nominated by the convention method.[3] Fifty years ago this would have been the normal pattern and those states with primaries would have been the exceptions. Now, the direct primary movement has become so widespread that the reverse is true.

It is interesting to note that three of the four states which retain the nominating convention are two-party states. This peculiarity can hardly be explained simply by that fact, however, for a much greater number of two-party states now use the primary. It is also very difficult to use the experience of these states to prove or disprove the claims concerning the effectiveness of the convention system. Since these states seem to have produced a fair share of outstanding governors, it may be that the evils of the convention system have been overrated. On the other hand,

[3] As was noted previously, the convention is also used in Rhode Island for gubernatorial nominations.

those states which have adopted the primary have also produced outstanding governors from time to time.

In view of the lack of conclusive evidence on the side of those who wish to return to the convention system, it seems probable that the primary will be retained in a majority of the states. While it is true that the primary as presently operated in most states can produce minority candidates, it has the basic advantage of allowing the voter to have a direct choice in the nomination as well as in the election of the governor. The powers which the average American governor wields are now very substantial, and the trend seems to be toward an increase rather than a decrease in those powers. Under these conditions, the question of popular control over the governorship becomes a matter of increasing importance. Considerable emphasis has been given to the importance of popular election as one method of popular control. Equal importance should be given to popular control of the nominating process.

It seems too much to expect that any nominating process either by convention or primary will actually place this control in the hands of the people. "The people" do not make a daily business of politics. At best they seem to forsake their daily pursuits only to come to the polls and vote, frequently in very small numbers. In the face of this lack of interest, no system will place the control in the hands of the people. Unless the majority of the states' citizens are willing to take a more active part than they have heretofore displayed in politics, real popular control will continue to be lacking. However, in spite of this political inertia, perhaps we should say because of it, the primary seems to offer more hope than the convention for more citizen participation in the nominating process. The average citizen seems reluctant to take any active part in politics, but he will come out and vote when he will do nothing else. Hence, the primary, based on a choice between candidates who are nominated by a fairly simple petition process, seems to offer more hope than a convention which experience has shown is not likely to be made up of average citizens.

The emphasis on the importance of the primary in the process of nominations and elections which recurs in all three of these sections may seem to be the result of some sort of obsession on the part of the writer. Hence, such emphasis may appear to be out of proportion to the real importance of this aspect of the selection process. While this emphasis may be misguided, it is certainly deliberate, for the results of this study seem to show, to the writer at any rate, that the real key to the whole process of selecting our governors lies in the procedures by which they are nominated. The key in turn to these procedures lies in the nature of the party pattern behind the formal legal framework. Hence, three chapters have largely been devoted to rough sketches of the party patterns found in the states in these three groups. Behind the gross party patterns lie the ramifications and complexities of the factional structure of the major parties themselves. This factional organization has barely been suggested in the discussion of the normally Democratic or Republican states and the discussion of the two-party group. It was discussed in more detail in the description of the one-party group, where it is of paramount importance.

As we have seen the groupings themselves, not to mention the party patterns within the groupings and the factional pattern of the individual parties, are not absolute. For the period covered the division of the states into three major groups and the party patterns within those groups seem to bear some resemblance to the actual party situation in the respective states, but states have shifted from one group to another and probably will continue to shift. Some of them, as has been indicated, seem to have already shifted from one party allegiance to another and others may be in the process of shifting.

The first four chapters of this book have been more descriptive than analytical, although in the nature of describing and classifying the states judgment must inevitably play a significant part. If they have succeeded in fulfilling their purpose, what they have attempted is to characterize the states as to the broad outlines of their party pattern in the period 1930-1950. This characterization, it is hoped, has some relation to the party patterns which actually existed in the states over this period. If it has, then the categories which were suggested for the states may be of some use in the better understanding of gubernatorial politics as a background for the governor's performance of his major functions.

The American governorship is primarily a political office in both senses of the term. A governor must begin by being a "politician" in the first sense of the term because he must first be elected. Only then can he exercise the function of policy formation which is a second aspect of gubernatorial politics. The way in which the governor was nominated and elected, the friends he made, and the enemies he made, his status as the real or simply the titular head of his party, his status as a leader of the majority faction of his party, or his status as a man opposed by an important faction of his party may all stem from his election and will have important implications in the exercise of every function of his office, particularly in his dealings with the legislature and the "party bosses." If any one point has emerged clearly from this study, it is the fact that the alleged distinction between "politics" and "administration" has little application at the state level, and that the governor's exercise of all his functions whether they be administrative or legislative is conditioned by the political process which brought him into his office and by the political considerations he may have for the future. Many of our governors have indeed developed into statesmen of no inconsiderable stature in their terms of office but first of all they have been politicians and by the nature of the system of popular elections must remain such in order to function under our system of checks and balances and peculiar patterns of party government.

It is primarily because we do not really have party government at the state level that the governor must continue to play the role of the politician even after his election. This matter will be explored in more detail in the chapter on the governor's relations with the legislature, but the same sort of factional politics which has emerged in our analysis of gubernatorial elections is also present in the election of our legislative bodies. The idea of disciplined parties in the legislature who work with the governor to execute a party program is largely a none-too-effective myth at the state level. The governor is elected in an atmosphere of factional politics and he continues to operate in that atmosphere in his dealings with the legislature, with his department heads, and with the other members of the executive branch.

5. CAMPAIGN TECHNIQUES AND COSTS

THE TECHNIQUES used by gubernatorial candidates in the primary and general election form a fascinating chapter in political history which can be only briefly sketched here. The answer to the intriguing question of what it costs to become governor can also be dealt with only in its general outline. Both of these aspects of gubernatorial politics are a study in themselves. The material presented in the following sections is not the result of a scientific approach to these problems but rather is a summary of some of the sidelights collected in the course of interviews which were directed primarily to determining the governor's function. Nevertheless, the comments of those interviewed brought into focus some interesting aspects of the techniques and financing of gubernatorial campaigns.

CAMPAIGN TECHNIQUES

The techniques used by gubernatorial candidates vary considerably from state to state and even within a state with the passage of time and the changing personalities of the candidates. What is sure-fire campaigning in Alabama may be completely ineffectual in South Dakota. A recent governor of the latter state told the writer that his opponent used a calliope in campaigning against him. The governor felt, however, that this had not only been expensive but actually had cost his opponent a considerable number of votes. The best campaign in South Dakota, according to the ex-governor, was one which involved personal contact with as many voters as possible. He favored short speeches to small groups of voters in which he presented his program in a matter-of-fact and fairly closely reasoned fashion. He felt that the voters in South Dakota put considerable emphasis on the candidates' programs. He added, with a laugh, that most candidates were forced to use at least a part of this technique because in a large state with a scattered population a small group of voters was the most a candidate could hope to get together in any one place.

In Alabama a calliope might be just the kind of campaign device which would appeal to the voters. After all, Gordon Persons was elected governor of Alabama in 1950 after a campaign in which he used a helicopter to land in the court house squares and other strategic spots for short talks. Crowds were attracted by loud speaker trucks which preceded the candidate into town and told one and all that he would descend in a few hours for a speech at the county seat. In Alabama, however, the audience is also likely to be small and personal contacts are important.

The flamboyant campaign antics of southern politicians are a matter of considerable amazement to people outside the South. At first glance it is perhaps difficult to understand how, in a sizeable section of the nation, voters can be influenced by such methods as clambakes, fish-fries, hillbilly bands, helicopters, replicas of the state capitol on wheels, and flaming oratory. The answer lies in part perhaps in the old proverb that "you have to cut a garment in accordance to the cloth" and that the cloth in the South is largely homespun and must be cut accordingly. However, the composition of the electorate is only part of the answer. The South is rapidly becoming industrialized and is losing much of its homespun flavor. The major reason for the difference in technique found in the South is the absence of the highly formalized and institutionalized political party organization which is found in two-party states. Except for the Crump machine in Tennessee and the Long machine in Louisiana, the party organizations of ward clubs, precinct captains and paid party workers who assiduously push door bells is virtually unknown in the South. Hence, the party does not have a latent organization which need only be activated and given a candidate's name to swing into action. Furthermore, the party ordinarily does not use the machinery which it does have to support a candidate in the primary where the crucial battle is fought. As a consequence, politics, while everywhere a highly individualistic art, is even more personalized in the South than in other sections of the country. In the primary campaign each candidate is thrown on his own resources and must build whatever organization he deems necessary from the ground up. Under these circumstances it is not surprising that candidates must replace organization with denunciation, ward clubs with fish-fries, and doorbell pushing with hillbilly bands.[1]

Ellis Arnall, the liberal former Governor of Georgia, well summarized the necessity for this sort of campaign in the South. Mr. Arnall had been asked in an interview to comment on the use of the Strawberry Pickers, a tireless aggregation of hillbilly musicians with whom Big Jim Folsom had successfully stumped the State of Alabama in the 1946 gubernatorial campaign. Said Mr. Arnall, "It was necessary for Folsom to use color and showmanship to win the governorship. The parlor liberals and advocates of good government in every state must realize that you have to have some showmanship and be a politician before you can develop into a statesman."[2]

In a one-party state and to a large extent in a normally Democratic or Republican state, the candidate is strictly on his own in the primary. Since there are few clear cut issues and many candidates in the average primary, the appeal to the voter tends to become one of personalities. Many forces are at work to impel candidates to try to attract attention by what they do rather than what they think. In two-party states, while personalities also tend to obscure issues, the successful candidate in the primary may expect party support in the general election and hence is not entirely on his own in his attempt to win the governorship. The race for the governorship is decided in the general election and in the voting in that election we begin to see the results of party discipline, a factor unknown in the South.

Warren Moscow points out that in New York, in comparison to one-party states in the South and the two-party system elsewhere, we find not only one but two actively functioning minor parties. These parties are big enough to be factors in determining an election. This is true because it is possible for the minor parties

[1] For an example of an "organized" type of campaign in the South see Estes Kefauver, "How Boss Crump Was Licked," *Collier's,* October 16, 1948.

[2] Birmingham *Post,* January 15, 1948.

to nominate the same candidate as one of the major parties and to have its votes counted for that candidate in the general election. In spite of this, New York is representative of the traditional two-party system. As a result of the contest between these groups, Moscow feels that

> . . . there is less chance for a political mugwump to get places in New York than there is elsewhere. New York sees no goat-gland doctor coming close to election as governor because of the panaceas he purveys by radio. No hillbilly bands or biscuit-passers threaten the established political order. New York's voters are tied more closely to the state's recognized political parties than is the general rule elsewhere, and only the regularly nominated candidates figure importantly in the election results. The Democratic and Republican parties have taken turns as the dominant party in the state. The American Labor and Liberal parties, one formed in 1936 and the other in 1944, can contribute to the success or defeat of either major party by alliance with one or the other or by taking independent action, but neither the ALP, the Liberals, nor any other independent group can come close to electing a candidate for high public office on a state-wide basis.
>
> Both parties have developed a sense of statewide responsibility. They know they have to run their candidates in Yonkers as well as Penn Yan, in Syracuse as well as Canarsie. The result is a democracy calculated to do the most good for and secure the most votes of the greatest number of people.[3]

In two-party states where the governor may expect some support from the party in the general election, the kind of campaign which he wages will probably be dictated in large measure by his past political experience, the political exigencies of the moment, and his own personality. One example of a highly organized, whirlwind campaign which used all the latest communication devices was that of Dan Thornton, who was the successful Republican candidate for governor in Colorado in 1951. This campaign was exceptional because circumstances dictated that it be confined to a five-week period. This was necessary because the Republican candidate for governor died shortly before the election, and the Republican leaders selected Thornton, then a state senator in his first term, to run in his place. Thornton conducted a whirlwind five-weeks campaign in which he traveled throughout the state by plane and car. He was preceded in each of the

[3] Warren Moscow, *Politics in the Empire State* (New York, 1948), p. 12.

towns in which he was to speak by a sound truck. The whole schedule was timed exactly so that Thornton arrived in each town a few hours after the sound truck had covered it announcing his forthcoming speech. The truck proceeded to the next town directly after each speech and had an audience collected by the time the candidate arrived at that location. Governor Thornton also had meetings at night and had lunch with smaller groups. This sort of campaigning is extremely strenuous but fitted well with the personality and background of the candidate, since Thornton was a relatively young man and a good extemporaneous speaker.

In normally Democratic or Republican states, campaigning tends to resemble that found in one-party states. This has been particularly true in California, where the unique cross-filing provisions tended to produce the free-for-all atmosphere found in most of the one-party states. Crouch and McHenry describe the California situation as follows:

> The conduct of a campaign in California differs considerably from that in states with strong political organizations. The primary, both partisan and nonpartisan, often is wide open, with nominations frequently won by dark horse or insurgent aspirants. Because many aspirants for nominations attempt to capture both party primaries, there is a tendency on their part to stress regional and personal issues, and to minimize partisanship. Since the partisan primary can be won by a plurality, aspirants often are numerous. This strengthens the position of the incumbent seeking renomination; his further advantage through cross-filing is obvious. The nonincumbent therefore may resort to spectacular antics, like a "hill-billy" campaign, or may support some farfetched panacea, such as a pension scheme, which will appeal to a considerable sector of the electorate.[4]

The advent of first the radio and now television as methods of mass communication has not been overlooked by aspirants for the governorship. The blessings that these two media have brought to political campaigning are not unmixed, for although both are effective in proper hands they are also expensive and may tend to place some advantage on the side of the individual who can afford to buy the most time on the air.[5] This is not necessarily

[4] Winston W. Crouch and Dean E. McHenry, *California Government* (Berkeley and Los Angeles, 1949), p. 62.

[5] See the following section on campaign costs for a discussion of this point.

true, however, for an individual must have a good radio personality in order to use this medium effectively and many individuals who are good stump speakers do not seem to have the same appeal on radio.

While radio has been used for many years as a part of the campaign techniques of most gubernatorial candidates, there has recently developed a new use of the technique which has proved successful in at least one recent gubernatorial race. This new development is the radio talkathon, in which the candidate takes to the air for 24 hours or more and answers any and all questions put to him by his listeners. Judge Francis Cherry is credited with the introduction of this device for the first time in gubernatorial campaigning in his 1952 campaign against the incumbent Sid McMath for the governorship of Arkansas. Cherry, who was a chancery judge from Jonesboro and virtually unknown outside his own chancery district, used the device to bring himself to the attention of the voters in the state at large. As a result of Cherry's vigorous campaign, he placed second to McMath in the first primary in July of 1952 and later overwhelmingly defeated McMath in the run-off primary in August. While there were many issues in the campaign, including "Trumanism," which may have accounted for McMath's defeat, the talkathon is credited by many local observers with bringing the Judge to the attention of enough of the state's voters to make him a state-wide "personality." While this is important in any gubernatorial election, it is especially important in a one-party state, particularly when the candidate is running against a well-established incumbent, who is not only well known in his home state but in the nation. At least a part of Cherry's success must be attributed to his talkathon technique.

No method, however spectacular, is uniformly successful even in the South. The same talkathon system was used by Jimmy Faulkner, a south Alabama newspaper editor in his campaign for the governorship of Alabama in 1954. Faulkner was regarded by many as a strong contender. However, he was decisively beaten in the primary by Big Jim Folsom who successfully made his second bid for the governorship after the compulsory four-year waiting period required by Alabama law. Faulkner did, however, become well known throughout the state and his talkathon may yet pay dividends in a future gubernatorial election.

It should also be noted that television is now coming into play in gubernatorial campaigning and is also being used by some governors for reports to the people and by at least one legislature as a reporting device. Governor Warren of California used television rather extensively in his 1951 campaign and also as a reporting device during his last term of office. The Governor had two weekly television programs which were in the nature of a report to the people on current issues. These programs were of the interview type, with the governor answering prepared questions which were put to him by an individual who interviewed the Governor on issues which had been decided upon in advance. This gave the program an appearance of spontaneity which would be lacking in a prepared address and also tended to hold the attention of the viewers. These programs were used primarily as a public relations device during the Governor's last term and were not, therefore, direct campaign measures.

Another interesting use of television which is not without potentialities as an indirect method of campaigning is the plan tried by the Oklahoma Legislature in a recent session. During the 1951 session, the Oklahoma law-makers were televised weekly by station WKY-TV. In order to insure an interesting program, the station's program director selected for television the house in which the calendar for the day looked most promising. Floor leaders of the respective houses arranged procedural matters on television days so that they were disposed of before the program went on the air. The first program included the governor's opening message to the Legislature and thus combined both gubernatorial and legislative coverage. The experiment, according to Paul Harkley, who is a member of the body, was generally regarded as successful. Mr. Harkley summarizes his description of the experiment by saying, "In Oklahoma most of us are convinced that the solid value fully justifies legislative television—that it is a genuine tool of democracy, for keeping government close to the people."[6]

[6] "Televising the Legislature in Oklahoma," *State Government,* XXIV (October, 1951), 260.

The fact that television can be successfully used in gubernatorial campaigning where the necessary coverage is available has already been demonstrated in the campaigns of Earl Warren in California, Thomas E. Dewey in New York, and G. Mennen Williams in Michigan. If the trend toward televising state legislatures and regular televised reports to the people by the states' chief executives proves effective, television may come to be one of our most important campaign techniques at the state as well as at the national level. The American people apparently like to see candidates as well as hear them. At least one governor is convinced that in so far as the chief executive himself is concerned the people are more interested in seeing "the governor" than in hearing him. When asked what he talked about at the innumerable banquets, luncheons, convention openings, bridge dedications, and the like that he was forced to attend, this governor replied, "I try to pitch my speech to the audience in so far as possible; if I am speaking to the state hog growers association, I always say something about the hog as a basic ingredient in the Nation's economy; if it's the cattle growers, I say about the same thing but replace hogs with cattle. It really doesn't make much difference; I am convinced that the people do not come to *hear* the governor speak, they come to *see* him." If this somewhat skeptical view of the interest of the populace in the state's chief executive is true, then television with its "see" potential should develop into a major campaign and publicity device.

CAMPAIGN COSTS

Any attempt to determine what it costs to become governor of any state is largely a matter of informed guesswork. Official sources of information on campaign expenditures are generally unreliable. In some states individual candidates are required by statute to report their personal expenditures in the campaign, but such laws are largely ignored, and the estimates reported, when they are reported, probably do not represent a reliable estimate of even the candidate's own expenditures. Furthermore, even if such reports were reliable, they would not portray the full picture, because the expenditures of the candidate himself form only a small part of the total spent in the campaign.

The picture given by various campaign managers, if they will discuss the matter, is also not entirely reliable. Since the candidate's campaign manager is conducting a campaign and not a business enterprise, he is not primarily concerned with bookkeeping, and frequently the manager himself does not know how much is spent in a campaign. The figures quoted in this section, therefore, are admittedly estimates based on the best information which could be obtained through interviews or in written sources.

The cost of campaigning varies from state to state and also from election to election within the same state because of such factors as the quality of the opposition, the presence of real issues in the campaign, the political following with which a given candidate starts the race, and, particularly in the case of men of great personal wealth, with the amount of money the candidate has at his disposal. State-to-state variations are also caused by the type of factional political organization found in the state itself, the geographical configuration of the state, and the size of the electorate.[7]

It was suggested earlier in this chapter that the cost of campaigning in two-party states is perhaps greater than in one-party states of comparable size and population because of the necessity for conducting two campaigns, one in the primary to secure the nomination and one in the general election. This is probably true in some instances but such is the variation from campaign to campaign caused by the other factors suggested above that it is difficult to document this observation. Furthermore, in most one-party states we find the double primary system which also generally forces the candidates to conduct two campaigns, one in the first primary and one in the second or run-off primary. This feature, together with the fact that factional politics places a premium on campaigning and showmanship, probably makes the cost of campaigning in the South as expensive as in many two-party states of comparable area and population.

Even within one-party states there is a considerable variation in campaign costs caused by the type of factional political organization which exists in the state and the type of primary which is used. For example, in Virginia the Byrd machine because of its extensive county organization and unusually weak opposition

[7] See V. O. Key, *Southern Politics* (New York, 1949), pp. 464-467 for a discussion of how these variables affect gubernatorial races in the South.

spends considerably less to finance the campaign of the organization candidate in the single primary than an individual candidate in Florida spends under the double primary system with its wide open competition in the first primary. A peculiar consequence of machine politics in Virginia is the fact that the anti-organization candidate can make a respectable showing, frequently polling one-third of the popular vote, with an expenditure of from $15,000 to $20,000. A similar situation prevailed in Tennessee prior to the recent Kefauver rebellion. In that state it was possible for the opponent of the Crump candidate to make a good race, sometimes polling as high as 40 per cent of the popular vote, for an outlay of as little as $10,000.[8]

While, on the surface, it may seem strange that it costs less to be an opponent of a well established machine than to be an independent candidate in a machineless state, the explanation is not extremely complex. The presence of an organization candidate in the race tends to rally all potential opposition, which frequently includes several influential newspapers, on the side of the anti-organization candidate. This individual is thus the recipient of a great deal of free publicity and leg-work and, consequently, can campaign with a relatively modest campaign fund.

It might seem from the foregoing analysis that it would be least expensive to run for governor in one of the normally Democratic or Republican states or in a one-party state with the single primary system. In either case the candidates do not have the added cost of a second primary and do not have as substantial opposition in the general election as do candidates in two-party states. On the whole this analysis seems logical but other factors may increase the cost of campaigning. For example, a candidate in New Hampshire estimated that he had spent $25,000 himself and that his backers had spent an additional $100,000 in a recent gubernatorial campaign.[9] This may be compared with an estimate

[8] Key, p. 466.

[9] This estimate is considerably out of line with the figures *reported* by a candidate in a recent election. Charles M. Dale, the successful gubernatorial candidate in 1946, reported that he received contributions of 50 cents and spent $6,800 in his campaign for the Republican renomination in the primary. On the other hand, this figure is very close to the $26,232 in campaign expenditures reported by Hugh Gregg in his successful bid for the Republican nomination in 1952. The figures *reported* by the candidate, even though accurate, represent

of $75,000 for a campaign in the one-party state of South Carolina, although that state has over three times the area and almost four times the population of New Hampshire. The $125,000 estimate for New Hampshire may not be out of line, however, if we take into consideration the fact that citizens in New Hampshire take their voting very seriously, approximately 80 per cent of the citizens of voting age turning out for recent gubernatorial elections. In South Carolina, on the other hand, less than 30 per cent of the citizens of voting age usually bother to go to the polls in the primary where the real choice for governor is made. While potentially the number of voters who must be reached in South Carolina is much greater than in New Hampshire, actually a candidate in New Hampshire must reach almost as large a number of voters as his counterpart in South Carolina. Furthermore, general political interest as reflected by voter turn-out seems to be at a higher level in New Hampshire. Party rivalry in New Hampshire is also rather sharp for a one-party Republican state, while in South Carolina the fight takes place entirely within the Democratic primary with the Democratic nominee commonly running unopposed in the general election. These factors may make it necessary to wage a more intensive campaign in New Hampshire than in South Carolina in the primary and especially in the general election and may tend to explain the higher cost of campaigning in the former state.

Average figures on the cost of campaigning for governor in the United States are relatively meaningless because of the great diversity of size, population, and political organization of the states involved. In addition, as was previously pointed out, it varies from election to election within a given state because of such variables as the quality of the opposition, the presence of real issues in the campaign, the political following with which a given candidate starts the race, and the amount of money a candidate has at his disposal. The money is also spent at different points in the campaign. In the two-party states the amount of money spent in the general election as opposed to the primary will be far greater than in the one-party states where almost nothing is spent in the general election. However, if there can

only a small part of what is actually spent in an election. Far more is spent by persons in support of the candidate than is spent by the candidate himself.

be an estimate of the cost of running for governor in the average state, $100,000 is a reasonable guess and one which does not necessarily imply any political skulduggery. This estimate would perhaps be too high for some of the more sparsely settled western states and would certainly be too low for the large, heavily populated states, such as New York, Pennsylvania, Illinois, Michigan, and California, or even for Texas and Florida. For example, in Florida campaigning for the governorship is very expensive. In the election of 1948, Governor Fuller Warren was supposed to have been elected to office on a campaign fund of no less than $462,000, of which $154,000 is alleged to have been provided (in spite of a law forbidding contributions by race track operators) by a dog track owner and $150,000 by a leading industrialist.[10]

In Texas Key estimates that a candidate must have in the neighborhood of $75,000 to have a chance of getting into the run-off primary and another $75,000 if he expects to make a reasonable showing in that primary. If he expects to win the nomination, he should have a total of at least $200,000 for both primary races.[11] Another source places the cost of "an active, state-wide campaign" as ranging from $50,000 to $500,000 or even more.[12]

In describing campaign expenditures in Illinois, Governor Stevenson writes, "When I ran for Governor in 1948, my campaign organization consisted of a Stevenson-for-Governor Committee in which persons of both parties participated. The contributions received by that Committee, both before and after election day, were lodged in a campaign account."[13] The amount "lodged" in this account according to the exhibit the Governor issued with this statement amounted to $172,203.00 of which $153,458.04 was spent to forward the Governor's campaign. This was undoubtedly not all that was spent in support of Stevenson's candidacy, but at least gives some indication of the amount spent by one major group backing his campaign.

[10] See *Time,* July 24, 1950, and March 17, 1952, for a further discussion of the alleged sources of the Governor's campaign funds.

[11] Key, p. 465.

[12] Stuart A. MacCorkle and Dick Smith, *Texas Government* (New York, 1952), p. 32.

[13] Boston *Sunday Herald,* September 28, 1952.

These examples would certainly seem to indicate that the $100,000 estimate is much too low for the larger states. However, campaigning throughout the nation is not as expensive as in Illinois, Florida, and Texas, so that our estimate may not be too far out of line in the average state.

Perhaps the one thing that can be said with authority about the cost of gubernatorial campaigning is that it is steadily becoming more expensive to run for the governorship of any state. Oswald West, who was elected Governor of Oregon in 1910, is quoted as saying, "I was elected Governor with $3,000. All of the money came from my own bank account and that of one friend."[14] Governor West's $3,000 would not go far in a modern election in Oregon, however. By 1948 the cost of running for governor in Oregon had increased to about $50,000 a year, so that in a 38 year period the cost of campaigning had increased over 1,500 per cent.[15]

The expenditure of $100,000 in the average state is not prima facie evidence that the candidate is engaged in vote buying or other illegal campaign tactics. The cost of campaigning, like the cost of serving in the office itself, has gone up under the pressure of the inflationary spiral. What can be done to dispose of $100,000 with ease is illustrated by the *Arkansas Gazette,* which suggested that the "average candidate for governor" in Arkansas should have a fund of over $100,000. The *Gazette* itemized the major expenditures, as set out below, slyly remarking that a "former candidate for governor" would recognize the items listed. "Headquarters rent, $1,000; Salaries, $5,000; Postage, $4,000; Automobile and loud speaker rent, $2,000; Printing, $10,000; Traveling expenses, $2,500; Signs and banners, $2,500; Radio advertising, $10,000;

[14] Quoted in Dayton D. McKean, *Party and Pressure Politics* (Boston, 1949), p. 345.

[15] Oregon state senator Richard L. Neuberger writing in *The Reporter* for January 31, 1950, stated that "it took a treasury of $50,623 to elect one of our colleagues to the governorship in 1948." While this figure is only about half of the $100,000 suggested as a reasonable estimate for the average campaign, it probably does not represent the entire cost of running for governor in Oregon. However, campaigning in that state may be less expensive than in other states. Louise Overacker in *Money in Elections* (New York, 1932), p. 67 found that of the 27 candidates for the Republican nomination for governor of Oregon during the period 1910-1928 only one reported that $10,000 had been spent in his behalf; four reported totals ranging from $5,000 to $9,999; twelve reported totals ranging from $1,000 to $4,999; and ten reported less than $1,000.

Newspaper advertising, $40,000; Telephones and telegraph, $2,500; Run-off campaign, $25,000."[16] This pattern could easily be applied to other states, simply by replacing the $25,000 estimate for the run-off campaign with an estimate of $25,000 or more for the general election.

The introduction of radio and television in campaigning has increased costs tremendously and the outlay for even a minimum radio coverage is astonishing to the average voter. Radio costs for political broadcasts are relatively higher than for other types of programs. The gubernatorial aspirant naturally wants to reach as wide a listening audience as possible. This audience in most localities is at its peak during the evening hours between 6 p.m. and 11 p.m. Hence, the candidate is competing with regularly scheduled commercial programs during this period and radio time for this period is at a higher rate than at more undesirable hours. Furthermore, the radio address is usually in the nature of a single political advertisement and usually must break in on a regularly scheduled program. The cost for such single-shot programs is also higher than if the program is repeated at a scheduled time over a longer period. Ordinarily the gubernatorial candidate will contract with a state network to carry his message over all or most of the stations in the state. The total cost to the candidate is the sum of the costs of the charges of each station. If we assume that the average per-station cost of a political broadcast is about $30.00 per quarter hour, his total cost for one fifteen minute state-wide broadcast would be $30.00 multiplied by the number of stations carrying the program. The cost will therefore vary greatly from state to state because the number of stations varies and because our average figure of $30.00 per quarter hour will not hold true in all states. Using this figure as a basis, however, one state-wide fifteen minute broadcast in 1952 would cost $4,800 in California, $2,850 in New York, $3,180 in Pennsylvania, $2,010 in Ohio, $450 in Maine, $270 in Vermont, and $240 in Nevada. When we take into consideration the fact that not one radio broadcast but many broadcasts are made by the candidate or by

[16] The *Arkansas Gazette,* April 18, 1948, cited in Key, p. 468, fn. 9.

[17] This estimate is based on commercial rates. Actually political rates are considerably higher, being fixed somewhere between the commercial rate and the maximum the traffic will bear.

persons speaking in his behalf, it is easy to see that several thousand dollars can be legitimately spent in radio broadcasting alone.[18] For example, "in Texas dual-network time sells for $2,100 for fifteen minutes. The bedrock allowance, says a publicity man with political experience, should be fifteen minutes a week for ten weeks plus an additional half hour in the closing week or a total outlay of $25,200. In a smaller state, Arkansas, a candidate reports an expenditure of $12,000 for radio in a campaign costing around $65,000, far less than the typical total cost for that state."[19] If this more practical estimate of radio cost evaluation is applied to even a small state like Vermont, the cost can still be considerable. A fifteen minute state-wide broadcast in that state each week for ten weeks plus an extra half hour in the closing weeks of the campaign would cost just over $3,000 which is very modest compared to our Texas figures but fairly substantial in view of the disparity of size and population in the two states involved.

Similarly large scale newspaper advertising is very expensive. If the candidate wished to run one quarter page ad in all the newspapers in his state, he would have to lay out approximately $21,268 in California, $20,007 in Illinois, $1,716 in Maine, $1,519 in New Hampshire, $7,263 in New Jersey, $20,938 in New York, $1,230 in Nevada, $15,553 in Ohio, $19,029 in Pennsylvania, $19,147 in Texas, and $1,362 in Vermont. Practically speaking, one quarter page ad would be completely inadequate for even a local campaign, much less a state-wide race for governor. Actual outlays for newspaper advertising are tremendous. For example, in Arkansas, where full page state-wide coverage costs $7,000 a page, a recent gubernatorial candidate ran ten full page ads, the total bill for which ran to $70,000.

In some states direct mail advertising is used extensively. This form of political advertising is probably the most costly in terms of its coverage and effect. Much of it is by second class mail, but even so it involves a substantial cost for postage alone, not

[18] The Atlanta *Journal* (August 10, 1948) estimated that during the 1948 gubernatorial campaign in Georgia, incumbent Governor Melvin Thompson averaged about 100 station-hours a week, probably a record. At a conservative estimate of $100 per hour this coverage cost $10,000 a week. The Governor's regular Monday night rally was carried by 49 stations.

[19] Key, p. 469.

counting the time and money involved in preparing the letters for mailing. To place a piece of campaign literature in the hands of all potential voters over 21 years of age in California would cost $144,320 in postage alone. In Illinois it would cost $119,180, in Maine $11,536, in New Hampshire $7,055, in New York $204,960, in Texas $96,140, while in Nevada it would cost only $2,143. It is not likely that such entirely indiscriminate mailing would take place, but to cover a mailing list of even 50,000 names would cost $1,000 and if the same individuals are contacted by mail more than once, as they generally are in a mail campaign, the outlay can be very substantial. The use of first-class mail, which is sometimes used on the theory that a first-class letter is more likely to be read, would up this figure to $1,500 for a one-shot coverage.

It is very easy to spend considerable sums of money in a gubernatorial race entirely for legitimate purposes, and it is difficult to be elected without considerable financial backing. It might be mentioned in this connection, however, that the candidate need not always have large sums at his command to begin a campaign. It is sometimes possible to begin campaigning on a more modest scale and by demonstration of some popular support to attract more substantial financial backing. The "poor but honest" candidate is under a considerable handicap, but his role is not always an impossible one. If he can demonstrate popular support, he can probably attract the necessary financial backing. He must, however, have a good deal to offer in the way of personality, identification with a particular cause or group, and the like, in order to attract this support.

In summarizing the cost of gubernatorial campaigning we might say that if we add to the two major items of newspaper and radio advertising the cost of maintaining a campaign headquarters, travel costs for the candidate and his staff, bills for extensive long distance telephone calls, the cost of posters, printing, and postage, the $100,000 which was suggested above as an average soon melts away. Added to these legitimate expenditures, we also find those which border on the illegitimate. Payments which are made to local political leaders to "cover the costs of local campaigns" for the gubernatorial candidate verge on bribery. The amount which must be spent in this kind of payments varies greatly from state to state and varies almost as greatly from election to election. A general election in a two-party state which is thought to be close calls for much more of this sort of thing than does one in which the candidate is regarded as a shoo-in. The same is true in the normally Democratic or Republican states and in one-party states, although in the latter instance the money is spent in a close primary or in the run-off.

The mention of these practices brings up the question of so-called corrupt practices legislation which is found in most states. This type of legislation is based on the concept that it is desirable to limit expenditures in state campaigns (including gubernatorial campaigns) either in terms of the total amount spent or in terms of the amounts which can be legally spent for certain items. Some 39 states have some form of limitation on campaign expenditures. In 25 of these the limitation applies to both the primary and the general election; in fourteen it applies only to the primary. The most common forms which these restrictions take are (1) a fixed dollar limitation with no exceptions (twelve states); (2) a fixed dollar limitation with exceptions, as for example, no limit on travel expenses (thirteen states); (3) a percentage of the salary of the office sought, such as 50 per cent (nine states); (4) an amount which varies with number of votes cast in the preceding election, as for example $10 per vote (five states).

These limitations are seldom observed in most states and even where observed are largely ineffective because most of them prevent expenditures only by the *candidate*. One governor explained the ineffectiveness of the statute in his state by pointing out that, in the first place, it had been passed twenty years ago, when the cost of campaigning was not as great as it is at the present time. He said that he doubted that the $5,000 maximum was a reasonable figure even in 1932, but that it certainly was not realistic in 1952. Secondly, he said that the limitation of expenditures by the candidate was even more unrealistic. For example, he said that he had reported accurately about $3,500 as personal expenditures. This amount, however, covered only one item, his personal traveling expenses. This item, he added, was the least of the campaign expenditures. All of his radio time had been bought by a citizens' committee, and his newspaper advertising had been purchased by "friends of the candidate." In other words, while the candidate had been careful to spend well within the limit himself, he estimated that others had spent over *twenty* times as much in his behalf.

The most effective approach to concentrating the responsibilities for campaign expenditures in a gubernatorial race would seem to lie in a statute which would provide that all campaign expenditures must be made through a finance committee. The expenditures of this committee would be limited and individuals or groups would not be permitted to expend funds to aid a candidate except through the official finance committee. Perhaps major items such as radio and newspaper advertising could be controlled by this method, although it is doubtful that it would prevent borderline expenditures to local political chiefs, which is one of the chief reasons for such legislation.

PART TWO

THE EXECUTIVE FUNCTION

6. THE CHARACTER OF THE EXECUTIVE FUNCTION

AS MIGHT BE EXPECTED, in dealing with 48 states each with a different history, a different cultural heritage, and sometimes with considerable differences in forms of government, we find distinct variations from state to state in the governor's functions. Nevertheless, it is the thesis of this chapter that out of these variations emerges a hard core of gubernatorial powers and duties which are sufficiently similar in all states to warrant the formulation of what may be called "the executive function" at the state level. This statement of the governor's functions is primarily a practical one based largely on information collected in the course of field trips to some 25 states.

In the section dealing with demands on the governor's time, the governor's daily and weekly schedule is analyzed with a view toward discovering just what the governor actually does as a matter of daily routine and the proportion of time he spends on his various duties. In the section following, the views of several past and present governors are presented to give some idea of what the governors themselves regard as their most important functions.

Based on the data presented in these two sections a formulation of the governor's functions is presented in the final section of the chapter. Briefly stated, this concept of the governor's functions is that the modern American governor is primarily concerned with three broad areas of operations—policy formation, public relations, and management. Each of these functions will be considered in some detail in succeeding chapters but may be briefly summarized here by way of introduction.

The role of the governor in policy formation includes his attempts to formulate and place in operation policy in the fields of legislation, administration, and partisan politics. These three aspects of policy formation are, in practice, very difficult to separate. The governors in their daily activities, in describing their functions in interviews and sometimes in writing about the office, fail to make any clear-cut distinction among their activities in these three fields. Consequently, in presenting these aspects of the governor's functions in the chapter on the governor's role in policy formation we have followed actual practice in describing the various aspects of policy making as interrelated parts of one central process.

Politics and administration at the level of the state governors seem to be part of a continuous-flow process, so much so that it is difficult to separate the two other than to indicate that a particular action falls closer to the policy end of the scale than to the administrative end or vice versa. Nevertheless, some attempt has been made to differentiate between the governor's role in legislative policy and his role in administrative policy because these two can be separated in some instances, at least for the purpose of discussion. The governor in forming and implementing policy in these three areas finds himself playing a triple role as legislative leader, administrative chief, and head of his political party or as head of a particular faction of that party. He may be playing these roles separately at different times or he may be acting in all three capacities on any particular policy matter. His functions in this area are frequently described by the governors themselves in such terms as "securing legislative co-operation," "explaining policies to my department heads," or "consulting with party leaders." Whatever the terminology used, however, a major function of the governor is setting the policy for the government of his state during his term of office and he is quite likely to be judged in the eyes of the general public primarily by how successfully he performs this aspect of his functions.

The governor's role in public relations, while perhaps not as important as his role in policy making, is the most time-consuming of his functions. His duties in this area involve many personal interviews, voluminous correspondence, numerous phone calls, and a large number of public speeches, radio addresses, and personal appearances. So great, indeed, is the drain on the governor's time occasioned by excessive demands in this field that most governors find this function interfering with their efforts at policy formation and encroaching upon the time which they might otherwise devote to management.

The governor's role in management is closely related to his policy functions on one hand and to his public relations functions on the other. In a way it occupies a middle ground between his attempts to formulate a legislative program and see that program enacted into law, and his efforts to explain the program, both before and after its enactment, to the public. The governor's role in management is that of establishing the policies which govern the day-to-day operations of the executive branch, of securing policy co-ordination among the agencies which make up the executive branch, and of very general supervision to make certain that his policies and those which have previously been established on a continuing basis are carried out properly.

This description is not intended to suggest that each succeeding governor proceeds to establish an entirely new set of administrative policies. Most of the programs which the governor is expected to administer are accepted as continuing programs in the major substantive fields of government such as education, public welfare, and highways. The governor, primarily through the budget, will seek to establish new programs in some of these fields, will seek to emphasize certain aspects of old programs, and occasionally will establish an entirely new program for the state in a virgin field of state endeavor. In all of these, however, he is concerned not only with the establishment of the program in legislative terms but also with the establishment of the administrative policies which govern the execution of these programs old and new. Consequently, the governor's role in management is also a policy role but one which is of a slightly different character than his role in legislative policy formation. Here, he is dealing primarily with a new group, the heads of the agencies which make up the executive branch. His relations with this group are of a different character than those with the legislature, although they are influenced to a considerable extent by the governor's relations with that body. The governor in dealing with his department heads must obtain their co-operation in carrying out the policies which he endorses and in carrying out those policies in such a way as to reflect credit on his administration. The central problem then becomes one of policy co-ordination. It is complicated by the fact that the governor frequently has no legal control over the department head in terms of appointing power or removal power and because many departments are not subject to the executive budget or to other fiscal control procedures. The governor must then operate largely through persuasion. These and other complications in management are discussed at more length in a subsequent chapter. It is sufficient to note here that the governor, handicapped on one hand by the lack of time due to the press of his functions in policy formation and public relations, and limited on the other by his lack of control over the executive branch, is far from being the chief executive he is so often styled in the public press and even in some of the state constitutions. In the state executive branch the governor's relation with the other executive officers is more accurately thought of as being the first among equals.

Cutting across all of these functions is the question of the governor's staff. While the staff concept is well developed in a few of the larger states, the staff of most governors is rather inadequate. Consequently, a later chapter of this book discusses not only the present organization of the governor's office but also puts forward some suggestions for possible improvements in the staffing pattern.

It should be emphasized at the outset of our discussion that while the writer believes this formulation of the governor's functions has considerable practical validity, it can by no means be applied as a formula which automatically defines the executive function in a given state under a given governor. The functions which are actually performed by the governor of a particular state depend on several factors, among the more important of which are the powers and duties given the governor by the state constitution, the attitude of the legislature on the question of the proper scope of gubernatorial power, the power or lack of power which arises out of the governor's position in his party, and the powers and limitations which have attached themselves to the office as a result of custom and tradition. The functions and duties of the office also vary considerably, even in the same state, with the concept of those functions and duties held by succeeding incumbents of the office. The following section gives some indication of the effect that these "conditioning factors" have on the actual operations of the governor and of the variations which may be expected from state to state as a result of the operation of these factors.

CONDITIONING FACTORS

The functions performed by the modern American governor are conditioned by many rather complex factors. One of these is the fact that the constitutional basis for the governor's powers is more limited in some states than in others. The attitude of the legislature over the years in either giving the governor increased power through the statutes or in limiting or attempting to limit the governor's constitutional powers is another important consideration. The governor's position in his party is also a factor which tends either to strengthen or weaken his power in relation to both his legislative and management duties. Equally important, however, are the custom and traditions of the state which, over a long period of time, seem to set the tone of state government. In some states the cumulative effects of custom and tradition tend to make the governor more powerful than he would appear to be from an examination of the statutes, while in others they seem to limit the governor's powers, although he may be equally as strong from a constitutional point of view. Added to these considerations is the view of the governor's proper role held by succeeding incumbents of the office. While this view tends to be shaped by the customs and traditions of the state and hence tends to be similar in succeeding governors of the same state, the governor's own version of his proper function is nevertheless quite significant. This is particularly true in the question of which aspect of the governor's duties shall receive the major emphasis during his term of office. Granted that he must perform certain functions under the statutes, the governor still has considerable leeway in determining which functions will receive the most emphasis, and this emphasis is an important factor in determining practical operations. As an illustration of the effect of these conditioning factors on the exercise of the gubernatorial function, we may examine the effect of the interplay between the force of custom and tradition in two selected states and the constitutional power of the governor in those states with particular reference to legislative policy formation.

In the field of legislative policy determination and implementation all governors have certain constitutional powers which prove valuable in presenting and securing the enactment of their legislative program. The governors of all of the states have the power to recommend legislation and all of them except the governor of North Carolina have the veto power. However, whether or not a given governor actually provides legislative leadership depends not so much on his constitutional or statutory powers as on his strength as a party leader, the presence or absence of a tradition of gubernatorial leadership in his state, and the concept which the governor holds as to his proper role in legislation. Most governors feel that legislative leadership is an important segment of their responsibility and many, as we shall subsequently point out, give it first rank. In states where the governor takes this view, he will certainly make an attempt to provide policy leadership for the legislature. On the other hand, if the governor takes the view that his role is primarily that of "seeing that the laws are faithfully executed," he will not place the same emphasis on legislative leadership, and this function will be subordinate to other functions.

The contrasting situations in the states of Alabama and Nevada furnish a good example of how the effect of tradition and the personal concept of the office held by succeeding governors shape the powers of the office. In Alabama the customs and traditions of the state and the governors' views of the gubernatorial function have made the governor a very strong legislative leader. In Nevada, on the other hand, the reverse has been true, although the legal powers of the governor in Nevada are similar to those of the governor of Alabama. Both governors have the usual power to recommend legislation. Both executives also have the power to call special sessions of the legislature, although the legislature in Nevada can consider only those subjects specified by the governor in his call for the special session, while in Alabama the legislature can, by a two-thirds vote, consider other subjects. Both governors have a strong veto power, although the governor of Nevada is in a more favorable position in this respect since his veto may be overridden only by a *two-thirds* vote of all elected members of the legislature, while the veto of the governor of Alabama may be overridden by a *majority* of all elected members. On the other hand, the governor of Alabama has an item veto and also has the power of executive amendment. The governor of Nevada possesses neither of these powers. On the whole, both governors are in a strong position legally in regard to the legislature, with the governor of Alabama in perhaps the slightly stronger position of the two. Nevertheless, the slight legal edge held by the governor of Alabama certainly does not explain the decidedly greater emphasis, in practice, on the exercise of legislative leadership by the governors of that state.

The answer seems to lie primarily in the concept of the governorship held by successive governors in the respective states and in the customs and traditions of the states in question. The situation in Nevada is explained by one student of the state's governmental processes by saying that

> The influence which the governor wields as legislative and political leader is largely dependent upon the character and personality of the individual incumbent. Over the years, however, the attitude of most incumbents toward the powers, duties and responsibilities of their office has tended to be substantially the same—namely, highly restrictive and conservative. The reason for this can partially be explained by the independent nature of the people of the state, by its culture and traditions, and by the basic distrust of a strong executive prevalent at the time of the adoption of the Nevada constitution. . . .
>
> Recognizing the legislature as a co-ordinate branch of government, the governor has been most careful to avoid any impression that he is dictating to it. On the contrary, he has gone to the other extreme; many problems which should be faced by the legislature with the advice and guidance of the governor have been left solely to the legislature. It is not that the governor is indifferent; it is just that he believes that such problems are not properly within the scope of his office.[1]

The situation in Alabama is quite different and Hallie Farmer, a long-time student of the legislative process in that state, finds that the governor is the "chief legislator" in Alabama. In explaining this phenomenon she says in part

[1] Albert Gorvine, *The Governor and Administration, State of Nevada,* An Abstract of a Dissertation Presented to the Faculty of the Graduate School of Arts and Science, New York University (March, 1950), pp. 22 ff.

> In spite of the fact that the fathers of the Constitution of 1901 attached much importance to the separation of powers, government as it has developed under that Constitution has made the chief executive the most powerful single factor in the legislative process in Alabama. . . . Much of the Governor's legislative power, however, rests upon custom rather than upon constitutional authority. By custom, every candidate for election to the office of Governor presents an elaborate platform to the people. The platform of the successful candidate is taken to represent the will of the people and it is presumed to be the duty of the Legislature to enact that will into law. Insofar as there is a general legislative program, it is furnished by the Governor's platform.
>
> By custom also the Legislature is organized under the supervision of the Governor. The Speaker of the House of Representatives is the man approved by the Governor for that position. The chairmen of the standing committees are selected by the Governor and, if that officer desires, the members of the committees are selected in the same way, though nominally appointed by the presiding officers of the two houses. The floor leader in each house represents not the house but the Governor, and is commonly referred to as "the Governor's floor leader."[2]

The distinct contrast in these two states in respect to the governor's role as a legislative leader points up the fact that the concept of the gubernatorial function held by the respective governors and the traditions of the state are factors which often have as much to do with the shaping of the gubernatorial function in a particular state as do the constitutional and statutory powers granted the governor. A listing of the legal powers of the governor, therefore, would be only a beginning in the understanding of those powers and would tell us little of their relative importance. It is for this reason that the following analysis of the governor's functions is made from the point of view of what a governor actually does rather than from the traditional point of view of his legal authority and responsibilities. The section below describes a "typical" day in the life of an American governor and reviews several case studies of the amount of time spent by certain governors on their various functions. The succeeding section summarizes some representative statements of the gubernatorial functions made by the governors themselves. These two sections should serve as a basis for a realistic summary of the

[2] Hallie Farmer, *The Legislative Process in Alabama* (Bureau of Public Administration, University of Alabama, 1949), pp. 167-168.

governor's principal functions. This summary will, in turn, serve as a basis for a more detailed consideration of these functions in the chapters of this book which follow.

DEMANDS ON THE GOVERNOR'S TIME

One of the facets of the governorship which is least understood by the average citizen is what a typical governor actually does with his time. The many requests from citizen groups that the governor speak at local meetings of various kinds, the constant stream of visitors who flood the governor's office, and the innumerable letters containing every conceivable request, all indicate that the average citizen thinks, if indeed he considers the problem at all, that the governor is an official who not only has unlimited time for the problems of individual citizens but also has equally unlimited power to solve those problems. It seems to the citizen to be inconceivable that the governor does not have time to settle a boundary dispute between two neighbors or that he does not have the power to "get my boy John" out of the United States Army. This concept has been encouraged by many governors who have adopted an "open-door" policy under which any citizen of the state can come to the capitol and see the governor. This is undoubtedly in accord with the democratic tradition in this country and with local tradition in most states. However, such a policy is not without severe limitations, not the least of which is the fact that if the governor spends all of his time on interviews with the state's citizens, he has little time left to attend to the state's business. The governor of most states is a very busy individual who follows a daily schedule which leaves him very little personal life. The schedule following is a composite of those of the governors in the states visited in the course of this study. It will not be valid for all states, particularly for the larger states such as New York, California, and Illinois, where the governor spends much less of his time seeing people than he does in the average state.

The time devoted to various activities also varies from state to state with such factors as the population of the state and the personality of a particular governor. In the smaller states the office tends to be more personal. The governor has a small staff and does more business through personal interviews and personal

TABLE VI

The Governor's Day

Time	*Activities*
8:30 to 9:30 a.m.	Reading and answering previously screened correspondence.
9:30 to 10:30 a.m.	Conferences with department heads or legislators.
10:30 to 11:00 a.m.	Press conference.
11:00 to 12:30 p.m.	Interviews or conferences with public, legislators, and department heads.
12:30 to 2:00 p.m.	Lunch, during which the governor welcomes some group meeting in the city or has a luncheon conference.
2:00 to 4:00 p.m.	Additional conferences with public, legislators, and department heads.
4:00 to 4:30 p.m.	Press conference.
4:30 to 6:00 p.m. or later	Clears up additional correspondence, makes phone calls, plans work with staff, etc.
7:00 p.m.	Frequently attends a banquet or similar gathering where he is either the principal speaker or must "put in an appearance."

telephone calls and less through his staff and by correspondence. In the larger states his schedule is more formalized and his office is larger and more highly organized. He spends a good deal less time seeing people since much of this work is delegated to members of his staff.

The governor's personality and work habits also have a marked effect on his schedule. For example, some governors do little correspondence at their office and prefer to take care of this chore at home after office hours. On the other hand, some governors like to begin the day by clearing up a major part of their correspondence. Others begin the day with a press conference or with conferences with their department heads. In some states the governor handles a great deal of business by telephone, while in others more business is handled through personal interviews and correspondence.

It should be understood also that the governor is not in his office every day. As a general rule, he is out of the office at least one or two days a week because he spends considerable time traveling throughout the state to deliver speeches, attend various meetings and participate in other activities away from the capitol. In general, however, the sample schedule in Table VI is representative of the various types of activity which make up the governor's daily routine when he is in his office.

An analysis of the time table presented here reveals that the governor devotes approximately four and one-half hours a day to conferences and interviews exclusive of press conferences. This figure seems, at first glance, to be rather startling but it is supported by several actual analyses of the governor's work load. For example, a "desk audit" of the Governor of Arkansas over a four-day period revealed that the Governor received 100 callers in this period, or an average of 25 persons a day. If each of these visitors spent only ten minutes with the Governor, these interviews would occupy over four hours of his time. However, interviews usually cannot be dispensed with so expeditiously and telephone calls and interruptions greatly increased the time they took.[3]

A detailed study of the activities of the Governor of New Hampshire over a three-week period reveals that the governor of that state spends about three and one-half hours a day on interviews and conferences.[4]

An average of several one or two day samples obtained by the author during this study and the estimates of the governors' executive secretaries in the states covered indicate that the average American governor sees from ten to 25 persons a day. The period during which the state legislature is in session is the busiest time of the year from the point of view of conferences. When the

[3] See Coleman B. Ransone, Jr., *The Office of Governor in the South* (Bureau of Public Administration, University of Alabama, 1951), p. 18 ff. for a more detailed discussion of this analysis including tables showing a list of the governor's visitors on representative days. The four days mentioned were selected as being representative on the basis of a month's record of the visitors to the governor's office. This analysis is based on that made by Daniel Grant in an unpublished Ph.D. dissertation, "The Role of the Governor of Arkansas in Administration" (University of Chicago, 1948).

[4] "What Does a Governor Do?" *The New Hampshire Taxpayer,* XII (January, 1950), 1.

legislature is not in session, the governor probably sees an average of fifteen persons a day, but when the legislature is in session the total is closer to 25. For example, the Governor of New Hampshire ordinarily sees about ten persons a day, but on August 2, 1951, which was a legislative day, he had already seen ten persons between 8 a.m. and 10:30 a.m., and interviews with legislators were scheduled for most of the rest of the day.

In regard to press conferences our schedule shows that the governor holds two half-hour press conferences a day. This is typical of most governors, although frequently the conferences do not last for the entire period scheduled. In some of the smaller states there are no formally scheduled conferences. For example, in Vermont only two correspondents regularly cover the capitol beat. Under these circumstances there is no need for two formal press conferences a day. When the governor has an item of interest to the press, he calls in the press representatives for a conference or gives them the information when they drop into the office informally to check up on the latest developments. As a result of this setup, the Governor of Vermont spends only about twenty minutes a day on interviews with the press. In South Dakota, the governor finds it necessary to have only one press conference a day at 9:30 a.m. and spends only about thirty minutes a day on this aspect of his duties.

The schedule for handling press relations depends primarily on two factors, the number of correspondents covering the capitol beat and the presence or absence of both morning and afternoon papers. If there are a large number of correspondents at the capitol, it is a more economical use of the governor's time to call in these representatives as a group for a press conference and thus relieve the governor of the necessity of seeing them individually. If there are only one or two press representatives at the capitol, press relations can be handled more informally and the governor can afford to see the representatives of the press individually on matters which they, or he, consider to be newsworthy. In several small states, however, the governor has two press conferences a day or is available for two interviews at different times because the capitol beat is covered by representatives of both a morning and an evening paper. Since these papers have different deadlines, one press conference a day would give the advantage to the evening paper if it were held in the early morning or to the morning paper if it were held in the afternoon. The timing of important announcements by the governor is a matter for nice calculation, and he must try to release an equal amount of important news at each press conference or at least alternately at the morning and afternoon session throughout the week.

Typically, therefore, we find two press conferences a day used by most governors because there is ordinarily coverage of most capitols by both morning and evening papers. It might seem to the uninitiated that these conferences could be handled by the governor's press secretary, or his executive secretary, with the governor appearing in person only on very important occasions. In some instances this is done, but the general rule is that the governor appears personally at the conference. The press looks with suspicion on press releases or second hand information, and such is their power of persuasion that they generally carry the day in demanding a personal appearance. This was not true in New York, however, where Governor Dewey did not have regularly scheduled press conferences. Apparently this is the only state in which the governor has not complied with the concept of the press that the governor's personal attendance at regularly scheduled press conferences, or availability for frequent interviews, is the sine qua non for adequate coverage of the capitol beat.

It may be, however, that more careful planning of the governor's press relations can result in a reduction of the number of press conferences. In California, for example, the governor has a press conference only twice a week, on Tuesday and Friday. Since the capitol in Sacramento is covered by a substantial number of newsmen, and since the importance of the governor's pronouncements in California may be assumed to be not less than those in other states, it seems probable that two press conferences a week might be adequate in some of the smaller states which continue to have two sessions a day. Routine matters might be adequately covered by press releases and by the understanding that the governor's press secretary or executive secretary is authorized to speak for the governor in the interim between regularly scheduled press conferences. In view of the time which most governors devote to press relations, it seems that the present system is too time-consuming and burdensome on the governor.

Most governors interviewed, however, took the position that press conferences were an inescapable part of their duties and several took the position that it was to their advantage to have at least daily contact with the press. The average American governor is well aware of the advantages of a favorable press and, as we shall see in analyzing the governor's staff in a later section, has a press secretary or designates a member of his staff to assist him in handling this important function.

A third duty of the governor as revealed by his daily time table is answering correspondence, telegrams, and telephone calls. The amount of time devoted by the governor to this aspect of his daily routine varies considerably from state to state and appears to be determined more by the governor's own view of the amount of time which should be devoted to this function than by the volume of correspondence, although the latter, of course, has some effect. A few statistics will give some idea of the work load in various states. These figures are based either on estimates by the governor's staff or by actual tabulations maintained in those states which have a highly developed correspondence system. Strangely enough, most of the states keep no records on correspondence, so that in only a few instances could the actual figures be obtained. In Wyoming, South Dakota, Vermont, and Utah the correspondence work load is between thirty and fifty letters a day. Correspondence in Kansas averages fifty to 75 letters a day; in Minnesota 75 to 100 letters a day; in New Mexico and Colorado about 100 letters a day; while North Carolina, Georgia, Michigan, California, Texas, and New York all average well over 100 letters a day. In California during Governor Warren's first eight years in office, the governor's office had received 333,076 numbered pieces of mail or about 41,600 pieces a year. In Michigan, figures for random years reveal a decided growth in gubernatorial mail. In 1943 the governor's office received 46,000 letters and sent out 40,000 replies; while in 1950 it received 62,000 letters and sent out 45,000 replies. The discrepancy in the figures representing incoming and outgoing mail, as for example, in 1950 when the office received 17,000 more letters than it answered, is accounted for by the fact that these letters were referred to the appropriate department for answer. Volume of mail is not dependent entirely on the population of the state, as witnessed by the fact that in 1945, 40,000 letters were written by the governor's office in North Carolina, almost on a par with Michigan and California.

The governor, of course, does not read or answer all of this mail personally. In some offices, such as California, an effective system of tabulating and sorting mail has been established with an inter-office routing slip to show the action on each piece of mail. In most offices a more informal system is in operation under which the mail is sorted by a clerk by previously agreed-upon areas so that the mail may be routed to one of the governor's assistants for reply. In smaller states the executive secretary reads all incoming mail and screens it so that out of thirty or forty letters a day the governor will actually see only a half a dozen. Some governors, however, like to read all their mail and spend several hours a day reading and answering correspondence. Estimates on the amount of time which the governor spends on correspondence range from one hour and thirty minutes to three hours a day, with the average time being about two hours a day.

In most offices the mail is delivered twice a day—in the early morning and late afternoon. The late afternoon mail is read and screened by one of the governor's staff and is ready for action by the governor early the following morning. The morning mail is read and screened during the day and is ready for action by the governor in the early afternoon, although he usually does not get to the mail until late in the afternoon or after normal working hours. Several of the governors interviewed said that they frequently took home the major part of their correspondence and answered it after working hours. One governor said that he regarded correspondence as his homework and that it took a large proportion of his free time. His wife confirmed this statement indirectly by saying that the governor worked until 12 or 1 o'clock each night and that in her opinion the executive mansion was too close to the capitol. The handling of correspondence is an important problem in most executive offices and probably could be improved by the installation of better procedures, as will be pointed out in a subsequent chapter.

In addition to correspondence, the governor makes and receives a large number of phone calls each day, most of which are to or from distant points in the state or throughout the United States.

These phone calls are frequently almost as time-consuming as correspondence. The relative amount of time spent on phone calls and correspondence varies considerably from state to state and seems to depend to a considerable degree on the geographical configuration of the state and on the density of population. For example, the Governor of New Hampshire, a compact rather densely populated state, spends about an hour and thirty minutes a day on correspondence and only 35 minutes a day on telephone calls. This ratio of three to one in favor of correspondence is unusually high and two to one ratio would be more in keeping with most of the states in the New England area. On the other hand, in those southwestern states which are characterized by a large area and a small population such as Wyoming, Colorado, and Nevada, much of the governor's business is handled by long distance telephone calls. Several of the governors pointed out that the long distances involved made it relatively difficult for citizens to come to the office with their problems and that they used the telephone as a substitute for a personal visit. In these states the ratio is probably two to one, or approximately even, on phone calls as compared to letters. In Nevada it was estimated that 80 per cent of the business of the governor's office was done by phone and only 20 per cent by correspondence and personal interview. In New Mexico, the two were the same, the estimate being 100 telephone calls and 100 letters a day. In Utah the governor's office receives approximately thirty to forty letters a day and about twenty telephone calls a day.

While no typical pattern emerges from these figures, it appears that a considerable amount of the business of the governor's office is conducted by telephone, with the use of the telephone being greater relative to written communications in the southwestern states. In the rest of the nation, the volume of correspondence equals or exceeds incoming and outgoing telephone calls.

This analysis of the governor's day reveals that he is occupied principally with conferences with department heads, legislators, and the general public; with press conferences; and with the handling of correspondence and telephone calls. In addition, he has a great many functions after hours, which one governor termed his extra-curricular activities. These functions, such as speeches, banquets and radio and television appearances, are very time-consuming and together with press conferences and the majority of interviews form the core of the governor's public relations activities.

More important than understanding what the governor does in terms of the time he spends on various activities is an understanding of the kinds of people he sees and the kinds of decisions he makes in the course of his day's work. The areas in which the requests for the governor's assistance fall tend to vary with national policies as well as with state conditions. For example, during the Korean conflict matters involving the armed forces of the United States became an important problem for the governors. In spite of the fact that the draft legislation was administered as a federal program, the number of requests for the governor's assistance on draft matters increased sharply. Several of the governors interviewed during this period listed it as the problem on which a majority of their visitors, among those not connected with the state government, were seeking the governor's aid. In most cases the governor has no control over these matters, although it is hard to convince the average citizen that this is the case. The fact that several national guard units were called into service intensified these demands on the governor, since the average citizen does not realize that a national guard unit on active military service is no longer under state control.

Perennial areas in which the governor's aid is sought include highway construction or repair, old-age assistance, pardon, parole, and prison matters, and patronage. As was stated at the beginning of this section, to judge from the variety of requests which are made of American governors, the average citizen views the governor as an individual with unlimited time for the consideration of his personal problems and as an executive with unlimited powers to solve those problems. As a result, much of the governor's time, particularly in the smaller states, is spent in interviews with the state's citizens who come into his office with a variety of requests. These requests range over the whole governmental process and frequently include matters which are not within the scope of the state government at all. The analysis which follows reveals something of the variety and number of these requests. It is based on a four-day representative sample taken from a month's schedule of the Governor of Arkansas.[5] Many of these requests fall in the general area of state management since they concern such matters as requests for state positions or special favors in certain administrative programs. They might, therefore, be classified as a part of the governor's management function. It seems more reasonable, however, to classify them as a part of the governor's duties in the field of public relations because, from the governor's point of view, these contacts with the state's citizens are important primarily in terms of the citizen's reaction to the governor and to his administration. More often than not the governor must turn down these requests but must do so in such a way as to engender a favorable reaction from the person interviewed. The following table summarizes the purposes of the governor's callers and thus casts considerable light on the reasons

TABLE VII

*Analysis of Visits to the Governor's Office in Arkansas**

Purpose	*Per Cent of Time Consumed*
Requests for State Positions	23
Requests for Special Favors	13
Requests from Civic, Church or School Organizations	12
Problems of Administrative Officials	10
Purpose Unknown	8
Criticism of Governmental Policy	7
Social Calls	6
Reports of Confidential Information	5
Requests for Executive Clemency	4
Press Conferences	3
Requests for Information	2
Requests for Extradition	2
Invitations to Board Meetings	2
Board Meeting in Governor's Office	1
Report of Parole Violation	1
Conference with Personal Tax Consultant	1
	100

*Based on 100 visits.

[5] This study was made by Daniel Grant of Vanderbilt University. See Ransone, p. 18 ff. for a more detailed presentation of this analysis.

why various individuals sought to see the governor and the type of problem which their visits produced.

While most of the classifications give a fairly good indication of the visitor's business, it may be useful to comment briefly on the four leading groups. The single largest group (23 per cent of all visitors) were those seeking public employment. These individuals either wished to be appointed to a state position, retain a state position which they were about to lose, or sought to influence the governor's appointments to county vacancies. The first-place position of this group would not be typical of all the states. In those states having a merit system, this percentage would be sharply reduced. Slightly more than half of the states do not have a state-wide merit system, however, and while it might not be entirely correct to place these job-seekers in the number one position in these states, they certainly would be near the top of any list of gubernatorial visitors. Even in the merit-system states the governor must make some appointments and whenever an appointment is to be made there will be persons seeking that appointment either for themselves or for their friends. Job-seekers and persons who wish to influence the governor in making his appointments are one group which can be found in the governor's office in any state in the nation, although the extent of this pressure is markedly lessened in merit-system states.

Thirteen per cent of those who came to see the Governor of Arkansas were in quest of some special favor. Most of these favors had a financial aspect, such as obtaining the governor's assistance in making sales to state agencies, securing permits to operate a business, or securing the governor's assistance in the settlement of a claim against the state. For example, two of the individuals in this group sought to have the governor reverse the decision of his revenue commissioner who had denied these individuals a permit to engage in the business of selling alcoholic beverages. On two other occasions committees representing local groups offered to exchange political support for the governor's influence in having certain roads paved. Of course, a few of the individuals who sought the governor's aid in Arkansas had a legitimate claim for the governor's assistance. Most of them, however, had no legitimate reason to see the governor and many were seeking to have the governor go over the heads of his cabinet officers and grant requests which had been refused by these officials. Others apparently sought the governor's assistance because they were ignorant of the proper channels for their requests. These were relatively few, however, for most of this type were steered by the governor's secretary to the proper department or agency handling the matter in which they were interested.

Favor-seekers, of course, are not confined in their operations to Arkansas and they make up a rather large group of the governor's visitors in any state. The governor may grant some of these requests on a political basis. It is not unknown, for example, for a governor to barter a few well placed roads for political support. In the main, however, he is unable or unwilling to grant these requests, because most of them represent an appeal from an already established procedure. If the governor makes too many exceptions to the established procedure, he will not only weaken the authority of his department heads but will also find himself performing their functions. If it becomes known that the way to secure a liquor permit is to appeal to the governor, then the governor will become the person who issues liquor permits instead of, as is the case in Arkansas, the revenue commissioner. Sound politics as well as sound administration would seem to require that the governor interfere as little as possible with the normal processes of government. This is not true in some states however, where it might be said that the state is administered "from the governor's office" rather than under the direction of the governor.

Close on the heels of the favor-seekers came the 12 per cent of the governor's visitors who represented civic, church, or school organizations. These callers usually requested the governor to speak at a gathering sponsored by their organization or sought his influence in behalf of some "worthy" cause. Some, however, merely wished to meet the governor. For example, this was the case with a committee of 4-H Club members, a large group of school children who were addressed by the governor in his reception room, and a group of boys from one of the state schools. Among the groups requesting the governor to speak were included a committee from a Sunday School class, a committee representing the Chamber of Commerce in an eastern Arkansas city, a committee from a Rotary Club in one of the cities of the state, and a committee which invited the governor to address a high school graduating class. The "worthy" cause representatives included an individual who requested the support of the governor for the statewide promotion of Thrift Clubs, and the president of the State Garden Club, who asked the governor to make a proclamation of a special garden week.

This type of visitor is familiar to the average American governor. The governor is always beset with individuals or, as was the case in Arkansas, with committees who invite him to speak. If he actually accepted all these invitations, he would be able to do nothing else. If he fails to accept the invitations, he runs the risk of alienating a particular group which is making the request. This is a problem of considerable dimension, since these groups want the prestige attached to the governor's personal appearance and a substitute is unacceptable. Similarly, the representatives of "worthy" causes are legion and, in at least one state, this has become such a problem that the determination of which causes the governor will support is a part of the regularly assigned duties of one of the governor's staff. Except for the youth groups, who simply wanted to meet the governor, most of these problems could have been handled by correspondence. However, other individuals also like to meet the governor incidental to their extending to him an invitation to speak or to support a "worthy" cause. Consequently, it is difficult for the governor to escape from visitors with this sort of mission.

It is particularly interesting to note that administrative problems as presented by department heads and officials of state agencies and institutions accounted for only 10 per cent of the total number of callers received by the governor. Of the ten visits recorded, seven were visits by individual department heads and three were group conferences with two or more department heads. The governor, therefore, probably saw a total of some fifteen agency department heads during the period in question. The estimate of 10 per cent for administrative matters is probably a little on the low side, since there were several brief conferences with department heads which were sandwiched in between the governor's regular appointments and which were not recorded on the table. If these visits were added, it might bring the total time spent on administrative matters to about 15 per cent. Even so, this percentage may seem unreasonably low to those who view the governor primarily as the state's general manager. However, the average governor spends relatively little time on conferences with his department heads on administrative problems. While the percentage might be increased slightly in those states where a more sophisticated concept of the governor's management functions has developed, the 15 per cent figure would not be atypical of most states.

The purpose of the visits of eight of the governor's callers was either unknown to the governor's receptionist or she could not recall the visitor and hence 8 per cent of the governor's visitors must be listed as "purpose unknown." These visitors, however, probably would be distributed in about the same proportion as the governor's other callers and hence would not affect materially the percentages.

This analysis of the purpose of the visitors to the governor's office in Arkansas is influenced by the conditions peculiar to that state. The fact that Arkansas is a spoils-system state accounts for the large number of visits concerned with state employment; the relatively small size of the state and the "open-door" policy maintained by the governor accounts in part for the large number of visitors whom the governor actually saw. If these two factors are taken into consideration, however, the kinds of people who came to see the governor and the reasons for which they came would be familiar to most American governors. In some of the larger states like California, New York, Illinois, and Massachusetts, most of these people would never actually see the governor but would be handled by members of the governor's staff. However, in most of the states in the South, the Southwest, and in the smaller Midwestern and New England states relatively informal operations persist and the pattern would be fairly typical.

Another form of analysis which combines that used in Arkansas and our previous analysis of the governor's day was that made by a recent reorganization commission in its study of the state government of New Hampshire. This study is based on an analysis of the daily engagement book kept by the Secretary to Governor Sherman Adams. It covers three weeks, selected at random, beginning April 4, May 23, and December 12, 1949. The first two weeks covered were during the period in which the legislature was in session and the week of December 12 was after the legislature had

TABLE VIII*

Weekly Schedule of the Governor of New Hampshire

Activity		*Average Time Spent in Activity*
Correspondence		9 hrs. 40 min.
Phone Calls		3 hrs. 30 min.
Interviews		20 hrs.
With Members of the Legislature	5 hrs.	
With Department Heads and Officers	4 hrs. 20 min.	
With Citizens	4 hrs.	
With Job Seekers	1 hr. 20 min.	
With the Press	1 hr.	
On Industrial Development	1 hr.	
With Party Leaders	1 hr.	
On State Reorganization	1 hr.	
On Employee Reclassification Study	40 min.	
On Miscellaneous Matters	40 min.	
Meetings		7 hrs. 20 min.
Of Governor's Council	4 hrs.	
With State Boards and Commissions	2 hrs.	
On Political Matters	1 hr. 20 min.	
Making and Writing Speeches		3 hrs. 30 min.
Travel		10 hrs. 30 min.
'Dignitary' Matters (Such affairs as christening *U S S Pickerel,* bill-signing ceremonies, meeting groups of school children, acting as honored guest at various meetings)		9 hrs.
Total Time Spent on Week's Activities		63 hrs. 30 min.

*Based on figures taken from "What Does a Governor Do?" *The New Hampshire Taxpayer,* XII, No. 1 (January, 1950), 1.

adjourned. This analysis shows that the work week of the governor was 68, 67, and 56 hours respectively during these three weeks. The governor's average work week would, therefore, be approximately 63½ hours which would be broken down as in Table VIII.

While the material which has been presented in this section shows considerable state-to-state variation, it also shows that the governors have many duties and functions in common in carrying out their daily routine. Perhaps the most significant point which emerges is the amount of time which the governor spends on correspondence, telephone calls, interviews, travel, and speech-making. While all of these may be concerned with either policy or management, they may also be classified partly as public relations. Most of the governor's correspondence and telephone calls as well as the majority of his interviews are concerned with problems which are presented by the state's citizens rather than by party leaders, legislators, or department heads. These contacts with the citizens of the state together with the governor's public speeches, his radio and television appearances, and his attendance either as a speaker or otherwise at numerous banquets, cornerstone laying ceremonies, state fairs and rodeos all fall in the general category of public relations. This aspect of the governor's functions emerges as the most time-consuming if not the most important of his duties on the basis of the evidence presented in this section. It is interesting to compare the findings of this section with the views of the governor's functions presented by the governors themselves in the following section. Such a comparison reveals that, while the governors do not give public relations as high a ranking as the time actually spent on the function would indicate, it nevertheless is a segment of their duties of which most governors are well aware and to which they give considerable weight.

THE EXECUTIVE FUNCTION—THE GOVERNORS' VIEWS

Another approach in determining the gubernatorial function is to examine statements of the governors' duties and responsibilities as formulated by the governors themselves. These statements are taken either from interviews with the governors or from articles and speeches by the governors. The governors' own evaluation of their duties and responsibilities tends to be in terms of their relative importance rather than in terms of the time spent on these functions, although several of the statements combine both approaches. The time a governor spends on a particular function is one indication of its importance, although it is not an infallible guide since for statutory or other reasons the governor may be forced to spend considerable time on a function which he personally regards as unimportant. Apparently, most governors are not given to philosophizing about the nature of the office, for speeches or articles in which the governor describes his functions are relatively rare. However, several of the governors have been moved to describe their version of the functions of the state's chief executive in fairly complete form and several others have made statements pointing to the importance of certain functions of the office. All of the governors interviewed were asked to comment on this aspect of the study and most of them had quite definite views. The initial statement of their functions given by most governors tended to be a fairly standard list of their legal duties such as the appointment of certain state officers, recommending bills to the legislature, and the preparation of the budget. In the more detailed questioning during the interviews, which was designed to reveal the governor's concept of the relative importance of his functions, rather interesting sectional differences developed. On the whole, the southern governors tended to place the greatest emphasis on the governor's function in the area of legislative relations, while the governors interviewed in the southwestern, midwestern, and western states tended to place more emphasis on the governor's managerial functions. Of the two governors interviewed in New England, one followed the line of his southern counterparts in emphasizing legislative leadership, while the other tended to follow the line of his colleagues in the Southwest, West, and Midwest.

These sectional differences are difficult to explain, but there is at least one factor which may have had considerable effect on the governors' views. In the South the one-party system prevails. In terms of gubernatorial leadership, this means that the governor, if he is to be the leader of the legislature, must develop an organization for legislative control from the ground up. In a one-party state the governor has no ready-made majority in the legislature as he generally has in a two-party state. In a two-party state, while the governor cannot depend on party responsibility alone to get his program through the legislature, there is in theory at any rate a common bond between the governor and the members of his own party in the legislature. Presumably these party members, who in normal circumstances would make up a majority of the legislature, can be called upon in the name of the party to support the governor's program as a party program. Thus the governor's role as a legislative leader in a two-party state may be somewhat easier than in a one-party state and the importance of this function may not loom as large in the governor's mind.

In a one-party state, on the other hand, members of the legislature are elected on a personal platform, which usually has little relevance to the governor's avowed program. In this sort of situation there can be no successful appeal to party responsibility or regularity. The governor must painfully build up his own factional group within the legislature to achieve and maintain sufficient strength to have the major part of his program enacted into law. The construction of this factional machine is a time-consuming process involving a great many personal interviews and not inconsiderable patronage. Hence, the southern governor may have some grounds for feeling that the legislative aspect of his functions should be given more importance than is assigned to it by his counterpart elsewhere in the nation. Most southern governors seem to feel that the electorate tends to judge them primarily on their ability to secure the passage of a major part of their program. Hence, whether they are correct in their analysis or not, they have a considerable motivating factor in devoting a substantial part of their energies to this aspect of their functions if they have future political aspirations.

The statements quoted below are fairly representative of the views of the governors on the scope and importance of their duties. No one formulation can be said to be typical, however, for the opinions of the governors reflect not only state-to-state variations but also the governor's own interpretation based on his personal prejudices and convictions. Nevertheless, there seems to be common agreement on the principal functions of the governor. If these functions on which there is general agreement are taken together with the information presented in the first section of this chapter, a reasonably accurate and realistic pattern of gubernatorial functions emerges.

In 1947 Millard F. Caldwell was serving the last year of his four-year term as Governor of Florida. The campaign for his successor was about to begin, and he took the opportunity presented by a request to address the annual meeting of the Florida State Chamber of Commerce to summarize his impressions of the duties of the governorship.[6] The Governor began his talk with an introductory comment to the effect that some problems were too big for one state acting alone to handle and that, therefore,

[6] Millard F. Caldwell, "The Governor's Duties and Responsibilities," an address before the 31st Annual Meeting of the Florida State Chamber of Commerce at St. Petersburg, Florida, December 2, 1947.

the governor must work harmoniously with the governors of the other states. He then presented a "factual description of the powers and responsibilities of the Chief Executive of Florida," the major points of which are as follows:

> . . . A Governor's first responsibility starts with his campaign. The dominant party in Florida prepares no gubernatorial platform and the determination of the objectives to be followed during the succeeding four years is largely left to the candidate. The Legislature, by long standing custom, has adopted the practice of treating the successful candidate's platform as the public mandate. . . .
>
> After the Governor's election comes the duty of intimately acquainting himself with the details of administration and the selection of department heads and staff. The judgment evidenced by the appointments will determine whether the State will enjoy four years of politics or four years of capable government. . . .
>
> . . . The Governor of Florida serves as Chairman and member of numerous Boards such as: The Budget Commission, The Board of Commissioners for State Institutions, The State Board of Education, The Department of Public Safety, The Trustees of the Internal Improvement Fund, The Board of Administration, The Pardon Board, The State Board of Pensions, The State Board of Conservation, The Board of Drainage Commissioners, The Labor Business Agents Licensing Board, The Agricultural Marketing Board and others. . . .
>
> After the Governor has selected and appointed his official family, his next big job is to look to the future and prepare a four-year program to be incorporated in the message to his first Legislature. That session comes quickly on the heels of his inauguration and fast, careful work is necessary if his recommendations are to be characterized by feasible soundness.
>
> One of the problems a new Governor will be interested in and will devote considerable thought to is the organization of the State administrative functions to the end that efficiency be improved and cost reduced. But, unfortunately, until one has served as Governor he is not qualified by necessary experience to recommend a far-reaching program of this sort, although incidental steps may be taken in that direction. He has not acquired the necessary knowledge to make his recommendations in time for the first session, and the second Legislature is generally unsympathetic to sweeping programs of a new order.

Thus the functions of the governor of Florida may be summarized as preparing a program for his campaign, preparing and presenting a four-year program to the legislature, acquainting himself with the details of administration and appointing his major department heads and staff, serving as chairman or member of numerous boards and commissions and devoting some thought to administrative reorganization.

In an interview, Governor J. Strom Thurmond described the duties of the governor of South Carolina as falling into six major categories. These may be briefly summarized as the execution of the laws, legislative leadership, membership on boards and commissions, appointments, pardon and parole (in conjunction with a Board of Pardon and Parole) and acting as the representative of the state in dealing with other states and the Federal Government.

On the whole, the southern governors tend to emphasize the policy-making aspect of their duties, particularly the role as legislative policy maker. For example, former Governor R. Gregg Cherry of North Carolina in commenting on his first year in office said, "The vast majority of my energies was spent in connection with the function of the General Assembly which was in session for the greater part of the first three months of the year."[7] Governor Folsom of Alabama also emphasized this aspect of his duties. In a radio talk on the governor's functions he said that the state's chief executive is supposed to "first recommend policies and programs to the legislature." Governor Folsom also viewed the governor's role in policy making to include that of setting the policy of certain executive departments and recommending party policies.

These summaries of the gubernatorial function by the southern governors, which emphasized the governor's role in policy making, may be contrasted with those of other sections of the country by an examination of the following statements by governors Johnston Murray of Oklahoma, Earl Warren of California, and Sigurd Anderson of South Dakota. In one of his regular weekly radio talks to the people of Oklahoma, Governor Murray developed his concept of the proper functions of the governor. In introducing his remarks he expressed sentiments which must have been shared by most governors at the close of a legislative session. In part Governor Murray said

. . . In most departments of your state government, peace and

[7] Raleigh *News and Observer,* January 2, 1946.

quiet reign once more. Administrators and state workers generally are breathing easier. The reason for this sudden return to normalcy, of course, is the fact that the state legislature has gone home. After a hectic four and one-half months, its work is finished for another two years. . . .

Which brings us to the job ahead. As I see that job, it is to administer all this new legislation in such a way as to benefit the greatest possible number of Oklahoma citizens. That job isn't going to draw as many bold-type newspaper headlines as the hot and heavy oratory from the legislature. But it's a lot more important. The *administration* of our laws is the final and supreme test of those laws. Good laws, poorly administered, can sometimes become bad laws. By the same token, the wise administration of a poor law can make it into a good law. . . .

As I see it, the primary job of your governor is one of administration. . . . Up to this point, I have been involved almost exclusively in the legislative end of being governor. And I don't mind saying that it's going to be a distinct pleasure to get better acquainted with other aspects of the office. . . .

I intend to spend as much time as possible in months ahead doing what I consider two important things. First of all, I want to determine what the people of Oklahoma are thinking, what their problems are, and how they hope to overcome those problems. And the only way I know of to determine it is to get among 'em. . . . So, I intend to spend a good deal of time in informal visits in all sections of the state. As governor, it's my job to represent all the people. It's my opinion that I can represent them better if I know at all times what they're thinking and doing. . . . While touring the state, as time permits, I also intend to have a first-hand look at all our state institutions.[8]

Governor Warren, of California, approached the problem of the governor's functions primarily from the point of view of certain problem areas in which the governor must be interested.[9]

In California, the Governor said, some of the most important of these areas were state finance, public works, and prison matters. The Governor explained that the proper operation of the state government depended first of all on the ability of the governor to get the state in a solvent financial condition and to maintain that status. If this is not done, the governor not only leaves himself open for criticism but also is greatly handicapped in carrying out

[8] These selections were taken from the text of the Governor's radio speech recorded for broadcast at 6:45 a.m., Saturday, May 26, 1951. Italics are the Governor's.

[9] Interview with Governor Earl Warren, Sacramento, California, June 25, 1951.

any other programs in which he might be interested. Public works, particularly highways and water projects, are of great importance in California. A good transportation system is essential for a state that is large in both area and population and has several densely populated metropolitan areas. Water is also a major problem in California, as it is in many western states. Most of the state's available water supply is in the northern part of the state, while the heaviest concentrations of population are in the south-central portions. Since it is not feasible to have a mass relocation of population, the only way to get the water supply and the people together is to bring the water to the people. This is actually what is being done in California and the state has one of the largest state-owned systems of water resource development of any state in the nation. The third area, that of prison affairs, is one which is receiving a great deal of attention throughout the nation. It is an area which is important not only because of the substantial sums of money involved but because of its human aspect. Governor Warren had been interested for many years in this particular area and through his experience as a prosecuting attorney and as Attorney General had personal first-hand experience with many of the problems involved. One of his first moves after being elected Governor was to revamp the entire prison setup in California. The present California system with its Adult and Youth Authorities and modern plans for the rehabilitation of prisoners has attracted wide attention throughout the United States.

Action in these areas cannot be undertaken by the governor entirely on his own initiative. While considerable progress can be made in improving administrative procedures without legislative action, most of the more basic changes require legislation. Governor Warren was well aware of the legislative aspects of his office and his staff was well organized to handle this particular side of the governor's duties. In spite of his approach to the functions of the governor in terms of certain major problems, I believe it would be fair to say that the Governor would emphasize not only his administrative functions in carrying out these programs but also the necessity of achieving legislative co-operation to have the programs enacted into law.

A slightly different type of approach to the functions of the governor was taken by Sigurd Anderson, Governor of South Dakota.[10] Governor Anderson summarized the governor's functions under three heads. First, he said the governor must provide for the proper administration of state government by seeing that all the various officers, boards and commissions operate efficiently. This involves supervision of those agencies under the governor's direct control and also the appointment of the proper individuals to carry out these functions. Secondly, Governor Anderson said the governor must provide guidance for the state government. The governor of South Dakota serves on a great many boards and commissions and through his membership in these bodies can provide personal guidance and direction for the state's affairs. Also included in this aspect of the governor's functions would be the guidance and leadership necessary to secure the enactment of the governor's program by the legislature. Third, the governor should bring the government to the people. This was interpreted by Governor Anderson to mean that the governor should speak to the people at various meetings, banquets, and other affairs, take the government to the people through the press and through the radio and by talking to those who came to see him at the capitol. Governor Anderson said that he planned to institute a regularly scheduled radio program as one means of accomplishing this end.

A very interesting discussion of the governor's functions which gives a good deal of the flavor of actual operations is found in an address by former Governor Forrest C. Donnell, then Governor of Missouri, given at the National Governors' Conference in June of 1943. The title of Governor Donnell's address is indicative of his approach to the governor's functions in that he spoke on "The Usual Duties of the Governor." The Governor began his address by stating that the two principal duties of the governor were that of the faithful execution of the laws and that of recommending measures to the legislature. "In connection with this duty," the Governor said, "should also be mentioned the power of veto which, I believe, exists in the Governor in all but one of the states. The word 'Governor' is derived from a Latin word signifying 'to steer a ship.' The duty of recommendation by the Governor to the legislature of his state and his power of veto

[10] Interview with Governor Sigurd Anderson, Pierre, South Dakota, July 10, 1951.

are important in enabling the Governor to steer, or at least to assist in steering, the ship of his state." The Governor then went on to describe the governor's "usual" duties in these terms.

> When, however, each Governor here present shall, a day or a few days hence, have returned to his office in the capitol of his state, he will find himself confronted not only with questions arising from the war but also with *ordinary* business of his state which engages, day by day, a large proportion of his time. If the legislature of his state be in session, bills from that body will be upon or about to reach his desk and, in nearly every such state, each of those bills will require his decision as to whether it shall be approved or vetoed. Proceedings for the extradition of persons charged with crime will require his attention. Applications for pardons or paroles may be present or near at hand for his action. Flood conditions or threatened violence may present to him the necessity for early decision as to whether he shall call out troops of the State Guard for enforcement of the law, preservation of property, or protection of life. Vacancies in local offices, with petitions and letters from advocates or opponents of persons who seek appointment to fill those offices, may require of him early and discriminating attention. State administrative boards and commissions will have before them practical questions requiring prompt joint thought and action of their members, of whom he is one. Financial problems, perhaps of eleemosynary or educational institutions, will require his assistance and counsel. Methods of punishment in penal institutions of his state may be presented to him for study and decision. In addition, constantly arriving correspondence from constituents and others, on a variety of types of subjects, may necessitate early personal consideration and response by the chief executive of the State. In short, the Governor . . . will on return to his office resume not only the function into which the war has projected him but also those more prosaic, but nevertheless extremely essential, duties which devolve upon him in the management of the ordinary current affairs of his state.[11]

THE EXECUTIVE FUNCTION—A SUMMARY VIEW

In the preceding sections we have attempted to examine the functions of the governor from several different points of view. In the introductory section we noted the effect which conditioning factors such as custom and tradition have on the exercise of the governor's powers. In the next section we analyzed the governor's

[11] Governor Forrest C. Donnell, "The Usual Duties of the Governor," an address before the National Governors' Conference on June 23, 1943, *Proceedings of the Governors' Conference 1943,* p. 118 ff.

daily and weekly schedule with a view to discovering what he actually does with his time, and in the last section we presented the views of several present and past governors on the nature and scope of the gubernatorial function. If these sections are considered together, we find, in spite of the different emphasis in each section, that there seems to be a hard core of agreement as to the duties, responsibilities, and powers of the governor.

The governor of the modern American state is concerned primarily with three broad areas of operations: policy formation, public relations, and management. Of these three, the governor's principal role seems to be that of policy formation, since the compelling force of policy considerations runs like a thread through all the governor's other functions. Most governors, sooner or later, find themselves enmeshed in the problem of formulating a legislative program and securing the acceptance of that program by the legislature. They also discover that they must be concerned with establishing the administrative policies which will govern the execution of this program and other programs which have been established on a continuing basis. Intertwined in both of these attempts are the governors' endeavors to exercise policy control over their party or over the faction of the party with which they are associated. This control may be either a direct control, as an adjunct to an attempt to establish legislative or administrative policy, or it may be more indirect in that the governors' concern with the control of the party organization may be based on a desire to influence the nominating process in connection with their renomination as governor or their nomination for some other office. Policy considerations also are an important force in the governors' role in public relations, since much of that effort is directed toward explaining or justifying their programs, either actual or proposed, to the people of the state. The American governor is deeply concerned with policy—legislative, administrative, and political—and while he is seldom conscious of the particular area in which he is operating and may be operating in all three areas simultaneously on a given problem, he is certainly active in the field of policy-making and decision-making.

Perhaps his most easily identified activity as a policy-maker takes place in the legislative policy field. The governor of the modern American state does not wait for policy to be handed to him by the legislature in the form of a legislative statute and then set about to carry out this policy. As numerous studies of the legislative process in the states have revealed, and as will be emphasized in a succeeding chapter on the governor's role in policy formation, the majority of important legislative policies embodied in the major pieces of legislation passed by the average state legislature emanate from the governor's office or from the offices of his department heads. The separation of powers theory, which still enjoys lip service among state legislators and constitution makers, is no great impediment to the governor in his role in the legislative process. In all states the governor is recognized by the constitution as having some part in the formation of legislative policy, and the development of the office has been such in most states that the governor has emerged as a powerful force in legislative affairs. The entering wedge in the governor's development as a leader in legislative policy is his power to report to the legislature on the condition of the state and to make such recommendations for legislation as he deems appropriate. Gradually over a period of time this power to recommend has been implemented by such powers as the veto, the executive amendment, and the power to call special sessions of the legislature. These formal powers have become more meaningful because the governor's popular election has greatly increased the prestige of the office. This prestige also has been increased through the example of forceful leadership presented by recent occupants of the office. The effectiveness of the governor's leadership in legislative matters also has increased with the development of informal arrangements to secure the passage of legislation. These arrangements seem to form an "influence cycle" which begins with the organization of the legislature, continues through such persuasive techniques as personal conferences with individual legislators and the judicious use of patronage, and finally ends with the veto, which generally is used as a last resort if other methods fail. All of these powers and techniques place the governor in a position to wield considerable influence in the legislative process. Whether he in fact assumes the role of legislative leader is another matter and depends on such factors as his party leadership, the customs and traditions of the state, and the governor's own view of his proper functions.

The southern governors tend to place more emphasis on this aspect of policy formation than do those from other sections of the country. In the South, legislative leadership probably would be ranked first in a listing of the governor's functions. In the rest of the nation, the governor's role in administrative policy formation probably would receive equal emphasis. However, the problem of legislative policy formation and the corollary problem of securing the enactment of a legislative program is one with which all governors are concerned and, hence, will be examined in some detail in Chapter 7, "The Governor's Role in Policy Formation."

The governor's role in forming party policy or acting as party leader generally is not considered by the governors to be separate or distinct from their roles in legislative or administrative policy formation. In practice, the governor seldom acts as a party leader except with some specific objective in mind, such as using this power to insure the passage of a particular piece of legislation. Demands on the governor when acting in this role also generally take specific form, such as pressure by party leaders for recognition in the determination of the governor's appointments. Furthermore, party leadership in most states is apt to be split between the governor and some other leading political figure. This rival is likely to be the senior United States Senator of the state but may be another elected officer of the state or even a political boss who holds no elective office. The use of the term "party leader" is, therefore, somewhat restricted in a consideration of the governor's functions.

The term "party leader" is also not an entirely accurate description of the governor's status because of the nature of state political parties. The analysis in Part I of the process by which governors are nominated and elected revealed that there are a great many states in which there are no effective opposition parties. As was pointed out, there are some fourteen states which make up a one-party group. In addition, there are some twenty states which may be characterized as being normally Democratic or Republican. In these 34 states the governor is the leader of one faction of his party. He is not, therefore, a party leader in the generally accepted sense of the term. Within this normally Republican group, the governors of Nebraska and Minnesota are in a rather peculiar position in regard to party leadership. The governor is elected on a partisan ticket but the legislature in both cases is nominally non-partisan. It may be proper to regard the governor as a party leader in these states but again his leadership does not follow the accepted pattern at least as far as his legislative leadership is concerned.

In the remaining states, which generally are regarded as two-party states, there are some states which meet the specifications generally suggested for a two-party pattern. In these states, the governor is the party leader in fact as well as in name. He is the head of the dominant party and that party controls both the governorship and the legislature. The governor, therefore, is in a position to use his party leadership to implement the party program. However, as will be suggested in Chapter 7, the states which fit this description are not as numerous as is sometimes thought. In a great many states, a pattern of party control has developed in which one party generally controls the governorship while the other party controls one or both houses of the legislature. In this case, the governor is still the leader of his party but that party does not have the control necessary to make a party program effective. Hence, the governor, if he desires to see his program enacted into law, must build a power base which must include at least some members of the opposite party.

The fact that the governor in the South and in the normally Democratic and Republican states is primarily a factional leader, coupled with the fact that many of the so-called two-party states fail to follow the prescribed pattern, leads to the conclusion that if the governor is a party leader, he acts in a fashion which does not follow the prescribed pattern. In practice, it seems to the writer that the governor must build a bloc of votes from whatever source he can and that in only a few states are the members of his party alone a sufficient basis for such a bloc. Consequently, while the governor's effectiveness as a party leader should not be judged entirely in legislative terms, it seems clear that the term cannot be used in its generally accepted sense in referring to the governor of most states. While the governor may be a party leader in terms of the state party's relations to the national party, he is a factional leader in terms of the organization of the party within the state. The term "party leader" as used in this book in connection with the governor's role in policy formation should be understood to mean the governor's leadership of a faction of his party in most states and of the majority of his party in those states where a true two-party situation prevails. This function is so closely connected with the governor's functions in legislative and administrative policy formation that we will not attempt to consider it in a separate chapter in this book. This, however, is not intended to minimize its importance but merely to consider it at those points in the succeeding chapters where it has the most relevance.

The governor's role in management is also a policy role to a considerable extent, since the governor is concerned primarily with the establishment of the policies which will govern the operation of the executive branch during his administration. This aspect of policy formation has been distinguished from the governor's role in legislative and party policy formation primarily for the sake of emphasis, but it does have a different character because of the nature of the individuals with whom the governor deals. In attempting to establish administrative policy, the governor must deal with the heads of the agencies which make up the executive branch. In many ways the governor is in a weaker position *vis-a-vis* some of these agency heads than he is with the legislature. While the governor is supposed to be the state's chief executive, he is actually the chief executive only in the sense that he is the first among several executives. Because many of the other executive offices also are popularly elected, they are on the same level with the governor and draw their authority from the same source. Consequently, the governor is not in an ideal position to establish administrative policy because he does not control the department heads who will theoretically be bound by that policy and who will carry out the governor's programs. The position of the governor is further weakened by the fact that in many states he has only a two-year term and some of his department heads may have terms longer than that of the governor. This means that in addition to being confronted with other elected officers who share his executive power he also is faced with one or more department heads who have been appointed in previous administrations and who are probably of the opposite political party. These are only a few of the complicating factors which make the governor's role in management a very difficult one. These factors will be discussed in more detail in Chapter 8, but it might be well to point out that the governor's central problem in management is the establishment and co-ordination of administrative policy in an administrative environment which is far from ideal. In attempting to achieve his goals, the governor is forced to depend primarily on such persuasive devices as cabinet meetings and personal conferences and on the executive budget and financial controls in those states where he is given these powers. In spite of the various state reorganizations which have been carried out in the last fifty years, it does not seem that the governor has yet become the state's chief executive. The governor's role in management is one of his most difficult functions and probably that in which he is least equipped in terms of powers and staff to do an adequate job. Curious as it may seem in many states, the governor is actually placed in the anomalous position of having far more influence with members of the legislature than with his own department heads. Under such conditions it is small wonder that his primary concern is with legislation rather than administration.

The governor's role in public relations also is closely related to his roles in policy formation and management. The preceding analyses of the governor's daily routine and the governor's own views on the gubernatorial function have covered this aspect of the governor's functions in some detail and it does not seem necessary to cover this function in a separate chapter. It will, however, be considered at relevant points in the two chapters on policy formation and management and will be returned to in a consideration of the governor's staff in Chapter 10.

The governor's function in the field of public relations is considered as separate in this formulation of his duties because so much of his time is devoted to public appearances, press conferences, correspondence, and interviews with the state's citizens on matters which have importance primarily in terms of the governor's relation to the public. It is perfectly true that in his major speeches he may be dealing with questions of policy or may be attempting to build up public support for his legislative program. It is true that his press conferences may be devoted to the announcement of appointments or to answering questions on some phase of administrative affairs. It is true also that the citizens of the state come to see him with personal problems in relation to state employment, old age assistance payments, highways, and a multitude of other matters which are directly related to administration. However, when the governor makes a public address explaining policy, or answers the questions of the press on a prison riot, or talks to a citizen about a job for a son-in-law, he is primarily engaged in explaining his program or the workings of one of the programs of the state government to the public, the press, or the individual citizen. The late James Forrestal put the matter very aptly in his diary when he said, "The difficulty of Government work is that it not only has to be well done, but the public has to be convinced that it is being well done. In other words, there is a necessity both for competence and exposition, and I hold it is extremely difficult to combine the two in the same person."[12] The governor's position is such that he must be constantly engaged in exposition. He must not only prepare a legislative program and see that it is enacted and establish administrative policies and see that they are adhered to, but he must also constantly assure the citizens that these functions are being well done and that he is carrying out the promises which he made in the election. It is, indeed, extremely difficult to combine the talents for policy formation, management, and exposition in one person, but any governor must constantly attempt to perform this difficult feat.

Perhaps this need for constant exposition is the feature which most clearly distinguishes the occupant of a key government post whether it be legislator, cabinet member, or governor, from important positions in business. While public relations is now recognized in both fields, it reaches much further into the inner workings of the government than it does in business. The government's whole scheme of fiscal operations is an open public record. Every policy which is considered by the legislature, not just those which are successful, is put before the public for scrutiny. While the press occasionally complains of closed hearings of certain

[12] James Forrestal, *Diaries,* edited by Walter Millis and E. S. Duffield (New York, 1951), p. 300, quoted in "Distinguishing Characteristics of Public Administration," by John J. Corson, *Public Administration Review,* XII (Spring, 1952), 125.

boards and commissions, the general tendency at the state level is for the operations of the executive as well as the legislative branch to be open to the press and the public. Pitiless publicity can be focused at any moment on any part of the whole governmental process and the office of governor is a favorite target of the spotlight.

The governor's every move is worthy of front page reporting. He has no private life and his day's work is not finished when he goes home from the office. One governor, who also had served several terms in Congress, said that he would rate the difficulties of the duties of the two offices about even but that the governorship was a much more strenuous position than that of a Congressman because the governor had no private life at all. "In Washington," the governor said, "a Congressman soon discovers what invitations he can refuse and what invitations he must accept. As a result, he has some time to spend with his family like other normal human beings. Such is not the case with the governor. When he goes home to the executive mansion, he discovers that he is still as close to the citizen as his telephone and that citizens think nothing of dropping in to see the governor at any time of the day or night." The governor lives in a goldfish bowl and cannot call his life his own until he leaves the office.

All of this emphasis on exposition means that the governor spends a tremendous amount of time on what has been called here the public relations aspects of his functions. It seems fair to say that the governor spends at least half of his time on such activities. This means that public relations is so time consuming that it limits the governor's other functions. The governor has only 24 hours in the day, and while it is not uncommon for him to devote twelve to fifteen of these to public business, there is a limit to what one man can accomplish.

The concept which we have developed in this country of a chief executive, whether he be President or governor, is that of a man who is expected to be simultaneously a legislative leader, a political chief, a general manager, and the ceremonial and public representative of the state. This concept places on any but the most exceptional individual an almost impossible burden. It seems abundantly clear that the average governor does not have the time to perform all of the functions which he is now called upon to carry out. The only way to give him sufficient time is to reduce the number of functions, reduce the time spent on certain of his functions, or to give him sufficient institutional aid to assist him in coping with these many responsibilities.

None of these approaches in itself is the entire answer, for none of them can be carried out completely enough to give the governor the additional time he needs. However, by a combined approach on all three fronts considerable progress can be made in this direction in most states. In many states it is also necessary to consider a closely related problem, that of giving the governor more power in those states where the office is still too weak for effective action.

It does not appear that the governor can abandon his major functions as policy maker, public relations man, and general manager, nor is it desirable that he give up any of these roles entirely. However, it is possible, as the experience of several states has shown, to reduce materially the minor duties of the governor, most of which have been saddled on him by legislative enactment, as for example, the commissioning of notaries public, appointment of justices of the peace, the approval in writing of all state contracts, and the like. This reduction in minor duties will save some time which can then be used for more important functions. In addition, better office management in the handling of correspondence and interviews should result in a reduction of the amount of time spent on these functions. This reduction in minor functions and the reduction of the time spent on those functions remaining is not a real frontal attack on the problem. What most governors need is some high-level assistance in performing their major functions, most of which cannot be completely delegated because of their very nature.

In the policy field, for example, the governor himself in the last analysis must make the policy decisions. Even in this role, however, he can be given some help. If the burden of decision-making cannot be transferred from his shoulders, much of the spade work preliminary to those decisions can be done by an able staff. Our experience with the Presidency and with developments in some of our states shows the desirability of what might be called a policy staff. This proposal is discussed at some length in Chapter 10 on the governor's staff.

Some progress can also be made through proper organization, scheduling, and staffing in reducing the governor's work load in the field of public relations. This is the most time-consuming of the governor's functions, but it is also one in which the people, particularly of the smaller states, are least likely to accept a substitute. Considerable public education as to the nature of the office will probably be necessary before substantial progress can be made in this field, but a beginning in the direction of a reduced work load is certainly in order. The primary complicating factor is that the governor's public-relations role is so closely affiliated with his role in partisan politics and with his future political aspirations that it will be exceedingly difficult as a practical matter to curtail.

The field in which the greatest progress has been made in delegation and staff assistance is in management. Here, we already have an example of what can be done in the Executive Office of the President, in the well-developed executive offices of several of our larger states, and in the recent development of the concept of a department of administration in some states. While none of these solutions has a complete transfer value, the experience at the federal level and in those states which have tried these devices should prove valuable to those states which have not yet explored such an approach. Some suggestions are put forward in succeeding chapters of this book as to the kinds of functions which can be successfully delegated or institutionalized and the kind of staff which may prove of the most assistance to the governor in his role as general manager.

If we accept as a basic premise that the office of governor is an essentially political office, we have taken a step forward in a better understanding of the kind of staff the governor needs. If the three-fold nature of the governor's functions is recognized, then his staff may be organized in such a way as to assist him in policy-making and public-relations functions as well as in management.

7. THE GOVERNOR'S ROLE IN POLICY FORMATION

ONE OF THE MOST significant points which has emerged from our study of the office of governor up to this point is the essentially political nature of the office: the governor's primary concern seems to be determining the policies of the state government during his term of office. As was suggested in our summary of the gubernatorial function, the effort made by the governor to determine these policies involves him in an attempt to mold the policies of his party and to influence the policy decisions of the legislature. It is also instrumental in causing the governor to promulgate policies which he hopes will guide the executive branch of the government. This three-fold aspect of policy-making is sometimes described by saying that the governor "wears three hats," i.e., acts as party chief, legislative leader, and the state's chief administrator.

These distinctions are partially valid and are useful in studying the governor's role in policy formation, but it should be pointed out that most governors do not seem to be conscious of these distinctions in carrying out their duties or to worry about the particular hat they are wearing when they make any given decision. The tendency to ignore the subtleties of these distinctions is probably due in large measure to the fact that the effects of almost any decision are felt in all three fields. For example, most governors, even in merit-system states, make a great many appointments. Some of these are appointments to major positions such as that of a department head or a member of important boards or commissions, but the majority are to positions of a less important character. It is easy to see how a major appointment can be used to pay a political debt, or to influence a particular group in the legislature, or to build favor with a powerful interest group. It is also obvious that the appointment of a department head or a commission or board member is exceptionally important in terms of the control of administrative policy. What is not quite so obvious is that minor appointments which are sometimes considered to be merely routine administrative decisions also have considerable significance outside the field of administration or management. The effect of these decisions is felt particularly in the fields of party control, legislative influence, and public relations. Because of their repercussions in these fields, minor appointments are frequently more troublesome to the governor than major appointments. It is these lesser appointments which are the primary concern of the party managers who seek to influence the governor's selection in order to strengthen party organization. These appointments are also significant in legislative terms because the average legislator is more concerned with securing one of the more numerous minor positions for one of his constituents than he is with influencing the governor's selection of a department head. Minor appointments in the aggregate are also quite significant in terms of public relations. This is particularly true of appointments which impinge upon what are usually regarded as local functions such as appointments to drainage districts, conservation districts, levee boards, or county fair boards. It is also true of appointments to local offices whose incumbents are normally elected by the people of the community concerned but which are filled on a temporary basis by the governor on the death or resignation of the incumbent. The cumulative effect of a series of "bad" appointments to such minor positions can be quite serious by creating unfavorable public relations for the governor.

The governor's decision on minor appointments is only one of the many so-called routine administrative decisions which he must make during his term of office. Without attempting to multiply these examples, it seems fairly obvious that the process of policy formation at the state level involves a series of decisions, large and small, by the governor over a period of several years. The cumulative effect of the governor's decisions during the course of his administration probably determines his effectiveness in all three aspects of his role in policy determination. Some decisions are at a much higher level and are much more dramatic than others. Certain of these can be dissected and found to impinge more upon administrative policy than party policy or more upon legislative policy than administrative policy. Even so, it is difficult and probably misleading to try to categorize the governor's decisions in policy formation as being entirely within any one of these fields. It is for this reason that the governor's role in policy formation will be considered in this chapter as a continuous process with decisions in any one field having definite policy implications in one or both of the other areas of policy formation.

The major distinction generally made by the governors themselves in discussing their role in policy formation is between party and/or legislative policy on one hand and administrative policy on the other. While many governors stressed the importance of both aspects of their policy function, most of them gave the greater weight to the party-legislative aspect as opposed to the administrative aspect. This is particularly true of the southern governors who, almost without exception, placed party, and particularly legislative leadership, in the first rank of their duties. The reason for this emphasis is not entirely clear, but it seems to be partly explained by two conditions which are found in combination primarily in the South. One of these is the fact that the South has a one-party system and as a result the governor must build a working majority of the legislature from among a group of competing factions. He does not have a majority party to serve as a basis for this bloc as does the governor of a two-party state. Thus, it may be somewhat more difficult for the southern governors to build a successful legislative bloc. This may tend to focus their attention on legislative matters, since the construction of a successful legislative organization requires considerable time and effort. This emphasis on legislative policy making at the expense of administrative policy formation is reinforced by the lack of power to control the executive branch which is characteristic of the office in many southern states.

This hypothesis receives some support from the interviews with governors in states in which the governor had more power over administration and in which a greater degree of administrative sophistication prevailed. In many of these states the governor tended to emphasize his role in administrative policy formation. The general position taken on the governor's role in policy formation by most governors interviewed is well illustrated by the comments of Governor Walter J. Kohler, Jr. of Wisconsin. In discussing the governor's role in policy making Governor Kohler pointed out that the governor is "the spokesman for his party and a formulator of many of its policies." He also felt that "one of the major responsibilities of the governor is to develop and recommend to the Legislature and to the citizens of the State programs and policies for the conduct of the State government and the improvement of the economic and social conditions of its citizens." The Governor added that he felt that a governor had not discharged his duties in policy formation simply by recommending policies to the legislature but that he should "urge these policies upon them in every honorable way."[1]

THE DEVELOPMENT OF THE POLICY FUNCTION

The emphasis on the governor's role in policy formation is a fairly recent development in the history of the office. It has not been too many years since the governor could be characterized properly as a figurehead. This characterization is hardly true in most states today, for the modern American governor is an individual who commands considerable respect and who has a decided influence on the formation of policy. The rise of the office to its present status in this field is the result of a gradual growth over a long period of time.

The first step in this direction was the early insertion in the majority of state constitutions of the seemingly innocuous provision that the governor should recommend a program to the legislature. Many of these provisions follow the wording of Section 3 of Article II of the United States Constitution. This section provides that the President "shall from time to time give to the Congress Information of the State of the Union, and recommend to their Consideration such Measures as he shall judge necessary and expedient." An examination of the debates in the Constitutional Convention leads us to believe that the founding fathers apparently did not envisage a chief executive who would be an

[1] Governor Walter J. Kohler, Jr., "The Governor's Office," *Wisconsin Magazine of History,"* XXXV (Summer, 1952), 243 and 245.

of policy formation. The next significant development was the provision for the selection of the governor through a state-wide election. The importance of this development was obscured when it was first introduced by the fact that not only the office of governor but also offices of a number of other executive officers were made elective. This Jacksonian concept, which was expressed in annual elections in many states, was a hampering influence in the development of the governor's power. However, in the long run the provision for the popular election of the governor was perhaps the most important single step in the governor's development as a policy maker. Through state-wide election the governor was placed in position to develop as a sort of people's tribune who could speak for the people of the state as a whole as opposed to the legislature, which spoke with a voice of many sections and many factions.[2] This is, of course, an over-simplified version of what actually took place but a development along these lines seems to have occurred in many states. Thus, in the governor's popular election we find an important impetus in the development of his present role in policy formation.

The development of this role has been very gradual in most states and is much farther advanced in some states than in others. It has been accelerated in recent years because of the high caliber of men who have come to occupy the office and because of modern means of communication which have enabled the governor to reach the people swiftly and directly and thus build up a backlog of popular support if he needs to appeal to the people over the heads of the legislature.

During the recent history of the office and even prior to World War I many able men were elected to governorships. These men were not content to act simply as the executor of the laws or as a check on the legislature. They had definite policies on governmental problems and they attempted to see those policies enacted into law. State-wide election had increased the prestige

[2] This is not to suggest that the governor may not speak with the voice of a faction or a section. Indeed, there is considerable evidence to show that he now speaks with distinctly urban overtones, as is pointed out in a later section of this chapter. In spite of this, however, the people seem to view the governor as a spokesman with a state-wide viewpoint, whether this is actually the case or not.

of the office and the governors were gradually able to focus the attention of the voters on their role as a representative of the people. The development of first the press, later radio, and now television has aided the governor considerably in this endeavor. While these facilities are open to the legislature and to the other elective officers, the governor is in the best position of any of these individuals to exploit the potentialities of these devices. There are many legislators and sometimes a considerable number of elected officials, but there is only one governor. Many of the governors elected after World War I were colorful and dynamic personalities and were able to utilize the press and later the radio to build up a powerful following among the voters who, of course, were also constituents of the legislature. Many of the successful governors of the modern period have not hesitated to carry their program directly to the people in the case of conflict with the legislature or simply to build public support for their program before or during the legislative session. In addition, the governor in most states also was given gradually the power to appoint an increasing number of state office holders. This appointing power can be used as patronage and hence is also useful in dealing with the legislature.

Added to these powers was the fact that by the beginning of the present century the governor had been given the power of veto in every state except North Carolina. This power considerably improved his position *vis-a-vis* the legislature and has been used to good effect in most states. However, as we shall point out in a subsequent section, it is generally a power which is used only after other methods of dealing with the legislature have failed. Furthermore, while it represented an important additional weapon in the governor's arsenal of persuasive powers, it does not seem entirely logical to maintain that this was the key factor in the governor's rise as a legislative policy maker. To do so is to ignore the fact that the governor of North Carolina, who was not given this power, apparently has been very successful in his dealings with the legislature of that state.

As a result of the increased prestige of the office through state-wide election, the example of gubernatorial leadership furnished by the governors of some states, the improved methods of mass communication, the provision for additional appointments by the governor which could be used as patronage, and the strengthening of his position through the veto, the office has developed into its present position of relatively high esteem and the governor has been able to make effective his power to recommend programs to the legislature. The governor's role in policy formation began in the area of legislative policy formation, since it was in this area that he was first given effective powers. At the same time the governor began to develop as a party leader largely because the same powers which enabled him to deal effectively with the legislature also enabled him to become a political leader in his own right. His state-wide election focused upon the office the attention of the voters and resulted in his legislative program receiving considerable popular endorsement. The office gradually became the central focus in state elections and became a sought-after position in terms of political preferment. The governor became a spokesman for his party and the leader of his party in the legislature. His powers of patronage and veto could be used not only to secure the passage of legislation but also to build a political following within his own party. The governor's emergence as a party leader seems to have been parallel to his emergence as a legislative leader. In a way he was forced into party leadership in an attempt to secure the enactment of his legislative program. Over and above this aspect of party leadership the governor in many states also became a party spokesman for his state in party councils at the national level. The governorship then gradually returned to its post-Revolutionary prominence as a stepping stone to higher political office, and many candidates for the presidency and a large number of senatorial candidates have come from the gubernatorial ranks. Thus, the forces which tended to shape the office toward a legislative orientation also tended to develop the governorship as a locus of party leadership.

The role of the governor in the establishment of administrative policy followed his emergence as a legislative and party leader in the states as a whole and has grown to an effective level only in those states where the office has developed sufficiently on the administrative side to enable him to operate as a leader in administration. In most states the administrative aspects of his role in policy formation have not yet been fully realized.

In spite of the theory that the governor is the state's chief executive, his powers in the executive branch in a majority of the states are not yet as fully developed as his powers in legislation. Consequently, the governor seeks to formulate policy in those areas where such policy will be successful. At the present stage of the office in the majority of the states these areas remain those of party and legislative policy.

The emphasis which we find on legislative policy formation has been partly forced on the governor by the state legislatures themselves. Not only have the legislatures frequently proved inept and sometimes obviously subject to corruption and pressure group domination in their attempts at policy formation but also they have demonstrated a definite tendency toward attempting to restrict the governor in the execution of the laws. Many state constitutions and most state statutes are characterized by an over-abundance of detail. As the structure of state government became more complex and, therefore, more difficult to understand, state legislatures seem to have developed the view that not only the policy control of the government but also the administration of the laws would slip from their grasp unless the governor and his department heads were rigidly controlled by statute. Hence, the statutes setting legislative and administrative policy began to be laid out in great detail. A governor coming into office with a program involving any real change in the status quo is immediately faced with the fact that the implementation of his program will require changes in legislation already existing or the passage of new legislation. The governor, therefore, must direct his energies to the formation and passage of legislation which will embody his announced program. As a result, his first moves in policy formation tend to be in the field of legislation.

In those states in which the governor prepares the budget, this power makes possible many of the policy changes which the governor wishes to see enacted. The governor's budget message, therefore, is a policy document of considerable importance in most instances. However, in some eight states the governor is not directly responsible for the budget, usually sharing the power of preparation with a board or commission. In some states this board is made up of the governor and elected officials, while in others it is made up of the governor and representatives of the legislature. In Arkansas the old legislative budget still remains and the governor is not, officially at any rate, responsible even in part for the preparation of the budget. Under the systems of commission and legislative budgeting, the budget does not necessarily represent the governor's views and is not as important a policy document as it is in states with the executive budget. Even in those states without the executive budget, however, the governor attempts to have incorporated in the budget as many of his policies as possible and incorporates in his general message to the legislature those policies which he could not persuade the budget commission to accept.

It should also be pointed out that in many of the forty states with an executive budget the budget document seldom reaches the high goals set for it as a policy device. One of its primary limitations is the fact that the budget actually covers only a part, sometimes as little as one-quarter, of the state's income and expenditures, since the majority of the state's income is from earmarked revenues which are dedicated to predetermined purposes.

Another limiting factor is the poor timing of the budget. In many states it must be submitted shortly after the governor takes office and before he has time to make a thorough analysis of the major policy problems involved. Frequently much of the governor's substantive program which should have been a part of the budget must be presented later in the session. These and other limitations reduce the effectiveness of the budget as the central focus in the process of policy formation. Nevertheless, it is an important part of the over-all process in a majority of the states.

POLICY PLANNING FOR A LEGISLATIVE PROGRAM

The initial role which the governor will play in forming legislative policies in his state is conditioned to some extent by the political setting. For example, in the one-party states the governor has a very free hand in the formation of his platform, which presumably serves as the basis for his legislative policies. In a one-party state, the party has no platform except those of the individual members of the party who are running for office. The real contest is in the primary. In this contest the platforms of the candidates for the governorship, the other elected executive offices, and the state legislature represent the views of the candidates and need not, and usually do not, contain uniform provisions. As a result, when the primary is over and the winners are known, the platform of the winning gubernatorial candidate, the other elected executive offices, and those of the winning legislators are not necessarily related. The party itself has had no platform in the primary, and since the general election is a formality, it develops no platform in that contest. As a recent governor of Florida puts the matter, "The dominant party in Florida prepares no gubernatorial platform and the determination of the objectives to be followed during the succeeding four years is largely left to the candidate. The Legislature, by long-standing custom, has adopted the practice of treating the successful candidate's platform as the public mandate."[3] While the latter half of this statement is open to some question, as we shall subsequently point out, it is generally true that the party's platform is that of the winning gubernatorial candidate. Under these circumstances, the governor in a one-party state starts out with the advantage of having a platform which represents "the objectives to be followed during the next four years" although in several one-party states this should be amended to read "for the next two years."

In the normally Democratic and Republican states the governor is in much the same position, since he is actually elected in the primary, and the platform on which he was elected is one of his own choosing. In the general election that platform may be changed slightly to conform to the party's concept of what its program should be in the succeeding four years. However, most of the planks will be those taken from the platform which the gubernatorial candidate used in his successful primary campaign.

In a two-party state, the governor may have to accept further alterations in the name of the party because the platform must be one on which an entire slate of candidates including the state legislators can campaign. However, the governor in his campaign can choose rather freely the issues which he will stress and those

[3] Millard F. Caldwell, "The Governor's Duties and Responsibilities," an address before the 31st Annual Meeting of the Florida State Chamber of Commerce at St. Petersburg, Florida, December 2, 1947.

which he will ignore and thus runs primarily on a platform of his own making.

The governors of all states, therefore, go into office with a platform of sorts, much of which is dictated by the gubernatorial candidate and his advisers. In the one-party states and in the normally Republican or Democratic states, the governor has a somewhat freer hand in the exact provisions of the platform. In all states, however, the platform will tend to reflect enough of the governor's major policies so that it will form a satisfactory basis for operation, if he actually desires to implement the program thus outlined.

The actual effect of the party platform on the process of policy formation is not entirely clear and varies greatly from state to state and within a given state from one campaign to another. For example, in most of the normally Democratic or Republican states the governor generally accepts the platform. However, this is not always the case. This is particularly true if the governor and party regulars are not in complete agreement. For example, Governor Warren did not accept all the planks in the Republican state platform in California in the 1950 campaign. However, during the campaign he publicly stated which planks he accepted as those which he would support as governor and thus went into office with his attitude toward the platform clearly understood.

While the governors are not always so explicit in their attitude toward the platform, this attitude clearly emerges during their first legislative session. At that time there is a further redefining of the issues stated in the platform through the selection of the issues which are actually presented to the legislature in the governor's first message. In addition, changes in the state or national political or economic scene may bring to the fore issues which were not crucial during the campaign itself. Thus, on some occasions entirely new issues are presented in the governor's messages. Generally, the governor's program is further refined in practice by the fact that not all of the bills introduced will actually receive full gubernatorial support. For political reasons it may be necessary for the governor to advocate certain policies in his messages and to have bills introduced which will embody those policies. His real program, however, will consist only of those bills which actually are pushed with all the resources at the governor's disposal. In the final analysis, therefore, the governor's program will embody only a part of the party platform and may, in addition, contain measures which are not mentioned in the platform at all. The party platform, consequently, is a part of the policy-forming process only to the extent that some of its planks find their way into the governor's real program.

The mechanics by which a "gleam in the governor's eye" becomes a concrete proposal which can be put before the legislature for consideration vary considerably from state to state. Some of the major agencies used for research and bill drafting include the governor's immediate staff, the budget agency, the regular departments of government, the agents of interest groups, facilities of the state educational institutions, and the legislative research and bill-drafting agencies of the state government.

It may seem strange at first glance that the governor would use an agency of the legislature in the preparation of his program. Yet, in several states this is a regular practice and one which seems to be spreading. Both the governors and the state legislatures are gradually beginning to realize the need for expert assistance in research on proposed legislation as well as in the drafting of legislation. In some instances the governor initiates the use of expert assistance and is followed by the legislature in securing its own legislative aids. In other states the legislature has pioneered in this field and has been followed by the governor. As an example of the first situation, we may take the present Legislative Reference Service in Alabama. That agency originated in a small research staff set up for the governor by the Bureau of Public Administration of the University of Alabama to assist him in the preparation of legislation. The legislature soon saw the advantage of expert research assistance to the executive and proceeded to take over the agency complete with its director and re-establish it as a legislative aid. The Legislative Reference Service, however, still retains the function of drafting bills and performing research for the governor as well as the legislature.

Perhaps the most startling example of the governor's reliance on the state bill-drafting agency not only for assistance in drafting legislation but also assistance in program formation is to be found in Oklahoma. In that state, Governor Roy J. Turner (1947-51) stated publicly that he had adopted the legislative program suggested by the Oklahoma State Legislative Council. This unusual reliance by the governor on an agency of the legislature is not typical of the states as a whole but serves to emphasize the role which can be played by a legislative research agency if the governor chooses to utilize its services.

In addition to using the services of the state bill-drafting agencies, the governors sometimes make use of the research facilities of the state university and in particular of the various bureaus of public administration or their equivalent which have developed in many states in recent years.[4] Some of them, as for example Governors Kohler in Wisconsin, Battle in Virginia, and Stevenson in Illinois, recruited a part of their staff from academic life. Many governors, however, regard the academic mind with some suspicion and do not utilize the resources of the state educational units as fully as they might.

The preparation of legislation also is influenced by pressure-group action and many "administration" measures probably are prepared by the legislative representative of these groups. It is difficult to determine just how much of the governor's program originates with these sources but certainly some of it may be attributed to pressure-group activity. It may be, however, that a smaller part of the governor's program should be attributed to these groups than frequently is credited to them, especially by members of the press. While many potent pressures are brought to bear on the governor, some of these pressures are directed toward influencing the governor's administrative policy rather than his legislative policy. For example, a highway contractor who contributed heavily to the governor's campaign while definitely interested in seeing that the governor emphasized a program of new highway construction also is very much interested in securing certain contracts for highway equipment or supplies. It is quite probable that both candidates for the governorship had a highway construction program which would be acceptable to the contractor. What he is interested in primarily is dealing

[4] See Rowland Egger and Weldon Cooper, *Research, Education and Regionalism* (Bureau of Public Administration, University of Alabama, 1949), pp. 120 ff. for a discussion of the role of the Bureau of Public Administration as a research agency for Alabama governors.

with the administration once the governor has come into power. This possibility is emphasized by the findings of a committee which was appointed by Governor James E. Folsom to investigate alleged irregularities in the Alabama Highway Department. In one section of their very illuminating report the committee said

> It has come to the attention of the Committee that there is an established custom in Alabama, over a long period of years, for highway contractors to make sizeable donations to political campaigns. One highway contractor testified that in the last ten years he had donated approximately $15,000 to political campaigns. . . . While all of the contractors before the Committee denied that there was any advantage in being on the successful side in a political campaign, or close to an administration, yet the highway contractors are striving desperately to gain such a position. . . . It goes without saying, that once a contractor has contributed materially to a successful candidate, or to any political campaign in which an Administration is interested, that there are advantages which he will receive and other advantages which he will expect to receive.[5]

In addition to the use of legislative research facilities, the facilities of state universities, and the services of the legislative representatives of interest groups, the governor also makes use of the resources of his own office. Here also the actual part played by staff members in influencing the governor's policy determinations is difficult to determine. In some states the governor's staff or certain members of his staff are quite influential in determining the content of the policies which they draft for the governor, while in others the staff members are used more for technical assistance in drafting legislation than for advice on its policy content. In general, staff members play a substantial role in policy determination if for no other reason than the fact that they are in constant touch with the governor and, hence, are in a position to influence his decisions through their recommendations on policy matters both pending and proposed. Since the arrangement of the staff and the determination of their duties are at the discretion of the governor in most states, responsibility for the preparation of legislation which is delegated to staff members does not follow a fixed pattern throughout the states.

[5] This statement is taken from an untitled mimeographed report of the Committee dated August 18, 1948.

In most states this responsibility is not placed on any one member of the staff, but in a few states the pattern has become fairly formalized. For example, in New York the Governor's Counsel is responsible for the preparation of the governor's legislative program, and many of the key measures introduced for the governor originate in this office. Furthermore, there was established under Governor Dewey a system of clearances under which all proposed legislation sponsored by the various departments of the executive branch was cleared with the Counsel's office before it reached the legislature. This system was similar to that established in the Federal Bureau of the Budget and apparently worked even more effectively than its federal counterpart. The counsel's office in the New York hierarchy was very close to the top of the governor's immediate staff and the occupant of the office wielded considerable power.[6]

In several states, including Florida, North Carolina, Vermont, and California, the governor has a special legislative secretary or legislative assistant who aids him in the preparation of legislation. However, the primary function of this individual is not preparation of legislation but keeping the governor informed on what is happening in the legislature and pushing those bills which the governor has had introduced and blocking those to which the governor is opposed.

Policy formation during a governor's term does not operate as a one-way street. When the newly elected governor takes office, particularly when this represents a change in political parties, he is generally forced because of lack of time and lack of confidence in the personnel already in office to have most of his program prepared by the members of his own staff or by some of his confidential advisers, who may be entirely outside the government. If a governor stays in office for more than one term in a state with a two-year term, or if he is in his second legislature in a state with a four-year term, many of his "administration" measures are the products of the departments under his supervision. The governor cannot be an expert in all the fields under his direction, and if he has confidence in the ability of a depart-

[6] For other examples of staff divisions which are used by the governor in legislative research and policy formation see Chapter 10.

ment head in a given field, he tends to accept his suggestions for changes in the existing program or for new programs in the area over which that department head has jurisdiction. The increasing technicality of legislation in many fields of state government reinforces this tendency, since their very complexity prevents the governor from being fully acquainted with all the details of necessary legislation. A great many of the governor's legislative proposals, therefore, originate with his department heads and are drawn up by the staff of the department concerned. This tends to insure their technical adequacy and also assures the governor of the assistance of whatever pressure groups the department can muster to aid in securing the passage of the legislation.

Out of this complex of the governor's personal desires, the party platform, the work of various research agencies, the planning of the budget agency, the prepared programs of pressure groups, the work of the governor's staff, and legislation prepared by the governor's own department heads come the major pieces of policy legislation. No definite pattern seems to emerge as to the relative importance of the contribution of each of these groups to the over-all program. In the case of a newly elected governor it seems likely that major reliance must be placed on the governor's own staff, with some assistance from advisers either within or without the government for the preparation of the governor's initial program.

PRESENTING THE LEGISLATIVE PROGRAM

Several of the governors interviewed pointed out that a newly elected governor is at a considerable handicap in attempting to present a carefully prepared program to his first legislature because of the brief period which he has for preparation. The primary problem is the proper timing of the initial session of the legislature after the date of the governor's election. The pattern in Arizona is typical. The governor is elected in November of even years and takes office on the first Monday in January, following his election. The legislature, which is also elected in November, meets on the second Monday in January. The first session of the legislature, therefore, follows a week after the governor's inauguration and about two months after his election. This gives the governor very little time to prepare his legislative program. While the governor of a state with a two-year term such as Arizona has this problem with each session of the legislature, the governor of a four-year state has the problem only with his first legislature. However, the first legislature is generally the key to the success or failure of the governor's program, and, consequently, the problem is as important in states with a four-year term as with a two-year term. This view is substantiated by a recent recommendation of Governor J. Bracken Lee of Utah, who suggested in his message to the second session of the Utah Legislature that a constitutional amendment was in order shifting the first session of the Legislature from the second Monday in January following the general election to the first week in March. Governor Lee apparently had experienced some difficulty in preparing a legislative program between his election in November and the opening of the Legislature on the second Monday of the following January. In support of his proposal the Governor said in part:

> . . . The newly-elected officials, including the Governor and most members of the Legislature, are faced with the tremendous task of preparing for a legislative session immediately upon taking office.
>
> I believe it would be in the interests of better government if biennial sessions of the Legislature were scheduled to begin the first week in March, or even February, following a general election, since the newly-elected officials would then have more time to prepare for their first session.[7]

The governor in a one-party state is in a somewhat more favorable position for program planning than is the governor of a two-party state. While he technically is elected in November and must present his program to the legislature which generally meets in January, he actually is elected in the Democratic primary which is held in May, July, or August. Thus, the successful candidate in the primary has a period of from five to eight months in which to plan his program.

Of course, there is nothing to prevent a candidate in a two-party state from preparing a carefully-worked-out program which he can hold in readiness in the event that he is elected. However,

[7] Message of Governor J. Bracken Lee to the Twenty-ninth Legislature of the State of Utah, 1951.

it is difficult to work out such a program in the heat of a political campaign, and it seems reasonable to give the governor at least two months, after he is actually in office, as Governor Lee suggests, to prepare a program. There are a tremendous number of things which a newly elected governor must do in his first few weeks in office. Among other things he must give prompt attention to major appointments and must deal with the horde of well-wishers and favor-seekers who flood his office. Two months go very swiftly under these circumstances and certainly it is not too long a period if the governor is to prepare a budget and a comprehensive legislative program.

In formal recognition of the separation of powers theory, the governor and his cabinet officers may not participate in the proceedings of the state legislature as they would under a cabinet form of government. This formality, however, is no bar to the introduction of the governor's major pieces of legislation. In fact the same constitutions which prevent the governor from taking a direct part in debates in the legislature generally provide that he shall, "from time to time, give to the legislature information on the state of the government, and recommend for its consideration such measures as he may deem expedient." As has been pointed out previously, provisions of this type not only permit but require that the governor make recommendations to the legislature. The only power which is lacking is that of actually introducing the legislation. In most states with the executive budget even this minor omission has been remedied in regard to financial legislation. The governor's budget message actually is submitted to the lower house of the legislature as a concrete proposal and frequently by statute must contain a draft of the proposed appropriation bill.

In any event, the introduction of legislation is the easiest step in the process of policy determination as far as the governor is concerned. In the two-party states the governor has access to the floor of both houses in the person of the leader of his party in each house. This is true generally in the normally Democratic and Republican states, where it is also customary for the two parties to have leaders in each house. In the one-party states there is usually no formal party organization, but the governor secures the introduction of legislation through a friendly legislator or through an individual who is known as "the governor's floor leader," whose functions are discussed in some detail in a succeeding section.

THE GOVERNOR'S BATTING AVERAGE

In most states the measures embodying the governor's program are known as "administration" bills. This designation ordinarily does not give the bill any official standing but in some instances the bills based on the governor's budget are given a preferred position.[8] In most instances, however, "administration" bills are no different from any other bills in so far as the rules of the legislature are concerned. In practice, the designation of the bill as an administration bill does have great significance in connection with its actual position in the order of business and with its passage, as will be pointed out in the next section, when the methods at the governor's disposal to expedite such legislation are considered.

The American governor in the past fifty years has had considerable success in obtaining the passage of administration bills embodying his major policy proposals. No over-all box score on the number of administration measures which have been passed is possible because the detailed studies of executive-legislative relations in the respective states which would be necessary to compile such a presentation are not available. However, on the evidence which is available, the governor's success is quite marked. For example, a careful study of legislative action on specific recommendations made in the governors' messages during the regular sessions of the Alabama Legislature from 1903 to 1943 reveals that out of a total of 207 recommendations, 116 (or 56 per cent) were enacted into law. The batting average of the Alabama governor is even more impressive than this over-all figure would indicate. Only three out of the eleven governors who served during this period had less than 50 per cent of their recommenda-

[8] For example, in California the constitution requires that no appropriation bill be passed except for legislative expenses until action on the budget bill has been completed. The budget, which is presented in even-numbered years, usually requires consideration for a major part of the session. See Crouch, McHenry, Bollens, and Scott, *State and Local Government in California* (Berkeley, 1952), pp. 65 and 119.

tions enacted into law and some had as high as 80 per cent. There also seems to be a trend toward greater executive dominance during the latter quarter of this period, since the average for the last four governors was 71 per cent.[9]

Studies of a recent legislative session in Tennessee and a much longer period in Virginia furnish additional proof of the governor's dominant role as legislative leader. In the 1947 session of the Tennessee Legislature, the governor or his department heads sponsored and wholly or partly drafted more than 100 public bills which were enacted into law. These bills formed almost one-half of the 237 public acts passed by the Legislature and included most of the major measures enacted. The bills covered a wide range of major governmental functions, including a new sales tax, appropriations, educational programs (a nine-month school term and teachers' retirement, among others), state bond issues, public health, conservation, and highways.[10]

In a recent study of gubernatorial leadership in Virginia, George W. Spicer finds that "through the vicissitudes of more than a century and a half the chief executive of the Old Dominion has emerged as the leader both of legislation and of administration."[11] In support of this statement, Professor Spicer marshals some imposing statistics on the legislative efficacy of the governor during the period between 1934 and 1941. For example, Governor Harry F. Byrd, the founder of the present Byrd "organization" in Virginia, compiled an outstanding record as a legislative policy maker. Of the approximately 75 recommendations made to two regular and one special sessions of the legislature only seven failed of passage. This gives Governor Byrd a very creditable batting average of approximately 91 per cent. His successor, Governor John Garland Pollard, also made a substantial record. Of approximately fifty measures introduced at two regular sessions, only eight failed of passage, giving Governor Pollard a score of approximately 86 per cent. Governor George C. Perry, who suc-

[9] The figures on which this estimate is based are taken from Hallie Farmer's *The Legislative Process in Alabama* (Bureau of Public Administration, University of Alabama, 1949), pp. 167 ff.

[10] Data furnished by Frank W. Prescott of the University of Chattanooga.

[11] George W. Spicer, "Gubernatorial Leadership in Virginia," *Public Administration Review,* I (Autumn, 1941), 441.

ceeded Pollard, had considerable success with his first session of the Legislature, with only two of the twelve recommendations in his inaugural address failing to receive legislative approval. He was not so successful with the next regular session, however, and the majority of his program of social legislation did not receive legislative endorsement. This rebuff may be attributed to the Governor's failure to provide the necessary crusading leadership, since at an extra session called later in the year, substantially the same program was enacted into law. The next Governor of the Commonwealth, James H. Price, is something of an anomaly in Virginia politics; he was elected without the support of the Byrd organization and did not have a specific program in the primary. In spite of these handicaps, he had a good record in the first session of the Legislature in 1938 but was unsuccessful in his reorganization proposals in the 1940 session. This failure Professor Spicer attributes to bad techniques in presentation, timing, and petty partisan politics. If the Governor had presented this rather substantial reorganization program to the first session of the Legislature rather than the second, and if it had been a part of his primary program, he might have achieved more success in spite of the control of important segments of the Legislature by the Byrd organization. Whatever the reasons for Governor Price's lack of success, his administration is not typical of the pattern of executive-legislative relations in Virginia. The governor of Virginia is traditionally in a very strong position in regard to both legislative and administrative leadership.

The governor's success as a leader in legislative policy is not confined to any one section of the country or to any particular pattern of party politics. The governors of the southern states, with the exception of South Carolina and Texas, are traditionally very effective in their legislative leadership. Governors in most of the normally Democratic or Republican states also have creditable records in this regard. For example in Kentucky during the 1948 session of the General Assembly Governor Earle C. Clements or his department heads had introduced 43 Senate Bills and placed 42 measures before the House. All of the bills introduced in the House and 39 of the 43 measures introduced in the Senate were enacted into law, which would give the Governor an average of almost 96 per cent.

Even in a state like Wisconsin, which has a considerable tradition of legislative independence, an astute governor can provide effective leadership. In June of 1951 Governor Kohler, addressing a joint meeting of the Legislature at the close of the regular legislative session, summarized executive-legislative relations during the session in the following terms:

> . . . I am pleased, too, because this legislature has dealt so thoughtfully with the program recommended in my messages to you. I realized, when I addressed you in January, that my suggestions were more elaborate, detailed and numerous than has ordinarily been the case.
>
> Honest differences of opinion must always be expected on problems of government and experienced observers did not expect this legislature to adopt all of my recommendations. Today, however, I can report to you that of 55 pieces of legislation specifically recommended by me in those messages, 47 have been enacted into law by the 1951 legislature. This extraordinarily high level of agreement is extremely gratifying, and I thank you for your support. . . .

Governor Kohler's record in securing the passage of 85 per cent of his proposals is indeed an excellent one and is probably not matched by the average governor. Nevertheless, there are many governors in other states who can point to a record of probably 50 per cent or more of their recommendations being enacted into law. This is a fairly creditable performance in view of the differences of opinion, honest and otherwise, which inevitably arise in the considerations of problems of government.

The percentages quoted in the preceding section are necessarily quantitative rather than qualitative and, therefore, may be quite misleading as a criterion of gubernatorial success. For example, a recent governor of Vermont estimated that he had been successful in securing the passage of 22 out of 27 administration bills but added that the five on which he was defeated were very important, particularly the Legislature's failure to increase the motor vehicle and gasoline tax in order to raise sufficient funds to meet available federal grants for highway construction. The governor said that repercussions from this failure were already reaching his office in the form of delegations from various sections of the state, telephone calls, and letters, all complaining of poor highway conditions.

In this instance and probably in other instances which may have been covered by our statistics, the qualitative aspect of the measures on which the governor was defeated may have outweighed the quantitative aspect of those measures on which he was successful. Statistics on the governor's batting average, therefore, are no infallible guide to judging the governor's success or failure as a legislative policy maker. However, the judgment of those who were responsible for the statistics quoted and the preponderance of the opinions of those interviewed in the course of this study all seem to point to the conclusion that the qualitative aspects of the governor's legislative program tend to average out over a period of years and that the figures quoted are a fairly reliable index to the governor's ability to get his major programs through the legislature.

It is also true that the program which the governor presents to the legislature may be tailored to fit the kind of proposals which the governor thinks that body may pass. This, however, is one of those imponderables that cannot be taken into account in a statistical presentation. Furthermore, this sort of reasoning is probably balanced by a tendency on the part of many governors to present a much more ambitious program than they feel the legislature will pass. By so doing they hope to put the legislature on the spot in the public's mind for the failure of the governor to live up to some of his more exaggerated campaign promises.

The pattern of success suggested above is reinforced also by an examination of the other aspects of the governor's relations with the legislature. For example, another device which may be used in roughly measuring gubernatorial power *vis-a-vis* the legislature is to examine the success with which the governor has been able to make his veto effective. If an examination of the ability of the governor to get certain proposals through the legislature is accepted as a positive measure of his strength, then the ability of the governor to make his veto stick might be called a negative measure of his strength. An examination of the relevant data shows that the American governor has been remarkably successful in this aspect of executive-legislative relations.[12] While

[12] Frank W. Prescott has made several very useful studies of the executive veto. See particularly: "The Executive Veto in American States," *The Western Political Quarterly,* III (March, 1950), 97-111, and "The Executive Veto in

the use of the veto has varied greatly from state to state in the course of the history of executive-legislative relations in this country, its greatest use and effectiveness has been in the twentieth century. From one-half to three-fourths of the total number of vetoes of legislation by the governors have occurred since 1900. This has been due in part to the fact that during the present century the volume of legislative business has increased substantially. It is interesting to note, however, that the average percentage of bills vetoed has remained about the same. On the other hand, the effectiveness of the veto has increased markedly in recent years. For example, in 1923 the governors vetoed 7 per cent of all legislation passed and their vetoes were overridden 9 per cent of the time. In 1945, while the percentage of bills vetoed remained about the same (5.1 per cent), the governors' vetoes overridden were only 1.05 per cent, and more than half of these were in one state, Wisconsin. In 1947 of the 24,928 bills which passed both houses of the legislatures of the respective states 1,253 (5 per cent) were vetoed. However, the governors' vetoes were overridden in only 22 instances (1.72 per cent). It is also interesting to note that ten of the total of 22 overridden vetoes were confined to Arizona and Kentucky. In Arizona the controversy between the governor and legislature was non-partisan and was based chiefly upon the alleged activities of pressure groups. On the other hand, in Kentucky the governor was Republican while the 1946 legislature was controlled by the Democratic Party. In this instance, the sources of friction may be more nearly attributed to partisan politics and perhaps to differences in regard to state policies.

In a rather substantial group of states the governors' vetoes have been overridden so infrequently that they have become almost absolute. This is true in the entire bloc of one-party states in the South, where only 101 of the 1,501 vetoes cast by the governors in the past decade were unsuccessful, and more than half of these occurred in Florida's torrid session of 1939-41. Illustrative of the absolute nature of the veto in some of the southern states is the governor's veto record in Alabama, where

---

Southern States," *Journal of Politics,* X (November, 1948), 659-675. The figures cited in this section are from these articles unless otherwise noted.

only 38 of the governor's 108 vetoes between 1903 and 1943 were overridden. Of these rejections 36 were in a single session in 1931, when Governor Miller and the legislature differed over the proper handling of state finance and on the matter of private legislation. The other two vetoes were overridden in 1915 when Governor Henderson and the legislature differed on the question of prohibition. These rejections are definitely the exception rather than the rule, as is shown by the fact that in nine of the eleven regular sessions during this period not a single veto of the governor was overridden.[13]

The governor's record in certain other states is fully as good as in the South. The record shows that only 28 vetoes have been overridden in California in the present century; only thirteen in Michigan during the period 1909-47 inclusive; and only three in Illinois since 1870. In addition, there have been but four vetoes overridden in Iowa since 1838; one in Pennsylvania since 1900; and none in Kansas since 1923.[14]

On the basis of the evidence, therefore, it seems clear that the American governor has been even more successful in his negative role in legislation through the use of the veto than he has been in his positive role in securing the passage of administration bills. It should be pointed out, however, that the use of the veto, while essentially a negative aspect of the governor's relation to the legislature, also has its positive side. The veto, and particularly the threat of veto, can be used to push measures which the governor favors as well as to kill those which he does not favor. This aspect of the veto power will be treated at more length in the subsequent section on the ways in which the governor may influence legislation.

In addition to the veto power, the governors of four states, Alabama, Massachusetts, New Jersey, and Virginia, have the power of executive amendment. This power enables the governor to return a bill without his signature to the house in which it originated with his suggestions for changes in the measure which would make it acceptable to him. A bill returned in this fashion is said to have received an executive amendment. Under the system used in Alabama, which is similar to that in the other states, when the

[13] Farmer, pp. 181-182.

[14] Prescott, "The Executive Veto in American States," p. 103.

bill is returned to the house of origin with an executive amendment, the amendment may either be adopted or rejected by that house, but the bill may not be further amended. If the bill, as amended by the governor, is passed by the house of origin, it is sent to the second house which can either approve or reject the bill as amended but which may not further amend it. If both houses agree to the governor's proposal, the measure is returned to him to be acted upon by him as he acts upon other bills. If the two houses refuse to agree to the executive amendment, they can enact the measure by a majority vote of the full membership in each house.

This power of the governor to enter into the legislative process through the means of the executive amendment is a device of considerable importance in the shaping of legislation. During the period 1903 to 1947, inclusive, the governors of Alabama sent 235 executive amendments to the legislature. Out of these only seven were rejected and in nine sessions no executive amendments were acted upon unfavorably by the legislature. During the last three legislative sessions the governor returned 33 bills with executive amendments. Most of these passed both houses unanimously or with very little opposition. For instance, in 1945 fifteen bills were returned; all passed the Senate unanimously and all but two also were accepted unanimously by the House.

In Virginia and Massachusetts the results are much the same. For example, in Virginia during the last sixteen years four governors have returned a total of 150 bills to the General Assembly with executive amendments and only two of these have failed to receive approval. The relative importance of the executive amendment as compared to the veto is indicated by the fact that during this same period the four governors vetoed only twenty bills during the legislative sessions and only two of these vetoes were overridden.[15]

In Massachusetts the governors generally have been successful in their use of the executive amendment, although the Legislature seems less inclined to accept the governor's suggestions automatically or *in toto*.[16] New Jersey has adopted only recently the

[15] Spicer, p. 450. Spicer points out that many of the executive amendments were used to correct technical defects in legislation.

[16] Prescott, "The Executive Veto in American States," p. 105.

executive amendment and it is too early to pass judgment on its usefulness. It might be noted in passing, however, that in the 1948 session of the Legislature that body approved only two out of the seven bills returned by the governor with suggested changes.

Because of the tendency of the legislature in those states which have the executive amendment to accept the governor's suggested amendments, many of his objections to legislation are handled in this manner and the need for the frequent use of the veto on policy matters is greatly lessened. While in Virginia the executive amendment seems to have been used primarily to correct technicalities in legislation, in Alabama and Massachusetts it is a real instrument in policy determination. In Alabama it has come to be primarily a policy device, and the veto has been reserved for measures which were technically deficient. This development has the desirable feature of enabling the governor to play a positive rather than a negative role in legislation and places more squarely in his hands the responsibility for important legislation. The recognition of such a responsibility and the provision of means to implement it seems highly desirable if the governor is to supply real leadership in solving the social and economic problems which beset the states.

The analysis which has been made of the governor's batting average and the corollary analysis of the exercise of the veto do not furnish us with conclusive proof that the governor is a successful legislative policy maker. Most of the evidence, however, does seem to point in this direction. While in some states there is a tradition of weak gubernatorial leadership in the last fifty years, these states now seem to be in a minority. It also is true that even in states which have a tradition of strong gubernatorial leadership there are occasionally governors who are completely ineffective in a policy-forming role. On the whole, however, the average governor in the United States in the past fifty years has proved to be a legislative policy maker of no mean stature. This policy, however, is not made in a political vacuum, and the governor cannot function effectively as a policy leader unless he can secure the support of a working majority of the legislature. It is to the governor's relationship with that body that the next section of this chapter is devoted.

THE NATURE OF EXECUTIVE-LEGISLATIVE RELATIONS

One of the most interesting aspects of executive-legislative relations revealed by this study is the substantial degree to which these relations depart from what frequently is regarded as the typical pattern at the state level. According to one theory which is current on the nature of executive-legislative relations, the typical situation is one in which both the governorship and a majority of both houses are controlled by the same party. The governor in dealing with the legislature, therefore, is supposed to work through the leaders of his party in each branch. His program is supposed to be based on the party platform and, consequently, receives the support of the members of his party in each branch of the legislature. The party, therefore, serves as a coordinating device to produce harmony in the relationships of the two branches.

While on the surface this description may seem to fit the facts in most states, an examination of the actual political situation in those states shows that such a pattern is the exception rather than the rule in more than half of the states and, therefore, cannot be regarded as typical. As has already been pointed out, at least a quarter of the states fall in the one-party category, which means that the governor upon his election finds an overwhelming majority of his party in both houses of the legislature. On the surface this follows the typical pattern, since both the governorship and the legislature are controlled by the same party. Actually, such control in party terms is meaningless. In a one-party situation there can be no successful appeal by the governor to party solidarity because there is no opposition party. There is no party platform because the party is simply a holding company for competing factions. The platform on which the governor was elected is his own and usually has no relation to the platform on which the legislators were elected so that they do not necessarily feel bound by it. In these states the "typical" pattern simply does not fit, because there is no opposition party to perform its time-honored and necessary functions. The governor in dealing with the legislature is dealing with factions, not parties. Generally, these factions are transient groupings which change with the changing issues before the legislature. Sometimes, however, the factions are fairly consistent throughout a legislative session.

An example of a fairly fixed factional situation is to be found in the 1946 and 1948 sessions of the Alabama legislature during the first administration of Governor James E. Folsom. Here, two factions formed, one of which favored the Governor and his program and one of which was opposed to almost every measure which he had introduced. The pro-Folsom and anti-Folsom factions were as bitterly opposed as any in the state's recent political history, primarily because the Governor represented the liberal wing of the party (in this case, the small farmer and labor), whereas the majority of the legislature was conservative (i.e., represented the large farmer and the major industrial groups). The pro-Folsom faction was much the weaker of the two numerically, but it was backed by whatever influence the governor could wield and by his veto power. Consequently, while it was unable to secure the enactment of the governor's program, it was able to prevent the opposing faction from pushing through any legislative program of its own. This resulted in a four-year legislative stalemate which caused Governor Folsom to characterize his administration as "the outstanding failure" of any in the state's history so far as any progress on a "fundamental program" was concerned.[17]

This deadlock situation is not typical of executive-legislative relations in Alabama nor is it typical of the one-party states as a whole, for the governor of a one-party state is normally a very effective policy maker. However, a situation of this nature sharpens and brings into focus the factional nature of legislative politics in the South.

Legislative factionalism is not confined to the one-party states but seems to be equally typical of the normally Democratic or Republican states. In these states the majority of the dominant party in the legislature is usually substantial, although not as great as in a one-party situation. Here, the governor may be able to call upon the legislators in the name of the party to support his program, but the effectiveness of this appeal is diminished by the lack of a really challenging opposition. The major party

[17] Governor's Day address at the Univeristy of Alabama, May 20, 1949 as reported in the Birmingham *Post,* May 20, 1949.

generally is broken up into factions and the governor's strength comes largely from one faction of his own party. In some situations his strength is drawn from a faction of his own party plus a part or all of the opposition party. This is particularly true when the governor is a liberal and a substantial number of his own party are conservative or vice versa. In the first case the governor seems to draw his strength from the liberal wings of both parties and is opposed by the conservative faction of his own party as well as by the conservative faction of the opposition party.

The cross-filing system for state legislators in California so obscures party lines that it probably would not be easy to say whether Governor Warren was supported by the Republicans in the legislature or by the Democrats. It would seem, however, that he was supported largely by the liberal elements of both parties and was opposed by the conservative elements, including a substantial number of the old-guard Republicans. In Warren's case he was able to successfully surmount the handicap of being at odds with the former leaders of his own party and with their representatives in the legislature. Such was not the case in the first term of Governor Folsom in Alabama. While he achieved the unusual feat of winning the primary without the support of the party regulars, he was not able to command sufficient strength in the legislature to have his program enacted into law over their opposition. While in Warren's case it was a question of drawing sufficient support from both parties, and in Folsom's case it was a question of drawing sufficient support from two wings of a single party, the problem faced by the two governors was very similar. Each needed a bloc of votes to put his program across; one was successful in obtaining this support, the other was not.

In theory the situation of a governor in a two-party state *vis-a-vis* the legislature is quite different; in practice the situation may be such as to produce substantially the same results as in a one-party situation. This is true because it does not seem that the typical pattern of one party controlling both the governorship and the two houses of the legislature is in operation in many states. For example in New York over the period 1900-1950 the Democratic party controlled the governorship for 26 years and the Republican party controlled the governorship for 24 years. Yet the Democrats controlled *both* the governorship and both houses of the legislature for only two years and the governorship and one house of the legislature for only four years. Hence there was a period of twenty years in which the Democrats controlled the governorship but neither house of the legislature.

Under this sort of situation Governors Smith, Roosevelt and Lehman could hardly be expected to operate according to the "typical" pattern of executive-legislative relations. Apparently they were able to operate effectively as governors only because they built a bloc of votes on key issues both from members of their own minority party and from certain members of the opposition. The Republicans in New York, on the other hand, were able to control both the House and the Senate for the entire 24-year period in which their party was in power. Consequently the pattern of executive-legislative relations under the Republicans was, at least on the surface, an example of the typical pattern. It is significant, however, that in a state which is frequently cited as an example of two-party politics the executive-legislative pattern in the fifty-year period under consideration was such that while each of the two major parties controlled the governorship for about the same period only one of them succeeded in controlling both the governorship and the legislature. Thus, in New York it does not seem that the typical pattern of executive-legislative relations applies unless the Republicans are in power.

Patterns similar to that in New York emerge from a study of executive-legislative relations in the states as a whole over the last twenty years. Table IX presents a comparison of party control of the governorship with party control of the legislature over the period 1930-1950. The data in Table IX shows that the governors of the states found themselves confronted by either one or both houses of the legislature under the control of the opposition parties approximately 34 per cent of the period. Thus during this time, a presumably atypical situation prevailed in which the governor, in order to secure the enactment of his program, had to deal with at least one house and usually with both houses controlled by the opposition party.

The Democratic governors fared far worse than their Republican counterparts in that they faced a legislature controlled in at least one house by the opposite party for 25.6 per cent of the period while the Republican governors faced opposition for only

TABLE IX

*Party Control and Executive-Legislative Relations 1930-1950**

Type of Relationship	*Per Cent of Period*	
Governor and a Majority of Both Houses of the Legislature of the Same Party		65.7
Democratic Governor and Legislature	30.0	
Republican Governor and Legislature	35.7	
Governor Faced by a Majority of the Opposite Party in One or Both Houses of the Legislature		34.3
Governor Faced by a Majority of the Opposite Party in *One* House of the Legislature		
Democratic Governor-Republican Opposition	10.7	
Republican Governor-Democratic Opposition	4.9	
Governor Faced by a Majority of the Opposite Party in *Both* Houses of the Legislature		
Democratic Governor-Republican Opposition	14.9	
Republican Governor-Democratic Opposition	3.8	
Total		100.0

*Data on which this table was based were taken from the New York *Legislative Manual* and the Gallup *Political Almanac*. Independent and third-party governors were excluded from these calculations. Party control in those sessions in which one house of the legislature was evenly divided was determined by the party allegiance of the legislative officers and chairmen of important committees.

8.7 per cent of the period. It is also significant that the Democratic governors found themselves opposed by a majority of the opposite party in both houses of the legislature almost four times as often as did the Republican executives. This Democratic dilemma in part reflects the fact that, outside the South, state legislatures tend to be dominated by the Republican Party and that a swing in popular sentiment sufficient to elect a Democratic governor is seldom sufficient to elect a Democratic legislature. Most state legislatures outside the South have been successfully gerrymandered to provide an almost automatic Republican majority that will be returned regularly regardless of state-wide popular sentiment. Democratic governors elected by a popular shift in state-wide sentiment therefore tend to be in for rough sledding in the legislature.

This is also true in reverse in some of the normally Democratic states which have a built-in Democratic majority in the legislature. It is also true for the states in the South, although in these states no Republican governor is likely to be elected to be faced by the Democratic majority. However, since there are more states with a gerrymandered Republican majority in the legislature than with a Democratic majority, the Democrats fight a somewhat hopeless battle for the control of most of the state legislatures.

The overall figures in Table IX show that the same party controls the governorship and both houses of the legislature about 66 per cent of the time. This is certainly a sufficient percentage to lend support to the theory that this pattern is indeed "typical" if the control by the same party represented a shift in party control from election to election. This was not the case, however, and the figures in Table IX consequently fail to give a true picture of executive-legislative relations. Concealed in the over-all totals is the fact that there are certain states which account for a disproportionate share of both those states in which the governor and the legislature tend to be of the same party and those states in which the governor tends to be opposed.

During the twenty-year period under consideration there was only *one* state in which the governorship and the legislature actually shifted simultaneously in terms of party control. In South Dakota when there was a shift from a normally Republican situation and a Democratic governor was elected there was also in each instance a shift of the legislature to Democratic control.

There were, of course, many other instances in which both the governorship and the legislature changed hands simultaneously during this period. However, the one-party states in which control of neither the governorship nor both houses of the legislature shifted during the entire period account for about 34 per cent of the elections of the period in which one party controlled the governorship and both houses. A substantial proportion of the remaining period in which there was agreement between the executive and legislative branches is accounted for by the normally Democratic or Republican states. In these states the complexion of the legislature changed only very infrequently, although the minority party occasionally captured the governorship.

In the normally Democratic group the most outstanding exceptions to this statement were Rhode Island, in which the governor was opposed approximately 54 per cent of the time, and Nevada, in which the governor was opposed almost 64 per cent of the time. In the remaining normally Democratic states he was opposed only from 10 per cent to 36 per cent of the time.

In the normally Republican states we find that the governor generally was not opposed to any appreciable extent in the legislature except in North Dakota, where he was opposed about 36 per cent of the time, and in Oregon, where he was opposed about 30 per cent of the time. In the remaining states there were one or two Democratic governors elected who were generally opposed in one or both houses of the legislature.

On the whole, however, in both the normally Democratic and normally Republican states the governor of the dominant party generally had a very strong majority of his party in the legislature. In fact, this majority in many cases was so great that it seems evident that the governor could not make a successful appeal to the legislators in the name of the party in order to secure the enactment of his program. In such a situation he would probably be forced to rely on appeals based on other grounds to individual legislators or to a bloc or blocs of legislators in the dominant majority.

The states in which the governor was opposed the greatest percentage of the time generally fell in the two-party group. For example, the governor found himself confronted by opposition majorities in one or both houses of the legislature in Connecticut for 72 per cent of the twenty-year period, in Massachusetts for 63 per cent of the period, in New York, Wyoming, Rhode Island and Indiana for 54 per cent of the period, and in Montana, Washington, Delaware and Colorado for 45 per cent of the period. Opposition control of one or both houses never fell below 27 per cent of the period in the two-party states and this low was reached only in Michigan, Idaho and Illinois. In general in the two-party states the governor was faced by one or both houses controlled by the opposition party for over 45 per cent of the period under consideration.

Within these states there are a substantial number where this division of control has become the typical pattern, particularly when the governor is a Democrat. For example, in New York each succeeding Democratic governor in the period was faced with both houses controlled by the Republicans, and the same situation prevailed in Massachusetts except in one session in which the

Democrats controlled the governorship and one house by a narrow 50.6 per cent and the second house was evenly divided.

If one considers the over-all picture of executive-legislative relations during this twenty-year period the situation in practice is somewhat as follows. Of the 46 states covered in the study there are fifteen states which fall in the one-party category.[18] In these states there was always agreement in party terms between the governor and both houses of the legislature, since party control always remained with the dominant party. These states, however, do not actually support the theory of obtaining executive-legislative co-ordination through the party, for "the party" is a meaningless term in this connection in these states. In the remaining 31 states which are made up of the normally Democratic or Republican groups and the two-party group there were sixteen states in which the governor was opposed by one or more houses of the legislature in 36 per cent or more of the sessions. Thus, in the states outside the one-party group the governor found himself with one or both houses controlled by the opposite party in more than half of the states. Even more significant is the fact that these sixteen states in which the most opposition occurred include all of the two-party states.

In view of this situation there is some doubt that the party can perform its alleged function as a co-ordinating device, simply on the basis that it cannot co-ordinate what it does not control. It would seem, therefore, that a more realistic view of executive-legislative relations might be based on the premise that the governor will either be dealing with individual legislators or with factions as is the case in the one-party or normally Democratic or Republican states, or that he will be dealing with one or both houses controlled by the opposition party as is frequently the case in the two-party states.

The concept that the governor must deal with legislators on an individual basis or on a bloc basis is not new. However, it is certainly worth more emphasis than it is sometimes given in discussions of party control and executive-legislative relations. The governor must deal with individuals or blocs in his own party in the one-party states because there is no effective opposition party.

18 Minnesota and Nebraska are not considered in these calculations because the legislature in these states is selected on a "non-partisan" basis.

He must deal with individuals or blocs of his own, and occasionally of the opposite party, in the normally Democratic or Republican states because his own party dominates the legislature to a marked degree and the opposition is not effective in party terms because of its relatively small size. Even in most of the two-party states the governor cannot deal with his own party as a unit, because that party does not control both houses of the legislature. Consequently he must deal with the opposite party, or with a bloc or individuals in the opposite party, in order to secure the number of votes needed to get his program enacted. It is not that this is a new concept which is stressed here but that this tends to be the typical situation in the fifteen one-party states and comes close to being the typical situation in some sixteen other states as well. There are situations in the two-party states in which the governorship and the legislature are controlled by the same party and where, given some party discipline, the governor may be able to make an appeal to the legislators on the basis of a party program. These situations, however, tend to be infrequent. If in addition one's definition of two-party politics contains the notion that there should be parallel shifts in party control and the governorship, he finds little supporting evidence in this study. The American governor must concern himself with building legislative support from among clusters of legislative factions. In only a few states does the party actually play its traditional role.

If we approach the governor's role in legislative policy making as a process which must be carried on in the context of factional politics, then his role becomes one of seeking to build support wherever he can find a suitable power base. Two of the factional bases which are at hand in most legislatures are those on which has developed a rural-urban division of the legislature. Most state legislatures are controlled by the legislators from the rural areas because the apportionment of the legislature was established fairly early in the state's history. The apportionment base or formula was thus established before the present concentration of population in large metropolitan centers. The failure of the rural dominated legislatures, except in a few states, to reapportion on a basis which would give adequate representation to the cities has left the metropolitan areas definitely under-represented. As a consequence, most governors face a legislature which is controlled by the rural legislators, the men from the "cow counties," the "branch heads," or the "Delta," or the "upstaters," or "downstaters."

On the other hand, the governor because he is elected on a state-wide basis tends to become the representative of the "big city" voters. This seems to be true not only in the states which generally are thought of as having a metropolitan tinge, such as New York, Connecticut, or Illinois, but also in many of the one-party states in the Deep South. While about one-half of our governors actually are selected in the primary in the one-party states and in the normally Democratic and Republican states, this factor does not mitigate the rural-urban division. The primary, like the general election, is a state-wide affair. Consequently, the important element is the total number of votes for the candidate regardless of the section of the state in which they were cast, except in Georgia, where the county unit system assures rural control. The impact of metropolitan voting on the selection of the governor has not become as pronounced in a state like Alabama as it has in New York because there is still no one metropolitan area in Alabama which is comparable on a proportionate basis to New York City. It is still possible to be elected governor of Alabama without polling a sizeable vote in Birmingham, while it would be almost impossible to carry New York State without polling a considerable vote in New York City. Nevertheless, the influence of the urban voter on the selection of the governor in the states in the South is becoming more marked with each election. The metropolitan areas are increasing in population and are becoming more conscious of their political power. This development is obscured, however, by the absence of an opposition party. On the other hand, the rural-urban cleavage in many of the two-party states is highlighted by the fact that it is paralleled by a Democratic-Republican division. For example, the vote of New York City is traditionally Democratic, while the rural upstate vote is traditionally Republican. The same situation prevails to a considerable extent in Massachusetts, where Democratic Boston is opposed to the rest of the state, which is largely Republican. In Illinois, Chicago and Cook County provide a large proportion of the Democratic vote, while the downstate vote is predominantly Republican. In Connecticut there is no one metropolitan area which is exactly comparable to Chicago or New York, but most of the major urban centers are Democratic and most of the rural and village areas are preponderantly Republican. While a rural-urban cleavage exists to some degree in all states, there seems to be a special sort of rural-urban division in these states because the great metropolitan areas in each state contain such a substantial proportion of the state's population that it is large enough to form in itself the basis on which a state party can be built. If the same proportion of urban population is scattered throughout the state in smaller cities, it may provide a less stable base for a state party.[19]

However, there seems to be a moderating factor in this potential struggle between the governor representing the urban areas and the legislature representing the rural areas. Even in states which have a sufficient concentration of population in one or two large metropolitan areas to form the basis for a state party, it usually is not possible for the successful candidate to build a winning combination solely on the strength of his party in that area alone. On the other hand, the candidate of a party which has a largely rural base cannot ordinarily secure the election with the vote of the rural areas alone. For example, in New York the hard core of the Republican Party is the rural upstate Republican vote. Yet, Governor Dewey in his successful campaigns for governor carried the state by being able to retain most of the upstate vote while cutting into the vote of his Democratic opponent in New York City. An analysis of the vote in the 1946 gubernatorial election shows that Dewey by no means picked up all of his votes outside New York City. While he did poll 1,643,363 votes outside metropolitan New York to 771,227 for his Democratic opponent, James M. Mead, he also polled 1,182,270 within New York City to 1,367,255 for Mead. Dewey lost New York City by only 184,985 votes, while he carried the rest of New York by 872,136 votes. This gave him a winning margin in the state as a whole of 687,151 votes, but this margin would not have been forthcoming if he had not received a very substantial Republican vote in traditionally Democratic New York City.

It is difficult to translate the rural or urban base of a state

[19] See V. O. Key's analysis of these states and his comments on the urban or rural base for state parties in *Politics, Parties, and Pressure Groups,* 3rd. Ed. (New York, 1952) pp. 324 ff.

party as revealed by the vote for governor into a rural-urban division of the legislature. What we can do, however, is look at the kind of program a successful gubernatorial candidate proposes and, more important, the kind of program which he is able to get enacted. In the case of Governor Dewey it is fairly obvious that his legislative program did not neglect the interests of the voters of New York City in spite of the predominantly rural upstate basis of his election support.

In the process of playing both ends against the middle, Dewey became a governor scarcely fitting the caricatures of a reactionary Republican. In 1950 Dewey could boast of his program of rent control, public housing, fair employment practices, public health services, and other measures that Washington Democrats might claim as their own. Moreover, he interpreted his election as a mandate for state development of St. Lawrence power. The major difference between party candidates for governor in New York may not rest in their policy differences but in their success in persuading the electorate of their integrity and of their capacity to carry out the program which more or less accords with the prevailing public sense of justice and priority. However that may be, competition for the New York governorship takes quite as much a two-party form as does competition for the Presidency.[20]

The rural-urban split, while present in one-party states, is more difficult to pinpoint than in other sections of the country because of the dominance of the Democratic Party. The usual urban under-representation is present in the South and, in fact, is even more pronounced than in some other sections with Birmingham, Alabama, being the most under-represented major city in the nation. Due to the absence of permanent factions in most southern states, it is difficult to evaluate the rural-urban split in factional terms, and the factions cannot be compared with parties as they function in two-party states. Perhaps the best example of a faction of some permanence which illustrates the rural-urban division in southern elections if not in the southern legislatures is to be found in Georgia. Gene Talmadge built his political following on a strong rural basis and attracted a considerable number of votes by a vitriolic denunciation of the big cities. V. O. Key after a careful analysis of the vote for Talmadge in the primaries during the period 1934 to 1946 explains Talmadge's support in these terms:

[20] Key, *Politics, Parties, and Pressure Groups,* p. 324.

It is not in sectionalism, however, but in an urban-rural cleavage that the most persuasive interpretation of Talmadgism is found. . . . In no county with a town of over 13,000 did he receive a majority in the four gubernatorial races that he entered after 1932. In only 10 of 53 counties with medium-sized towns (for Georgia) did he receive consistent support. But in almost half the counties without incorporated places over 2,500 he could count on a majority in all four elections.[21]

While the rural-urban division is very apparent in the selection of Talmadge as Governor, the same division did not carry over completely to the legislature. This is shown by the fact that in a major test of Talmadge's power in the legislature in 1947 the Talmadge faction did not draw its strength entirely from the rural areas nor did the anti-Talmadge faction draw its strength entirely from the urban areas. The test arose when Gene Talmadge, who had been elected governor in the 1946 elections, died before being sworn into office. The legislature which met in January, 1947 was divided into two groups over the question of the choice of a successor. The Talmadge partisans maintained that the legislature had the power to select a successor and favored Herman Talmadge, Gene's son, for the office. The anti-Talmadge faction maintained that the proper individual to succeed to the governorship was the Lieutenant Governor-elect, M. E. Thompson. When the issue came to a vote in the legislature, representatives of almost a fifth of the counties which had supported Talmadge in the July primary failed to give unanimous support to Herman's candidacy. On the other hand, legislators from about half of the counties that opposed Gene Talmadge in the primary failed to vote solidly against Herman.[22] This peculiar conduct does not mean that there is no urban-rural split in the Georgia legislature, but it does seem to indicate that this division which was quite marked in the primary did form the basis for an entirely similar faction in the legislature. The division in the Georgia legislature might well be characterized as pro and anti-Talmadge factions, but these factions are not necessarily parallel to the rural-urban split.

In most southern states the rural-urban split is not the basis for major factions which tend to fall on sectional lines rather than on rural-urban lines. For example, in the Alabama legislature

21 V. O. Key, *Southern Politics* (New York, 1949), pp. 115-116.

22 Key, *Southern Politics,* p. 110.

the representatives of the Black Belt, which runs through the center of the state and is a very conservative area of large planters, form a loose coalition with the representatives of the large cities and generally are opposed by the representatives of the small rural counties of North and South Alabama. However, on an issue such as reapportionment the rural-urban lines are rather clearly drawn. In the Alabama legislature the rural legislators are so strong that reapportionment bills which are introduced regularly in almost every session seldom come to a vote. However, in 1939 Governor Frank Dixon, who was from Birmingham, called a special session of the legislature to consider reapportionment and a House bill actually came to a vote. It was defeated by sixty nays to 31 yeas. An examination of the vote shows that the representatives of only three South Alabama counties, Mobile, Houston, and Coffee, voted for the bill. All of these counties are urban in character. However, Montgomery, which is the other urban county in South Alabama, voted against the bill. The northern urban areas supported the bill but thirteen North Alabama counties, all rural, voted against the bill. Thus, the vote on reapportionment showed the small rural counties of North Alabama combining with the rural counties of the Black Belt against the large urban counties of both North and South Alabama.[23]

This situation probably would be typical of the reapportionment votes in most other southern legislatures. However, reapportionment is only one issue and rural-urban lines are not as clearly drawn on all issues. The factions in one-party states generally have a sectional rather than a rural or urban base, but they do not seem to be constant enough to be regarded as the equivalent of political parties. They tend to form and re-form on the basis of personalities, particularly on the basis of the governor's personality, and shift with the changing issues before the legislature. The governor of a one-party state, therefore, must build his support wherever he can in the legislature. If he was elected with substantial urban support, as is generally the case, he may be able to count on the urban votes as a basis for his working majority. In most legislatures, however, because of the acute urban under-representation this can be only the beginning of a bloc of votes sufficient to carry out his program. He must have the sup-

[23] Farmer, pp. 38-39.

port of a substantial number of rural legislators in order to see his program enacted into law. Consequently, even though the governor may be regarded by some as representative of the urban interests, he must tailor his program to fit the rural as well as urban interests if he is to be successful. Thus, he is faced with much the same problem as the governor of a two-party state such as New York. The major difference is that in a one-party situation the governor does not have the votes of his party to serve as a basis for his working majority and that there are no parties representing either the rural or the urban vote, as may be the case in two-party states where one or the other of the two major parties has come to speak either for the big city voters or for the branch heads.

It would seem that factional divisions also appear in the normally Democratic and Republican states. For example, in California there is both a north-south division and a rural-urban division. The north-south division, however, is based in two great metropolitan areas. The north, led most of the time by San Francisco and the Bay district, dominated California politics from 1850 until about 1930. This control was based at first on a concentration of population in the north during the Gold Rush and the earlier development of agriculture and manufacturing in that area. The south, led by Los Angeles, rapidly matched the population growth in the north but was held in political subjection by the over-representation of the north in the legislature. In two violent reapportionment struggles in 1931 and 1941 this over-representation was corrected to a considerable extent in the lower house of the legislature. However, the south is still under-represented in the Senate.[24]

In addition to a north-south division, California politics also is characterized by the same rural-urban conflict which has been evident in the other states. In California, like most of the southern states, this conflict has been subordinated to a sectional division. However, the so-called federal plan of apportioning membership in the State Senate represented a rather complete victory of the rural over urban forces. The rural areas

were able to establish this system in 1926 only with San Francisco support, which was given to spite Los Angeles and has been re-

[24] See Crouch *et al.*, p. 37 for a further discussion of this sectional conflict.

gretted many times since. The California politician who would win votes or influence legislation must defer to rural sentiment. The formation of state policy often touches upon the regional or sectional interests of the rural areas. Party groups, urban elements, individual politicians, and pressure groups—all must bow to the supremacy of the "country" or "cow counties" in the state Senate.[25]

The general proposition that the governor represents the urban interests while the legislature represents the rural interests is a useful generalization but, in most states, it is too broad a statement to give the whole picture. The governor does tend to represent the urban interests in many states because he is elected on a state-wide basis and the greatest concentration of population and, hence, of voters is in the urban areas. The legislature, on the other hand, tends to represent the rural interests because its members are elected from single-member districts and because the number of rural districts, as the legislatures are now apportioned, outnumber the urban districts. However, to stop here in this analysis of the nature of executive-legislative relations is to oversimplify a rather complex relationship. As was pointed out earlier, in Connecticut, California, Illinois, Massachusetts, and New York, rural-urban cleavages do exist. They are even found in such supposedly rural states as Alabama and Georgia. Even in the urbanized states, however, the division of political power is such that a candidate must appeal not only to the urban but also to the rural vote in order to be elected. Furthermore, the rural over-representation in the legislature is such that he must compromise even further in his legislative program if he is to be successful in the formation of legislative policy. Hence, the governor usually does not, in practice, attempt to secure the straightforward execution of his party's program if that party has an urban base or to push exclusively the interests of the urban centers of the state if he is operating in a one-party situation. Executive-legislative relations are primarily a process of negotiation and compromise. It is rare that a governor can afford to ignore entirely either the rural or urban voter in his campaign or the representatives of either group in his subsequent legislative program.

The rural-urban cleavage which is present to some extent in all legislatures is highlighted in some two-party states such as New York by the urban basis of one major party, in this case the

[25] Crouch *et al.*, p. 38.

Democratic Party, and the rural basis of the opposing party, in this case the Republican Party. On the other hand, it is concealed in many of the one-party states by the fact that the cleavage finds an outlet only in two factions of the same party and that this cleavage frequently is obscured by other factional arrangements. The rural-urban split is, nevertheless, one of the hard facts of political life with which a governor must deal. To assume that this is the only factional division in the legislature is to ignore the presence of other groups based on other considerations which may be equally important. There are many other bases for factional divisions in our state legislatures which must be considered by the governor of any given state in dealing with the legislative body. As was seen in Alabama and California, there is a sectional division in those two states based on geographic, economic, and traditional patterns which in most cases is more important than the rural-urban division, although this division is present in both of these states. These two factional divisions are only two examples of the multitude of factions which exist in the legislatures of the 48 states. Space does not permit a state-by-state analysis to illustrate this point, but it seems that a good case can be made for the proposition that the governor in either a two-party or a one-party situation in many states actually is dealing with factions and not with parties in his relations with the legislature. As was pointed out at the beginning of this section, the basic problem facing the governor is to build a bloc of votes which will be sufficient to enable him to have his program enacted into law. This bloc of votes may have as a base the members of his own party in the legislature, and in a real two-party situation the governor may be able to use his position as party leader to control enough votes to enable him to put through his legislative program in the face of opposition by the minority party. However, this situation seems to be the exception rather than the rule. The governor certainly cannot operate in this manner unless his party controls both houses. In many states this is not actually the case and, hence, the governor must deal with a faction of the opposing party in order to get his program enacted. In the one-party states the governor faces a body which is made up almost entirely of members of his own party who are loyal neither to the party nor to the governor and who must be dealt with either individually or on a factional basis. Consequently, it would seem that the governor in most states must begin upon his election, or preferably even before his election, to build up a bloc of votes on which he can rely for support for his legislative proposals. In the following section some of the methods open to the governor to build such support will be considered briefly. The methods in general are well known and have been widely discussed and, hence, need not be covered in any great detail here; but an attempt will be made to illustrate a sort of cycle which seems to exist in most states.

METHODS OF INFLUENCING LEGISLATION

The methods by which a governor will seek to secure the passage of his legislative program or attempt to block those measures which he feels are inimical to his program vary from state to state and also within the same state under succeeding governors. In general, however, there are a number of methods of influence of steadily increasing degrees of pressure which seem to be used in a sort of influence cycle which affects each important piece of legislation.

The first step in this cycle actually takes place prior to the legislative session in the caucus of the majority party in a two-party state or in informal meetings of the various legislative factions in a one-party state. In these caucuses or meetings the decisions are made as to who will be selected for the important posts of speaker of the house, president pro tem of the senate, the chairmen of important committees and, in states with two functioning parties, the majority leader in the two houses. The governor is vitally concerned with this process because the fate of his program will depend on the treatment it receives in the legislature, and this treatment in turn depends primarily on the actions of the individuals who hold these important positions. If the governor is adept at politics, he will have his nominees for these posts selected and their subsequent election or appointment assured long before the first meeting of the legislature.

The speaker and president pro tem are formally elected by their colleagues in the house and senate. This, however, presents no real obstacle to an alert governor-elect who, if he has any semblance of strength in the legislature, will be able to secure the election of members of his choice to these important posts.

If he cannot, it probably is indicative of a rough road ahead in his relations with the legislature.

In most state legislatures, the committee chairmen and committee members are appointed by the speaker of the house and either the lieutenant governor (as president of the senate) or the president pro tem of the senate. These officers, if they are supporters of the governor, will make sure that individuals friendly to the administration are selected for important committee posts and thus insure prompt and friendly consideration of important administration measures in committee. This is vital to the passage of these measures, for state government, like national government, is largely "government by committee." The fate of important bills usually is decided before they reach the floor, and, in fact, it is only by favorable committee action that they will ever come before the legislative body for consideration. Hence, the governor must concern himself with all phases of the legislative process. He cannot be content simply with drafting legislation or even with having it introduced by a friendly legislator. If he is to see his program enacted into legislation, the stage must be set with a careful organization of the legislature which runs from the presiding officers down to the individual committee members. This "interference" by the governor in legislative affairs probably was not foreseen by those who drafted the early state constitutions, but it has come about as a necessary corollary to the governor's role in policy formation.

The governor in a two-party state is in a somewhat more favorable position *vis-a-vis* the legislature than his counterpart in a one-party state, since he has access to the legislature through the presiding officers in both houses and also through the majority leader in each house. These individuals are supposed to work with the governor on party measures and to represent his point of view in the legislature. In a one-party state, on the other hand, there is no formal party organization, but the governor still needs a channel to the legislature. This channel generally is established either through the speaker of the house, the president pro tem of the senate, or through an individual who is known as the "governor's floor leader." This individual, as has been pointed out, does not occupy an official party position. He is selected by the governor from the prominent leaders in each house and is frequently the chairman of a key committee such as the finance committee. He is expected to represent the governor's views on measures before his house both on administration bills and on legislation which is introduced by individual members. The legislators who make up the governor's faction look to the floor leader for guidance in much the same way as members of the majority party look to the majority floor leader in a two-party situation.

The intra-party politics involved in the selection of the speaker of the house, the majority leader, or the governor's floor leader are sometimes quite bitter, and the scars which result may have an important influence on the ability of the governor to get his program enacted into law. For example, a recent popular governor of New Hampshire was singularly unsuccessful in getting through the legislature a program of increased taxation which he regarded as basic to his whole legislative program. Increased taxation is never popular with a legislature, and is particularly unpopular with the legislators of New Hampshire, many of whom are retired persons living on a fixed income and who represent constituents who are in the same position. However, some well-qualified local observers credit the defeat of the governor's program in large measure to an intra-party battle in the Republican Party for the speakership. One of the two leading candidates had been active in the governor's campaign and expected the governor to support him in his race for the speakership. This support, however, was not forthcoming and his opponent was elected. As a result, the defeated candidate spearheaded a bloc in the legislature which opposed the governor's taxing program and which was largely responsible for its defeat. This economy bloc, together with the Democrats who voted solidly against taxation, proved too strong for the governor's faction even though it was headed by the speaker of the House and the majority leader.

The governor's role in the selection of legislative leadership is a very delicate matter in most states, since the legislature is inclined to regard this as interference in legislative affairs. Yet, the governor has a very real interest in the selection of these important officers and must attempt to make his weight felt without giving offense to the legislature.

The second step in the influence cycle is the presentation of the subject matter of the proposed legislation as a part of the governor's message to the legislature. This at least makes the legislators aware of the fact that the governor does have a concrete proposal in this particular field so that the bill which is later introduced to implement this proposal is recognizable as an administration bill that is a part of the governor's over-all program and will be backed by the governor's not inconsiderable legislative powers. The fact that the governor presents his message to the legislature in person tends to highlight the importance of the program, since it is widely summarized in the press and in radio and television newscasts and discussed both by newspaper and radio commentators. Hence, the program is brought to the attention not only of the legislature but also of the people of the state as a whole. Consequently, the governor's program as presented to the legislature becomes a document of considerable persuasive power because of the attendant publicity. The legislators are aware that their constituents are informed of the governor's program and may ask embarrassing questions about the legislator's failure to vote for the program. Hence, the legislator has some reason to go along with the program if only because its existence as a program is well known to the folks back home. On the other hand, when word of the governor's program gets back to the legislator's constituents, they may deluge him with requests to work against certain of the governor's proposals. The chances are good, however, that the reaction of the legislator's constituents will be favorable in most instances, since many of the proposals were probably a part of the governor's platform which had been endorsed only recently by a substantial number of the voters in the general election or primary.

This popular endorsement has more effect than is sometimes credited to it. Several of the legislators who were interviewed pointed out that unless they were violently opposed personally to a measure in the governor's program or unless they were sure that their constituents were violently opposed to it, they would be inclined to go along with the governor's program, since after all it recently had been approved by a large number of the state's voters. The average American legislator, while acutely conscious of the views of the folks back home, usually is not bent on sabotage of the governor's program simply for the sake of sabotage.[26] Consequently, there are a good number of measures on which something close to general approval can be secured without resort to strong pressures and sometimes without great effort on the governor's part.

Sooner or later, however, one of the governor's proposals will be viewed by a legislator or a group of legislators as being personally obnoxious, opposed to the best interest of their constituents, unacceptable to their faction, or for some other reason a measure which they will not support. At this point the influence cycle usually comes into its third phase, which is based primarily on persuasion. In these situations, one of the most effective methods which the governor can use is a conference with an individual legislator or with a group of recalcitrant legislators. This group may be a party caucus or it may be the leaders of a faction. In the conference it may not be necessary for the governor to promise the legislators anything tangible in the way of patronage or other rewards. Frequently, the prestige of the governor's office coupled with a forceful presentation of his views may be all that is necessary. Most legislators are well aware of the governor's additional persuasive powers which he can use if forced. Therefore, it is probably fair to say that this knowledge plus the prestige of the governor's position as chief executive coupled in some instances with his prestige as party chief tends to maximize the effectiveness of his arguments. The use of persuasion as a technique is well summarized by Governor Kohler in explaining what he considered to be "honorable" ways of influencing the legislature. In part the Governor said

> I have attended, when invited to do so, the caucuses of my party in the two houses and invited its members to support bills or resolutions which I deemed in the public interest. I have spoken,

[26] There are, of course, many situations in which this generalization is not true. For example, in a two-party state when one or both houses are controlled by the party opposing the governor, it is sometimes true that the legislators, motivated by partisan considerations, do engage in what certainly looks like sabotage for the sake of sabotage. The same thing is sometimes true in a one-party state when the governor is of one faction of the party and a majority of the legislature is of another. Most of the legislators with whom the writer talked, however, seemed to be far less inclined to be obstructionists than they are sometimes represented to be.

through members of my staff, at hearings when matters of this type were before the standing committees of the Legislature for consideration. I have met at regular intervals with the leaders of my party in both houses to discuss with them the legislative program before their houses and to receive the benefit of their advice and counsel on how best to solve problems of state concern. I have met with most members of the Legislature individually and urged upon them the importance of the measures which I have recommended. I have also received from them a great deal of helpful advice in discharging my responsibilities.[27]

Lest this view be thought unsophisticated it must be remembered that it is this governor who was successful in getting 85 per cent of his program through the legislature in a state in which that body is noted for its independence. On the other hand, it would be naive to suggest that there are not some situations in which a tremendous amount of pressure is brought to bear on individual members of the legislature. This was true, for example, in another midwestern state which the writer visited in which the senate was evenly divided between the Democratic and Republican parties while the governor and his party controlled the house. In this case the governor was able to get his major measures through the house but needed one or two votes to secure their passage in the senate. In these circumstances, local observers reported that one or two members were being "bought" regularly to secure the passage of important administration measures. Here, the governor used not only his best powers of persuasion but also used the promise of patronage and the threat of veto. On several occasions, he went so far as to veto a measure in which a particular legislator was interested because the legislator had refused to go along with the governor on an important measure. In this crisis a good deal of rather nasty political in-fighting went on and not all the methods used can be placed in Governor Kohler's list of honorable ways of influencing legislation.

Faced with these two situations as examples of the possible role of the governor in influencing legislation, the question arises as to which of these is the typical pattern. There can be no pat answer to this question, but the hypothesis may be advanced that as the unfavorable aspects of the local political situation become dominant or as opposition to a particular measure in-

[27] Governor Kohler, p. 245.

creases so also does the frequency with which such high pressure techniques as patronage and the threat of veto are used. In many states the writer found very amicable relations existing between the executive and legislative branches of the government and found that the governor was able to get his program across primarily by using the first three steps in what has been called the influence cycle. Most legislators expect the governor to have a program and they expect him to push that program. Strange as it may seem even the legislators of the opposing party understand this as a part of the governor's functions and are willing to go along with him to a considerable extent. In one of the southwestern states where the governor was faced by a majority of the opposite party in both houses of the legislature, the writer interviewed the speaker of the House, the acknowledged leader of the opposition party. This individual complained that he had found it difficult to co-operate with the governor because the governor had not proposed a concrete program. In the view of the speaker of the House the governor had been remiss in one of his most important functions, and the speaker was rather bitter about this dereliction of duty. The governor, the speaker said, should have known better, since he had been a member of the legislature himself. While this view probably is not typical of the attitude of opposition leaders toward the governor's program, it is indicative of the fact that most legislators, even of the opposing party, expect the governor to have a program.

The first three steps in the influence cycle seem to follow a general pattern in most states. The first step is the organization of the legislature, which is followed by the introduction of the subject matter of proposed legislation by the governor in his messages. These two steps in turn are followed by individual or group conferences with legislators to explain the governor's program and secure their support. If these three steps fail, then the governor may resort to other methods and the steps in the cycle will not follow necessarily in any particular order since the influence used must be tailored to the situation at hand. Among the more common methods used are the threat of veto and patronage. The latter may take the form of the appointment of a protege of the legislator to a government position or the promise of a future appointment to the bench or to some other position for the legislator himself. It also takes the form of awarding contracts to a firm in which the legislator is interested or paving of certain highways and even private roads in the legislator's district.[28] Occasionally, the governor will use his pardoning power as a lever in influencing legislation. In this case, the governor pardons one of the legislator's constituents in exchange for the legislator's vote.

The extent to which it is proper for the governor to use the powers of his office to reward his supporters or to secure the passage of legislation is, of course, open to some debate. One side of the controversy is well represented in a recent frank statement by Governor Gordon Persons of Alabama. In response to some newspaper criticism of the way in which contracts for the purchase of state automobiles were being let, the Governor released a statement to the press explaining his views on state purchasing. In this case the governor was not speaking directly about using the awarding of state contracts to influence the passage of legislation, but rather was concerned with their use in rewarding those who had helped him in his campaign. The reasoning, however, would seem to apply equally to friends either in the legislature or in an election. In part the Governor said

> There are a few things I'd like to get straight. It's true that we don't seek competitive bids for our vehicle purchases. The law doesn't require it, but if we pay more under our system, then we're wrong.
>
> But we're not paying more. We're getting fleet prices, the same as any large business organization can do. The fleet prices are set by the manufacturer and any dealer who tries to raise or lower that price will get his franchise yanked in a hurry by the manufacturer.
>
> Fleet prices are determined by how many cars we buy and how often and the types. So no matter where we bought them in the state, the price to us would be the same.
>
> There are two types of people I can buy from. Those who helped me get elected and those who didn't. I may be wrong, but I'm getting them from my friends.[29]

[28] See Coleman B. Ransone, Jr., *The Office of Governor in the South* (Bureau of Public Administration, University of Alabama, 1951), pp. 88-96 for a more detailed discussion of patronage methods. While these are discussed in the southern framework, they are quite similar to those found in most states.

[29] This statement was made in a news release which was quoted in the July 4, 1952 issue of *Alabama*, p. 6.

The idea that a governor may use patronage or the threat of veto to build a bloc of votes in the legislature or to pay political debts undoubtedly is obnoxious to those who seek good government. However, it seems to be one of the realities of political life which must be accepted. While much can be done by the governor through the prestige of his office and through personal contact with legislators, there may come a time when certain legislators must be dealt with more or less on their own terms. The use of such methods is disavowed by many governors who stress, quite rightly, what can be done inside the legal framework. Yet, there is much truth in the observation of one practicing politician of considerable success in Arkansas who told me, "Perfessor, I don't know nothing about books on government, but I do know that you got to have votes to be elected or to get your bills through the legislature. If you don't give the boys what they want, you won't get the votes. The only way you can beat a machine is to build a better one." The alternative of building a better machine in the legislature is not always easily accepted by a governor who feels that the legislators should see eye to eye with him on matters affecting "the public interest" without additional persuasion. However, when the governor is faced by a well organized opposition whether it be party or faction, he must build a better machine if he is to beat that opposition. The governor, even in merit-system states, has a considerable number of appointments at his disposal and has considerable influence over such matters as highways and contracts in most states. If he uses some of this power to repay political debts resulting from his campaign or to smooth the path of his program in the legislature, he should not be judged too harshly. Behind his actions is a long history of the use of such methods by former governors and the practical necessity of securing the enactment of his program, sometimes under very adverse political circumstances. The chances seem better than fifty-fifty that the governor will have as good a concept of the public interest as the members of the legislature who are selected from single-member districts of widely varying populations and many of whom represent the American equivalent of the rotten borough. In such circumstances, there may be considerable justification for the governor's using such methods.

If we assume, however, that it is undesirable for the governor to use such methods as patronage to influence the passage of legislation, there are still other ways in which this can be done within the accepted exercise of his power. One of these methods is the attempt by the governor to build public support for his program through direct appeals to the legislators' constituents. This method has become increasingly effective with the improved coverage of the press and the advent of radio and later of television. As was discovered in the analysis of the governor's day, many governors use weekly or bi-weekly radio or television programs in which they explain to the people the major issues before the legislature and the governor's position in regard to those issues. Other governors use a daily or weekly newspaper column for this purpose. Added to these means of direct access to the citizen are the twice-daily press conferences held by most governors. While all of these avenues of communication are open to the legislature as well as to the governor, the governor's position as the state's chief executive is of incalculable value in his contest for the public eye and ear. No single legislator or even a group of legislators can hope to command the audience which is the governor's simply because of his position. Any governor gets a tremendous amount of free publicity during his term of office. Not all of this publicity will be favorable, but if the press and radio representatives are handled properly, the governor finds himself with very effective channels to the voter. The net effect of all this publicity on the legislator's constituents has not yet been accurately determined, but many governors feel that the result is favorable climate of opinion for the governor's proposals.

Another device at the governor's disposal in most states which can be used to center public attention on particular aspects of his legislative program is the special session. The power given the governor to call a special session of the legislature has its origin in the belief that certain emergencies might arise, such as war, invasion, or economic collapse, which would make it desirable for the legislature to meet at some time other than that regularly appointed by the constitution. As a matter of practice, real emergencies are fairly rare, but the business of government is pressing enough so that the governor feels compelled to call special sessions to put before the legislature business which could be handled in a regular session if all the states had annual sessions of the legislature. In some instances the special session is used deliberately as a device to influence legislation. The governor in calling a special session centers the attention of the state on the problem or problems for which the session is called and thus places the legislature in the position of either acting on these proposals in the manner in which the governor suggests or taking the political consequences which can be serious if the electorate really is concerned with the problem before the session. In many states the governor has the sole authority to designate the subjects which may be considered at the special session and no other subjects can be considered by the legislature. In several states the stringency of this provision is relaxed by the fact that the legislature by a two-thirds vote or some other extraordinary majority can take up subjects beyond the call for the special session. In these states a special session frequently becomes simply another session of the legislature and in practice many matters are taken up which were not suggested by the governor in his call for the session.

The fact that the governor has authority in many states to limit the subjects to be considered in a special session has brought up the interesting problem of whether the governor may be impeached at a special session which was called for another purpose. This situation actually occurred in New York, where the impeachment of Governor Sulzer took place during a special session in 1913 which the Governor had called for the transaction of other business. The courts in New York took the view that impeachment was a judicial and not a legislative process and, hence, that the impeachment was constitutional.

The chief value of the special session as a means of influencing legislation comes from the fact that the subjects to be considered are more or less those of the governor's choice and because of the attention focused on these particular issues by the calling of a special session of the legislature. This method is not always effective as is witnessed by the fact that in 1947-51 Governor James E. Folsom of Alabama called six special sessions of the Alabama legislature to consider the problem of reapportionment but was unsuccessful in securing a reapportionment bill from any of these sessions.

In addition to these methods, the cycle in its final phase comes around to the use of the veto and in some states to the use of the executive amendment. Generally speaking, these are methods of last resort, since neither of them is generally used until the governor's other resources for influencing legislation have been exhausted. Of the two powers, that of executive amendment has a much more positive aspect and seems to recommend itself for consideration in the states at large. Nevertheless, at present only four states, Alabama, Massachusetts, New Jersey, and Virginia, have given the governor this power. Its principal advantage over the veto is that it enables the governor to make suggestions for changes rather than simply vetoing the legislation.

As has been pointed out previously, the governor has been very successful in making his veto effective. Less than 2 per cent of the governors' vetoes are usually overridden. Hence, the governor has a very powerful negative voice in legislation when he chooses to exercise this power. Because of the effectiveness of the veto and the knowledge on the part of state legislators of this effectiveness, the veto, even when not used, is a very powerful conditioning factor in securing legislative co-operation. The fact that the majority of vetos which are overridden occur in situations where there has been a complete breakdown of executive-legislative relations points to the last resort nature of this power. In normal circumstances the governor does not have to veto legislation, for the legislature generally is willing to adapt its legislation to the governor's concepts of what is desirable so that the legislation may be passed with the understanding that it will not be vetoed. The veto, therefore, has not been listed as the last of the governor's powers to influence legislation because it is unimportant. On the contrary it is quite important and is basic to many of his other powers. However, it does seem to come last in point of time since generally it is used only when other methods have failed.

If this analysis of the importance of the veto power is correct, it is difficult to explain the governor's leadership in North Carolina, where the governor has no veto power. While the governor of North Carolina has not been as effective a legislative leader as the governors of some states, it would not be fair to say that he has been ineffective. Most of the evidence on administration bills and the comments of local observers seem to show that he has been rather effective in getting his program through the legislature. An examination of the situation in North Carolina shows that the governor uses all the methods which have been discussed to secure the passage of legislation but that the veto is not a powerful conditioning factor, since he does not have that power. A two-fold explanation may be advanced to explain the governor's success in spite of his lack of the veto. First, the legislature seems to have developed some sense of legislative responsibility since there can be no buck passing of undesirable legislation to the governor with the knowledge that the governor will veto the bill in question and thus take the burden from the legislature. Secondly, the governor seems to have made very effective use of the legislative powers which he does have and also has used effectively his rather considerable powers in the field of finance to back-stop his legislative powers.

Even so, there remains the interesting possibility that the governorship might have developed in other states to its present status even if there had been no veto power. It is difficult either to prove or to disprove this proposition with only the example of North Carolina on one hand and the contrary example of all the other states on the other. It seems that the importance attributed to the veto in the states as a whole is based on a sound analysis of the actual development of the office in those states. On the other hand, it certainly is true that the office of governor in North Carolina is not the weakest in the nation by almost any standards that might be chosen. The governor of North Carolina generally is a much stronger legislative leader than his counterpart in the neighboring State of South Carolina, where the governor does have the veto power. It is obvious, therefore, that the development of the governor as a legislative leader cannot be attributed entirely to the veto power.

As this analysis has attempted to bring out, the governor's power to recommend was basic to the development of the governor's role as a legislative leader. This power, in itself, would not have resulted in the present importance of the governor's activities in the field of policy formation had not the office and its powers undergone other important changes. One of these changes which enabled the governor to take a more meaningful part in the policy process was the increased prestige which gradually became attached to the office. This was in part the result of the introduction of the system of state-wide election as the method for selecting the governor. It was also a result of the higher caliber of the individuals who have served as the governors of many of the states, particularly since the first World War. In addition, the governor gradually began to build his legislative influence through such devices as the "organization" of the legislature, the judicious use of patronage, the use of special sessions to center public attention on certain aspects of his program, and appeals to the people of the state to bring his program to the attention of the legislators' constituents. The growth of the press, radio, and television greatly increased the governor's effectiveness in such public appeals. Also in all the states except North Carolina the veto has been a backstop to the other methods of influencing legislation.

8. THE GOVERNOR'S ROLE IN MANAGEMENT: ENVIRONMENT

POLITICS AND ADMINISTRATION at the state level form a seamless web and the distinctions which are made between the governor's role in policy formation and his role in management are largely of degree. The responsibility of the governor for policy does not cease when he has presented his policies to the legislature or even when those policies have been enacted by that body. The formation and the execution of policy are but two phases of the same process. In the early stages of this process there is more emphasis on the governor's relations with the legislature and in the latter stages there is more emphasis on the governor's relations with the department heads who will be responsible for the application of these policies. The process itself, however, is really a continuum. The governor must deal with the legislature initially on the policy questions which are raised in legislation introduced by the governor or by his budget. Once the legislature has decided these questions, however, the process of policy formation does not cease. Policy continues to be made through the application of these general prescriptions to specific situations in accordance with the department head's interpretation of legislative intent. On the other hand, the legislature, through its investigating committees, the approval of the governor's appointments, its legislative budget staff, and its post-auditing agent continues to wield sporadic but powerful control over the administrative process. Furthermore, the governor's position *vis-a-vis* the legislature is a very important conditioning factor in dealing with his department heads and with independent boards and commissions. Frequently, the governor's ability to control the executive branch is as dependent on his power base in the legislature as it is on any particular institutional arrangements within the executive branch.

The governor is concerned not only with the administration of policies which he may have recommended to the legislature but also with the statutes which were in effect when he took office. In most administrations these will form the bulk of the legislation under which the agencies of the executive branch will operate. While the governor through the budget and through other legislation may have suggested new programs, most of the budget will be concerned with the degree to which existing programs will be implemented in terms of the amounts appropriated for those programs. The governor is vitally concerned with the administration of established programs in the fields of highways, health, social welfare, agriculture, and the other major substantive fields of government. Through the budget he probably has emphasized the importance of one or more of these substantive fields or of a particular program in one of these fields. He must see that such programs are carried out in a manner which will coincide with his interpretation of the public mandate as revealed in his election. His program in one or more of these fields may, indeed, have been based on certain changes in the administration of a particular law, or in the structure of the agency administering the law, rather than in substantive program changes. These two objectives—program changes and administrative changes—may well be a part of one major plan. For example, if the governor has promised the voters that he would clean up the prison system in the state, then he will be concerned with both policy and administrative changes to accomplish this end.

Even if the governor has recommended no major policy change in a particular program and even if he has promised no administrative shake-up in a particular department, he, nonetheless, is concerned with the proper administration of the major departments of government. This is true because the focus of public opinion is not alone on legislation but also on administration. While the view was expressed by some of those interviewed that the people of the state "weren't interested in administration," this statement is not entirely true. The people are interested in administration because the point of contact between the citizen and his government is frequently at this level. The citizen may not be entirely aware of the action of the legislature on the highway program in general, but he is aware of whether or not he has to drive to town on muddy roads. The citizen knows and cares about the kind of treatment he receives when he is stopped by a state highway patrolman who accuses him of speeding. The citizen who has children generally is aware of the condition of the schools and of the kind of educational program to which his children are exposed. He is less aware of the condition of the state prisons or state mental institutions because most citizens have no first-hand knowledge of either of these programs. Similarly, he may not know a great deal about the state's program for the care of the indigent aged because no member of his family may be in this category.

Nevertheless, the state's program in any of these fields and the administration of that program can become a hot issue at any time. The press helps to keep the citizen aware of the programs with which he has little personal contact. To be sure, few stories emerge on the favorable side, because good administration seldom makes good copy; poor administration, particularly if charges of cruelty, graft, or corruption are involved, makes much better copy and, hence, at any time any department of the state government may suddenly find itself in the publicity spotlight. The public makes no fine distinctions between those departments over which the governor has considerable control and those which are relatively independent. As the average citizen views the situation, the governor should "do something" about whatever department is at fault or is alleged to be at fault. Consequently, the governor is impelled from time to time to concentrate his attention upon certain departments of government.

A good example of this sort of situation was the wave of prison riots in 1952 in such states as Illinois, Ohio, Michigan, New Mexico, and Massachusetts. In each instance these were regarded as being of such importance that the governor personally took charge of the attempts to quell the disturbances. Governor Stevenson, who was then campaigning for the Presidency, felt that the situation was of such importance that he stopped campaigning long enough to fly to his home state to take charge of the situation. The governor is vitally interested in seeing that situations which furnish good copy, in the sense that this implies maladministration or an administrative crisis, do not arise. Hence, the governor, if impelled by no other motive than political self-preservation, has a considerable stake in the honest and efficient management of the state's business.

It seems clear, therefore, that the governor has a legitimate concern with management. On one hand it dovetails into his functions in the policy field and on the other it is an important part of good public relations. These two considerations, quite apart from a real desire on the part of many governors to provide the citizens of the state with effective, efficient, and honest administration of state services, are sufficient reasons for the governor to be concerned with management. This does not mean, however, that the governor can be, or should be, the state's "general manager" in the sense that he must personally participate in the day-to-day operations of the executive branch. His proper role is that of establishing the policies which govern the day-to-day operations, of securing policy co-ordination among the agencies of the executive branch, and of very general supervision to make certain that his policies and those which previously have been established on a continuing basis are carried out properly.

The governor in carrying out his functions in the management field usually does not regard these as separate and distinct from his other functions. Hence, the governor acts in a particular situation as the occasion demands, using whatever powers are at his disposal, be they derived from the constitution or statutes, from his position as party chief, from his support in the legislature, from the custom and traditions of the state, or from his influence with the electorate. Consequently, administrative decisions are made in a distinctly political atmosphere and the governor's functions in the field of management are carried on within the larger framework of the total environment in which the state government operates in a given state. A realistic appraisal of the governor's role in management, therefore, requires that his operations in that field be regarded simply as a part of his over-all duties and as a role that is to be distinguished from his other functions only for the purposes of discussion. The factors which go to make up the environment of administration are the same factors which go to make up the total environment in which the governor operates in a particular state. Consequently, the factors which are discussed in this section have as much relevance to the governor's role in legislative policy formation and public relations as they do his role in management. They are emphasized here, however, because there is sometimes a tendency to regard the governor primarily as a general manager who can and should operate in a way that is somehow apart from the partisan world of party politics, legislative relations, and policy formation. In the writer's opinion such a view of the governor's role in management is highly unrealistic, for it disregards the facts of political life at the state level. The governor as general manager operates in an environment where the major emphasis is on politics. His moves in the management field are dictated by policy consideration and, hence, are political in the broad sense of the term and are frequently also political in the narrower sense of partisan politics.

The governor in managing the executive branch operates both within the framework established by the constitution and statutes and within the framework established by the political pattern of the state. The inter-relation of these two frames results in a series of very interesting and frequently very different environments which cannot be explained adequately except on a state-by-state basis. The fact that the statutes establish an executive budget or a merit system and that a state is listed in the standard references as being among the merit-system states or among those states with an executive budget does not mean that this is actually the case. A closer look at one of these states may reveal that, in fact, the governor does nothing more than pass departmental estimates along to the legislature and that by custom his so-called "budget message" is actually ignored by that body. Similarly, a study of the merit-system states reveals a wide difference of interpretation of that term. In one state which has a merit system there is no real central control over appointments, since these by the dictates of custom are made by the department heads who are the sole interpreters of the term "merit and fitness." In another state, a closer look reveals that the governor's former campaign manager is the personnel director and that the merit system operates as a very effective patronage bureau.[1]

[1] See Coleman B. Ransone, Jr., *The Office of Governor in the South* (Bureau of Public Administration, University of Alabama, 1951), pp. 129-149 for a

The imposition of a particular legal pattern on a particular political pattern may produce such wide variations that the governor's actual position may be very different in states where his legal position is technically the same. This makes generalizations in the area of management fully as hazardous as in the field of policy formation. As was brought out in discussing the governor's role in legislative leadership, the surface pattern of executive-legislative relations conceals a multitude of local variations. So also in the governor's role in management the "legal" pattern may not be the actual pattern. Nevertheless, there are certain facets of the governor's legal position which should be discussed, since these apparently have a considerable effect on his ability to perform his functions in the management field even though the presence of a certain legal provision is no guarantee of uniformity. Some of the legal factors which contribute to the environment of administration are: the governor's constitutional position as the chief executive; the effects of the salary paid the governor on the type of talent the office can command; the effect of the two-year term and of provisions which prohibit the governor from succeeding himself; and the limitations imposed on the governor's control over administrative policy by the chaotic conditions in the executive branch in many states.

The factors which go to make up the political pattern of the respective states already have been discussed in previous chapters and will be summarized only briefly in this section. In the first four chapters an attempt was made to divide the states into one-party states, normally Democratic or Republican states, and two-party states. The variations in political setting in these groups of states are reflected in the governor's position in his party and in his position *vis-a-vis* the legislature. These in turn are of considerable significance in his attempts to carry out his management functions.

In addition to the factors which related particularly to the political or legal pattern in the state, there are several which do not lend themselves to easy categorization. These include the limited time which the governor is able to devote to management,

---

discussion of legal theory versus custom and tradition in the governor's relation to personnel management in the southern states.

the governor's own view as to the importance of this aspect of his duties, the differences in the environment of administration which are the result of the size of the state, and the impact of federal grants-in-aid on both the policy and management aspects of the governor's functions.

This chapter will seek to illustrate the proposition that the governor must attempt to carry out his management functions in an environment which is made up of many diverse and sometimes contradictory influences. These influences may come from the legal pattern of the state government, from its political pattern, or from its social or cultural pattern. Some of these factors are common to only part of the states while others, like the federal grant-in-aid system, are of significance, though not of equal significance, for all the states. Some factors like the size of the state in area are influences which have been at work since the founding of the state and remain constant. Others like the population of the state are constantly shifting, and a sudden growth in population may be of very recent origin and only now beginning to influence the government which serves this larger citizen body. This chapter, therefore, will be devoted to a consideration of how the legal, political, and other factors suggested above go to make up the environment of administration in which the governor attempts to carry out his management functions.

FIRST AMONG EQUALS

The concept of the governor being primarily responsible for the management of the executive branch has not yet gained a firm foothold in most states in spite of some rather substantial reorganizations. As will be pointed out in Chapter 11, the concept was challenged by a great many of those interviewed and apparently has not yet been accepted generally by the voters in many states. Except in a few states in which the reorganizations of the last fifty years included constitutional revision of a substantial nature, the concept also has not yet been accepted as a basis for the organization of the executive branch.

The governor's constitutional powers in the field of management are relatively limited in most states and on the whole are probably not as important as his statutory powers. Nevertheless, they have influenced the development of the governor's powers in this field and in some cases his lack of certain key powers forms a barrier to effective management.

In most state constitutions there is what might be called a grant of "general executive power." For example, the Michigan constitution of 1908 has a provision which vests "the chief executive power . . . in the governor." In Michigan as in most states this phrase has not been regarded as an independent grant of authority. It not only indicates the superior status of the governor in that he has the *chief* executive power, but it also suggests that his executive authority is shared. This is indeed the case since the voters elect not only the governor but also the lieutenant governor, attorney general, auditor general, treasurer, secretary of state, highway commissioner, superintendent of public instruction, the board of agriculture, the board of regents, and the board of education. In Michigan the elected officers are given few specific functions by the constitution and thus differ somewhat from most states where many of the elected officials are given certain duties by constitutional provision. However, in Michigan as in most states the governor is not the only executive in the government and is the chief executive only in the sense that he is the first among many executives.[2]

The presence of other constitutional elected executive officers is not a serious threat to the governor's ability to control the executive branch if those officers do not, in fact, exercise important executive powers. The presence of an elected secretary of state, for example, may be of minor practical significance if that officer performs mainly ministerial duties, many of which are of a minor character, and few of which have any real policy connotation. The presence of an elected superintendent of public instruction who has views divergent from that of the governor on the state's education policy, or the presence of an elected commissioner of agriculture who is strongly opposed to the governor's announced agricultural program, or even the presence of an attorney general who is, as is sometimes the case, of the opposite party and of a hostile disposition, is a horse of another color. These officers, as well as many others who are elected in certain states,

[2] *General Management of Michigan State Government,* a Staff Report to the Michigan Joint Legislative Committee on Reorganization of State Government, Report Number 30 (Lansing, November, 1951), Part II, p. 11.

actually perform functions which are quite significant to the governor's program. Their presence, therefore, may constitute a real divisive force in executive policy and management which is of considerable practical significance to the governor.

From a constitutional point of view, therefore, the governor cannot be said to be the chief executive of most states except in the sense that he is the chief among several executive officers. This is a point which is well worth remembering, since it is an unspoken assumption which underlies the arguments of many of the elected officials and others interviewed who did not feel that the governor should be a general manager. Part of their rationale certainly is that if the governor is not the chief executive then there is little reason to assume that he should be the state's general manager.

The provision in most state constitutions which gives the governor a general grant of executive power and the provision which generally also is found charging the governor with the faithful execution of the laws are only points of departure from which the governor's role in management has developed. While the governor's role in management is still fairly limited in many states, many of the powers which give him even a limited effectiveness are based on statutory rather than constitutional provisions. In some states the legislature has given the governor increasingly more important powers in such matters as appointments, the executive budget, and fiscal controls over the spending process. These powers tend to overshadow his constitutional powers so far as practical administrative operations are concerned in many states and from a substantial part of his powers in those states where they have been granted.

THE SALARY/PERFORMANCE RATIO

One of the criticisms frequently made of state government as a whole and also frequently applied to the office of governor is that in most states the salary paid the state officials is too low in relation to the duties they are expected to perform. This is generally true, and the governor of many of our states is a rather poorly paid individual to judge by present standards in industry or even by those of the federal government and some of the larger cities. It is very difficult, however, to show that there is a direct correlation between the salary paid the governor and the kind of administrative talent that the office will command as a result of setting his salary at a particular level. The salaries paid the governors in 1952 ranged from $4,500 per annum in Maryland to $25,000 per annum in California and New York. Seventeen of the states, however, pay their governor $10,000 or less; and, in view of the financial burden placed on him in maintaining an establishment commensurate with the dignity of his office and the necessity for doing a considerable amount of official entertaining, this sum is probably inadequate to cover the actual cost of the office. However, it should be noted also that some 34 states provide housing for the governor, and an allowance for official expenses is also customary in most states. Even if the governor's housing and expense accounts are taken into consideration, few, if any, governors receive a salary sufficient for them to live in luxury, and many of them, according to their own statements, find that the governorship is a losing proposition from the financial point of view.

The author is convinced from discussing this problem with a number of governors and with their wives, who have the problem of running the executive mansion, that the popular concept of the governor's mansion as the epitome of luxurious living is largely without foundation. Many governors live in a "mansion" which would pass unrecognized in any good residential area. Others live in a large house which from the point of view of size might qualify as a mansion but which was built many years ago and in many cases does not have the modern conveniences of an average home of one of the state's well-to-do citizens. Indeed, the situation in one of the southwestern states a few years ago had the ingredients of a Hollywood movie. The governor and his large family started to move into the "mansion" only to find that the departing governor and his wife had removed most of the furnishings and left the house in such a state of disrepair that several months' work was necessary before the governor and his family could move in. The legislature made an appropriation for the renovation and while the work was in progress the governor "camped out" in one of the upstairs bedrooms until the work was completed. The funds for renovation, however, were not sufficient to cover such items as draperies, silverware, and linens. For some time, the governor and his family lived in the mansion without draperies or other light furnishings and were forced to do their official entertaining in a local hotel because of a lack of staff, silverware, or linens to entertain at home. Not all governors live in luxury, and those who seek to live on their salary alone are sometimes hard put to make ends meet.

The relatively insecure financial position of some of our governors leaves open the possibility that the governor will use extralegal methods to augment his salary. Thus, the way is opened for "expense accounts" from large corporations, the selling of pardons, and other devices which may seriously impair the efficiency of administration. Whether the governor actually does use such methods seems to depend largely on the character of the incumbent, and such actions cannot be attributed directly to the low salaries paid. It may be, as some writers maintain, that raising the governor's salary to a higher figure would partially remove this temptation and thus would tend to produce a more honest administration.

It also may be true that since the salary paid many of the governors does not compare favorably with that of an executive of even a medium-sized corporation within the state, many of those who would be qualified by experience or training for the position, at least from an executive point of view, prefer to devote their managerial talent to more lucrative pursuits. However, individuals do not run for the governorship simply to make a living, and, therefore, it does not seem entirely logical to assume that raising the salary to a higher level will have any startling effect on the caliber of personnel occupying the office. Those who argue that it will do so ordinarily use the same line of reasoning as do those who argue for an increase in the salaries of civil servants on the grounds that the best talent can be obtained only by setting the rate of pay of government employees at a level more nearly comparable to that found in private industry. While this argument is valid in its application to the civil service, if that service is under a sound merit system, it is not necessarily valid when applied to an elected administrative office, particularly the governorship.

The motives which influence a candidate for the governorship are complex, but on the whole the rewards which he expects from the office tend to be of a political rather than an economic nature.

Social prominence, the opportunity to wield considerable power, and the concept of the governorship as a stepping stone to a further political career as a judge, senator, or perhaps even as a presidential candidate all seem to weigh heavily in this determination. It is probable, therefore, that we cannot expect an increase in the caliber of the candidates for the governorship proportionate to an increase in the salary offered. On the other hand, it seems in keeping with our democratic philosophy of government and a common sense precaution to establish a salary for the governor which will at least enable him to live on his official income without resort to extra-legal means. While it must be admitted that few of the state's citizens will, practically speaking, have the "political availability" which is so necessary for a successful candidate, a low salary should not be established as an additional handicap to the well intentioned citizen seeking the office. Perhaps what is needed here is a dual approach which includes a salary increase for many of our governors who are indeed underpaid and an examination of the possibilities of reducing the cost of campaigning for the office. The latter, perhaps even more than the low salary, is the real barrier for "poor but honest" aspirants to the governorship.

A BIRD OF PASSAGE

More important than the possible effects of the low salary on the caliber of men who occupy the governorship is the weakening of the governor's position by provision of only a two-year term of office in 22 states and provisions which prevent him from serving two consecutive terms in the majority of four-year states. As a result of these limitations, the chief executive in these states is considerably handicapped, both as a policy maker and as administrative chief.

While accountability of the chief executive to the will of the people as expressed at the polls is a basic consideration in state government, as it is in any democratic system, there must be a limit to the frequency with which he is put to the test. It seems probable that even four years is a very short period for the governor to develop and put into operation programs in which there is any substantial change from the *status quo.* Every state administrative machine has its own set of customs and traditions, its own methods of "doing things."[3] Many state administrative practices are antiquated, and the thinking of many state administrative officials is centered on the past, or at best on the present, instead of on the future. The time and effort required for the re-tooling of such human machinery is considerable. To ask the governor to perform such a feat in two years is to place him in a very difficult position. If we add the time and energy required to formulate his program and get it through the legislature, it readily becomes apparent that two years is far too short a period for the task at hand. Yet, we ask the governnor to do all this and at the same time to keep his political fences mended so that he may be able to continue in office for at least another term.

All of the governors interviewed who now have a two-year term were in favor of the extension of this term to at least four years for their successors. The quotations which follow are representative of the views of the "two-year" governors on the necessity of the state's chief executive having at least a four-year term.

Governor Walter J. Kohler in a recent message to the Assembly and Senate of Wisconsin summarized his view and that of the preceding governor on the question of a two-year term versus a four-year term as follows:

> Governor Rennebohm, in his recent message to the Legislative Council, offered a number of recommendations to the legislature based upon his experiences as the Chief Executive of Wisconsin. He suggested that our citizens suffer a loss of service because of the present two-year term for elected state officials. The pressure of legislative business during six months of the term, and the requirements of speaking engagements and the biennial campaign for office during the remainder of the term, consume too much of the time which the governor should devote to improvement of state administration.
>
> Our state would benefit from the adoption of a constitutional amendment extending the terms of the state constitutional offices from two to four years, with election in the even numbered years between presidential elections when the national campaign does not distract attention from state issues.

A succinct summary of one of the major disadvantages of the

[3] See Donald C. Stone, "Notes on the Governmental Executive," *New Horizons in Public Administration* (University, Alabama, 1945), pp. 48 ff. for a more complete discussion of the effect of institutional environment on the functions of the executive.

two-year term was given by Governor Mechem of New Mexico who said, "I am running for office 365 days a year."[4] He indicated that this constant "running for office" consumed valuable time which could have been spent profitably in the exercise of his many gubernatorial functions.

A governor of one of the New England states pointed out that for the past twenty years the governors of his state had generally been elected for two two-year terms and thus actually had served for four years. However, the governor contended that running for re-election every two years was a needless waste of money as well as time. He estimated that it cost at least $100,000 to be elected governor of the state. Thus, the cost for two gubernatorial campaigns in a four-year period would be $200,000. The governor felt that not much more than $100,000 would be spent in the election if it were held every four years and, therefore, the cost for campaigning for governor would be reduced by almost half if the governor were given a four-year term. While this argument may be attributed to New England emphasis on thrift, it is also true that the cost of gubernatorial campaigning is a real barrier to the "poor but honest" aspirant for the governorship. Hence, the installation of a four-year term might be of some value in reducing campaign costs.

The need for a four-year term was also stressed by another of the New England governors, Harold J. Arthur of Vermont. In his retiring message to the General Assembly, Governor Arthur said: "By my experience in state government, extending through twenty years, I am inclined to believe that the state would greatly benefit if the term of chief executive were extended to four years without the right of succession."[5]

Governor George T. Mickelson of South Dakota stressed the possibility that the two-year term would weaken the governor's hand administratively. The Governor said in part:

> I think we should have a four-year term for probably all of our state officers, but certainly for our Governor. . . . We would be giving him a chance to select his appointive officers on a four-

[4] Interview with Governor Edwin L. Mechem, Santa Fe, New Mexico, June 9, 1951.

[5] Retiring Message of Harold J. Arthur, Governor of the State of Vermont, to the General Assembly, January 4, 1951.

year basis. I want to tell you, it is not too easy to secure well-qualified men, especially during these times when they can make so much more money in private business than they can working for the state. It is not easy to induce a person to work in a responsible position for the state when you can promise him a position for only two years. I have been a bit proud that we have been able to secure the caliber of people that we have to head up our departments. But, I am frank to tell you that I have had to get them in my office and really sell them the book.[6]

The major arguments presented by the governors interviewed who favored a four-year term as opposed to a two-year term may be summarized as follows: (1) the two-year term places the governor in the position of constantly running for re-election. This is not only expensive but it also wastes time and effort that could, and should, be placed on other duties. (2) The two-year term handicaps the governor in his relations with administrative officials. Many of these officials have terms longer than the governor and do not feel in any way obligated to him or responsible for the execution of his policies. Furthermore, it is difficult to get high-caliber people to accept appointments which, if the governor is not re-elected, may last for only two years. (3) The two-year term handicaps the governor in his relations with the legislature. In some cases the legislature has a four-year term while the governor has only a two-year term and, in any event, the legislature realizes that the governor may be only a transient and is reluctant to make any major policy changes to implement his program.

The primary arguments advanced by those who opposed the extension of the governor's term to four years, principally department heads, were: (1) the governor, if he desires a second two-year term, generally can be re-elected and, therefore, serves the equivalent of a four-year term. (2) The two-year term is more democratic because the governor must "go to the people" for a

[6] Excerpts from an address titled, "South Dakota, Yesterday, Today, and Tomorrow," delivered before the Sioux Falls Chamber of Commerce. October 3, 1950. Published in pamphlet form as *Improving State Government* by the Political Science League of the University of South Dakota (Vermillion, South Dakota, 1950). Governor Mickelson is well qualified as an observer of the state governmental scene, having served as a legislator, Speaker of the House of Representatives, Attorney General, and Governor of South Dakota for two terms.

renewal of authority every two years instead of every four years.

When carefully analyzed these arguments do not seem to the author as compelling as those advanced by the governors in favor of a four-year term. An examination of the history of the office in the two-year states does seem to bear out the contention that a governor usually can be re-elected. While there are some notable exceptions, the general rule seems to be that a governor who has been elected to one two-year term usually can be a successful candidate for a second term if he elects to run. It also should be noted, however, that frequently it is the tradition in two-year states that no governor is elected for a third term, so that four years tends to be both the accepted minimum and customary maximum for governors in these states.

However, the argument that two two-year terms are the equivalent of a four-year term fails to take into consideration several factors. In the first place, whenever the governor fails to be re-elected for a second term or does not run for a second term, there will be a turnover in top administrative personnel and in those states without a merit system substantial shifts in the lower reaches of the service as well. One of the two-year governors estimated that in his state a 50 per cent turnover in personnel was not unusual with the advent of a new governor. This turnover, particularly in the higher reaches of the service, has serious implications for administrative efficiency. At least a minimum degree of continuity in public office is desirable for the orderly development of sound public policy and for the execution of plans stemming from those policies. A change of department heads every two years does not lead to such continuity.

Secondly, proponents of a two-year term do not take into consideration the fact that a two-year term of office for the governor leaves him in a position where he must spend the first year of his term getting acquainted with the office and the second year campaigning for re-election. This campaigning is a considerable drain on his time and energy, as well as a conditioning factor in dealing with the legislature and with department heads. A governor who is elected for a four-year term is in a more favorable bargaining position with both groups than is a bird of passage who may not occupy the office beyond a two-year period. The time and effort which is devoted by the governor to this constant running for re-election is time and effort which the citizens have a right to expect him to devote to the management of his office.

While the governor must be held accountable to the people, it also is true that some degree of continuity is desirable. If the governor is to perform his many functions effectively, he must be given a reasonable period in which to establish his policies and carry them out. A four-year term is a desirable step in this direction.

In addition to the two-year term, many states have inherited another expression of the fear of constitution makers of the possible abuse of power by the executive branch. This fear has expressed itself in a limitation on the number of consecutive terms a governor may serve. Thirteen states with four-year terms have constitutional provisions which make the incumbent ineligible to succeed himself.[7] Three others restrict the governor to two four-year terms, while eleven states with four-year terms have no limits. This latter group includes California and New York, two of our largest states.

In twenty of the 22 states having a two-year term there is no limitation on the number of terms which a governor may serve. In New Mexico a governor who serves two consecutive terms is ineligible to hold office during the next two years, while in Tennessee the governor is not eligible to hold office for more than six years in any eight-year period. South Dakota does not limit the number of consecutive terms which a governor may serve, but the legislature has enacted a statute which provides that the governor may not run in the primary more than twice. This would seem to limit effectively his securing the nomination of a major party and thus make it unlikely that he could be elected for more than two terms. It should also be pointed out that when there is no legal limitation to prevent the governor from serving more than two two-year terms, it is usually traditional in the two-year states to limit the governor to two terms.

The effect of these provisions, both legal and traditional, is a limitation on the number of years which the governor can serve either successively or in total. The most important limitation is that which prohibits the governor from succeeding himself. If it is desirable, as was argued in the first part of this section, that

[7] In these states provision is made for the re-eligibility of the governor after a lapse of one term.

the governor have a four-year term, then it also is logical that the governor should be able to succeed himself.

The limitations on the governor succeeding himself, whether they are legal or traditional, are usually defended on the grounds that they prevent the establishment of a "machine" by the governor and thus prevent the establishment of autocratic control. This argument, however, does not seem to be supported by the facts. What this self-denying ordinance may do is to prevent the people from re-electing a public servant who has given them effective and machine-free administration. The administration of Governors Price in Virginia, Arnall in Georgia, and Jones in Louisiana are cases in point. These men, though unlike in many respects, were elected as anti-machine candidates and gave their respective states sound and honest administration. It is quite possible that they may not have been elected for a second term, but under the re-eligibility provision of those states the people were not given an opportunity to pass judgment on their administration. None of these men was able to transfer his own popularity to other (and perhaps weaker) reform candidates, and the result was that the machine came back into power in the succeeding elections in Virginia and Georgia and two elections later in Louisiana. Further, it may be argued that the well organized political machine is not as dependent upon personalities as is a reform candidate who is running for the governorship. In Virginia the face in the governor's office changes every four years but except on rare occasions such as the one mentioned above the policies of the Byrd "organization," as it is called in Virginia, continue to prevail. Thus, it would seem that those who attempt to buck machine politics are being handicapped in as great a degree as those who possibly may be seeking to establish or maintain a machine based on long tenure in the governorship.

The result of these provisions on re-eligibility has been an enforced rotation of the governorship in those states with such provisions. Many of them were adopted in preceding decades when the fear of executive dominance was stronger than it is today, and it is doubtful whether they would all be retained if the matter came before the people for a vote today. Anderson and Weidner point out that these provisions tend to a weak governorship which is only an interlude in a man's political career rather than to the type of governorship which has developed in New York, where from 1922 to 1954 the office was filled by only four able men securing successive re-elections. They also note that one of the striking facts about the American state governorship is the average shortness of tenure. For example, the New York average since 1777 is 3.6 years, the Minnesota average since 1858 is 3.4 years, while the Mississippi average since 1817 is only 2.6 years. It is probable that the national average since 1776 would not be much above three years, although in recent decades the average probably has gone up. The average governor is, therefore, a bird of passage who comes from other walks of life and after a short stay in the governor's office moves on to other places.[8]

In view of this shortness of tenure, it seems highly desirable that the idea should not be fostered that the governorship is merely a stepping stone to higher political office. Certainly, preventing an able man from succeeding himself in the governorship encourages him to look elsewhere for higher office. It is doubtful whether the majority of able men will be content to make the governorship the apex of their political career but they might at least be encouraged to pause a little longer on this particular stepping stone by being allowed to succeed themselves in office.

If a governor is allowed to succeed himself, he has considerable incentive during his administration to give the people that kind of stewardship which will insure re-election. On the other hand, if he cannot succeed himself and seeks no further political preferment from the people, he may be placed in a position where, as one department head maintained, "the governor has no incentive for good administration other than his own desire to perform efficiently."

The governor's inability to succeed himself not only has serious implications administratively but also has a very deleterious effect on the governor's relations with the legislature. This is true particularly in the second half of his term, when the legislators are more concerned with the programs of the potential candidates for the governorship than with the incumbent who cannot be looked upon as a candidate for at least another four years, if at all.

The common-sense view that a governor who has given faithful

[8] William Anderson and Edward W. Weidner, *State and Local Government* (New York, 1951), p. 398.

service should be allowed to continue his program is very appealing, and the continuity of policy which could result seems sorely needed in state administration. A four-year term with no bar to re-election seems a highly desirable goal for future constitution makers.

CHAOS IN EDEN

The fact that the executive branch in most states is an unplanned tangle of boards, commissions, departments and other agencies which, like Topsy, "just growed" has been well established by the analyses of the various groups which have studied state administrative organization in the last fifty years. This growth has now reached substantial proportions as the perusal of any of the recent "Little Hoover Commission" studies will reveal. The problem seems to afflict large and small states alike and the size of the state is no criterion by which to judge the size of its administrative organization in terms of the number of agencies. For example, Nevada, which is one of the smaller states in terms of population, had, at the last count, some 99 agencies. The heads of thirteen of these are elected by the people, twenty are *ex-officio* agencies solely, eleven are jointly *ex-officio* and appointive, the members of 48 are appointed solely by the governor, one is filled by the legislature, and the directors of six are appointed in various other ways.[9] The State of South Dakota has some 77 agencies, the heads of which are also appointed in a variety of different ways.[10] The Commission on State Government Organization in its survey of Connecticut government reports that "at our last count we had the names of 184 agencies in the executive branch alone. There may be more."[11] The Minnesota Efficiency in Government Commission reports that the executive branch consists of 105 separate agencies over which the governor has relatively little control because the terms of office of most department heads are longer than that of the governor and that, consequently, "he

[9] Albert Gorvine, *Administrative Reorganization for Effective Government Management in Nevada,* a report prepared for the Nevada Legislative Counsel Bureau (Nevada Legislative Council Bulletin No. 4, 1948), p. 16.

[10] W. O. Farber, *State Administrative Organization in South Dakota* (The Governmental Research Bureau, University of South Dakota, Report No. 20, July, 1949), p. 6.

[11] *The Report to the General Assembly, Governor of Connecticut,* Commission on State Government Organization (February, 1950), p. 23.

does not have opportunity to appoint many of the major department heads until he is serving a third term."[12]

These are but samples of the size and diversity of the administrative structure of our states. Upon close examination the executive branch is revealed as a large and chaotic collection of agencies, the heads of which are chosen in every way that can be devised by the ingenuity of successive legislatures. This aspect of the environment of administration in which the governor must operate has obvious and unhappy consequences for his effectiveness in management. The number of agencies in the average executive branch, even if these agencies were headed by single directors appointed by the governor for a term coterminous with his own, would stretch his span of control to such an extent that no real supervision would be possible. The problem of unwieldy size is compounded by the fact that the governor actually does not appoint the heads of most of these agencies. Many of the agency heads are elected, and some of those who are elected have terms longer than those of the governor. Others are selected by the legislatures for varying terms. Still others are selected by a board appointed by the governor. Frequently, however, there is a provision that the board have staggered terms so that any one governor may appoint only one board member during his term. Many agencies are headed by a board or commission which may be elected, appointed by the governor, appointed by the legislature, or nominated by private interest groups. The ingenuity of state legislators in devising systems of appointments is astounding and the end is not yet in sight.

The chaotic condition of the executive branch tends to limit the governor's efectiveness in management in almost all states. It is mentioned here as one of the factors which make up the environment of administration and one which, in this instance, tends to make that environment seem a jungle land of bureaucracy to the uninitiated chief executive. The implications of this chaos will be considered at more length in Chapter 9. At that point, the attempts of the governor to deal with the complicated administrative structure of the executive branch in order to secure some

[12] *How to Achieve Greater Efficiency and Economy in Minnesota's Government,* the recommendations of the Minnesota Efficiency in Government Commission (December, 1950), p. 3.

vestige of policy co-ordination and policy control are discussed.

POLITICAL PATTERNS AND MANAGEMENT

At the very beginning of this book the view was expressed that one of the things which was of considerable significance in an understanding of the governor's functions was an understanding of the political background against which those functions were performed. A part of this background is the process by which the governor is nominated and elected. This process, particularly the informal process of political selection that underlies the legal procedures, is significant for administration because it determines to a considerable extent the kind of individual who can be elected to the governorship. The caliber of this individual, his previous governmental experience, the deals he has made to secure the nomination, the appointments he has promised, and a multitude of other political aspects of the process are all relevant to the kind of administration which will be forthcoming.

The process of nominations and elections is but one part of the political pattern of the state. The party organization of the state is also a significant part of this pattern. In Part I it was suggested that the states could be classified in terms of their political structure as one-party, normally Democratic or Republican, or two-party states. It also was suggested that in the first two groups the dominance of a particular party encouraged factionalism and that these factions tended to replace political parties while not furnishing the advantages of a well organized and well disciplined party. The governor in dealing with the "party" in these states is in practice dealing with a group of factions of varying strength and importance. This situation is carried over into the legislature so that the governor must build support for his program wherever he can find that support among the various factions represented in that body. This also is true to a certain extent in many of the two-party states. In some of these states a pattern has emerged which threatens to become typical in which the governor's party controls only one house of the legislature while the opposition party controls the other house. In this situation the governor must build his support not only among members of his own party but also among the members of the opposition party if he is to be successful in his legislative program.

The implications of this factional situation in the one-party states, the normally Democratic or Republican states, and in some of the two-party states for gubernatorial leadership in the legislature are fairly obvious. What is less obvious but none the less of crucial importance to the governor in his management role is that the power base which the governor establishes in the legislature is a factor which conditions the whole relationship between the governor and his department heads. The typical situation in most states is that the governor is dealing with many department heads who are independent of his control so far as appointment and removal is concerned. In the case of a disagreement between the governor and the head of such a department, the governor's most potent weapon is a threat to reduce the department's appropriations through a reduction of its part of the executive budget. This reduction will stick only if the governor is in a very strong position *vis-a-vis* the legislature. When the governor is not in a strong legislative position, the department head knows that he can secure a reinstatement of the reduced item and, consequently, he can flout the governor's authority with impunity. Even under a strong governor there will be one or two departments or bureaus in certain departments which have such strong legislative backing that the governor must act with considerable circumspection in regard to their program.

While there are no Army Engineers at the state level, there are such potent organizations as the agricultural extension services, the bureaus of fish and game, which are the preserve of the state's sportsmen, and other agencies varying from state to state which represent potent political power and which even a strong governor must treat with respect. A governor with weak legislative support is virtually helpless in enforcing his administrative edicts, save in those departments which he can control by appointment. Even here he is likely to be stuck with his original appointee since in many states the governor's removal power does not extend even to the officers whom he appoints. This particular aspect of the inter-relation between the governor's role in management and his role in legislation is sometimes overlooked, but it is of great significance in practical administration.

The more obvious connections between the governor's role in management and his role in policy formation were pointed out in the introduction of this section. The governor must go to the legislature initially with his budget and with other policy proposals. If he is in a strong position with that body, the program which he will be called upon to administer will be largely one of his own choosing. If he is in a weak position with the legislature, the policies which he will administer are less likely to be those of his own choice. In either case, the legislature after the policy decisions have been made is still in a position to influence the administrative process. Acting through its investigating committees, through the power of the senate to approve appointments, and through its post-audit agency, the legislature can harass the governor in the execution of policy, if it so desires. Whether the powers of the legislature are used in this fashion depends largely upon the governor's relations with that body. Let those who see a distinct separation between policy and administration attempt to carry out a program in the face of a hostile legislature and they will quickly become converts to the theory of policy and administration as a continuum.

Even if the governor enjoys good relations with the legislature during its first session, that body is apt to become more recalcitrant in its second session as the governor's power tends to wane. The legislative controls over administration in any state tend to become sharper and more searching during the last two years of a governor's term.

Since the governor in most states lacks the kind of executive control furnished by substantial appointive and removal powers, his most potent weapon of control tends to be the executive budget in those states where he has actual control over the budget process. However, even this control cannot be implemented if the governor does not have appreciable legislative support. In those states where the governor has neither the appointing power or the executive budget, he must rely almost wholly on persuasion to establish his policies in the executive departments. Such persuasion will be effective only if it is backed by the knowledge, on the part of the department head, that the governor will be supported in his actions by the legislature. Consequently, the political setting of the state and, in particular, the governor's position *vis-a-vis* the legislature is of great significance in his role in management.

ONLY TWENTY-FOUR HOURS IN A DAY

The governor in "managing" of the state must operate not only within the legal framework and the political pattern of the state but also under the compulsion of the limited amount of time which he can devote to the managerial side of his duties. It was suggested in Chapter 6 that the governor probably spends no more than one-half and possibly no more than one-fourth of his time on management. The determination of the exact proportion of his time spent on management as opposed to policy formation and public relations will depend to a considerable extent upon the way in which the desk audits and other data in Chapter 6 are interpreted. For example, the governor spends a substantial proportion of his time in interviews. The weight of the evidence seems to indicate that most of these interviews are of a non-management character and are concerned with party or legislative policy or with the complaints and suggestions of the state's citizens. However, if a portion of the time spent on interviews with citizens is allocated to the management category on the basis of the fact that some of the citizens' complaints concern management problems, then the total time spent on management might be increased. Another way in which the time computed for management functions might be increased is to consider the process of budget formation as both a management and policy function and allocate a part of the time which the governor spends on the budget to management. However, even if these more liberal interpretations are used, it is doubtful whether it can be said that the governor spends more than half of his time on management. Governor Kohler of Wisconsin, one of the governors who are firmly convinced of the importance of the governor's role in management, estimated that the governor spends "probably more than half" of his time on policy and public relations, thus leaving somewhat less than half of his time for management. A reasonable estimate of the amount of time spent by the governor on management would seem to be one-half or less of his total working hours over the course of his administration.

It seems unlikely that the amount of time which can be devoted to management can be substantially increased. The governor's policy function is both important and time consuming and is perhaps his greatest contribution to effective state government. His public relations function is less important but is of such a nature that much of it demands the governor's personal participation and, hence, cannot be delegated satisfactorily.

Nevertheless, the governor can be given some additional time by a streamlining of procedures in his office and by the elimination of a multitude of routine chores which are an utter waste of gubernatorial time. As was suggested in Chapter 6, the routine of the executive office can be improved so that the governor spends less time on correspondence, interviews, and public appearances. Furthermore, the governor's duties in each state need to be carefully reviewed so that those duties which are not vital to his three principal functions may be delegated or eliminated. It is nonsense for the governor to waste even two or three hours a week signing hundreds of commissions for notaries public or for justices of the peace. It is equally senseless for him to spend two or three hours a day interviewing job seekers or approving personally of every request for out-of-state travel. Careful consideration should be given to the elimination of these and other similar duties so that the governor may use his limited time to operate at his proper level in policy formation, public relations, and management.

It is probable, however, that even with the elimination of such duties and the improvement of procedures in the executive office the governor will find that he still has a relatively limited amount of time to devote to management. This places an emphasis on the determination of his essential functions in management and on the kind of staff which can be provided to assist him in this aspect of his functions. It is the writer's view that the governor can use his limited time to best advantage if he confines himself to the establishment, co-ordination, and control of policy in the executive branch. The methods by which this may be accomplished are discussed in the next chapter. The problem of providing the governor with the proper staff is discussed in some detail in Chapter 10.

THE GOVERNORS' VIEWS ON MANAGEMENT

The limited amount of time which the governor devotes to management is not entirely indicative of the relative weight which the governors give this function. While there was a definite difference of opinion among the governors interviewed as to the relative weight which should be assigned to management, an over-all evaluation seems to indicate that the management function should be placed second in terms of its importance. That is, management would be considered more important than public relations but less important than legislative policy formation.

This over-all evaluation, however, conceals some rather distinct differences of opinion. At one end of the scale would be the evaluation of the southern governors who on the whole find that policy formation and public relations are more important to their operations than management. As has been suggested previously, this evaluation may be due to the presence of the one-party system in the South, which places primary importance on legislative leadership, and to the weakness of most southern governors in the field of management in comparison to their rather substantial legal and customary powers in legislative policy formation.

At the other end of the scale should be placed some of the governors of the Midwest and Far West who tended to give first rank to management. For example, Governor Johnston Murray of Oklahoma took the position that the management aspect of the governor's functions was of primary importance. He explained this view in one of his weekly radio reports to the people of Oklahoma in May of 1951 by saying that "the *administration* of our laws is the final and supreme test of those laws. Good laws, poorly administered, can sometimes become bad laws. By the same token, the wise administration of a poor law can make it into a good law. . . . As I see it, the primary job of your governor is one of administration."[13]

Most of the governors interviewed would not place such extreme emphasis on the importance of the administration of the laws since the majority seem to feel that the formation of policy is fully as important as its execution. All of them, however, probably would agree that the governor has a definite stake in seeing that his policies are properly administered.

The relative evaluation of the management function is complicated by the time element referred to in the previous section. Many of the governors in discussing this function pointed out that while the management function was important they did not have enough time to devote to this phase of their duties. Hence, the ranking given which placed the function in second or third place is de-

[13] Radio address, May 26, 1951. Italics are the Governor's.

pendent, in large measure, on its inter-relation with policy formation and public relations in terms of time. As has been suggested throughout this book, the attempt to separate policy, public relations, and management is not a fruitful endeavor. This evaluation of the relative importance of these three functions is advanced only to indicate that the governor's primary role in terms of time and of the governors' own evaluations is that of policy formation. This function is the core of the governor's duties but shades into management on one hand and public relations on the other in such a manner as to make a complete separation of the three highly unrealistic.

SIZE—A DIFFERENCE OF DEGREE OR OF KIND?

Some of the raw material out of which state management is fashioned includes the number of persons employed by the state and the total expenditures of the state. Viewed in these terms, the business of the average state is large enough to warrant considerable attention even in these times of astronomical federal expenditures and employment. There is, however, a tremendous variation in the expenditure and employment figures from state to state. For example, in 1950 the total expenditures of New York were $1,375,275,000, while those of California were $1,367,576,000, Pennsylvania $962,283,000, Michigan $655,943,000, Illinois $609,-161,000, Ohio $591,801,000, and Texas $478,121,000. On the other hand, Nevada had a total expenditure of only $21,534,000, Vermont $31,537,000, Wyoming $37,789,000, Delaware $42,172,000, New Hampshire $44,758,000, and Idaho $54,326,000.

The same contrast is found in employment figures, although those states with the greatest expenditures do not always have the largest number of employees or those with the lowest expenditures the smallest number of employees. The pattern, however, is fairly consistent and those states with large expenditures are likely to be those with the largest executive establishments in terms of the number of persons employed by the state and vice-versa. New York in 1950 had a total of 83,300 employees, while California had 73,400 employees, Pennsylvania 68,700 employees, Illinois 41,600 employees, Texas 41,300 employees, Ohio 38,900 employees, and Michigan 37,800 employees. In contrast the State of Nevada had only 2,000 employees, Wyoming 3,000 employees, Vermont 3,600 employees, Delaware 4,300 employees, New Hampshire 6,600 employees, and Idaho 5,900 employees.[14]

A comparison between the two extremes in these sets of figures reveals that the ratio of employees in New York as compared to Nevada is about forty to one while the ratio of expenditures is about sixty to one. Judged on these two standards, therefore, the governor of New York is dealing with an administrative organization which is at least forty times as large as that which must be "managed" by the Governor of Nevada and one which spends sixty times as much money in the course of a year's operation. The variation in size between the operations in New York and those in Nevada is so great that in practice it becomes almost a difference in kind. The fact that the governor of New York must deal with an administrative structure which is so large and complex that it is greater in scope than the governments of many independent nations means that he has a tremendous burden in the field of management. If he is to carry out his management functions in New York, the governor must either devote more time to management or establish rather elaborate institutional devices to assist him in carrying out this aspect of his functions. In New York the latter alternative has been adopted and through several fairly substantial state reorganizations the executive branch has been streamlined so that it has become a more manageable organization. In addition the governor has been given very substantial powers in the field of management, so that he is now one of the best equipped of the states' chief executives in terms of the authority-responsibility ratio. The impact of the vast administrative structure of the state is also seen in the governor's executive office, which under Governor Dewey grew to over forty persons. Additional managerial aids are to be found in a well-organized budget office and a modern personnel agency, although the latter is not entirely under the governor's control. On the other hand, the governor of Nevada is dealing with a much less complex administration and, therefore, can afford to give personal attention to more of the details than can his counterpart in New York. The relatively small size of the

[14] All employment figures are for April, 1950 except those for Michigan which are for March, 1950 and New Hampshire which are for July, 1949. Figures on both expenditures and employment are from *The Book of the States 1952-53*, p. 185 and p. 232.

administrative organization in Nevada is reflected also in a rudimentary budget system and in the fact that the governor has one of the smallest staffs in the United States, with an average of only two persons other than the governor in the executive office. It is quite probable that the governor of Nevada is understaffed, as will be pointed out in Chapter 10, and that his managerial aids are not adequate to the task at hand. However, the fact that he is able to operate with such a small staff and with such limited managerial aids is a reflection of the relative simplicity of the management problem in Nevada.

In discussing the governor's role in management there are very few generalizations which are valid. It is obviously absurd to suggest that the governor of Nevada needs a staff of forty to assist him in management simply because the governor of New York has an executive office of that size. It is quite another matter, however, to suggest that his present staff of two is probably inadequate and might well be increased to five. This would seem to be simply a reiteration of the obvious were it not for the fact that some of the groups which have studied the organization of the executive branch in our states tend to recommend a more or less "standard" pattern of organization and staffing without due regard to the raw materials of administration. The administrative procedures and organization which have proved to be effective in New York cannot be applied in toto to the situation in Nevada without carefully considering which, if any, of these procedures are really applicable to an administrative organization which is only 1/40 the size of that in which the procedures proved effective.

On the other hand, there seems no reason to assume that a device such as the executive budget cannot be applied to states whose expenditures vary greatly if reasonable modifications are made to fit the local situation. Similarly, an organizational device such as a single personnel director who will head the state's personnel agency probably can be used in states which have a considerable variation in their total employment. The key factors in the question of the proper organization for personnel management in a given state may not be the size of the state but the political atmosphere and the customs and traditions of the state in question. While the problem of size should be considered, the key problem is a political one in that those who are to determine the proper type of personnel agency must decide whether or not the ecology of government in the state is favorable to any kind of a merit system. If this decision is in the affirmative and a merit tradition exists, it is probable that a single director will be acceptable. On the other hand, if there is a distinct anti-merit tradition in the state, it may be that the commission form would be more likely to produce the popular confidence necessary for the initial establishment of a merit system of any sort. The size of the state is but one of the factors which must be considered, but it does deserve more consideration than is sometimes accorded it.

Because of the variety of factors to be considered in an analysis of the proper powers and institutional arrangements which should be established in a given state so that the governor may be able to play his proper role in management, the proposals made in this chapter and in Chapter 10 on the governor's staff should be viewed simply as suggestions for application in any given state. Most of the suggestions are based on procedures and institutional arrangements which have operated successfully in one or more states. This does not mean that they will necessarily operate successfully in any given state and the fact that these proposals are advanced certainly should not be taken as an attempt to establish them as immutable principles. However, if state government is to progress and if it is to perform in any measure as a laboratory of government, then what has been tried in one state and found to be successful should serve as the basis for the solution of similar problems in other states. What is suggested here is that we must be sure that the problems are actually similar. If the difference in the scope of state functions in one state is so great that the difference becomes not only one of degree but of kind, then the situations are not similar and it is foolhardy to propose the same solution to the problem. Nevertheless, the experiments in management which have been undertaken by some of the states should be examined carefully by those who are concerned with management in a given state, and if the difference is found to be one of degree rather than kind and if the other factors in the ecology of government seem favorable, the new device might well be attempted in the state under consideration.

Of course, the size of the state does not determine the strength or weakness of the governor in the management field and does not determine his need or lack of need for additional power. Some of our smallest states, like Nevada, are those in which the greatest administrative confusion reigns and those in which the governor's powers are at their lowest ebb. On the other hand, some of our larger states, like New York, are those in which the governor is best equipped in terms of power to perform his management functions.

In addition to the question of size and the governor's legal powers, the customs and traditions of the state regarding the proper role of the governor should be taken into consideration. Ordinarily, such customs and traditions tend to form an upper limit as to what is politically feasible in any attempt to revise substantially the governor's powers and sometimes also affects the type of institutional aids which can be expected to operate with any degree of success.

What is suggested here is that the determination of additional powers needed by the governor and the institutional arrangements which should be made to facilitate his role in management should be based on the needs of the state and that no ideal organization or set of powers is equally applicable to all our states. This view receives support from the lack of success in some of the recent reorganization attempts. This lack of success may have been due in part to an effort to equip the governor with a more elaborate set of powers and aids than the state required and its present administrative development permitted.

THE NEW FEDERALISM—BANE OR BOON?

Thus far in this analysis of the governor's functions, the discussion has been centered largely on these functions as they were performed within particular states as though these states were separate entities. It was suggested in Chapter 1 when the political structure of the states was discussed that concentrating on the internal political situation of the states revealed a pattern which was false to a degree because it ignored the national connections of the state's political parties. Similarly, in this chapter the concentration on the governor's functions in relation to management within the limited frame of reference furnished by each state presents a pattern that is also false to a degree, since the state government over which the governor presides actually does not operate as a separate entity in our federal system. Instead, the state governments primarily through the existing grant-in-aid programs have been integrated into a network of partially federally financed but generally state administered programs in such fields as highway construction, land use, social security, employment security, public assistance, forest management, hospital construction, tuberculosis and venereal disease control, airport construction, civil defense, and the construction of school facilities in areas overburdened by federal activities, such as atomic plants and military bases. The impact of these programs on state policy in these fields and their implications in state finance and administration should not be ignored in considering the governor's position.

The policy implications of the federal grant-in-aid system are fairly obvious and can be readily illustrated from the examination of any one of these programs. In the field of highway construction, for example, the governor may campaign on the basis of more farm-to-market roads. When he gets into office, however, he may discover that because of a recent change in federal highway policy the state has far more funds available from the federal treasury for the construction of major highways than it can hope to obtain for farm-to-market roads. If the governor persists in his attempt to construct farm-to-market roads, many of these roads may have to be constructed on state funds alone or on state funds matched by some local funds. Under these conditions the expenditure of the same amount of state money might result in a smaller mileage of farm-to-market roads than of primary roads, since state money used on the latter could be matched dollar for dollar by federal funds. The governor, therefore, finds himself impaled on the horns of a nasty political dilemma. If he continues with his avowed policy of farm-to-market roads, he may be able to retain the political support of those who were in favor of this program. On the other hand, his opponents in a succeeding election can claim that he was profligate with the state's funds, since he did not use them for the type of highway construction which would produce the greatest miles per tax dollar spent, and this argument may be very effective in discrediting the governor's administration.[15]

[15] This is not entirely a hypothetical situation since the 1950 campaign in Alabama was partly concerned with just such an issue. Governor James E.

Even if it is assumed that the federal policy remains constant during the campaign and at least for the first year of the governor's term, it is still obvious that his stand on highway matters in the campaign and, hence, his recommendations to the legislature will be influenced by the federal policy on grants-in-aid for highway construction. If the federal policy stresses primary highway construction and makes available federal money on a matching basis for this purpose, a gubernatorial candidate will think twice about advocating farm-to-market roads which do not fall in the category which will receive federal aid.

Every year in almost any state there are examples of programs which are undertaken primarily because there is federal money available for these programs on a matching basis. The programs themselves may be highly admirable, and it is doubtful if any of them do not benefit the state. However, it is debatable whether the programs undertaken under the influence of available federal grants are *more* beneficial to the state than other programs which could be undertaken. The governor and the legislature in making policy decisions among the many programs urged upon them for their consideration by various groups within the state are not as free as they were prior to the development of the federal grant-in-aid system to make a choice of the programs on the basis of their relative merit. It is not suggested, of course, that these are the grounds on which the decision would necessarily be made in any case. What is suggested is that the presence or absence of a federal grant-in-aid program in a given field is a powerful factor which conditions the legislature and the governor in making alternative policy decisions. In practice, therefore, the governor finds that his policy decisions are conditioned by the policy decisions which have been made in Washington in these fields. To be sure

---

Folsom (1946-50) had concentrated his highway program on farm-to-market roads, some of which were built largely out of state funds. Gordon Persons, one of the candidates for governor in the Democratic primary, used this as an issue in his campaign and promised that, if elected, he would begin a program of major highway construction. Governor Folsom was not a candidate, since under Alabama law the governor may not succeed himself. Philip Hamm, the Governor's Director of Finance, was a candidate, however, and was necessarily running on the record of the Folsom administration. After a hot race, Mr. Persons was elected.

the governor does not have to accept federal funds and may, if he desires, recommend to the legislature that no state program be undertaken in certain of these fields. The lure of "free money" is a very powerful one, however, and it is doubtful whether the state legislature would go along with any proposal which was drastically counter to federal policy in these fields. In many of the poorer states, the funds received from the federal government have become the first or second major source of revenue for the state. In such situations, it is quite clear that federal policy will be a powerful influence on state policy and that state funds tend to be diverted to those areas of operation in which federal funds are available. It is not within the scope of this study to attempt to determine the desirability of the grant-in-aid system or the desirability of the present formulas for the distribution of funds and the standards established for the administration of these programs. It is pertinent, however, to point out the very considerable influence of these programs on state government both from the point of view of policy and of administration.

From the administrative point of view a federal grant-in-aid program may tend to weaken the governor's channels of communication with the agencies which receive federal funds and to weaken his control over those agencies. The pattern of administration which has developed in some of these programs involves a good deal of direct contact between individuals at the state level and the agency of the federal government which supervises the program. The governor, to a considerable extent, is by-passed in this line of communication and finds that his control over both policy and management of the agencies which administer these programs at the state level is weakened considerably.

The imprint of federal policy also is found in the administrative structure and the procedures of the state agencies participating in federal grant-in-aid programs. One obvious example of the influence of federal policy on state administrative procedure which has fairly important implications for the governor's role in management is the requirement under the present Federal Social Security Act that the employees of state agencies which receive funds under this legislation must be chosen under a merit system. This has resulted in the establishment of merit systems covering these agencies in those states which did not have a merit system acceptable to the federal authorities. In most of these states this federally inspired merit system is still the only merit system in the state government. The employees of the other departments of government are selected under a spoils system developed in the particular state.

While the writer personally accepts the merit principle of personnel selection as being conducive to good management, it should be pointed out that the imposition of such a system from the outside does not necessarily strengthen the position of the governor. In many states where these systems were adopted, it seems fair to say that they were adopted with the unwilling acquiescence of the governor. The presence in the executive branch, but presumably independent of the executive, of a personnel agency which controls under guidance from Washington the personnel policies of the agencies which it serves may weaken the governor's hand in management. This situation, however, and others which result from the sometimes reluctant acquiescence of state authorities to federal standards are illustrations of the rather substantial effect which grants-in-aid have on administrative procedures and administrative structure at the state level.

Because of the policy and administrative implications of the federal grant-in-aid system some governors are inclined to take a rather dim view of the effects of such a system on the governor's position. For example, one of the governors interviewed took the position that if the federal grant-in-aid programs are extended gradually to cover all the major fields of state governmental operation and if the conditions attached to these grants continue to look toward a standardized organization and procedure and, in practice, a standardized policy at the state level, the governor would become the "manager" of an executive branch which is made up primarily of agencies really operating under the administrative direction of Washington. He contended, moreover, that the governor is so limited already in his dealings with certain departments of the state government and so circumscribed in his preparation of the budget because of the persuasive power of the lure of available federal funds that he is no longer the master of his own household. This view is not typical of that of most of the governors interviewed, but many of those who did not take this extreme position did express concern over the effects of the federal grant-in-aid system on the powers of the governor in both policy and management.

The problem suggested here is only a symptom of a much more basic problem which seems central to the proper operation of the federal system itself. That problem is the proper division of tax resources between the states and the federal government. This problem was stressed by several of the governors interviewed and was regarded as the central problem in federal-state relations by the heads of most of the revenue and budget agencies interviewed. What has happened in the last fifty years is that the federal government gradually has invaded more and more fields of taxation which were once regarded as the province of the states. As this has come about, the states, who also have been feeling the pinch of inflation and the increased cost of government made necessary by citizen demand for new services, have been forced to use hitherto untapped tax sources, including the much-debated sales tax.

A complete discussion of this problem is beyond the scope of this book, but at least it can be pointed out that in the opinion of many governors a realistic view of federal-state relations requires that the whole system of federal grants to states be re-examined with a view toward developing a more rational basis for federal grants and especially of integrating the tax structures of the state and federal government.[16]

There is, however, another aspect to the federal grant-in-aid picture which should not be overlooked. While undoubtedly it is true that federal control in the form of standards and procedures tends to go along with federal funds, it also is true that the states occupy a key position in all of these programs, for it is the states rather than the federal government which actually administer the programs. The states stand as an intermediary between the federal government and the cities, towns, and the countless individual citizens who will be the recipients of the

[16] This general point of view is expressed in an article by Governor Alfred E. Driscoll of New Jersey in *The Tax Review,* VIII (December, 1947), 53-56, in which he argues for an over-all policy on federal grants, some of which he feels should be eliminated on the grounds that they do not fill a "demonstrated need." The Governor also argues for "an integration of federal and state tax structures which will free for state use those sources of revenue which are best adapted for state administration."

services provided by these programs. The states are the funnel through which this golden stream from the national treasury flows and are also the valve which regulates the volume of that flow, for in many of these programs no federal funds can be spent without prior approval by the states and the volume of the flow is in large measure determined by the state's willingness to match or partially match federal funds.

The states have become the focal point of national problems flowing downward and of local problems rising upward. To be sure, the federal government has gone into many fields which formerly had been the province of the states and may have reduced to some extent the state's prestige in these fields and the governor's control over these functions. But, and this is an even more important consideration, many of these programs are in fields into which the state government had never before ventured. Further, in speaking of a majority of these programs, it actually is misleading to say that the federal government has gone into these fields. What actually has happened is that the states with federal funds and under federal supervision have increased their programs in the older functions such as land use, highways, and health; and, under federal auspices, have started a number of new programs such as old age assistance and unemployment insurance in the social security field. While it is unrealistic to deny the factors of national control which are inherent in these programs, it is equally unrealistic to think of them as entirely national programs. The fact is that they are joint national-state programs in which the states have come to play an increasingly important role. The fact that the state, not the Federal Government, is the administrative unit to which the citizen and local units of government turn for aid and direction in these programs has increased greatly the prestige of state government. This increased prestige has been reflected in the increasing prestige of the office of governor. It may be, therefore, that the governor owes some of his present relatively high prestige to the very grant-in-aid programs which some exponents of states' rights see as handwriting on the wall predicting the doom of the states.

It seems highly unlikely that there will be any decrease in the federal grant-in-aid program. Indeed, the signs point to the adoption of new programs, particularly in the field of education and perhaps in the field of health insurance. Consequently, no matter what view is held as to the desirability of such programs it seems clear that they must be considered as a part of the environment in which state government and the governor as the state's chief executive must operate. The realities of present national-state relations call for the recognition of the importance of the grant-in-aid system to the state's governmental life and for devising ways and means by which the state government may best profit from its very substantial share in these systems.

One of the reasons why the federal government tends to deal directly with the heads of agencies in certain fields is that they are in practice quite independent of the governor and, hence, it is rather impractical to attempt to go through the governor in dealing with these agencies. The independence of agencies in many of these fields is not the result of any direct federal provision which requires their independence except in one or two cases such as the personnel boards previously mentioned. Much can be done to improve the organization of state government so that the governor will be in a position to control the agencies affected by federal programs and can be logically the focus of communications from Washington to those agencies.

There seems to be some recognition even at the federal level of the desirability of clearance through the governor when he is in a position to make that clearance practicable. For example, a report by the National Security Resources Board in 1950 suggested that "in matters of civil defense, the Federal Government will deal directly with the State, *i.e.*, with the Governor, or if he so delegates, with the civil defense director."[17] This sort of thinking at the federal level could do much to improve the governor's position in the management of programs which are partially federally financed if the organization of state government is such that the governor's participation is meaningful. What is needed in addition to federal realization of the desirability of making the governor a part of the process is the reorganization of the executive branch in many state governments to make such participation practicable.

Even without federal recognition of the desirability of including

[17] National Security Resources Board, *United States Civil Defense* (Washington, 1950), p. 5, quoted in *The Book of the States 1952-53*, p. 40.

the governor in the grant-in-aid process, the states can take some steps to improve the co-ordination of these programs. Some of the larger states have established a Washington representative who can deal with the federal agencies on policy matters, particularly in the fields in which federal grants-in-aid are of considerable importance. California, New York, and Massachusetts are three of the states which have such a representative, and in time it is probable that more states will join them in establishing this sort of liaison. This is only one approach to the problem and may not be the most desirable solution, since many of the smaller states may not be able to afford such a representative.

An alternative approach also exists in those states where the governor has a close relationship with the administration in Washington. In these states there is the tacit understanding that major policy changes will be cleared through the governor's office. A recent study of the governorship in the New England states points out that in Connecticut under Governor Bowles "the Governor was the focal point where Connecticut's part in the New Federalism centered. The Governor's office remained constantly briefed on the flow of grants-in-aid."[18] In this case the close relationship indicated was possible because of the friendly relations between the Governor and the Administration in Washington. It is doubtful whether such a close relationship prevailed between Washington and some state capitols whose chief occupant was not of the same political party as that in control in Washington.

The problem of federal-state co-ordination in relation to grant-in-aid programs is a difficult one. However, if the governor is to play his proper role as an instigator and co-ordinator of state policy some more uniform solution to this problem must be reached. The most fruitful approach seems to lie in a two-way attack on the problem. From the state side, the governor must be made the master of his own household so that he will be in a position to deal with the federal government on such matters. From the federal side, there must be a recognition that the governor has a legitimate interest in these programs and at least should be informed on major policy changes. Further, this co-ordination must not be left to chance or be subject to occasional co-ordinating

[18] Robert C. Wood, "The Metropolitan Governor," an unpublished Ph.D. dissertation (Harvard University, 1950), p. 50.

influence which comes as a result of the President's personal or political affiliation with the governor. Such personal liaison will, of course, continue to occur and is helpful to those states which are fortunate enough to have a governor with such contacts. This sort of arrangement, however, leaves the states whose governors happen to be of the opposite political party at a distinct disadvantage, and this does not seem to be an area which should be deliberately left to partisan influences. A recognition on the part of the federal agencies concerned that the governor, no matter what his political party, is the chief executive of the state and should be dealt with on policy matters would go a long way toward improving federal-state co-ordination on this very important segment of state affairs.

9. THE GOVERNOR'S ROLE IN MANAGEMENT: POLICY CONTROL

THE VIEW ADVANCED in the foregoing chapter was that the governor's primary function in management is the establishment of policies for the guidance of the various agencies which make up the executive branch and the general supervision of those agencies to ensure the proper execution of those policies. To a lesser extent, the governor must be concerned also with the coordination of the policies of these agencies when their programs fall in the same general area of governmental operation.

The essential problem of the governor in regard to management therefore is the control of the policies of the agencies under his "supervision." As was pointed out in the preceding chapter this "supervision" is more imaginary than real. The governor is not established by the constitution in most states as the sole executive but only as the "chief" among several executives. He is handicapped in his operations by having a short stay in office, since he has either a two-year term or is prevented from succeeding himself in most states with a four-year term. He is further restricted in his attempt to act as chief executive by the fact that he does not appoint and cannot remove the heads of many important agencies in the executive branch. In addition he is beset by a lack of time to devote to this aspect of his function and finds himself somewhat circumscribed in his establishment of administrative policies by the effects of the federal grant-in-aid system. Then, too, he finds that even if he is granted limited powers in management he can operate effectively as an administrative policy maker only if he has substantial legislative support.

It is small wonder that most governors faced by this array of discouraging factors choose to concentrate on legislative policy making or public relations and tend to make only halfhearted attempts to be the chief executive in fact as well as in name. However, some of them do make the attempt and many of them succeed in spite of the difficulties which confront them. It should be emphasized also that there are a few states in which the governor's administrative powers and the state organization are such that he is in a position for really effective management, granted at least some legislative support.

In spite of a series of state reorganizations, however, most of the governors do not find that they have available the powers which the literature on administrative reorganization generally prescribes as basic to gubernatorial control of the executive branch. These prescriptions invariably include the concept that first of all the governor must be able to appoint the heads of his principal departments and be able to remove those department heads at will so that he can control the policy of the respective departments. This power generally is reinforced with the power to make up the executive budget which is viewed as a device both for the establishment of policy and for policy control. The budget together with centralized accounting, the pre-audit, and a system of quarterly allotments serves as a fiscal control system for the orderly expenditure of funds. More recently there has been considerable emphasis on the need for centralized purchasing to go along with the other fiscal controls. In addition, it frequently is suggested that the governor be able to control personnel through his power to approve additional personnel for the departments, promotions, within-grade pay increases, and other personnel actions. All this is to be accomplished generally either through the governor's staff, through a budget and a personnel agency in the governor's executive office, through a centralized department of finance, through a department of administration, or through the appointment of a "general manager."

All of these devices have been used separately or in combination by one or more states. Most of the states have not attempted to establish a short ballot because this would require constitutional revision—deemed to be politically impractical. A few states such as New York, New Jersey, Virginia, and Tennessee have made substantial progress in establishing the short ballot by providing that the governor be empowered to appoint the heads of the major departments of government. In several other states the constitutional officers have been retained as elected officials, but the governor's appointing power has been extended by statute to include the principal department heads other than those prescribed by the constitution. On the whole, however, it would be fair to say that the governor's power of appointment, and particularly his power of removal, is distinctly limited in most states

The short ballot is certainly a desirable concept and should serve as a guide for future state reorganizations. It seems unlikely, however, that the short ballot will be established in the near future in many states because of the opposition of the present elected officers and their legislative supporters. The views of these officials on the short ballot are discussed in Chapter 11 in considering the question of democratic control over a reorganized executive branch.

Whether or not this prediction as to the difficulty of establishing the short ballot is correct, the fact is that at the present time the governors in most states must "manage" a large group of agencies, the heads of many of which are not persons he has appointed. Consequently, consideration must be given to the practical problem of how the governor can achieve policy co-ordination and control in a situation which is far from ideal from his point of view.

CO-ORDINATION BY PERSUASION

One of the devices which has been tried in a number of states in an attempt to secure policy co-ordination and control is the use by the governor of cabinet meetings of his department heads. This was one of the recommendations in the early state reorganizations and it remains as a part of the standard recommendations of most bodies which study the organization of the executive branch. The central idea is that the governor is to call together the heads of the major departments of state government either weekly or monthly to discuss current problems and to secure their advice on policy matters. These discussions are also to be used to inform the department heads of the governor's policies and to co-ordinate the programs of the various departments.

It is difficult to determine just how successful this prescription has been or how widely it has been applied. While the question was raised with most of the governors and with other officials interviewed, the answers were not uniform. In many states cabinet meetings are not used at all, and, consequently, no evaluation can be made of their possible efficacy. In other states the governor interpreted the term "cabinet" to mean informal meetings of three or four department heads in whom he had the most confidence. Judged by this standard the governor was using "cabinet" meetings and generally felt that they were useful in both policy co-ordination and formation. This sort of a cabinet meeting does not seem to be the kind of thing that the advocates of state reorganization have in mind in prescribing the cabinet as a coördinating device. In this section these meetings are called group conferences and are distinguished from cabinet meetings which presumably should include all of the major department heads. In a few states the governor actually does have meetings of most of his department heads which could be properly characterized as "cabinet" meetings. It was interesting to note, however, that even in these states the judgment of the governor and those who attended these meetings was not always the same as to their value. For example, in one midwestern state the governor felt that such meetings were valuable, one of the department heads who was in the cabinet felt that the meetings were valuable, while two others felt that the meetings were of little value. Consequently, it is not easy to make valid generalizations concerning the effectiveness of cabinet meetings as a policy co-ordinating and forming device. In the paragraphs below some of the experience pro and con is presented and an attempt is made to analyze the value of the cabinet in some of the states where it has been used.

In the South in recent years only three states, Virginia, Kentucky, and Alabama, have used the cabinet with any degree of regularity. In Virginia, cabinet meetings were held by Governor Byrd, but the use of the cabinet was not continued by his successors. In Kentucky there is a statutory requirement that the governor hold regular cabinet meetings. In spite of this provision, cabinet meetings seem to have been held with any degree of regularity in recent years only by Governor A. B. Chandler and Governor Earl C. Clements. In Alabama there was intermittent use of the cabinet under Governors Sparks and Dixon and there were fairly regular cabinet meetings under Governor Folsom. However, Governor Folsom's cabinet meetings consisted only of some of the department heads appointed by the Governor and, consequently, were more in the nature of a group conference than a full cabinet meeting. Governor Folsom in the last two years of his first administration also used the cabinet in a very interesting manner. He had a series of so-called "cabinet meetings" at various cities and towns throughout the state. Present at these meetings were the Governor and some of his principal appointed department heads. These meetings were open to the public and were designed, according to the Governor, to keep the people informed about the state's business. In practice, therefore, these cabinet meetings were a public relations device rather than a method for co-ordination or policy formation.

Before leaving the South, it should be pointed out that the term "cabinet" has a special meaning in Florida which seems to be peculiar to that state. While we do not find the collective responsibility in Florida which we do in Great Britain and other cabinet governments, there is some superficial resemblance between the two forms. In Florida there is really a plural executive system under which authority if not responsibility is lodged with six elected department heads, who, with the governor, make up the cabinet. This group is recognized by both the Constitution and the people as an important part of the governing process, and frequent reference is made in the press to cabinet actions. The collective responsibility of these officials as the cabinet, however, is very limited. In practice the executive responsibility is spread among officials who are independent of each other and responsible only to the electorate. These six elective officials (the attorney general, treasurer, commissioner of agriculture, secretary of state, superintendent of public instruction, and comptroller) plus the governor, serve as the body through which co-ordination is supposed to be obtained. A recent committee appointed to study the executive branch in Florida, however, found that co-ordination

> . . . may be obtained only by agreement. The Governor, charged by the Constitution as Florida's chief executive, has no direct authority over the Cabinet or the activities in the several departments headed by these cabinet members. Only through his prestige, personality, and party leadership can the Governor assume the

responsibility vested in him by the Constitution but also denied him by that same instrument in providing for the election of cabinet officials.[1]

A cabinet meeting in Florida is not like that in other states in that it is not looked upon as a meeting of the governor and his chief advisers but rather as a meeting of the major executive officials of the state with the governor presiding as chairman. The so-called "chief" executive has a vote and undoubtedly has a great deal of influence but can be, and sometimes is, outvoted by his colleagues. Under these circumstances, the governor is but one of several executives and can become the chief executive in fact as well as in name only if he is able to carry his cabinet with him. In commenting on the results of this system the Joint Committee reports:

> . . . Fortunately, the position of the Governor has on the whole been such that co-ordination has been the rule. To prevent friction from occurring, action has sometimes been postponed or not taken. This "do nothing" may be worse than friction. But, friction, independence of action, and failure to act has occurred in the past and there is no guarantee that they will not again develop in the future.[2]

The key position held by the Cabinet is further enhanced by the power vested in the cabinet as a group or in several of the cabinet members as various *ex-officio* boards. Florida has gone further than most of the states in providing for the conduct by *ex-officio* bodies of much of the State's most important administrative business. Most of the key administrative functions are handled by the four constitutional and 34 statutory *ex-officio* boards now in existence, and 32 of these 38 boards are wholly or partly made up of cabinet officers.

The governor serves on 24 of these *ex-officio* boards, the secretary of state on 15, the comptroller on 19, the treasurer on 21, the attorney general on 21, the commissioner of agriculture on 13, and the state superintendent of public instruction on 10.[3]

[1] *Report of the Special Joint Economy and Efficiency Committee of the Florida Legislature of 1943* (Tallahassee, 1945), p. 21.

[2] *Special Joint Economy and Efficiency Committee,* p. 21.

[3] *Special Joint Economy and Efficiency Committee,* p. 22. As might be expected, these extensive memberships are a great drain on the time of the cabinet members. The head of one department estimates that he spends 50 per cent of

Outside the South cabinet meetings have been tried in several states with mixed results. Leslie M. Gravlin, describing the Minnesota experience with a Department of Administration, discusses the use of the cabinet in that state as a device for co-ordinating administrative policy. He points out that the commissioner of administration serves as a sort of buffer between the governor and his department heads but observes that

> Obviously, no law can prevent department heads from going to the governor with their worries but in my own experience there was exceedingly little of that. In this connection it might be pointed out that an important instrument in promoting direct relations between the commissioner and the various departments was the cabinet meeting which was held at frequent intervals. At such conferences, presided over by Governor Stassen, the policies to be carried out through the commissioner of administration were clearly outlined for department heads. Thus the governor relieved himself of many individual meetings with the administrators of the operating agencies.[4]

The cabinet also has been used in the past two terms by Governor Kohler in Wisconsin. The Governor's explanation of why he instituted a regular meeting of his department heads and the values which he felt resulted from such meetings are most interesting. In discussing these points, Governor Kohler said that the

> . . . formal powers of the governor as state manager do not really constitute the necessary tools for leadership, and I and my immediate predecessor have found it useful to supplement them with many informal arrangements designed to keep us abreast of the current business of the State.
>
> In some respects the most useful device we have developed is the periodic meeting of the department heads, at which time we discuss numerous problems of general interest to the State. Such problems as reducing employe turnover and absenteeism, the proper use of state-owned vehicles, the type of planning that ought to be included in developing building programs, the weak spots in office management, the reduction in departmental publishing—all of these have been considered.
>
> The governor has received the benefit of the experience of the department heads while they, in turn, have heard his recommen-

---

his time on *ex-officio* board duties. He felt that the assignment of cabinet members to such posts has now "reached the point of diminishing returns."

[4] Leslie M. Gravlin, "An Effective Chief Executive," *National Municipal Review*, XXXVI (March, 1947), 139.

dations looking toward the most effective utilization of public monies. At some of the meetings early in my own administration I brought in experts in management from the outside to instruct us in and stimulate us to better practices.[5]

In several states, of which Colorado and California are two examples, an attempt has been made to secure some degree of inter-departmental co-ordination through what is known as the governor's council.[6] The governor's council in Colorado was established in 1941 and is made up of the major elected and appointed administrative officers. The council is supposed to meet monthly to discuss matters involving general administrative policies and inter-departmental relations. However, the council in Colorado does not seem to have ever been used as the statute directs and is inoperative at the present time.

The governor's council in California was established in 1927 and is a going concern, although it has not been used by all the California governors since its inception. Governor C. C. Young held regular monthly meetings, but these were discontinued under Governor James Rolph, Jr. Governor Frank F. Merriam held a few fairly unproductive meetings and his successor, Governor Culbert L. Olson, also held a few meetings of the council in the latter part of his term. Governor Earl Warren held council meetings regularly and the council apparently functioned more effectively under Governor Warren than under any of the California governors except possibly Governor Young.

[5] Governor Walter J. Kohler, Jr., "The Governor's Office," *Wisconsin Magazine of History,* XXXV (Summer, 1952), 311.

[6] The governor's council in these states is not to be confused with a body of the same name in Maine, Massachusetts, New Hampshire, and North Carolina. The councils in these states are composed of from five to nine individuals whose duty is to advise the governor on state policy and approve the governor's appointees. In Massachusetts and New Hampshire the members of the council are popularly elected, and in Maine they are chosen by the legislature. The North Carolina "council of state" is made up of four state officials serving *ex officio* and has some powers in the field of finance, such as the approval of expenditures from the governor's contingent fund. These councils are a relic of the colonial days and are really intended to serve as a check on the governor rather than to serve as policy-coördinating bodies. Their importance in state government varies from state to state, but in none of these states do they seem to be groups on which the governor depends for advice in policy formation. Because of their composition they seem not to be useful as co-ordinating bodies.

An interesting footnote on the experience of California with the use of the council is that it follows a pattern which was duplicated in the experience with the cabinet in Virginia and New York. In each case the governor under whom the state's first major reorganization took place, *i.e.,* Governor C. C. Young in California, Governor Harry F. Byrd in Virginia, and Governor Alfred E. Smith in New York, all used the cabinet or council during their term of office but the device was abandoned by their successors and has been revived only in the case of California. All three of these governors believed that the cabinet device had merit and all felt that it formed an important method of co-ordinating the state's business. Yet, the point of view of governors Byrd and Smith was not adopted by their successors, and the council was revived by Governor Warren in California only after a lapse of a considerable period of time. One of the reasons for this may be that the problems of reorganization are such that there is a great deal of new administrative policy to be threshed out among the department heads and that a cabinet is extremely useful in assisting in this operation. After the administrative structure and procedure has become more fixed, the problems of administrative policy are not as pressing and cabinet meetings do not have the same urgency.

As the council was organized in California under Governor Warren, it was composed of the heads of most of the larger state agencies. The membership of the council is prescribed by statute and the list of agency heads involved has been revised from time to time. Most of the agency heads who are members of the council by law are appointed by the governor. Governor Warren, however, adopted the practice of inviting the elected department heads as well as his own appointees to attend the council meetings. Thus, a meeting of the governor's council as constituted by law and by practice involves approximately 35 individuals who are the heads of the most important state agencies.

The council meets at Sacramento on the last Monday in each month. These meetings consist primarily of short reports by agency heads on developments in their departments which they believe will be of interest to the group as a whole. The reports do not cover in detail the activities of the department, since each department reports in writing to the governor several days before the council meeting covering the activities of his department during the period since the last council meeting.[7] These reports are sent to the governor's departmental secretary who analyzes and summarizes them.[8] This summary is sent to the governor, together with the original reports, and a copy of the summary also is sent to each member of the council. This summary has proved to be a very useful device for keeping the department heads informed on the activities of other departments and is one which might prove valuable in other states, even if no council or cabinet meetings are held.

Governor Young was a firm believer in the cabinet device. In his inaugural address of January 4, 1927, he recommended the reorganization of state government and a "governor's cabinet or council, to the end that at regular meetings there may be discussed in orderly fashion the various problems which confront the state." The council was established in 1927 and in his First Biennial Message on January 7, 1929, Governor Young reported that the council had been meeting regularly and that it was proving to be very valuable. In Governor Young's Second Biennial Message on January 5, 1931, he still felt that the council was a valuable device and summarized its purposes and values by saying in part

> The creation of a Governor's Council has served at least four purposes, each of them so important as to make it almost indispensable in any departmentalized form of government: First, it brings together those in charge of various governmental activities,

[7] The writer attended a meeting of the Governor's Council on June 25, 1951. The meeting was held in the office of the Superintendent of Public Instruction in Sacramento. Fourteen official members of the Council were present, together with eight invited officials, the governor's departmental secretary, and Governor Earl Warren. Each department head reported in turn on what he felt had been significant developments in the work of his department since the Council last met. Three of the department heads stated that they had nothing to add to their written reports. Governor Warren commented on several of the points raised and also commented on the general results of the legislative session which had just been completed. He felt that even though a number of important matters had been voted down by the Legislature, the educational work done on such programs as aid to the disabled, and some of the programs for seniles, the acute mentally ill, and alcoholics would bear fruit in future legislative sessions.

[8] The position of departmental secretary has interesting possibilities as a device for policy co-ordination and will be discussed in more detail in the chapter on the governor's staff.

and furnishes opportunity for unifying those activities such as would never be possible when boards, commissioners, or even departments have no contact, one with the other. Second, it keeps the Governor continuously informed as to the progress of the state's government from month to month, with only a fraction of the time and effort which would be required in a constant endeavor to learn about each department separately. Third, it gives to the Governor a body much like a President's cabinet, consisting of council members, each especially concerned with the work of his own department, but all acquiring a general knowledge of all departments, and consequently always available to the Governor for counsel and advice. And fourth, by the very necessity of these monthly reports to the Governor in the presence of his fellow directors, each director is stimulated to his best efforts to keep closely in touch with activities of each division in his department.

Governor Warren also was a firm believer in the council device and attempted to extend its possible value as an instrument for inter-departmental co-ordination by inviting some of the principal elected department heads to attend the meetings in addition to his major appointed department heads. He also attempted to improve the value of the meetings by introducing the system of written reports so that the meetings themselves could be devoted to developments after the written reports were submitted or to topics of general importance.

Most of the department heads interviewed in California who were members of the council felt that the meetings had considerable value. The two most often mentioned results of the council meetings were that they kept each department head informed on important developments in departments other than his own and that they gave each department head an opportunity to meet with the heads of other departments and thus become better acquainted with the agency head as well as with its program. Several of the department heads pointed out, however, that the council was too large and of too heterogeneous a composition to materially assist the governor as a policy-making body. They also pointed out that one of the principal defects in the California plan was the fact that the council meetings were open to the public and to the press. This makes it virtually impossible for the governor to discuss really significant policy matters, since any discussion which hinted at disagreement among the governor's department heads probably would be heralded in the press with the headline "Governor's

Appointees in Row Over Proposed Policy Changes." Consequently, the council meetings generally are devoted to fairly innocuous reports. According to the department heads interviewed, the important problems of inter-departmental co-ordination both on policy and administrative matters are handled by the inter-departmental committees of the council which meet with the governor in private in the afternoon following the general council meeting.

The California experience shows that the cabinet device can be useful in acquainting department heads with the work of their colleagues and in promoting mutual acquaintance among the department heads themselves. The Minnesota and Wisconsin experiences show that, in addition, the cabinet also can be used to explain administrative policies which are common to more than one department. This use of the cabinet was the one which was mentioned most frequently by the department heads interviewed in those states where cabinet meetings are held regularly. Some of the examples which they gave of the agenda of various cabinet meetings included such matters as forthcoming state-wide pay increases for state employees, the installation of a personnel classification system, certain changes which were to be made in the preparation of the budget, changes in the purchasing procedures, and policies on the use of state-owned automobiles. Most of these new procedures already had been decided upon by the governor in consultation with the commissioner of administration, the budget officer, the personnel officer, or other appropriate state officials and were, in effect, simply being announced and explained to the department heads. In some instances, these proposed changes were discussed in the formative stage and the comments of the cabinet members taken into consideration in their preparation. This consultation aspect of the cabinet meetings which was emphasized by Governor Kohler seems to be the exception rather than the rule in most states, and most of the meetings seem to be those in which administrative policy is "clearly outlined for department heads," to use Gravlin's phrase.

It seems probable from the experience in several states that the cabinet is useful as a device for explaining policy; it is not as clear, however, that it is equally as useful as a device for policy formation. It is interesting to note that many of those interviewed in states where there was a cabinet or a council pointed out that the present group was too large for effective action and that its heterogeneous composition, since in most states it was composed of both the governor's appointees and of elected officers, made it unsuitable as a policy body. The same two defects were pointed to by several of the governors who were not using the cabinet as reasons for their failure to hold cabinet meetings. One governor pointed out that if he called all of his department heads together, he would have "a mass meeting." On the other hand, he said that if he attempted to limit the cabinet to a manageable size, he ran the risk of alienating the support of those agency heads who were not included. Many governors probably would feel that the governor of California is fortunate to be able to hold a council meeting made up of his major department heads and the elected officers and still have a body of only about 35.[9]

Since the organization of the executive branch in most states is such that it contains a large number of agencies, if the governor attempted to call the heads of these agencies together as a cabinet, he would certainly have a "mass meeting." Of course, it would not be necessary to include the heads of all the agencies in his cabinet. However, if the group is to be limited, as it must be if it is to be of any practical value, a nice problem is presented as to which agency heads should be included in the cabinet. One logical basis on which to make this choice certainly would be the relative importance of the functions of a given agency. The choice here is not as simple as it might seem, however, for one immediately runs into the problem of overlapping functions. For example, when a state has a Department of Industrial Relations and a Department of Labor, as does the State of Alabama, and both of these agencies deal with the general problem of industrial relations, which of these two department heads should sit on the cabinet? This example can be repeated in any state in almost any of the various functional fields of state government, and, as a result, it is extremely difficult to select a cabinet of a reasonable size which is representative of the major state functions. This problem will continue to plague those governors who attempt to use the cabinet until a stage of state administrative development

9 See the foregoing section of Chapter 8 on "Chaos in Eden" and the studies of the organization of the executive branch of the respective states mentioned in this section.

is reached in the respective states at which the number of agencies is substantially reduced and the functional overlap and conflict now rampant is resolved by the establishment of a small number of functionally integrated departments. This millennium is far from a reality in most states and, unfortunately, does not appear to be just around the corner.

In addition to the problem of unwieldy size, the present system of selecting potential cabinet members is a very serious handicap in most states. If the cabinet is to be a group of advisers to the governor, then a minimum basic requirement is certainly that the individuals who make up the cabinet should be appointed by the governor. Again, this situation is approached only in a few states such as New Jersey, New York, and Virginia, and even here the governor does not have complete authority to appoint all of his major department heads. In the remainder of the states if the governor calls a cabinet meeting, he discovers that anywhere from one-third to two-thirds of his cabinet is made up of agency heads whom he did not appoint. These individuals are selected in a number of different ways. The variety of methods used seems to be limited only by the ingenuity of the respective state legislatures, and new methods of selection are constantly being devised by enterprising legislators. Among the most common selection methods are election by the people of the state as a whole, election by the voters in certain geographical districts (this applies primarily to boards or commissions), appointment by the governor, selection by boards or commissions which in turn may have been appointed by the governor or may have been elected, selection by the legislature, and selection by private organizations such as veterans groups or professional associations.[10]

It is obvious that the governor is not likely to turn to such a heterogeneous group for advice and counsel and that its use as a control and co-ordinating device is limited to the governor's persuasive ability. These defects are, of course, greatly aggravated

[10] Perhaps the extreme in the dispersal of authority is found in situations where a department head is selected by a private organization. For example, in Alabama the State Health Officer is appointed by the State Board of Health which is *ex officio* the Medical Association of Alabama. In this instance, one of the governor's principal department heads is actually selected by a private organization which is completely outside of the government.

when there has been a change in political parties and the governor discovers either that not all of his ticket for the elected offices has been successful and that some of his cabinet are newly elected members of the opposite party or that there are several "hold-over" officials from the past administration who because of their lengthy terms are still in office.

In view of the problems inherent in the size and composition of the body which would form the governor's cabinet, if it were called into session, it would seem that its usefulness in most states will depend in a considerable measure on basic changes in the structure of the executive branch. Those who envision the cabinet as a device for policy formation and co-ordination are obviously working from the premise that the executive branch will be made up of a small number of major integrated departments whose heads would be appointed by the governor. This actually is not the case in most states. Consequently, the cabinet cannot perform the functions suggested for it, because the structure of the executive branch is such that the premise upon which the cabinet idea is based is not valid; and, hence, the conclusions based on that premise are not valid. This leaves open the possibility that with substantial state reorganization to produce the conditions on which the premise is based that the conclusions could very well follow. The cabinet idea, therefore, may not be unsound but simply inoperable because the states have not yet reached the stage of organizational development where it can be tried under optimum conditions.

On the other hand, there is some reason to question the concept of the cabinet as a policy body even if the present handicaps of excessive size and heterogeneous composition can be overcome. The failure of some governors to use the cabinet probably is due to a considerable extent to the personality and working methods of particular governors. Apparently, there are some governors who do not feel entirely at ease in a large group of department heads and who prefer to work through individual conferences or conferences with two or three department heads as the need arises. Governors of this temperament will not be likely to use the cabinet even if it were administratively practicable.

A more serious defect in the rationale of those who advocate the cabinet as a device for policy formation is their failure to give sufficient weight to the basis on which the governor's appointments to cabinet posts have been made in the past and seem likely to be made in the future. The process by which department heads are actually selected does not seem likely to produce that kind of policy adviser that is envisioned as a department head by those who advocate the cabinet. At present, the heads of most of the departments of state government who are appointed by the governor seem to fall into two broad categories. The largest category is formed by those department heads who are appointed for political reasons. These appointments are made as a result of campaign promises, as rewards to the party faithful, as rewards for unusually large campaign contributions, to cement an alliance with a particular faction of the party, to help build a legislative bloc, or for some similar reason. The persons appointed as a result of these considerations may be qualified for the position to which they are appointed or may be totally inept in their role. It is fallacious to assume that appointments dictated by political considerations are necessarily "bad" appointments. Some department heads appointed in this fashion turn in very creditable performances, although many do not. The point at issue here, however, is not whether the appointments are "good" or "bad" but whether appointments of this type tend to give the governor a group of individuals to whom he will turn for policy advice. The answer is generally in the negative. To be sure, the kind of advice that the governor is seeking is political advice in the broad sense of the term and such advice must come from a group which is appointed for political reasons. However, a group which is appointed as a result of the kind of political pressures suggested above are not necessarily those whom the governor would appoint if he had a really free hand in the matter. Consequently, they generally are not individuals in whom the governor has confidence and to whom he would turn for advice on policy problems.

The other major category of department heads, which is increasing in number at the state level, is made up of professional administrators in certain substantive fields such as health, welfare, mental hygiene, social relations, corrections, and industrial relations. These men are appointed because of their presumed qualifications as administrators in a particular substantive field and frequently are drawn from other states, major cities, or sometimes from the federal service. Governor Warren of California made several appointments of this type. For example, in selecting a Director for the Department of Mental Hygiene, he appointed an individual who was then serving in a similar capacity in Los Angeles County and who had served with distinction in several other states. This appointment was made only after a competent committee had made a survey of possible appointees and had recommended the person actually appointed by Governor Warren as the best qualified individual available. The same system was used in the selection of a Director of Social Welfare. This type of appointing process, which is somewhat comparable to merit-system procedures for high level appointments, is coming into more general use in the states as a whole, particularly in fields where it is felt that the department head needs a professional background. This type of appointment has the very distinct advantage of producing a capable administrator who is well acquainted with the subject field with which he will deal. The transfer of personnel at the department head level from state to state and from city to state, while it has not reached substantial proportions, may be the forerunner of a sort of nation-wide career service for department heads in certain fields which is much like the career service that is now growing up among city managers. While this system of appointment produces capable administrators, it tends to move even further away from the type of individual to whom the governor will turn for advice on policy matters. If carried to its logical conclusion, this system will result in the governor's cabinet being a group of high level specialists in various subject fields. Such a group probably would not be the best possible cabinet for the consideration of broad policy matters.

In the writer's view it is too much to ask that a department head be able to run his own department effectively and at the same time serve as one of the governor's advisers on policy matters. Certainly, some department heads are both able administrators and able politicians, but the combination of a technically competent administrator with the kind of individual to whom the governor will turn for broad policy decisions is relatively rare. The average department head is involved in running a fairly complex operation of his own and tends to be immersed in the problems of his own department. He also tends to be the defender of the department against all comers, whether they be other department heads, the legislature, or the governor. Hence, most department heads are not equipped to take the broad view of the whole operation of state government necessary for an individual who will serve as an adviser to the governor on policy matters. Similarly, they are not as likely to see the political repercussions of suggested programs, particularly if their own departments are involved.

The history of state government, and of the national government for that matter, does not seem to point to the likelihood of the cabinet being used as a policy body. The past has seen the emergence of the "kitchen cabinet," the "brain trust," and other unofficial bodies which were used by the executive for policy advice. In many states there are such groups as the "little cabinet" in Florida, which is composed of a small group of the governor's advisers outside of the regular cabinet, and the now famous group of Governor Dewey's advisers which met every Monday night during the legislative session to plan the next week's legislative program. The composition of these groups is as varied as the personalities of the governors themselves and no valid generalizations can be made as to either their composition or their actual influence, although the latter seems considerable in some states.

The existence of these groups points to what at first glance might seem a serious problem for democratic government, namely the formation of policy and the wielding of considerable influence by persons who are not responsible to the public or to the legislature. However, it must be remembered that this group can speak only through the governor and that while his decisions may be influenced by this group, those decisions, if they are of far reaching importance, usually result in a proposal for legislation which then comes before the scrutiny of the public and more particularly the legislature. The governor must have advice, and if our system is not set up in such a way that that advice will come from the cabinet or other public body, it must necessarily come from a private body. The governor's staff needs in the policy field are fully as acute as his staff needs in the management field, although the need is not as generally recognized even by the various commissions which have studied the executive branch in recent years.

The question of a policy staff is quite important and will be discussed at some length in the succeeding chapter.

In most states the possibility of using the cabinet as a device for policy formation and co-ordination has either never been explored or its use has been rejected as impractical. The governor, nevertheless, is faced with the need for some method of securing policy co-ordination. In lieu of the cabinet, the most widely used method is the individual or group conference with certain department heads. If the governor has the kind of personality and managerial ability which enables him to work well with other officials, this device may prove to be fairly satisfactory. Nearly all of the governors make some use of this method and several of them have used it successfully under rather adverse conditions.

In some cases the governor is left with little alternative because of the peculiar structure of the state's government. For example, while the governor's council in Colorado has never been used as it was originally intended, most of the Colorado governors have used the conference method with some degree of success. The governor in Colorado is forced to use some sort of persuasive technique since the department heads in Colorado, unlike their counterparts in most states, come under the state's merit system. Consequently, it is possible for the governor to come into office with a full complement of department heads who have been appointed by his predecessors over a period of years. Therefore, it is essential that the governor of Colorado be able to persuade these department heads of the validity of his program and of the necessity for co-ordination. Some of the governors of Colorado have been able to do this with considerable success.

In most of the other states the governor appoints at least some of his department heads, but many of the others are selected in such a way that the governor has no direct control over them in terms of either appointment or removal power. Consequently, the individual and group conferences are widely used as a means of persuading the department head of the desirability of the governor's program and of the necessity for co-ordinating the work of his department with that of other departments.

Those who advocate that the governor should appoint all of his department heads sometimes do so on the basis that unless he is given this power total discord and stalemate will result. This possibility also has been suggested earlier in this book. In fairness to those who oppose this view, it should be reported that, in general, the elected department heads are inclined to go along with the governor. One of the department heads interviewed explained this by saying that after all the governor had a mandate from the people for a particular program, and if that program did not appear to be destructive of his department or actually contrary to the public interest, he was willing to go along with the program. It might also be pointed out that in the case of some of these department heads the governor has some community of interest through the fact that they are of the same party, or the same faction of the dominant party, as the governor. Consequently, they are inclined to follow the governor's leadership as the titular head of the party. Furthermore, the governor frequently has some control over these departments through his powers in connection with the executive budget and through appropriation and personnel controls, particularly if he has a strong power base in the legislature. This is not always true, however, since some of the department heads are virtually assured of an appropriation because they operate on revenues from certain earmarked taxes. If a department head is an elected official or if the agency is headed by an elected board or a board with long staggered terms and at the same time the agency has a virtually assured source of income, the governor finds himself in a very difficult position if a department so situated refuses to go along with his program.

In fairness to those who recommend that the governor appoint his major department heads, it also should be reported that there was considerable evidence that the governor is opposed from time to time by certain elected officials and that this opposition has had unfortunate results in terms of a unified program.[11] While

[11] See Coleman B. Ransone, Jr., *The Office of Governor in the South* (Bureau of Public Administration, University of Alabama, 1951), pp. 104-106 for a discussion of a recent conflict between the Attorney General and two successive governors in Florida. Another version of this lack of co-ordination is found when two of the elected officials engage in open warfare and the governor is powerless to resolve the conflict. Albert Gorvine describes such a dispute between the Comptroller and Treasurer in Nevada over the distribution of federal money connected with the Boulder Dam project in his pamphlet, *Administrative Reorganization for Effective Government Management in Nevada,*

such conflicts are not rare, the evidence collected in a fairly substantial number of interviews with state officials, both elected and appointed, does not show that open warfare between the governor and the elected officials is the usual pattern.

Nevertheless, the presence of a large number of independent department heads has greatly complicated the governor's already difficult role in management. Even if the department heads generally do "go along" with the governor, the fact that they are independent and that they must be persuaded either through personal conferences with the governor, by the implied threat of reduced appropriations or reduced personnel where this is within the governor's power, and occasionally even through the exercise of the governor's patronage power, simply places in the governor's way an additional hurdle in terms of securing policy co-ordination. There seems to be no counterbalancing advantage to this system either in terms of democratic control or more effective administration. Therefore, it certainly does not follow that such a hurdle is desirable simply because the governor manages to get over it in most instances. The governor has enough problems in the field of management, among which the problem of policy co-ordination is one of the most important, to justify any steps that might be taken to improve his chances of success in the management field. One desirable step would be to provide that the governor appoint and be able to remove for policy reasons the heads of the major departments in the executive branch.

In several states there has developed a system of inter-departmental committees which seems to hold some promise as a method for achieving policy co-ordination. For example, in California the governor's council is subdivided into a series of standing committees. These committees are relatively small and unlike the council their business is conducted in private. For example, the Institution and Social Welfare Committee which is one of the largest of the council's subcommittees is made up of the director of employment, director of the youth authority, chairman of the adult authority, director of corrections, director of industrial rela-

a report prepared for the Nevada Legislative Council Bureau (Nevada Legislative Council Bulletin No. 4, 1948), p. 32. Gorvine concludes that "when a serious controversy between two major officials becomes public knowledge, the entire administration appears to bad advantage in the eyes of the voters."

tions, director of mental hygiene, director of public health, director of social welfare, and the director of recreation. These gentlemen meet with the governor and discuss problems in the general field of social welfare. Their discussion may concern a new program which is being proposed or may concern the implementation of programs already in existence. Since the group is small enough for real discussion, since they meet in private, and since the department heads involved have a certain community of interest, some effective co-ordination can be accomplished, policy decisions made, and legislation, if this is felt necessary, can be decided upon at least in its broad outlines. This legislation can then be prepared and introduced by one of the department heads involved or can become a part of the governor's program. Most of the department heads interviewed were favorably disposed toward the committee system and emphasized the fact that the real business of government was carried on in these committees rather than in the council meetings themselves.

The inter-departmental committee system in New York is more elaborate and somewhat more formalized than that in California. It is based on the same basic concept but has been established independently of the cabinet, which was not used to any great extent under Governor Dewey. In New York there is a fairly elaborate system of inter-departmental committees at the department head level and also a series of inter-departmental committees below this level. Committees of the latter type frequently are appointed on a short-term basis by the heads of the departments involved to work out the co-ordination problems in a particular program affecting more than one agency or to plan a program in a particular field which will require legislative implementation. Most of the department heads interviewed in New York placed considerable emphasis on the system of inter-departmental committees and indicated that they have been useful in both policy formation and co-ordination.

The experience of New York and California with inter-departmental committees seems to have been in general rather satisfactory. However, the committees in these two states usually are made up of department heads who are appointed by the governor and, consequently, may be more effective than they would be if they were composed partly of the governor's appointees and partly of elected officials. This may be a limiting factor in the usefulness of the inter-departmental committee in states where many of the important executive officers are elected or are selected in such a manner that they are not under the governor's control. In spite of this possible limitation, the favorable results obtained in New York and California suggest that the use of such committees might be explored by other states in which the governor is having difficulty in achieving policy co-ordination.

The question of policy co-ordination and control remains as the governor's major problem in the management field. One approach to the problem is through such devices as the cabinet, individual and group conferences, and inter-departmental committees which were considered in this section as methods of co-ordination by persuasion. Another approach, which can be regarded either as an alternative to the first approach or as complementary to it, is through the medium of fiscal controls. This approach is considered in the next section of this chapter.

Before leaving this section, however, it might be well to point out that in several states the governor has attempted to delegate some of his duties in policy co-ordination to a member of his staff. Such delegation has proven reasonably successful in those states where it has been attempted and will be discussed in more detail in the following chapter on the governor's staff. It should be noted in passing, however, that such delegation cannot solve the basic problems which confront the governor when he finds himself in a position where persuasion does not seem to be enough and he lacks such punitive powers as the power of removal or of fiscal controls which can be used to back his persuasive powers. On the other hand, if the governor does have the requisite power, then the delegation to a member of his staff of the preliminary responsibility for inter-departmental co-ordination may prove quite useful. This is true even in a small state, but the environment of administration is generally such in the smaller states that the governor will find that he must participate personally in many administrative activities which can be handled by the governor's staff in the larger states. The development of such a position as the governor's departmental secretary in California or the director of administration in Minnesota holds much promise in the direction of reducing the governor's work load in policy co-ordination and control.

CONTROL VIA THE PURSE STRINGS

This phrase probably brings to the mind of most readers the classic position of the legislature as the agency which controls the purse strings and thereby determines the policies under which the executive branch will operate in a given fiscal period. In this section, however, the idea of fiscal control will be broadened to include those controls over the fiscal process which can be made available to the governor through the preparation of the budget and through the control of the spending process, once the legislature has enacted the budget in the form of an appropriation act.

The prerogative of the legislature in appropriating the funds for the operation of the executive branch is a jealously guarded right which on many occasions in the history of its development in England was the cause of hard-fought battles between the Crown and Parliament, some of which were literally military conflicts. In the Colonies under the Royal governors, the right of the legislature to appropriate continued to be a bone of contention between the governors and the elected assemblies. It is not surprising, therefore, that the primacy of the legislative branch in this field was assured in the early state constitutions by provisions which stipulated that no money was to be expended for the operation of the government save by an appropriation of the legislature. The democratic control over the appropriation process was further insured by the provisions in these constitutions that all money bills should originate in the lower house. The result was that early in the history of the state governments the legislature's authority to appropriate was firmly established.

This authority has not been challenged even in this era of rapidly rising state budgets. However, it actually may be somewhat modified in practice by the complexities of the modern budget and the failure of the legislature to provide itself with the proper staff in its important financial committees so that the budget may receive the thorough review to which it should be subjected. Its oversight of the spending process also is weakened considerably in several states by the fact that the post audit is performed either by an elected officer or by an official responsible to the governor.

It is the writer's opinion that the heart of the governmental process is the preparation of the budget and the legislative review of that document which results in an appropriation act establishing the pattern of the state's function for a given fiscal period. While the executive budget is essential to the governor's policy program and is one of his most important methods of fiscal control over the executive branch, it can become destructive of democratic government if it is not subject to careful legislative review and if the legislative authorization to spend is not carefully checked by an effective post audit conducted by a legislative agent. One of the serious weaknesses in state government at the present time is in the fiscal process. On one hand, the governor is given neither the time nor the staff to prepare an adequate budget, and that budget when completed does not cover all the major functions of state government. On the other hand, the legislature does not have the proper organization and staff to review the budget adequately. In addition, in many states the post audit is either not conducted by a legislative agent or is conducted by a legislative agent so poorly staffed that his review is several years behind the actual spending process.

The whole tenor of this book is to emphasize the need for a strong governor who is equipped with both the powers and staff necessary to do an adequate job in the formation of policy, in the explanation of that policy to the citizens of the state, and in the supervision of the agencies who will carry that policy to fruition. This emphasis should not conceal the fact that the writer is equally desirous of seeing a legislative branch which can perform adequately its function of reviewing that policy in the light of its interpretation of the public will. This interpretation may at times be different from that of the governor. Certainly at times the governor will feel that the legislature out of partisan considerations has sabotaged a program which he feels has overwhelming public support as evidenced by his election. On the other hand, the legislature will at times see itself as the guardian of the public interest against a "dictatorial" governor. Such differences in points of view are bound to arise under our particular form of democratic government and on occasion both sides probably are correct in their interpretation. At other times, the struggle is more clearly partisan and the delays involved less justified. Nevertheless, the submission of the governor's program to legislative scrutiny and review is a vital part of the process of democratic government. The delay entailed by such a process and the differences of opinion engendered may be a source of bitter comment by the governor, the legislature, or the public. The latter in particular is apt to mutter about the apparently needless jockeying back and forth and is apt to suggest rather forcefully that its elected representatives should get on with the business of government. Yet, it is out of these maneuverings that some consensus is reached as to the public interest and the programs which should be undertaken by the state. The legislature and the governor have the very difficult task of trying to match unlimited demands for governmental services with very limited state resources. This process takes time, and it involves much political give and take, but it is a vital part of the governmental process.

The organization which has evolved for handling executive-legislative relations at the state level is far from perfect and the need for improvement of this aspect of state government is nowhere more evident than in the field of fiscal affairs. The present trend toward the executive budget and a set of improved fiscal controls under the governor's supervision has improved greatly his position *vis-a-vis* the legislature in this field. These additional powers coupled with the governor's already substantial general powers in the fields of legislation represent a real challenge to legislative supremacy in the field of state finance. Increased attention should be given to the problem of implementing adequately the important legislative responsibilities in this field. While any complete prescription for this implementation is both beyond the scope of this book and beyond the capabilities of its author, it is suggested that a three-fold approach to this problem might prove useful. This approach might include consideration of the overhaul of the present committee system used in most state legislatures for the handling of the governor's budget. As presently constituted, the legislature's machinery for handling the budget in most states includes an appropriation committee in the house which receives the document and subjects it to initial review, a ways and means committee in the house which next considers the document from the revenue aspect, and two companion committees in the senate which actually repeat the process while maintaining the fiction that they have only the power to amend the house appropriation bill. This procedure is cumbersome, time-consuming, and ineffective. It could be improved by a consolidation of the two house committees into one finance committee which could consider the governor's budget as a unit, giving due consideration to both the spending and revenue-raising aspects of the document. To avoid the repetition of this process in the senate, the senate committees should be consolidated also into one finance committee which could meet with the house committee, thus eliminating duplicate review and at the same time strengthening the actual review of the document by allowing more time for more thorough consideration.

The second avenue of approach might be a consideration of legislative staff. The legislature needs more and better staff attached to these committees so that it may have an independent source of information on the state's fiscal affairs for comparison with the governor's estimates. The state budget is a very complex document to the average legislator, or to the student of government for that matter. The legislators need adequate information on which to base their evaluation of the governor's proposals. The question of adequate legislative staff is not an easy one. If carried too far, it results in a complete duplication of the executive budget agency, which is a waste of state money and can lead only to conflict and the destruction of the executive budget. If the legislature has no staff, it is not prepared to make anything more than a partisan appraisal of the governor's budget, which may do more harm than good. Obviously, the legislature needs more staff and a better trained staff, but the exact size and institutional arrangements which will be conducive to a good legislative product can be determined only after careful study of the individual legislature.

Finally, the writer feels that it is very important that the legislature have a post-audit agent who can render current and accurate reports on what the executive branch is actually doing with the funds which the legislature has appropriated. This elementary check over the executive is found in far too few states.

Certainly the evaluation of what agency X should have in the forthcoming fiscal year should be based in part on the use the agency made of the funds it was given in the previous year. At the least, the legislature would like to know whether the department head's new Cadillac was a product of an appropriation designed to buy several new trucks or was the result of a fortunate marriage. It also might want to know not only whether the money was spent honestly and for the purposes set out in the appropriation act but also whether the agency made efficient use of its funds. This is a much more difficult question for the auditor to answer and might require considerably more than the standard fiscal audit. Yet, with the proper staff a good auditor might be able to come up with a reasonable estimate. Even if the legislature does not wish to push its inquiry to this point, it certainly cannot act with any degree of effectiveness unless it can get an accurate picture of what the agency spent in the last fiscal period and for what purposes these funds were used. To be sure, the governor may include such a report in his budget or if it is not found in the budget, it may perhaps be found in the elected auditor's report, if he is within three or four years of current expenditures, or it might be found in the elected comptroller's reports. However, the legislature should not be forced to depend on these possible sources for its fiscal information. It has a right to get a complete, unbiased financial picture of state governmental operations, and, human nature being what it is, there is some reason to expect that its best chance of getting such a picture might be from its own agent.

There are indications that more and more state legislatures are beginning to adopt something of this attitude toward the fiscal process. In California, the legislature has established a legislative budget officer who is called the Legislative Auditor. This title is a misnomer, however, for the "Auditor" does not conduct the post audit but has the duty of maintaining liaison with the executive department on fiscal matters and of providing the legislature with estimates by which to judge the soundness of the governor's budget. The legislative oversight of the budget process in California even extends to having the legislative budget officer sit in on the budget hearings between the governor's budget officer and the department heads.

In Oklahoma, the legislature recently has created a "legislative audit committee" within the State Legislative Council. This committee is charged with the function of making "a continuous audit and analysis of the state budget, revenues and expenditures during and between sessions of the Legislature. It shall be the further duty of the Committee to ascertain facts and make recommendations to the Legislature and to the houses thereof concerning post audit findings, the revenues and expenditures of the State, and of the organization and functions of the State, its departments, agencies, boards, commissions, offices, authorities and subdivisions, with the view of reducing the cost of the state government and securing greater efficiency and economy." The same act also authorizes the State Legislative Council to appoint a Legislative Auditor who is to act as secretary of the audit committee and who is to conduct a continuous selective post audit of expenditures by the various state departments.

Wisconsin also has added two budget analysts to the staff of the Division of the Budget who are to work under the supervision of the budget director. These individuals are technically on the staff of the budget director and, hence, on the surface are under the direction of the governor, since Wisconsin has an executive budget, at least in theory. However, it is interesting to note that in discussing this addition to the budget staff with members of the legislature, these members referred to the new personnel as "our" budget analysts. In practice they probably will actually work on projects suggested by the legislature, if they follow the pattern which the legislature apparently envisages for them.

These are but three examples of an apparently widespread resurgence of legislative interest in the whole fiscal process. While this interest has not always taken the most productive forms, the fact that the legislature is awakening to the need for more staff and more information on the whole fiscal process is one which seems to be on the credit side of the ledger.

The present division of labor which has grown up in most states having the executive budget breaks down the fiscal process into four steps. Each of these steps is under the general control of either the governor or the legislature, although at any phase of the process the control exercised may be weakened considerably by the lack of proper powers, organization, or staff to handle adequately the demands of a particular step in the fiscal cycle. The first step in this process is the preparation of the budget. This function is assigned to the governor who includes in the budget both his plans for spending and his plans for raising revenue, if the latter are necessary to present a "balanced" budget. The second step is the review of the budget by the legislature for conformance with the legislative concept of proper state policy. This review is done primarily by the finance committees of the House and to some extent by their companion committees in the Senate. The third step is the control over the expenditure of funds through such devices as the pre-audit, accounting controls, purchasing controls, and a system of quarterly allotments. These controls should be under the supervision of the governor, but in many states they are badly split among several officers in the executive branch, such as the comptroller, treasurer, and auditor. These officials frequently are popularly elected officers and, consequently, are not under the governor's control. This usually leads to a rather involved fiscal system and sometimes may lead to an impasse in state fiscal operations. The final step is a post audit which should be conducted by an agent of the legislature. Again, there is little consistency in the assignment of this function which in some states is the work of a legislative auditor, in others of an elected auditor or comptroller and in still others, of an auditor appointed by the governor. This section is primarily concerned with the first and third steps in this fiscal cycle, since these involve the preparation of the budget and control over the spending process, both of which are legitimate concerns of the governor.

Some forty states are now listed as states having an "executive budget." However, it should not be assumed that there actually is an executive budget in all of these states or that the budget actually is an important device for policy formation and co-ordination. In theory the executive budget serves three purposes. It is the major vehicle of the governor in presenting his policy to the legislature; it is the major method by which the legislature reviews state policy; and it is an important means of internal policy control over administration. From the governor's point of view, however, if the executive budget is to attain the high purposes suggested for it, the budget process must meet certain qualifications in terms of gubernatorial control. In the first place, the concept of the budget as a major expression of gubernatorial policy and as an important method of administrative control generally demands that the governor be able to control the official who prepares the budget. In the second place, it is necessary for the budget officer to have an adequate staff of trained budget analysts who can prepare a budget which is an accurate expression of the governor's proposed program and who can analyze the estimates of the various agencies in the executive branch so that they can detect any policy overlaps or conflicts and any departures from the governor's major program outline. Thirdly, there must be an adequate period between the time the governor takes office and the time when the budget must be presented to the legislature so that the budget document can be thoroughly reviewed. It is obvious that the preparation of the budget is a matter which requires several months of detailed work. Therefore, an incoming governor cannot expect to be able to prepare an entirely new budget in the short time which he is now allotted in most states. Even if he were allowed a period of one or two months after he takes office, he would still have to accept much of the detailed work done by the outgoing administration. Nevertheless, a longer period would give the governor the opportunity at least to determine that the budget reflects his major policies. In order to assist the incoming governor in preparing a meaningful budget there should be some provision made for a smooth transfer of the budget function from one administration to the next. Finally, the budget should cover all the major departments of government.

Unfortunately, the executive budget systems of most states do not meet these criteria, and in so far as they depart from them the governor is weakened in his participation in the fiscal process. In the case of the first suggested qualifications, an analysis of the governor's relation with the official who prepared the executive budget shows a considerable weakness in the governor's position in fiscal management in some states. It also shows the fine gradations which develop through custom or through statutory prescription within what is rather loosely called "an executive budget system." If the states were ranked according to gubernatorial control over the budget officer, there would be a number of different groups of states ranging from complete control to almost no control.

This may be illustrated by three or four examples which by no means exhaust the possible variations. At one end of the scale would be a state like Virginia where the governor not only appoints the budget officer and can remove him at his pleasure but that official heads a division in the governor's executive office. Next would come a state like Alabama where the budget officer is one step removed from the governor's appointing and removal power. In that state the governor appoints the director of finance who in turn appoints the budget officer, who is the head of one of the divisions of the Department of Finance. The budget officer in this situation comes under the merit system, which covers division heads in Alabama, and, therefore, cannot be removed by the governor for policy reasons.

Following Alabama might be placed the system used in Wisconsin where the governor appoints the budget director with the advice and consent of the senate, but that official has a six-year term as compared to only a two-year term for the governor. Further, the budget director can be removed by the governor only with the consent of a majority of the senate, thus placing him for practical purposes beyond the governor's control for policy reasons.

Texas perhaps follows Wisconsin in descending order of gubernatorial control, although the situation in that state is so confused that its system cannot be placed with any accuracy. In Texas there are two budget systems and two budget directors. One of these budget directors is appointed by the governor and is located in the executive office. The other is appointed by the Legislative Budget Board and is properly regarded as a legislative agent. The results so far under this system have been that the legislature has ignored the governor's budget and has used that of its own budget officer as a basis for its actions of appropriation. This system has been established only recently so it is difficult to predict the outcome of the dual system. However, as it is presently arranged, it does not give the governor a very powerful voice in the state's fiscal affairs.[12]

[12] See Stuart A. MacCorkle and Dick Smith, *Texas Government* (New York, 1952), pp. 49, 99, and 160, for a discussion of this system.

Next in line would come those states which have a commission form of budgeting and at the far end of the scale, in theory at any rate, comes Arkansas, which still retains the old legislative budget.[13]

The experience of these states with these variations of the executive budget does not prove conclusively that the governor should be able to appoint and remove the budget officer at his pleasure. The experience in Virginia, where this is the case, has been very satisfactory and lends support to this line of reasoning. On the other hand, the governor in Alabama has not experienced any real difficulties from a control point of view with his budget officer and the governor in Wisconsin generally has also been able to make his policy views effective.

Perhaps the best arguments for making the budget officer a gubernatorial appointee with no strings attached to his removal come in the experience of such states as Texas with its confused dual system, or Arkansas with the legislative budget, or in the states with the commission budget. Here, experience has pretty clearly demonstrated the need for an executive budget under a director appointed by the governor with no competing budget officers and no shared authority. However, the proof of the pudding is in the eating and if such a system as that in Wisconsin, which seems to be an administrative anomaly, is functioning satisfactorily, there seems no reason to make a change simply for the sake of conformity. On the whole, it seems desirable for the governor to appoint the budget director and to be able to remove him for policy reasons. This is reasonable since the budget is, or at least should be, the governor's primary policy vehicle. However, the writer is no believer in attempting to change the customary pattern of a state simply for the sake of conformity to this concept

[13] The effects of commission and legislative budgeting on the governor's position in fiscal affairs is discussed at some length in Ransone, pp. 155-182. This book also spells out in more detail the various control devices used by the governor in his attempts to secure a degree of control over the spending process. While the states involved in this study are all in the South, it so happens that all three of the major budget forms are well represented in this area. Arkansas, which is the only state with the legislative budget, is in the South, as is Virginia, which is a good example of a budget system directly under the governor's control. The commission form also is well represented by the systems in Florida and South Carolina.

if the customary system is, in fact, a satisfactory one. On the other hand, for many states where the governor has little or no control over the budget and where the present system is not satisfactory in the judgment of those who have given the matter careful study it seems to be time for a change.

The governor's functions in policy formation and co-ordination require that if he is to present the legislature with a budget which actually will be "a work program in terms of dollars and cents," then he must be able to control the preparation of that document. This normally means that he must be able to appoint the budget director. It also means, however, that the budget office must be adequately staffed. The lack of staff is one of the most serious weaknesses in the executive budget system in those states in which the governor has actual as well as theoretical control over the preparation of the budget. While there are a few states in which the budget office has an able, trained staff which includes professional budget analysts and trained personnel in the organizations and methods field, such well-staffed states are in a distinct minority.

The budget staff and the governor must also have sufficient time to prepare the budget, certainly more time than is currently available to most incoming governors. It is obvious, of course, that the preparation of the budget is a project which requires months of work and cannot be started from the ground up after a new governor takes office. Much of the detailed work must be done under the outgoing governor because of the time-consuming nature of budget preparation. However, it is also reasonable to suggest that the governor have at least a month after he takes office to review the budget and make any major policy changes which he feels are necessary to bring the budget in line with his program. A system such as that used in Wisconsin where the incoming governor is authorized by statute to conduct budget hearings before he actually takes office has much to recommend it. The provision in the Wisconsin statute which makes it mandatory that these be open hearings is not conducive to the free exchange of information and does not allow the incoming governor to conduct the budget hearings in such a way that they will be of maximum benefit to him in the subsequent budget preparation. However, some system designed to effect an orderly transfer of the budgeting function from one administration to the next seems highly desirable.[14]

It also seems evident that if the state budget is to be a really meaningful policy document and if it is to be useful in terms of control, it must cover all, not just a small part, of the major functions of the state government. In the writer's opinion the most serious single weakness in the budgetary process at the state level at present is the fact that in far too many states the governor's budget covers only a fraction of the state's total expenditures. This is due in large measure to the fact that the budgets of the states as a whole are characterized by a remarkably large proportion of the budget being made up of expenditures from "earmarked" funds. In many states such expenditures are not included in the budget at all while in others they are included, but their inclusion only camouflages the fact that the governor has practically no control over such expenditures. For example, the functions of the highway department in many states are financed by a state gasoline tax and the receipts from this tax go into a special highway fund. The money in this fund can be spent only for certain specified purposes, primarily the construction and maintenance of state highways, the state's contributions to the Federal grant-in-aid system for highway construction, and the operating expenses of the highway department. In some states the estimates of the highway department are not included in the budget. In others, they are included but the governor has little option except to report the amount recommended by the highway commission, since the funds from which these expenditures will be drawn cannot be spent for any other purpose. Further, in several states the highway department is not subject to the usual fiscal controls once the legislature has appropriated. When the governor is confronted with a highway commission which is made up of popularly elected commission members whose term is probably longer than that of the governor, and

[14] It is interesting to note that the change-over in the National administration in 1952-53 was accompanied by an attempt to provide this sort of budgetary liaison. On the suggestion of President Truman the incoming President, General Eisenhower, appointed a representative to sit in with the Bureau of the Budget in the preparation of the final budget of the Truman Administration which would become the initial budget of the Eisenhower Administration.

at the same time this group controls a function which is financed from a special fund, he finds that he is dealing with an agency which forms its own little empire within the executive branch. When this example is repeated, as it is in many states, so that it covers 50 per cent or more of the state budget, it is obvious that the budget loses much of its meaning as an instrument for policy formation and co-ordination. In addition to the departments which are financed from earmarked funds, there are in most states certain departments, usually those under elected officers, which are exempt from the usual budgetary and fiscal controls either on the basis of statutory exemption or on the basis of custom and tradition. The net result of earmarked funds and exemptions from the governor's budget is that it turns out to be a budget for one-half or one-third or sometimes as little as one-fourth of the state's expenditures. Such a budget has little meaning in terms of policy or of administrative control, although the system may be admirable for the departments which it does cover. Great caution must be used lest the term "executive budget" delude the reader into thinking that a given state has a meaningful budget which lives up to the great potential of a truly comprehensive executive budget.

The various techniques used in fiscal control through the pre-audit, the quarterly allotment system, accounting controls, and purchasing have been well discussed in other writings. It is not necessary for the purposes of this chapter to review these methods. What is suggested here is that the governor's role in management should include not only the preparation of the budget but also the control over the expenditure of funds. The latter aspect of his fiscal functions is necessary if he is to exercise any real control over the executive department. This is important in all the states, but it is particularly important in those states where the governor's appointing and removal power is limited. If it is not practicable to secure the constitutional revision necessary to give the governor the power to appoint his department heads, it may be practicable to secure the centralization of the revenue and financial control functions in one or two departments whose heads are appointed by the governor. Through these departments the governor can exercise considerable control over the spending process in the respective departments, and this control can be made a real policy control over the programs of those departments.

In most states the governor probably will find it expedient to delegate the day-to-day operations in this field to a member of his staff or to a department head whom he appoints. Some of the institutional arrangements used in the respective states to obtain this end are discussed in a succeeding chapter. The exact institutional arrangement will depend primarily on the size of the state and on other factors which will have to be determined on a state-by-state basis. The important point for this discussion is not the particular institutional arrangement but the acceptance of the idea that the governor should have the power to control expenditures.

This theory has not been fully accepted in most states. One important departure from this concept is found in the fact that in many states the accounting function is centered in the comptroller or state treasurer who is usually an elected officer. This removes from the governor's influence one of the principal devices by which the fiscal control of the policies of the respective departments can be implemented. At the same time, it removes from his control the principal financial reporting device which he needs both in the preparation of the budget and in the supervision of the programs of the respective agencies as revealed by their spending. Frequently, the pre-audit also is performed by the comptroller or some other elected officer and this avenue of program control is removed from the governor's supervision.

In most of the states which have an executive budget, however, the budget officer or the governor is given the power to establish a system of quarterly allotments. When this system is examined at close range, it turns out to be in many instances merely a formality. In some cases this is the result of the budget law which fails to give the governor any authority to force the department head to desist from spending funds simply because they are available and have been divided on a quarterly basis. For example, in Alabama a system of quarterly allotments has been established in the Division of the Budget and no money may be expended by the agencies covered by the system unless the funds are a part of an approved allotment. However, the power of the governor to effect any economies by this quarterly review is distinctly limited by the fact that the statute establishing the system provides that the total amount of the annual appropriation to any agency shall not be reduced. Thus, in practice, if the request for an allotment is in the proper form and falls within the amounts provided in the appropriation act, it is approved as a matter of course.

This defect, however, is not the major weakness of the allotment system in Alabama. Its major limitation, like that of the allotment system in many other states, is that the system covers only a small part of the state's total expenditures. The allotment system covers only expenditures made from the general fund and from the special educational trust funds. It does not cover expenditures made from the majority of the 100 or more special funds which account for almost 90 per cent of the state's revenue. Since in Alabama thirteen of the sixteen major functions of government are financed wholly from these special funds and all of the major functions get at least a part of their support from one or more special funds, the allotment system covers only a very small proportion of the important state activities.

In many states the legislature encourages the department heads to regard an appropriation as a mandatory injunction to spend rather than simply permission to spend on gubernatorial consent. The reasoning of the legislature in taking this position is apparently that any interference by the governor in the spending process is an invasion of legislative authority on the determination of state policy. This is a point which certainly can be argued both ways. However, an expenditure appropriate at the time the legislature passes an appropriation act may not be so some six months to two years later. Conditions may change radically in a fairly short period in state government often under the impact of national or even international events which the legislature cannot readily foresee. In such circumstances, it may be desirable for the chief executive to be equipped with the power to limit the spending of certain agencies or even to prohibit the spending for certain programs altogether. The legislatures of some of the states have recognized this contingency in a back-handed fashion by providing that the governor may reduce the amounts appropriated if the revenues of the state fail to reach the estimated levels for the spending period in question. Most of these provisions make such a reduction mandatory so that the state cannot incur a deficit. These provisions are wise in so far as they go, but it is possible that the governor should have the power, probably through the system of quarterly allotments, to reduce the spending of certain agencies, if he sees the opportunity for a saving of state funds without destroying the program which was set out by the legislature.

The usefulness of the budget as a device for policy formation and administrative control, while potentially very effective, is limited in practice because the budgets in many states are not based on a comprehensive coverage of all the departments, because the governor does not always control the budget officer, because that budget officer does not have an adequate staff, and because there is no system for a smooth transition in the budget process from one administration to the other and the incoming governor does not have an adequate period in which to review his first budget.[15]

While the system of spending controls is well developed in a few states, there are many states in which these functions are either non-existent or are divided between the governor and other elected officers. Considerable work needs to be done in this area if the governor is to have a firm hand in the control over his departments. This is particularly true in those states where the governor's power to appoint and remove department heads is limited and where there seems to be little prospect of constitutional revision to improve this situation. Even without comprehensive appointing and removal powers, the governor can be given a very important control over the executive branch through the institu-

[15] To some extent the governor's second budget in those states where the governor has a four-year term or in those situations where he is re-elected for a second two-year term meets more fully the requirements suggested. Of course, the governor's second budget will be no more adequate than the first if the governor does not control the budget officer, and the budget does not cover the major functions of state government. However, the second budget has the advantage of being the product of the work of the budget staff over a considerable period of time and thus probably will be a better-prepared document. On the other hand, particularly in the four-year states, the governor's influence with his second legislature generally is weaker than with his first, and, consequently, the governor may have more difficulty in securing legislative approval of his program than is the case with his first budget.

tion of a centralized system of fiscal control under his supervision. It should be remembered, however, that the governor's actual control in this situation will depend not only on his fiscal powers but also on his legislative power base. If the governor does not have sufficient influence with the legislature to back up his budget cuts or other program changes, these fiscal controls will not prove to be of great practical importance. On the other hand, if normally good relations with the legislature prevail, these fiscal controls can go a long way in strengthening the governor's hand in administrative management, even though he does not have substantial appointing and removal powers. The short ballot is desirable, but it is only one of the methods of gubernatorial control.

If the governor is actually given the power to prepare a comprehensive executive budget and if he is equipped with the full complement of spending controls suggested above, he will be placed in a very strong position in regard to the whole state fiscal process. It is the writer's belief that these powers should be given the governor so that he can perform adequately his role in the preparation and execution of the budget. On the other hand, as it was urged earlier in this section, the legislature must also be strengthened so that it, too, can perform adequately its very vital part in the review of the budget and in the check on executive spending which comes through an adequate post audit.

REPORTING IS VITAL

The foregoing discussion of the problem of policy co-ordination and control is based on the premise that the governor has some way of actually knowing what is going on in the executive branch. This assumption is not necessarily valid, since the governor actually may be ill informed on the programs and activities of the various agencies. In fact, one of the difficulties faced by the governor in dealing with his department heads is that their more intimate daily contact with their departments gives them a knowledge of operations that the governor cannot hope to match. This places the governor at some disadvantage in his conduct of executive affairs, for it is obvious that if the governor is to co-ordinate and control the policies of these agencies, he must first know what these policies are. A system of reporting, therefore, is a vital part of the whole program of policy co-ordination and policy control.

Such a reporting system must be much more than formal annual, monthly, or even weekly reports from the department heads to the governor. These have a definite place in the reporting system but can be only one of several methods used, if the governor is to be kept adequately informed. Most of these methods have been discussed elsewhere in this chapter as devices for co-ordination and control. Devices such as cabinet or council meetings, informal individual or group conferences, inter-departmental committees and the other institutional arrangements discussed as methods of co-ordination and control are obviously also methods of reporting. Through cabinet meetings and conferences and through inter-departmental committee reports the governor seeks to keep informed on what is taking place in the executive branch, to discover the major problems of his department heads, and to ascertain what plans they are making. All of these devices are as much an attempt to understand the programs of the various agencies as they are an attempt to persuade the heads of these agencies to co-ordinate their programs with that of the governor or to dissuade them from programs which the governor considers unwise.

This also is true to a considerable extent of much of the executive budget process. The estimates from the various agencies are in the nature of a report in financial terms of their programs for the past fiscal year and on their proposed programs for the coming fiscal year. The system of pre-audit, quarterly allotments, and accounting controls are all a part of a financial reporting system which keeps the governor informed on the pattern of spending developing in the respective agencies.

The reporting aspect of these dual purpose devices does not have to be spelled out in any great detail. Reporting and control are closely connected and the separation suggested here is used simply to point up the fact that good reporting is an essential part of the process of co-ordination and control.

A more formal type of reporting, on an annual, monthly, or even weekly basis, is also useful. The experience of California with a system of monthly reports submitted to the governor by each department head prior to the monthly Council meeting points up both the strength and weakness of such a system. These monthly reports are potentially a very useful device for both the governor and the department heads. They keep the governor informed of the activities of the departments and, since a summary of the reports goes to each department head, they keep each department head informed of the activities of his colleagues. The usefulness of the reports has been reduced, however, by the fact that these monthly reports receive wide circulation, including transmittal to the press. This has changed their nature from that of a confidential report to the governor to a public relations handout which tends to emphasize the achievements of the department for the period covered and to gloss over its defects. If a monthly report to the governor is to be of any real value, it must be brief, well written, and highly confidential. The report should contain not only a summary of the programs in which the agency is making progress but also a summary of those in which it is experiencing difficulties and an analysis of the nature of these difficulties. From the governor's point of view, the latter aspect of the report is fully as important as the former. Nothing is more disconcerting to the governor than to discover a program weakness for the first time in the front page headlines of the local press or to be asked at his press conference to comment on a new program which has just been proposed by a department head when the governor has never heard of such a program. The governor is concerned to a considerable degree with what might be called preventive management. He would like to know about possible sore spots in his administration before they reach the crisis stage, not after. Admittedly, it is difficult to get this sort of report even from an appointed department head, and it is virtually impossible to get such a report from an elected official. Any administrator likes to appear successful in the eyes of his immediate superior and will be reluctant to burden the governor with a situation which he hopes to be able to work out satisfactorily or which he hopes will "work itself out." The problem of formal reports is a difficult one and is yet virtually untouched at the state level.

Most of the annual reports which are submitted to the governor are in the nature of publicity releases, as are the annual reports to the legislature and the reports of some agencies to the public at large. These are valuable for the purposes for which they were designed and more readable and informative departmental reports should certainly be encouraged since they stimulate legislative and popular interest in the department concerned. They do not, however, meet the needs of the governor.

In an attempt to establish a more adequate reporting system several governors have developed certain staff sections whose functions are primarily those of investigating and reporting on the operations of the executive branch. One of the most effective of these has been developed in Wisconsin where the governor's staff includes a Division of Departmental Research. Governor Kohler in describing the methods by which he sought to keep "abreast of the current business of the State" lists as important informal arrangements a periodic meeting of department heads, frequent personal conferences with department heads, the review through his financial secretary of year-end purchases, purchases of expensive capital items and unusual expenditures of other types, and the assistance of the Division of Departmental Research. In explaining the functions of this Division, he says in part

> The governor has been thoughtfully provided by the Legislature with a research division charged with continuing studies of department policies, practices, and procedures with a view to eliminating unnecessary, complex, expensive, wasteful, duplicating, and ineffective activities. Both my predecessor and I have tried to make the maximum use of this agency, although in a quiet, unspectacular, and friendly way so far as the departments are concerned. I have not sought to pillory public servants or to capture headlines by destructive criticism, but have ordered my staff to seek out questionable practices and work with the departments to correct them. The staff of this agency we have deliberately kept small and inexpensive to prevent it from seeking power or prestige from sheer weight of numbers. This division has aided me by multiplying my eyes and ears and bringing to my notice matters which I can discuss with the department heads.[16]

Governor Kohler's comments on this type of staff section point up the usefulness of such a division and also suggest the difficulties inherent in such an arrangement. The history of this Division in Wisconsin shows that it was established several administrations before Governor Kohler took office. However, it was used during the first years of its existence in such a way that public servants were indeed "pilloried" and headlines "captured" by the device

[16] Governor Kohler, p. 311.

of open hearings in which the department heads were questioned by the personnel of the Division. This kind of operation soon brought the Division into disrepute with the department heads, and after a rather stormy history, it was allowed to lapse in a succeeding administration. It was revived under Governor Oscar Rennebohm in 1949 and continued under Governor Kohler. Much of the success of its operations can be attributed to the director who served under both governors and who approached his task in such a manner that he regained the confidence of the department heads. Such a position calls for a maximum amount of tact and for a "passion for anonymity," to use the phrase of the President's Committee on Administrative Management.[17]

As is indicated by Governor Kohler's discussion, this Division is far more than simply a unit which keeps the Governor informed on the happenings in the executive branch. It is concerned with not only the discovery of administrative and program weaknesses in the various departments but also with the preparation of plans to remedy these weaknesses. The director, on occasion, also serves as a representative of the governor before the various legislative committees in connection with certain of the governor's administration bills and with the executive budget. In short, the section has developed into a general staff arm of the governor. One of its important functions, however, is investigation and reporting. The success of this Division in Wisconsin points to the possibility that such a staff aid might prove valuable to the governors of other states.

The position of departmental secretary to the governor found in California is of a slightly different character but is also designed as a part of the governor's reporting system. The function of the departmental secretary is to serve as a liaison officer between the governor and a majority of the department heads on administrative matters. Among other things, the departmental secretary serves as secretary to the governor's council. In this capacity, he receives all of the monthly reports submitted by the department heads to the governor. The departmental secretary reads these reports and makes a short summary of the pertinent points in

[17] Note the discussion of the public relations of this Division in Chapter 10. It is extremely desirable for such a division to remain in the background if it is to prove of maximum usefulness.

each. This summary is sent to the governor and briefs him on the activities of the departments for the month. It goes also to the department heads and serves to keep them informed of the activities of the other agencies in the executive branch. It would be highly desirable for a governor to read all of these reports himself, but in a large state this may be too great a drain on his limited time. If this is the case, such a summary as that prepared in California would be extremely helpful. As has been pointed out previously, the California system would be more useful if the reports were entirely confidential. The concept of a departmental secretary who can follow up on these reports and who can relieve the governor of many routine contacts with his department heads also seems to be a useful device. This possibility will be explored at more length in the chapter on the governor's staff.

This discussion does not exhaust the possible reporting methods, but it does serve to give some idea of their scope and importance. Reporting, co-ordination, and control are so closely interrelated that any device which serves one of these purposes will necessarily serve all three. Adequate reporting in the sense in which the term is used here is an essential ingredient in any meaningful system of co-ordination and control.

10. A STAFF FOR THE GOVERNOR'S OFFICE

IT IS DIFFICULT TO AVOID generalizations about state government which contain just enough truth to have the ring of authenticity and thus lead the reader to pass over the vast differences between the states which such generalizations conceal. Generalizations about the governor's staff are particularly dangerous and misleading, for the organization of the governor's staff in the respective states tends to reflect the variations in the size of the states, the scope of their functions, the distribution of population, the economic pattern, the state's customs and traditions, and a number of other factors which go to make up the ecology of government. The result of the interplay of these forces is that the governor's staff ranges in size from three to over forty and is quite varied in its organization, in the duties assigned to different staff members, in the titles given to the various members of the staff, in its mode of operation, and in the significance of the role which it plays in the day-to-day operation of state government.

Perhaps these differences can best be illustrated if the reader will imagine himself for a moment in the position of an individual seeking information about the governor's staff and collecting that information through personal interviews. As he travels from state to state, he begins to find that not only do the governors' staffs vary in size and in their organization but also the mode of operations, the atmosphere so to speak, of each state capitol has a distinctive character. For example, after a hot drive across some very wide open spaces, one might come to Carson City, the capital of the Silver State, Nevada. Carson City, which is the smallest state capital in the United States, reminds the casual visitor of a county seat in many of the southern states. Its atmosphere is unhurried and most of the town's business seems to be centered around the main street which runs the length of the town. The capitol itself is set back from the main street and is a rather unpretentious structure. The governor's office occupies a small suite of rooms in the capitol building itself, which is typical of the arrangements in most states. You go into the outer office and meet the Secretary to the Governor, a very pleasant individual who is an industrial engineer by profession. This is rather unusual, for most of the governors' secretaries whom you have met up to this point have a background as a member of the working press. After explaining your mission and discussing the general subject of the governor's position in Nevada, you inquire about the other members of the staff and discover that the governor's staff in Nevada consists only of the Secretary to the Governor and one stenographer. Further discussion reveals, however, that the staff might be interpreted to include the budget director and the director of civil defense. The former is an ex-newspaper man who is concerned not only with budgeting but also with public relations. The latter is in the governor's office, but his functions are such that he does not handle any of the regular business to which the staff devotes its time in most states. On the basis of the functions which they perform, it would seem that the secretary to the governor, the budget director, and the one stenographer make up the governor's staff. Therefore, the working staff in Nevada really consists of three persons which makes it one of the smallest staffs in the nation.[1]

The small size of the Nevada governor's staff is in part the result of the small population of the state, but it is also the result of the state's customs and traditions. One of these traditions is that the governor of the state will be available to any citizen for personal consultation. As a result, the governor of Nevada

[1] Other states in which the governor has a staff of three include Vermont, Utah, South Dakota, Wyoming, and New Mexico. The governor's staff in New Mexico consists of an executive assistant, a secretary, and a stenographer. The stenographer speaks both Spanish and English and serves on occasion as an interpreter for the governor, since the state is still bilingual and many of the governor's visitors either speak only Spanish or in the excitement of meeting the governor revert to Spanish to explain their missions.

has an "open door" policy in regard to interviews. Because of the small population of the state, the government still retains much of the face-to-face flavor found in the present small local governmental units in many states and characteristic of the states themselves at an earlier period. Governor Russell pointed out that government in Nevada is a very personal affair and that "everyone feels free to come to the governor with his problems." This is true not only of state officials and legislators but also of local officials and ordinary citizens. For example, when a county commissioner comes to Carson City, his first move is likely to be to drop into the governor's office for a chat on the problems of his county.

While many of these problems concern such matters as highways, old age assistance, and education, all of which are familiar problems to any governor, others are related to the particular ecology of government in Nevada. For example, because of the exceptionally light rainfall, problems involving water supply are very important and are likely to be the topic of discussion in many of the governor's interviews. Another problem is "gaming." Since gambling is legalized in Nevada and is one of the state's major businesses, many of the governor's visitors are likely to be concerned with some aspect of this business.

The governor's staff is small in part because a larger staff might seem to interpose a barrier between the governor and the public. Such a barrier would not be in keeping with the tradition of personal government which prevails in the state and which demands that the governor be readily available to any citizen.

The governor's staff in Nevada also reflects the legal and traditional powers of the governor and the influence which the governors' own ideas of their proper role have had over the years. The governor of Nevada is traditionally and by gubernatorial interpretation not the legislative policy leader which he is in some states. He also is legally in a rather weak position as the administrative head of the state. These facts are reflected in the gubernatorial staffing pattern. For example, there is no policy staff in Nevada and no legislative secretary who serves as the legislative liaison man for the governor. There also is no one staff member assigned to administrative matters, although the budget officer performs one aspect of this function. The budget officer, however, seems to concern himself primarily with public relations rather than budgeting. This is in part a reflection of his newspaper background and in part, as further investigation reveals, the result of the fact that the budget system in Nevada is a very rudimentary operation.[2]

The governor's administrative position is also a controlling factor in the allocation of his time. The administrative organization of Nevada is such that the governor spends more time on administrative matters than on legislative matters. This is true because the executive branch in Nevada is a loose confederation of some 99 independent departments, boards, and commissions. The heads of thirteen of these bodies are elected by the people, twenty are *ex-officio* agencies solely, eleven are jointly *ex-officio* and appointive, the members of 48 are appointed solely by the governor, one is filled by the legislature, and six are appointed in various other ways. The most important of these agencies are those whose heads are elected or which are headed by *ex-officio* boards and commissions. The governor of Nevada is a member of some nineteen of these *ex-officio* boards. Hence, his influence over administration though limited comes primarily as a result of his participation *in* administration rather than his directing of the executive branch, as is the case with some governors who have more extensive powers in the realm of appointments and fiscal controls.

The governor of Nevada is, therefore, in a rather weak position traditionally as a legislative leader and is also in a rather weak position legally as an administrative chief. His powers over the budget are fairly substantial on paper but in practice are greatly weakened because of the tendency of the legislature to earmark over 80 per cent of the state's funds. His control through the budget also is weakened by the absence of any controls over the

[2] See Albert Gorvine, *Administrative Reorganization for Effective Government Management in Nevada,* a report prepared for the Nevada Legislative Counsel Bureau (December, 1948), pp. 73-77 for a more detailed discussion of the governor's relation to the budget process in Nevada. Gorvine summarizes his conclusion on the budget process by saying that "the State of Nevada has a budget system in name only. In practice it is not a statement of financial policy; it is not a complete and well-organized record of receipts and expenditures; it is not an effective guide for legislative appropriations; and, finally, it is not an adequate instrument for fiscal control."

spending process. The staff seems to reflect the governor's position to a considerable extent. A larger staff would seem to interpose a barrier between the governor and the citizens which would not be in accord with the tradition of face-to-face government. The staff is not organized for policy leadership because this is not considered to be a function of the governor. It is organized, however, to assist the governor in carrying out his role in public relations. This aspect of the governor's functions is heavily emphasized in a state like Nevada with a population so small that the governor is almost expected to know every citizen, or at least to be readily available to any citizen who thinks he has a problem warranting gubernatorial attention. Staff operations are informal as befits a governor whose door is always open to the public. Nevada cannot be said to be typical of the smaller states, but a visitor from one of the smaller southern, midwestern, or New England states is quite likely to feel at home in Carson City. There is a genuine friendliness about operations in Nevada which is sure to appeal to those who think government has become too impersonal.

As you travel from state to state, you will find that the formality with which the governor and his staff operate tends to be in a rather direct ratio to the size of the state. The same informality found in Nevada usually prevails in the smaller states regardless of their geographical location. For example, in Vermont the writer first visited the governor's office fairly early one morning on a fine July day only to discover that the governor was out of the office and would not be back until later in the day. The governor's Secretary of Civil and Military Affairs kindly arranged an appointment for the late afternoon. At the appointed time, the writer came back for his appointment but found that the Secretary had stepped out of his office for a few moments. While waiting for his return, the writer fell into conversation with an individual who was sitting on the window sill in the Secretary's office. This individual the writer took to be a representative of the local press. Since the members of the press who cover the capitol beat are frequently an excellent source of information on governmental matters, particularly local politics, the writer began discussing his project and had been talking for two or three minutes when the Secretary came in and said, "Well, I see that you have met the Governor!"

This incident is not typical of most of the writer's interviews with the governors, but it does serve to give something of the flavor of the informality of operation in some of the smaller states. This informality has many good features and appeals to those who, like the writer, look with favor on a more personalized government. However, such informality, which is but an expression of more basic governmental features, is apparently doomed by the expanding functions of the states and by the press of business which has already forced the "formalizing" of the governor's staff and mode of operations in the larger states. Probably as the complexities of government increase, operations in the smaller states will gradually be formalized. Informality is not without its drawbacks, not the least of which is the considerable drain on the governor's time which an "open door" policy imposes.

Traveling West, our next stop is Sacramento, California. Here the situation is quite different, as might be expected in a state which is the second largest in the nation in terms of both area and population. The emphasis in California seems to be on expansion, as is witnessed by the fact that it has advanced from fifth to second place in population during the decade from 1940 to 1950. The governor's office has expanded along with the population, having grown from five persons in 1930 when the state had a population of 5,677,251 to 21 persons in 1943, when the state's population had increased to 7,795,000, and to 42 persons by 1947, when the state's population was about 9,000,000. This makes it one of the largest gubernatorial staffs in the United States. As these figures show, there is no exact ratio between the size of the governor's staff and the increase in population. However, as the population of the state has grown, the problems of the state have become more complex and the executive branch has increased in size. The governor has been forced to add additional staff to cope with the scope of his increased responsibilities. This growth of gubernatorial staff is paralleled in many of the larger states, and the largest gubernatorial staffs are now found in such states as California,

Illinois, Pennsylvania, and New York. While the governor's staff in most states has developed rather slowly, it is no accident that it has reached its greatest development in those large industrial states which have problems that are broader in scope than some of their smaller neighbors.

One of the effects of the large scale operation found in California is that the governor's staff is more elaborately organized and more formal in its mode of operations. You do not walk casually into the governor's office in Sacramento and expect to see the governor. Governor Warren's schedule of appointments was made out at least a week in advance and only those with pressing matters, either political or administrative, were actually likely to see him. The governor's staff now occupies a large and imposing suite of offices in a new addition to the capitol. A visitor to the executive office will first meet a receptionist who will attempt to determine his business and will refer him to the proper member of the staff. This group includes an executive secretary, private secretary, press secretary, departmental secretary, executive clemency and appointments secretary, legislative secretary, research secretary and an adjustments, invitations, and travel secretary. The clerical operation is so large that it requires an office supervisor who is in charge of six units covering correspondence, messenger service, bookkeeping, mails, files, and stenographic service. Many of the secretaries also have assistants and all of them have at least one stenographer. In short, in so far as operations in the states are concerned, this is what might be termed a large scale operation. Yet, in spite of the size of the operation something of the friendliness of the smaller states prevails and the visitor is not likely to get the "run around" to which he may be subjected in some of the other large states.

The governor's staff in California does its best to protect the governor from unnecessary callers, and attempts, with considerable success, to handle most visitors and most problems both from within and from without the government. There are, of course, many visitors who cannot be handled by the staff, but probably 85 per cent or more of those who come into the governor's office do not see the governor. Governor Warren, like most governors, was available to the heads of the agencies in the executive branch, but much of the business handled by individual conferences in other states is handled in California through the inter-departmental committee system which was discussed in Chapter 9. The governor also is available to members of the legislature, and during the legislative session, tries to keep his calendar free to consult with them on the legislative program. However, Governor Warren spent much less of his time "seeing people" in the sense in which the term was used in reference to the governor of Nevada. To be sure he spent a great deal of time in interviews, but these were with department heads, legislators, or members of the press rather than with the average citizen who wanted to talk to the governor about his personal problems. The pressure of the state's business is so great in California that the governor cannot devote as much time to this type of interview as do the governors of the smaller states.

The composition of the governor's staff in California gives us some clue to the position of the governor in that state and some indication of his more important functions. The executive secretary is in general charge of the entire staff and is responsible for co-ordinating the work of the various staff members. This is a considerable assignment with a staff as large as that in California and is accomplished partly through personal contacts with individual staff members and partly through a weekly conference of the major staff members. The governor's private secretary has a much more important position than the title would indicate in some states. In addition to being responsible for all the normal functions of a private secretary, she also is responsible for maintaining liaison with various women's organizations in California such as The League of Women Voters, The American Association of University Women, various parent-teacher organizations, and the like. The private secretary also is responsible for the final processing of all matters requiring the governor's signature, signs for bills which are sent to the governor from the legislature, and handles a part of the governor's correspondence. In addition, the private secretary maintains the governor's appointments calendar. The press secretary is responsible for relations with the metropolitan and capitol press, for radio and television arrangements, for public proclamations, statements and articles, and for recommendations regarding the acceptance of invitations for speeches and public appearances. The position of departmental secretary is an unique office which will be discussed at some length later in this chapter. As was pointed out earlier in a discussion of the Governor's Council, the departmental secretary serves as the secretary to this body and prepares summary reports of departmental activities on which the discussions in the Council are based. The primary function of the departmental secretary, however, is to provide liaison between the governor and the heads of the majority of the important agencies in the executive branch. Some of the other secretaries also provide liaison with certain selected agencies. The executive clemency and appointments secretary as his title indicates is responsible for pardon, reprieve, commutation of sentence, and extradition matters. His full title is "Secretary in Charge of Executive Clemency and Appointments to Public Office," which indicates that he also is in charge of processing all appointments for notaries public in the state and for the collection of information on recommendations for public office. In addition, he is responsible for the clearance of legal opinions from the attorney general. The secretary in charge of legislative affairs is responsible for assisting the governor in the preparation of his legislative program. In practice this involves not only program preparation but also close liaison with the legislature in order to see that the governor's program is enacted. The legislative secretary also is responsible for seeing all legislators who wish to talk to the governor and for scheduling such appointments. In addition, he is responsible for advising the governor on bills which come to him for his signature. The research secretary is responsible for factual research on any matter in which the governor may be interested. These assignments generally include the assembling of material for the governor's speeches and for research work on various aspects of the governor's legislative or administrative program. The secretary for adjustments, invitations, and travel is responsible for arranging the governor's travel schedule and public appearances. He normally accompanies the governor when he is traveling either in the state or on official business outside the state.

The organization in California is one of the most elaborate of that of any of the executive offices. In size, and to some extent in composition, it resembles that of New York, but it has certain peculiarities which reflect the emphasis which Governor

Warren placed on certain aspects of his functions just as the staff in New York reflects certain of Governor Dewey's concepts on the nature of the gubernatorial function. The organization of the governor's staff in no two states is exactly alike. Each of the 25 states visited had its own particular staffing pattern and its own mode of operations, and just as there was little consistency in the details of the staffing pattern, there was little consistency in the titles used to designate the governor's major assistants. The staffing pattern did seem to reflect the customs and traditions of the state in regard to the governorship and also seemed to reflect the scope of the governor's powers and the size of the state's business. Even in states of similar size, however, the staff pattern may be quite different because of the different view which is held by the governor or by the people of the governor's proper function or because of the difference in the scope of the gubernatorial power.

These brief analyses of the staff of the governor in Nevada and California are presented simply as examples of the diversity which exists in the staffing pattern in the governor's office in the respective states. Because of this diversity, one of the basic problems in this chapter is to determine whether or not there are any underlying similarities in this pattern which might serve as a basis for a suggested staffing pattern having rather general applicability. In the section which follows, such a pattern is suggested based on what appears to be the elements of similarity in the staffing problem in the states as a whole.

A BASIC STAFFING PATTERN

The question of who should constitute the governor's staff is closely related to the question of why the governor needs a staff at all. The answer to this question is found primarily in two very practical facts about state government. One of these is that even in the smaller states the operation of the state government is such a large enterprise that it is not easily understood or controlled by one man unless that individual is assisted by an able staff which is large enough to relieve the governor of some of his duties and to keep him informed on the operation of the various departments. A second fact is that the problems of state government whether they be in the realm of policy or administration are of such scope that they cannot be understood by one person unless he has considerable background data at his disposal. The range of these problems is so great that this data can only be collected by a staff of assistants.

If we can imagine a state which is so small and which has such simple problems that the scope of state government is within the understanding of one person and subject to his unaided control, then there is obviously no need for a staff. Such might have been the case fifty years ago in our smallest states. The writer would argue, however, that such is not the case today even in those states which have the smallest population and whose problems are perhaps somewhat simpler than those of some of their sister states. Even in the smaller states the governor's responsibilities are of such scope that he needs a well organized staff to assist him in his duties. It is obvious that the governor of Nevada will not need a staff as large as that of the governor of California. It is also obvious, however, that the governor of Nevada needs some staff and that his staff should be adequate to the needs of the office in Nevada. In reference to this standard, it is quite probable that the governor of Nevada actually needs a somewhat larger staff than he has at the present time. There is some reason to suppose that in Nevada, as in many states, there has been a time lag in the development of the governor's staff so that it has not kept pace with the governor's increasing responsibilities. While it might seem that the impact of the expanding functions of state government and the parallel growth in state personnel and expenditures would make itself felt immediately in the governor's office and, hence, force an immediate increase in staff or a change in staffing pattern, such is not usually the case. The typical pattern in most states seems to be that better staffing for the governorship follows increased functions and added responsibilities but follows only after a considerable lapse of time. Over a period of time as the state's organization becomes more complex and its problems become more acute, the governor is finally forced to add additional staff to help him cope with his expanded responsibilities. This addition in staff, however, seems to come fairly slowly and then only when circumstances force the governor into making such additions. Here and there, we find a governor who appreciates the real potentialities of a staff and in that state, at least during his administration, there may be an abrupt blossoming of the staff concept. The general trend in gubernatorial staffing in the last ten years has been toward larger and more adequate gubernatorial staffs with some increasing realization on the part of the governors as a whole of the advantages of completed staff work as a real tool in policy formation and management. This trend has not spread evenly over the states as a whole, and there are many states which seem to have been almost completely by-passed. As was pointed out in the case of Nevada, this variation is due to many complex factors, most of which are inherent in the ecology of government in a given state. In addition, it should be remembered also that not all states have reached the same stage of administrative development. Furthermore, the personalities of governors of the respective states are quite varied, so that not all of them will see the value of the gubernatorial staff concept, and among those that accept the concept there will be variations to fit the staff to a pattern acceptable to different gubernatorial interpretations. Consequently, it should not be surprising that the governor's staff has not reached the same stage of development in all states nor should it be felt that uniform development is necessary or desirable. The adequacy of the governor's staff in a given state can be determined only in relation to the functions of the governor of the state in question, the ecology of government of the state, the stage of its administrative development, and the size of the governmental operation. What may be an entirely adequate staff for the governor of Nevada may be wholly inadequate for the governor of California and may not even be suitable for the neighboring state of New Mexico. On the other hand, the elaborate organization which is necessary to do an adequate job in California would overshadow some of the line departments in Nevada or New Mexico and would be wholly inappropriate for those states. While there is no set yardstick which can be used to determine the proper size and composition of the governor's staff in any given state, it is suggested that the following considerations may be useful in making such a determination.

In the first place, it seems desirable in designing the governor's staff to use as one guiding principle the concept of the staff as an agency to assist the governor in carrying out his principal functions of policy formation, public relations, and management.

This guide for staffing must be balanced, however, with the realization that the governor's staff must be adapted to local conditions. This adaptation may require that one of the governor's functions be emphasized at the expense of the others and that, consequently, his staff must be designed to implement this emphasis. An attempt to tailor the staff to fit local conditions also means that the duties of the staff members must be assigned with a view to relieving the governor of the particular minor functions which are assigned to him by the constitution or statutes of the state, or are traditionally a part of the governor's duties in the state in question. These minor duties are so varied in character that no catalogue which might be suggested here would have general application but they would include such matters as commissioning notaries public or justices of the peace, signing a variety of legal papers such as deeds or contracts in connection with the state's business, and making a multitude of minor appointments. Because of the variety of minor duties which the governor may be called upon to perform, it seems desirable to start a consideration of the staffing pattern for a particular state with a careful review of the constitution and statutes to determine the exact duties of the governor. This review should be combined with a thorough desk audit of the governor's daily routine to determine which duties occupy the major portion of his time. These two analyses, taken together, should give a fairly accurate picture of the governor's duties and responsibilities. With this picture as a starting point, the governor's staff can be designed to fit the particular local situation. If at all possible, the majority of the governor's minor duties should be transferred to appropriate agency heads so that the governor may be free to concentrate on his major functions of policy formation, management, and public relations. If this is not possible, every effort should be made to transfer these minor duties to a member of his staff.

The governor's staff must be tailored to fit the particular governorship in question. While it probably should be designed around the governor's three principal functions, it also must be designed to take into consideration local duties and responsibilities which are assigned to the governor's office by the constitution, the statutes of the state, or by custom and tradition.

A third suggestion is that the staffing pattern be kept flexible. Successive governors should be able to change the arrangement of the staff to suit their own conception of the functions of the office and their own working methods. While in some states the members of the governor's staff fall under civil service, this does not seem to be a desirable arrangement, since it reduces considerably the flexibility of staff needed to secure adjustment to the personality of successive governors. For example, in Michigan all of the members of the governor's staff except his press secretary and executive secretary are technically under civil service. In theory, this means that some of the important members of his staff such as his personal secretary, executive aides, and legal adviser have permanent tenure and may not be replaced by succeeding governors. In practice this is not the case. While a number of the lower ranking staff members actually do have permanent tenure, there is a gentleman's agreement that the higher ranking staff members will be provisional appointees and, therefore, can be and are changed with succeeding administrations. This informal arrangement clearly shows the need for giving the governor a free hand in appointing his key staff members. It would seem desirable in Michigan and in other states which have similar arrangements to recognize legally this need for flexibility by removing the major positions in the executive office from the operations of the merit system. This would give the governor a free hand in appointing his principal assistants so that his staff might be adapted to his view of the executive function.

It also might be suggested that the governor's staff should be kept as small as possible while providing enough staff assistance to enable the governor to operate effectively. The governor in most states is already beset with enough problems in co-ordination without adding the problem of co-ordinating his own staff. In some of the largest states one of the governor's staff, probably the executive secretary, should be appointed as the governor's chief assistant for the purpose of intra-staff co-ordination. In most states, however, it should be possible to keep the staff small enough so that this co-ordination can be obtained on an informal basis and the governor can be relieved of the necessity of staff co-ordination to a considerable extent. It also might be pointed out that from a practical point of view a large staff will serve as a convenient target for the legislature, which may try to attack the governor through a reduction in his staff.[3]

The problem of the proper staffing of the governor's office is intimately connected with many of the larger problems of state government suggested elsewhere in this book. Such problems as a two-year term, the short interval which is now given the governor to prepare his program between the time he is elected and the time he takes office, the disorganized condition of the executive branch in many states, the problems inherent in our present methods of selecting the governor, and the lack of party cohesion, all have definite implications for the staffing of the governor's office. An improved staffing pattern cannot correct these major deficiencies. However, it may be some years before changes are made which will improve the governor's position in these matters, if they are made at all. Consequently, the problem of providing the governor with an adequate staff must be approached within the framework of the practical situation with which the governor is faced in most states. Improved staffing cannot be regarded as a substitute for more basic changes, but it can be helpful even if these changes cannot be accomplished.

It must be admitted that the concept of the usefulness of an adequate gubernatorial staff has not received wide acceptance at the state level. While it is mentioned in most reorganization studies and is well developed in some of them, the concept of an executive office for the governor has not been greatly emphasized by many of the groups which have studied the executive branch in the past and has received too little attention from some of the recent "Little Hoover" commissions. Furthermore, the idea of anything more than a minimum staff was not well received by some of the governors interviewed. On the other hand, in some states the governor was keenly aware of the desirability of an adequate staff and many governors have built up very effective staff organizations. Reaction was mixed on this point and the governors' statements ranged from that of one in the Midwest who said with some pride that he had gone into office on a

[3] Another reason for keeping the staff small was expressed by Governor Kohler of Wisconsin in discussing one of the divisions of his staff. He stated that "the staff of this agency we have deliberately kept small and inexpensive to prevent it from seeking power or prestige from the sheer weight of numbers."

platform of economy, and "I set an example by reducing my own staff" to a statement by one in New England that "I needed more staff and I got it."

In view of the varying degree to which the concept has been accepted both by those who have studied the executive branch and by some of the governors themselves, the practical problem of how to improve the basic staffing pattern of the governor's office in a given state is very real. Impetus for a staff reorganization might come from a reorganization commission as a part of their recommendations on the executive branch. If such a proposal has strong gubernatorial backing, it may well succeed. However, if it results in an increase in gubernatorial staff on a permanent basis, it probably would have to be embodied in a statute. This might be helpful if the statute were drawn in very general terms so as to preserve the necessary flexibility. It probably would be undesirable if the statute specified the titles and duties of the staff, for this would establish a rigid pattern of staffing which would become unrealistic with the advent of a new governor. For a staff to be really useful it must fulfill a demonstrated need. Hence, it seems probable that the demand for a more effective staff must come primarily from the governors of a particular state over a period of time. This demand probably will be based more on the growth of the state and the increasing complexity of the problems which face succeeding governors than on any realization of the desirability of the staff function as an abstract principle.

Nevertheless, it probably is desirable that some sort of basic pattern be suggested as a possible guide and that the experience of other states be analyzed to determine the kinds of staffing patterns which have proved to be useful. Based on this premise, a basic staffing pattern is suggested below in the nature of a recommendation which might be considered by those who are concerned with this problem. It is followed by an analysis of some of the staffing patterns which have proved useful in certain states and particularly by an analysis of certain positions on the governor's staff which have been especially helpful.

The major functions of the governor as they have emerged from this study are policy formation, management, and public relations. The basic staff of the governor should be designed to assist him in carrying out these three principal functions. In a very small state, therefore, the governor's basic staff would consist of three principal staff members. Using the terminology currently prevalent, these might be designated as a policy secretary, an administrative secretary, and a public relations secretary.[4] In addition, the governor needs a legal secretary who will advise both the governor and his other principal assistants on the legal aspects of the governor's functions and who will handle such quasi-legal functions as pardon and parole, executive clemency, and extradition. These individuals would, of course, be augmented by a clerical staff and perhaps by additional professional personnel if certain of the management functions discussed later are actually placed in the governor's immediate office. The number and duties of these additional staff members would be dictated by local circumstances but probably would include a private secretary for the governor, a receptionist who would also be a part-time stenographer, a file clerk, and one or two additional stenographers or clerks.

In general, the policy secretary should be responsible for the spade work which is necessary to change the governor's campaign promises into legislation. If the governor's actual program is to be different from his campaign program or from the platform of his party, these differences will, of course, be taken into consideration by the secretary in the preparation of the governor's legislative program. Since one of the major vehicles for the governor's program is the budget, the policy secretary should be responsible for the review of this document to determine its conformance with the over-all policy of the governor. As a corollary to his role in program preparation, the policy secretary should be responsible for the main outline of the governor's principal policy speeches, such as his initial message to the legislature and his budget message, if this is a separate presentation. He also

[4] There is no uniform terminology used to describe positions in the governor's office in the various states. The terms "secretary" and "administrative assistant" are used interchangeably for positions which cover some of the duties proposed for the policy and administrative secretaries. The four basic positions suggested above were all designated as secretaries to provide some consistency and to conform with general usage in that at least one of the governor's principal assistants is a "secretary" of some sort in most states. The modifying adjectives in each title were added to give some idea of the function of each position.

should be prepared to brief the governor on the exercise of his veto power, since this is sometimes the final step in the control of legislative policy.

The function of the policy secretary includes not only the preparation of policy but the co-ordination of policy. If proposed legislation affects the functions of already established agencies of government, or if it proposes new programs for those agencies, these items should be cleared with the agency heads affected. Similarly, if the agencies plan to sponsor any changes in existing legislation or any new legislation, they should clear such proposals with the policy secretary. These proposals may be integrated into the governor's program, if this is desirable, or cleared for agency sponsorship if the governor does not wish to make them a part of his major program. Of course, in those states where the governor has little direct control over agency heads, such clearances would have to be obtained, if they can be obtained at all, by previous agreement with the agency heads so situated. Any changes desired in proposals from these agencies probably would have to be negotiated with the agency head by the policy secretary or by the governor. Such negotiations will not necessarily be successful, but the policy secretary should make every effort to be informed on all policy proposals by the agencies of government and try to co-ordinate these proposals so that the governor's program may have unity.

The careful preparation and co-ordination which have gone into the governor's program will be of no avail if that program is not passed by the legislature. Consequently, the policy secretary should keep the governor informed of the program's progress through the legislature and notify the governor of the need for executive intervention if the program meets legislative resistance. In addition, the policy secretary should keep informed on major measures introduced by the legislators themselves so that the governor may have a clear picture of any measure which might be inimical to his program. Finally, if legislative action has been contrary to the governor's recommendations, the policy secretary should be prepared to brief the governor on the possible use of his veto power.

The advantage in having a policy secretary lies chiefly in allowing the governor to operate at his proper level in policy formation. Under this plan, the governor's role would be confined primarily to the establishment of major policy guide lines for the policy secretary and to policy co-ordination at a relatively high level. The details of the preparation of policy and such policy co-ordination and clearance which could be handled below the gubernatorial level would be taken care of by the policy secretary. This is an assignment of considerable scope even in a small state and is greatly complicated in many states by the governor's lack of authority over his department heads. However, the governor's role in policy formation can be expedited considerably by the assignment of the spade work on policy formation to one individual. This is not to suggest that any one person on the governor's staff will be the only source of policy information or that all or even most of the governor's principal policies will originate with his policy secretary. As was pointed out, these policies come from a variety of sources, including department heads, pressure groups, gubernatorial advisers outside the government, and the party platform. What is urged here is that the responsibility for the preparation of policy measures be centered in one individual so that this one person can obtain an over-all view of the program which is being proposed to the legislature. The governor's policy secretary need not even be an expert in the drafting of legislation, although this would be desirable. It is quite probable that he will call on experts in bill drafting in the legislative reference service or in some of the departments concerned for the actual preparation of many of these measures. While it would be desirable to have an expert in such matters on the governor's staff, it may be that this is not feasible because of the small size of the staff and that such expert assistance must be, as is now the case in many states, "borrowed" from outside the governor's office.

The proper location of the budget function is a difficult problem in the formation of a staffing pattern even for a small state. The budget is both a device for policy formation and a device for administrative control. The latter aspect of the budget process usually is reinforced by a system of fiscal controls, including the pre-audit, a quarterly allotment system, centralized accounting, and perhaps centralized purchasing. This two-fold aspect of budgeting raises the question of whether the responsibility for the budget should be a part of the duties of the policy secretary because of its policy implications or a part of the duties of the administrative secretary because of its implications for administrative control. The word "responsibility" is used advisedly in this connection, because it is obvious that even in a small state neither the policy secretary nor the administrative secretary can actually prepare the budget under the press of other duties. Nevertheless, the question remains as to the location of the policy decisions which have to be made in the course of the preparation of the budget and of its initial review before submission to the governor. To meet this dual problem, it is suggested that the budget division be under the supervision of the administrative secretary. This recommendation is made because of the implication of the budget and its corollary control procedures for the day-to-day management of the executive branch. It is further suggested, however, that because of the primary importance of the budget as a policy vehicle the policy secretary should be responsible for policy review of the document both during its preparation and before it is presented to the governor. This suggestion may seem to indicate a divided authority and responsibility which is inconsistent with the general thesis of this book, but the budget does serve two functions and to remove it completely from the province of the administrative secretary would weaken his hand in the necessary administrative control aspects of his duties, while to remove it completely from the jurisdiction of the policy secretary would leave a fatal gap in the whole policy program. In practice it is quite probable that the policy secretary and the administrative secretary will work in close conjunction on the preparation of the budget. They also must work closely with the governor on the budget. This is a policy function of such importance that it is the legitimate concern of the governor, who should not be isolated from the budget process but who should be protected from much of the detailed work he now does in many states. The governor is, and should be, vitally concerned with the policy decisions on the budget. These decisions are made in part before the budget process begins, in part while the budget is being prepared, and in part in a review of the document before it is sent to the legislature. Some governors have adopted the practice of outlining their major policy on the budget in a call for estimates. This may be nothing more than the injunction to department heads that the governor expects the revenues of the state to remain static or to decline in the forthcoming fiscal year and that in order to present a balanced budget he anticipates that it will be necessary either to reduce expenditures or to "hold the line" on governmental spending. The call for estimates may go beyond this and suggest a particular program emphasis for the ensuing year.

During the budget process, the policy and administrative secretaries will be called upon constantly to evaluate the various programs submitted by agency heads. Since there is never enough money to carry out all the suggested programs, they must decide on the desirability of one program as opposed to another or on the desirability of reduced programs in some areas as opposed to expanded programs in others. Pressure from agency heads to secure the adoption of the programs which they have proposed will be very strong, and it is quite probable that the resolution of the competing demands will have to be made in the final analysis by the governor.

After the budget document has been completed, it probably will be reviewed by the governor and the policy secretary and the governor's budget message prepared. Since this is primarily a policy message, the major responsibility for its preparation should rest with the policy secretary.

In a small state the policy secretary and the administrative secretary both might be able to sit in on the budget hearings so that both might be thoroughly familiar with the alternative programs presented by the various department heads. The present practice in many states is for the governor to spend several weeks in such hearings. This would seem to be an undue drain on the governor's time. The fact that such hearings are conducted in some states by the budget director without the governor's presence suggests that the governor himself need not be present at the hearings. The task of the governor in trying to decide which of the many demands made by the agency heads on the limited funds of the state should be incorporated in the budget and which of these demands rejected or modified is a task of Herculean proportions. The governor need not sit in on all budget hearings in order to make such decisions. The role of the administrative and policy secretaries is to sift this mass of data presented in the hearings and in the estimates submitted prior to the hearings and present to the governor their joint recommendations on the desirability and feasibility of such programs.

It is not suggested that such a process now goes on in all of the states or that the budget is now prepared in such a way that meaningful review and analysis is actually possible. The disorganized condition of the executive branch allows many departments to escape the budget process altogether or to present only a token estimate to the governor. In many states the budget covers only a small part of the state's expenditures. It is very difficult if not impossible in those states for the policy secretary and administrative secretary to perform the functions suggested above.

Nevertheless, the governor is still responsible for the preparation of the budget in a majority of the states. In many states he is desperately in need of the kind of assistance which can be given by an adequate staff. If he is to do anything more than collect departmental estimates and pass these on to the legislature as a so-called "budget," he must have assistance in making a real analysis of departmental estimates. The provision of a policy and an administrative secretary to assist him in such an analysis is one way of improving the quality of his policy program.

In some states the kind of budget analysis suggested as a function of the policy secretary is performed by a budget director. This individual is either on the governor's staff, as in Virginia, or he is the head of a budget office under the governor's immediate control, as in New York, or he is the head of a budget division in a department of finance, as in Alabama, or he is the head of a division of a department of administration, as in Minnesota. Occasionally, as in Alabama and Colorado, his position falls under the state's civil service, and he is not as closely under the governor's supervision as is a person whom the governor appoints and can remove for policy reasons. In some states the budget director comes under an agency which is not subject to gubernatorial control, as has been the case until 1952 in Massachusetts, where the budget director was under the director of administration who had a term longer than that of the governor and generally was an appointee of the previous administration.

Of course, in some states the budget is prepared by a commission which is not directly subject to gubernatorial control, and in Arkansas and Texas it is prepared by an agent of the legislature.[5]

Where an active budget agency exists which is subject to gubernatorial control, it may be that the present arrangement is satisfactory and that some of the duties suggested for the policy secretary might be assigned to the budget director, the director of finance, or the director of administration. However, even in a situation where there is an active budget agency there is some reason to assume that there is a case for having the budget reviewed in the governor's office by a person other than the budget director. In those states having a functioning budget system, the department heads interviewed frequently suggested that the budget director was inclined to think primarily in dollars and cents terms and tended to be an advocate of economy in government for the sake of economy. This may have been simply an expression of sour grapes resulting from an unsuccessful encounter with the budget director over certain pet programs of the department head. On the other hand, it may be an indication that there are several ways of looking at the desirability of a particular program, and that while the cost of the program is a very important consideration, other considerations may make the program desirable in spite of its cost. By having the governor's policy secretary make an over-all review of the budget in terms of the governor's general policies, a fresh point of view in budget review may be introduced.

The problem of criteria in budget review is fully as important at the state level in terms of the programs undertaken by the state as it is at the national level in terms of programs undertaken by the national government. It is an area in which a great deal of work still remains to be accomplished and in which relatively little has been done.[6] While the author has no panacea for this

[5] See Chapter 9 for a more detailed discussion of the relation of the governor to the individual who is responsible for the preparation of the budget. Texas actually has a dual budget system; one budget is prepared by an agent of the governor and the other by an agent of the legislature.

[6] See V. O. Key, "The Lack of a Budgetary Theory," *American Political Science Review,* XXXIV (December, 1940), 1137-44, and Verne B. Lewis, "Toward a Theory of Budgeting," *Public Administration Review,* XII (Winter,

problem, his study of gubernatorial responsibilities in policy formation, and particularly in budgetary policy, leads to the conclusion that this is an area in which those interested in better state government might profitably spend some time and effort. The suggestion made here for policy review by the governor's policy secretary, or by the governor himself for that matter, leaves unsolved the criteria on which such a review is to be based.

Nevertheless, the dual approach to budgetary evaluation may have some value. The administrative secretary can prepare an evaluation of the proposed programs of the various agencies based largely on fiscal considerations, such as the probable income of the state for the coming fiscal year, the prior commitments of the state for programs already underway or authorized, the available federal funds, and the like. At the same time, the policy secretary can review the programs for conformance with the governor's announced policies. This combined review should place the governor in a better position to evaluate the competing programs in over-all terms. This is admittedly a difficult feat of evaluation, and the final responsibility in these decisions must be that of the governor, subject, of course, to eventual legislative approval. Most governors simply do not have the information on which to base intelligent policy decisions of this nature. A series of conferences on the budget with his policy and administrative secretaries should go a long way toward giving him the kind of data on which an intelligent decision can be based. This would improve immensely the quality of the governor's policy planning process and enable him to carry out more effectively his major role in policy formation. At present the governor generally is successful in getting his program through the legislature; what is needed is a better program to be presented to that body. The two staff positions of policy secretary and administrative secretary are designed to give the governor the raw material for a better program.

The preceding discussion of the duties of the policy secretary clearly shows that a close correlation exists between the duties of this position and those of the administrative secretary. Never-

---

1952), 42-54 for a discussion of the difficulties in establishing budget criteria and for some suggested criteria.

theless, the administrative secretary has several important duties of his own falling in three principal areas of operations. In the first place, the administrative secretary should serve as liaison man between the governor and the heads of the agencies in the executive branch. Secondly, he should serve as an adviser to the governor on budgeting, fiscal control, personnel, purchasing, and other housekeeping functions necessary for the daily operation of the executive agencies. Finally, the administrative secretary should be responsible for the data on which the governor can make his appointment decisions.

In carrying out his first function, the administrative secretary has the very delicate task of attempting to handle as many of the more routine problems of the various department heads as possible without seeming to stand between the governor and the heads of the agencies in the executive branch. Particularly in a small state, there is usually a tradition of free access to the governor by the heads of the various agencies which make up the executive branch. Since it is quite probable that many of these heads are not the governor's appointees, the governor's position and relation to these individuals is precarious at best and will only be further endangered by an administrative secretary who tries to act as a buffer between the governor and the agency heads. As will be pointed out later in this chapter, a few states have experimented with a position of this nature. Comments from department heads interviewed in these states indicate that they are extremely jealous of their right of access to the chief executive. Only if the administrative secretary is an individual of recognized stature who is known to have the complete confidence of the governor and who is a person of considerable tact, can such a position be of practical value to the governor. If not properly handled, this sort of liaison can be very detrimental to the governor's relations with his department heads; many such relationships are very tenuous at best.

The second function suggested for the administrative secretary is really that which is performed by the director of administration in some of the larger states. The individual who occupies this position should be well informed on the so-called housekeeping functions of the state such as budgeting, purchasing, personnel, accounting, and the like. It is obvious that even in a small state, the administrative secretary will have a very difficult time trying to be a combination budget director, personnel director, director of centralized purchasing, and comptroller, and it is not suggested that he actually perform the details involved in these functions. His job is to keep informed on what is happening and to give policy direction to the agencies engaged in the day-to-day operations in these areas.

There are several institutional arrangements which might be used to achieve this end. If the state is small enough, the administrative secretary may be able to give fairly close supervision to these functions which can be carried out in divisions actually attached to the governor's office. Presumably, each of these divisions would be headed by a division chief of professional caliber who would supervise daily operations and report to the governor's administrative secretary who in turn would report matters of major significance to the governor. In somewhat larger states it might be desirable to have these units located in a finance department under a director appointed by the governor. The director would keep the administrative secretary informed of all major policy problems in this area but probably would need to deal with the governor on the most important policy matters. Another arrangement which has been used successfully in several states and has found favor with several "Little Hoover" commissions is to centralize these functions in a department of administration. All of these institutional arrangements are being used at present in various states, although few of them have an administrative secretary who performs the functions suggested here.

In many of the smaller states there is actually no functioning budget agency at present, although in most of them there is a statute providing for a so-called executive budget. The personnel agency, if it exists, is likely to be headed by an independent board not subject to the governor's control. The accounting system frequently is located in the office of an independent elected executive officer such as the comptroller or treasurer, and centralized purchasing frequently does not exist at all.

In such a situation, more typical than one might expect in view of all the reorganizations which have been proposed or attempted, the governor has no one person who can keep him informed on the management side of his functions. It is obvious that he should have such a person. In a small state with a small staff, the administrative secretary could play such a role and might have a fairly direct relation with the division head in the governor's office who would actually carry out the various management activities. In most states the administrative secretary would operate primarily at the policy level and would confine his activities to providing policy co-ordination for the units carrying out the management functions and to providing the governor with the information necessary for policy decision in the management field. The exact form of organization to carry on the management functions will have to be adapted to suit the needs of each state. The important point here is not the institutional arrangement but the recognition that there should be on the governor's staff an individual who is informed on management matters and who can advise the governor in respect to this part of his functions. In this area, a good administrative secretary can relieve the governor of much of the workload of detailed operations which he is now carrying.

Since the role of the administrative secretary involves both departmental liaison on administrative matters and on budgeting, it is obvious that his functions must be closely co-ordinated with those of the policy secretary. This relationship has already been discussed in regard to budgeting. In the field of departmental liaison the necessity for such co-ordination will be a continuing process. For example, many of the departments will have programs which require new legislation. Since many of these programs are inextricably entwined with administrative matters, the administrative secretary probably will be informed of such proposed programs in advance and should pass this information on to the policy secretary. It is essential that such co-ordination be accomplished by mutual agreement between the governor's secretaries or the governor will have to devote considerable time to the co-ordination of his own staff. Inevitably, there will be problems on which the governor's secretaries will not be able to arrange satisfactory solutions themselves. In this event, the governor will have to resolve the difficulties. However, it is desirable for the staff to solve as many problems of co-ordination as possible below the gubernatorial level, leaving for the governor only major problems.

Since all governors have to make a considerable number of appointments, it is desirable that some member of the staff be charged with the responsibility of collecting the data on which such appointments can be based. In the case of major appointments the governor undoubtedly will receive advice from many quarters and will make his decision primarily on political grounds. In the case of minor appointments, there is the problem of keeping track of all the appointments which must be made. This is a considerable task in most states since these appointments number from 500 to 1,000 in the course of the governor's term of office. In addition there is the problem of collecting recommendations from party leaders, department heads, members of the legislature, and local groups who may be interested in certain positions, and of accumulating a file on the persons suggested for various positions. The governor does not have time to go through all of this preliminary investigation, and his administrative secretary should be responsible for making such preliminary checks and presenting to the governor a list of names of individuals who meet the legal and political requirements for the position in question. This is usually a time-consuming task, and the functions described above generally are assigned to one of the governor's secretaries or an appointments clerk. It is highly desirable that the governor be relieved of most of these appointments. If that is not feasible, the most satisfactory temporary solution is to assign the task of collecting data and recommendations on possible appointees to a member of the staff. This function is suggested as a part of the duties of the administrative secretary, since he will be familiar with the detailed organization of the executive branch and will be in a position to know the legal requirements for the various positions which must be filled.

The primary functions of the public relations secretary are to act as a buffer between the governor and the public and to act as the governor's eyes and ears in obtaining reactions to his programs, present or proposed. In acting as a buffer for the governor, one of the secretary's major responsibilities is to handle as many of the governor's visitors as possible so that the governor's interviewing load may be reduced. This is a difficult role which requires tact and knowledge of the state government. Frequently the governor's visitors actually do not want to see the governor but are seeking some service which is under the control of one of the departments of the executive branch. Such visitors can be referred to these departments. Other visitors are well acquainted with the department with which they intend to deal but want the weight of the governor's office behind a particular request. These can be handled, if the secretary decides that the case warrants such action, by a call to the agency involved. Other visitors demand to see the governor personally, and in a state with an open door tradition these are hard to handle. However, the public relations secretary must make every effort to take care of as many of the governor's visitors as possible, and experience shows that this can be done to a considerable extent by an able secretary.[7]

In addition to acting as a buffer in handling visitors, the secretary must act in the same capacity in handling mail. In this capacity the secretary will screen the incoming mail and will answer or refer all but a few letters himself, reserving for the governor only those letters which raise important policy or political questions. At least a part of the incoming mail may be referred to the various departments of the executive branch on the basis of its contents, and some of it probably will be referred to the policy secretary or administrative secretary. The replies to the letters referred to the departments may be drawn up by the department for the governor's signature or the secretary may send a form letter to the person writing to the governor, informing him that his letter has been turned over to a certain department for reply. The letters referred to other executive departments and to the policy secretary and administrative secretary, combined with those replies which can be written by the governor's public relations secretary, should take care of the bulk of the mail, leaving only a relatively few letters of major importance to be answered by the governor personally. Frequently, even in these letters the governor can indicate in a one line memorandum the tenor of the reply and the public relations secretary can actually prepare the

[7] Estimates given by the secretaries to the various governors as to the number of callers they are able to handle range from 50 to 85 per cent. Even with this reduction the governor still has a very substantial interviewing load. See Chapter 6 for a further analysis of the governor's daily schedule of interviews.

answer which can be read and signed by the governor before it is dispatched.

Another important function of the public relations secretary should be the preparation of the drafts of most of the governor's major public speeches and radio or television broadcasts. In this area close co-ordination must be maintained with the policy secretary so that these speeches will be in line with current policy. Not all of the governor's speeches will actually be major policy speeches, since he makes a myriad of official welcoming speeches, cornerstone laying speeches, after-dinner speeches, and the like, in which major policy probably will not play an important role. However, in those speeches where the policy content is important, there must be close co-ordination between the governor's secretaries. In addition there may be need for co-ordination outside the governor's office with department heads and legislative leaders or party officials, depending on the nature of the speech. As a corollary function, the secretary should be responsible for arranging the governor's press conferences and preparing press releases. He should also prepare the drafts of proclamations on state holidays and on other occasions such as National Hog Week. In addition he should advise the governor on requests for the governor's endorsement of or contribution to fund-raising drives for charitable, religious, and philanthropic organizations, all of which at least want the governor's name on their letterhead and many of which are seeking a contribution.

While interviews, handling mail, preparing the drafts of public addresses and press relations probably will take up the bulk of the public relations secretary's time, he also should attempt to keep himself informed on the reactions of the public to the governor's program and to his public statements. In fact, he must try to anticipate the public's reaction to such programs and speeches and inform the governor as to the possible public reaction to a given program if it were put into effect. This is a function which is closely related to that of the policy secretary and which requires close co-ordination between these two. The public relations secretary must know in advance the new programs or changes in old programs which will be proposed so that he may try to gauge the public reaction and be prepared to explain or defend the programs either to the press or to citizens who write in for information or who are critical of the new programs.

It should be noted that the governor's public relations include not only those speeches, letters, proclamations, and the like, which emanate from the governor's office but also include the same sort of public contacts which are made by the various departments.[8] If favorable public relations are to be maintained with the state's citizens, the governor's public relations secretary must at least be informed of what the various departments are doing along this line. Bad public relations on the part of any one of the departments can be a very serious matter for the governor. Hence, his public relations secretary must not only see to it that the governor and his staff maintain good public relations but also that the departments maintain favorable relations with the citizens. This is a very large order, and it is doubtful whether such co-ordination can be achieved in many states. One device, however, which has proved useful in some states is a clearance procedure whereby major speeches and press releases which emanate from the departments are cleared with the governor's office before their release. If the governor's relations with his department heads are such that this sort of control can be enforced, such a procedure would be extremely helpful to the public relations secretary in his attempts to secure co-ordination in the field of public relations. If the device is used, it would seem logical for the public relations secretary to act for the governor in the clearance process.

In addition to the three positions thus far described, the governor needs a staff member who can provide him with legal advice. While in theory this is provided by the attorney general, in

[8] Actually the governor's public relations is an even broader problem than is suggested by this description. The average citizen is quite likely to receive his impression of the governor's program at that point at which the citizen comes into contact with the program through its application to his particular case by an employee engaged in carrying out one facet of the program. Hence, the real problem of public relations embraces the actions of a multitude of state employees. The treatment of the citizen by these employees so as to produce a favorable view of the program of the administration is not a matter which will be controlled by a system of press release clearances. See Ransone, *The Office of Governor in the South* (Bureau of Public Administration, University of Alabama, 1951), pp. 224-226 for a "case study" of the broader aspects of public relations in one southern state.

practice it is common for the governor to have his own legal adviser. This is true particularly in those states where the attorney general is an elected official and, therefore, may be of a different party or of a different faction of the governor's party. In this situation it is difficult for the governor to maintain the close relationship with the attorney general which is essential if the governor is to secure legal advice on the many problems which confront him daily. In particular he needs legal counsel on his proposed programs and on the constitutionality and legal implications of bills which come before him for signature. In this connection the legal secretary will be in a position to advise the governor on the legal aspects of legislation, while the policy secretary would advise the governor on the policy implications of legislation. Thus, these two staff members would work closely with the governor on the problem of whether to veto or sign a particular statute.

One possible solution to providing the governor with legal advice is to make the attorney general an appointive officer. This solution has been accepted by several states and seems to work very satisfactorily. In lieu of this solution, however, it seems desirable to provide the governor with a legal secretary in his own office. In addition to providing the advice suggested above, the governor's legal secretary could also perform the preliminary work on pardon and parole matters which is a part of the governor's function in most states. He also might be responsible for the preliminary work on requests for extradition from other states and the review of requests for extradition sent to other states. In this connection the legal secretary might hold extradition hearings where the case warranted such a hearing and make specific recommendations to the governor based on such a hearing and other data.

The basic staff of four persons which has been described above is rather small, even for a sparsely populated state. The description of their duties is admittedly oversimplified. Nevertheless, this description represents an attempt to design the governor's staff so that it can be of assistance to the governor in carrying out his three major functions of policy formation, management, and public relations. Even with an able staff, there will remain a great deal for the governor to do. However, if the staff performs its functions with some degree of effectiveness, those tasks which remain for the governor are primarily in the realm of policy decisions in these three fields. Consequently, the governor will be able to operate at his proper level in making major decisions and will not be overburdened by the multitude of detailed operations which now occupy a substantial part of his time.

It is quite obvious that the compartmentalization of duties which has been used here for the sake of emphasis is not something which in practice will follow any neat pattern. The governor's secretaries undoubtedly will perform additional duties and the governor probably will assign from time to time to any of the secretaries various tasks in any one of these three major areas of operation. One of the secretaries to a prominent midwestern governor who has been exceptionally effective in his role as the governor's principal assistant suggested that the governor's relations with the legislature were such as to demand a new face from time to time as a representative of the governor's office. This gentleman sagely observed that in the course of time a single legislative representative from the governor's office might be expected to wear out his welcome with the legislature. It would, therefore, be necessary to replace him with another representative. This undoubtedly is true in many instances. Consequently, in suggesting that the function of legislative liaison as one of the principal roles for the policy secretary, it was not intended that this individual be the only representative of the governor in dealing with the legislature. It may well be that the policy secretary may wear out his welcome, and one of the other gubernatorial assistants may have to take over the duty of serving as contact man with the legislature. This is primarily a tactical question, however, and it does not seem to detract from the necessity of centering the responsibility for policy review in one individual on the governor's staff. The policy secretary might still be responsible for the governor's program even if he did not personally serve as contact man with the legislature. In this connection it might be noted that the administrative secretary or budget division head might be called upon by the legislature to testify before the appropriations committee of the House on the governor's budget or on some other proposed program. This is common practice at present and undoubtedly will continue.

It is because of such practices and the possibility of the policy secretary becoming *persona non grata* with the legislature that it was suggested that the governor might find it necessary to shift assignments among the members of his staff as the occasion might demand. The governor's staff must be flexible in its assignments between various staff members much in the same way that the composition of the staff must be flexible over a period of time to adjust to the changing methods of succeeding governors. There also is nothing in the plan suggested here that would prevent the governor from using additional individuals from time to time either on a consultant basis or as temporary personnel in his office. What is urged is that provision be made on the governor's staff for able, high-level assistants to aid the governor in carrying out all three of his major functions.

The primary difference in the staff which has been suggested and that of the average governor is in the policy field. The governor must make policy decisions and in practice makes these as a matter of almost daily routine. He receives and will continue to receive advice on how he should make these decisions from a variety of sources both in and out of the government. The pressures from party leaders, interest groups, and department heads will continue and the presence of a policy secretary will not alleviate totally such pressures. What he can do is to give the governor a source of advice to which he can turn for an accurate analysis of the mass of data which must be considered in making most policy decisions. It is at this point that a small research staff under the policy secretary can become a valuable aid to the governor. Such a staff has not been suggested in the basic staffing pattern since it is doubtful whether it would be acceptable in a very small state. However, there have been several interesting developments along this line in some of our medium-sized states which point to the usefulness of this device in states with a fairly small population. These developments will be discussed at a later point in this chapter.

The staff described above is not a prescription for a particular state or even for all small states. It is designed to represent a concept rather than an exact institutional arrangement. Essentially, it is based on the simple proposition that the governor's staff should be designed to assist him in his three primary functions of policy formation, management, and public relations. As has been repeatedly pointed out in this study, this division of the governor's functions is primarily a classification of convenience for the purposes of discussion. Of necessity these functions are interrelated and overlapping to a considerable extent. Consequently, any individual positions set up to carry out these three functions will show in practice a considerable overlapping of duties and the need for careful self-coördination among members of the governor's staff.[9]

REDUCING THE GOVERNOR'S WORK LOAD

In the previous section it was suggested that the establishment of an adequate staff should be accompanied by the transfer from the governor's office of those duties which do not relate directly to his major functions. While it is very important that the governor be given those powers and duties which are necessary if he is to operate effectively at the policy level, it is also important that those duties which are not pertinent to this level of operations be abolished or shifted to other quarters. The particular duties which should be abolished or transferred will depend on conditions in each state. However, it is suggested that the guide to abolition or transfer should be the determination of whether or not a given duty or responsibility is necessary for the execution of one of the governor's three principal functions. If they are pertinent, they should be retained; if they are not pertinent, they should be abolished or transferred. One of the ways by which the governor can be given more time to perform his major functions is to limit the time which he must spend on his minor functions. Thus, a desirable corollary to the provision of an adequate staff is the elimination of minor duties which now occupy the time of the governor or which occupy the time of his staff.

The appointing power, an aspect of the gubernatorial function common to all states, might be used to illustrate the nature of this problem. In some of the states, such as Virginia, New York,

[9] In a large state the problem of staff co-ordination becomes one of considerable importance. In such a situation it probably is desirable for one of the secretaries to be designated as a co-ordinating agent. Policy differences within the staff might be resolved by this individual as a sort of chief of staff. A weekly staff conference also has been used successfully in several states to achieve better policy co-ordination. In some of the larger states co-ordination of routine matters is achieved through an office manager. All of these approaches seem useful if the staff is large enough.

and New Jersey, this power involves most of the major positions in the executive branch. In other states, like South Carolina, it is highly circumscribed by legislatively contrived standards and relates only to minor positions. In almost all states, however, the governor must make many minor appointments even if he also makes some major ones. While it is highly desirable that the governor be able to appoint and remove his major department heads, it does not follow that it is desirable for him to appoint all the notaries public in the state, or to appoint the members of twenty or thirty licensing and professional boards, or even the bulk of the state employees below the policy level. These minor appointments should be shifted to other quarters. For example, some states have had considerable success with a department of licensing and registration and have designated the head of that department as the governor's agent in making the necessary appointments to licensing and professional boards which operate within the department. Some solution similar to this seems desirable so that the governor may be relieved of this particular type of appointment. In the case of notaries public or such offices as justice of the peace, there seem to be no policy considerations which make it desirable for the governor to appoint these individuals. Experience in several states shows that a better system to obtain standards and control of these appointments can be secured by placing the job in one of the established departments of government.

The problem of the governor in the spoils-system states in regard to appointments is a more serious one. As the analysis of the daily routine of the governor of Arkansas revealed, the governor in a spoils-system state spends far too large a proportion of his time on interviews with prospective job-seekers. This time can be cut substantially by the installation of a merit system, according to several members of the governor's staff in Alabama who served under governors both prior to and after the adoption of the merit system. In that state the governor's burden in interviewing applicants was greatly reduced by the installation of a merit system and the transfer of the authority to make appointments to the department head in whose department the vacancy occurs. When the governor in Alabama is approached by a person seeking an appointment in one of the departments, the person is told that the position is under civil service and that he will have to take an examination for the position. This generally is enough to discourage most would-be applicants. As the governor's executive secretary put the matter, "Most job seekers are looking for a 'position' not for 'work'." The notion that they might have to work in the job and that it is filled on a competitive basis discourages all but those who have a legitimate reason for seeking state employment. Such individuals are referred to the director of personnel and, if qualified, are given an appropriate examination. Word on the procedure for filling state positions gradually spread throughout the state, and the installation of merit-system procedures reduced to a comparative trickle the flood of job seekers who once inundated the governor's office with each change of administration.

Several of the governors interviewed in states where the spoils system still prevails felt that patronage of this type was more of a headache than a benefit, and were in favor of the establishment of a merit system as much as a device to relieve the governor of his burdensome task in interviewing prospective job applicants as for the intrinsic worth of the merit system. Regardless of how the installation of such a system is viewed, it does remove a large part of the pressure on the governor in minor appointments and will be a distinct step forward in the provision of more time for major functions.

Similarly, it is possible to relieve the governor of much of the detailed paper work which he must now perform in connection with such matters as purchasing, contracts, deeds, personnel actions, and allotment changes. While at least some of these should be under the governor's control, this does not mean that he must personally sign each piece of legal paper. In most states the governor actually signs most of these documents without personal review on the assurance of his staff that the papers are in order. If the governor's personal review was what the legislature was seeking in establishing these processes, this is not now being accomplished in most states. The governor simply does not have time to review all of these documents personally even if it is assumed that it is desirable that he do so. Consequently, these functions might be shifted to the governor's administrative secretary, a director of administration, or some other appropriate official under the governor's control who could be delegated this responsibility under a revision of the statutes. In this connection the picture comes to mind of the governor's desk in one of the southern states visited in the course of the field work done in preparation for this book. The executive secretary spent some time with the writer and showed him around the executive offices, ending with a visit to the governor's office. Here, the writer found the governor's massive desk almost obscured by a vast pile of documents of all descriptions. The executive secretary pointed to the two overflowing "in" baskets and remarked that the governor had been out of town for three days and, because of the wording of the pertinent statutes, no one in the office could sign any of the documents for the governor. "What we need," he said, "is an assistant governor who could at least sign the governor's name in his absence."

This indeed would be one possible approach to the problem, but state legislatures and the public do not seem to have accepted the idea of an "assistant governor," at least by that title. In lieu of an assistant governor a parallel approach might be to revise the statutes so that these documents need never reach the governor's desk. It is this approach which is suggested here in recommending that the authority to sign such documents be transferred to the administrative secretary, director of administration, or, better still, to appropriate department heads if these are under the governor's control.

Another example, which also applies to most states, of the kind of duties which might well be delegated are the so-called "legal" powers of the governor. These include the power of the governor to pardon criminals convicted under the statutes of the state, to extend executive clemency for certain periods to those sentenced to die, to commute death sentences to life imprisonment, and to grant paroles to those serving prison sentences. These functions in some states are a considerable drain on the governor's time and are duties which cause him a great deal of personal anxiety.[10] It does not seem to the writer that these functions are among those

[10] See Alfred E. Smith, *Up To Now, An Autobiography* (New York, 1929), pp. 306-308. Not all of the governors interviewed felt as keenly as did Governor Smith the personal strain of such duties. However, one of them characterized his executive clemency functions as "a considerable burden and a great mental hazard."

which should be properly assigned to the governor. However, the fact remains that some or all of them are assigned to the governor in most state constitutions. Thus, we are faced with the problem of either shifting these functions to other quarters or of providing the governor with some assistance in their execution.

In Texas this problem has been approached by removing most of these functions from the governor and transferring them to a constitutional board. This board is composed of three members—one appointed by the governor, one appointed by the Chief Justice of the Supreme Court, and one appointed by the Presiding Justice of the Court of Criminal Appeals. The members serve six-year overlapping terms and are subject to Senate confirmation. Appointments to the board are made from a list of eligibles which is drawn up by a second board composed of the chairmen of the boards of Public Safety, Public Welfare, and Prisons; an appointee of the governor; and an appointee of the attorney general. The Board of Pardons and Paroles, as it is called, has the authority to recommend pardons, paroles, and other acts of clemency to the governor. The governor on his own initiative has only the power to grant one thirty-day reprieve to a prisoner and cannot act on pardon and parole matters except upon recommendation of the Board. The governor, however, may request the Board to investigate the advisability of executive clemency in particular cases.[11]

This arrangement tends to relieve the governor of the responsibilities connected with pardon and parole matters and makes his actions almost automatic in complying with the Board's recommendations. Similar boards of pardon and parole exist in other states and some arrangement to transfer the governor's responsibility to such a body seems desirable, although the board need not be constitutional in nature or the selection procedure as elaborate as that in Texas.[12] If such a transfer cannot be arranged, the

[11] Stuart A. MacCorkle and Dick Smith, *Texas Government* (New York, 1952), p. 119.

[12] It should be noted that the pardon and parole boards in many states were established primarily for the purpose of preventing certain abuses of the pardon and parole authority by the governor. In some states there has been considerable abuse of this power. While the board system has not always improved the situation, it seems to have functioned fairly satisfactorily on the whole. A by-product of the board arrangement has been to reduce substantially the governor's work load.

preliminary work on pardon and parole matters might be done by the governor's legal adviser, as was suggested previously.

The problem of the governor's power to grant requests for extradition[13] is not as serious in terms of time consumed as the problems relating to pardon and parole since requests for extradition are not as numerous. Nevertheless, this is a duty which does take some time, since extradition hearings generally are held in most states, and in several of them the governor presides at such hearings. In a few states the governor has, in practice, virtually delegated this function to the attorney general, who reviews the facts in the case, holds a hearing if he feels that one is warranted by the facts, and makes a recommendation to the governor as to the disposition of the case. This seems to be a desirable solution if there is a good working relationship between the governor and the attorney general. Another approach to the problem which is used in several states is to refer such cases to the governor's legal adviser, who reviews the case, conducts a hearing if necessary, and recommends appropriate action. This solution also relieves the governor of much of the time-consuming details of the extradition process and is perhaps the best solution in those states in which there is any frigidity in the relations between the governor and the attorney general.

While the time spent on extradition cases by most governors is not great, in view of the press of his other duties it seems desirable to reduce it to a bare minimum. The best way to achieve such a reduction would seem to be to delegate the details of the extradition procedure to one of the governor's staff. In the particular staffing pattern suggested in the first section of this chapter, the individual to whom such duties could most logically be delegated would seem to be the governor's legal secretary because of his training in law.

The minor functions of the governor which have been discussed in this section are but examples of the multitude of such duties which are placed upon him by the constitution and statutes in every state. While they are minor duties in terms of their importance relative to the governor's other functions, over the course of a

13 Technically this power is that of rendition, but most of the governors and members of the governors' staffs interviewed used the term "extradition" in describing this power, and consequently, that terminology is used here.

year these duties become almost major in terms of time consumed. The suggestions made here for the transfer of some of these duties and for delegation of others are based primarily on the premise that the governor must be relieved of such minor duties if he is to have time to carry out his major functions. Some of these duties, such as the approval of personnel actions or the approval of purchases and contracts, should be under the governor's control and, hence, should be delegated rather than transferred. Others, such as the commissioning of notaries public, do not seem to be a proper function of the governor and should be transferred to other quarters. The list given here is far from complete and a careful study of the governor's minor constitutional and statutory duties should be made in any given state before it is decided what duties should be transferred or delegated. Those duties which are directly pertinent to the governor's major functions of policy formation, public relations, and management should be retained by the governor himself. Those duties which are subsidiary to these functions and which serve to implement one or more of them should be retained by the governor, but the actual details of operations should be delegated to a member of his staff or to a department under his control. Those duties which do not directly or indirectly assist the governor in his major functions should be transferred to other quarters.

PROTOTYPES FOR GUBERNATORIAL STAFFING

The pattern suggested for the staff of the governor's office in the first section of this chapter was not based on the staffing pattern of any particular state. However, certain of the governor's assistants in some of the states will recognize in the descriptions of the positions in the basic staffing pattern a remarkable similarity to their own positions, and others will recognize that one or more of the duties of a particular position are those which they now perform. It may be useful, therefore, to consider in more detail the various prototypes which served as models for these positions to see how the basic staffing pattern was derived. The fact that similar positions do exist and that they have proven useful in their respective states also should be of interest to those who are concerned with practical problems of gubernatorial staffing in a given state.

In considering a staffing pattern for any state, both the size and composition of the staff must be taken into consideration. In the basic staffing pattern suggested in the first section of this chapter, the question of size was touched upon only indirectly, since the concept of a basic staffing pattern suggests that this pattern is subject to expansion to fit the needs of the governor in a particular state. Implicit in the suggestion that the governor have a policy secretary, an administrative secretary, a public relations secretary, and a legal counsel is, of course, the notion that the governor would have a staff of four persons at what might be called a professional level. It was suggested further that if the governor's office contained a division of budget, a division of personnel, or other similar divisions, there should be at least one professional person to head up each of these divisions. In addition, there probably would be at least three stenographers or typists to handle clerical chores, including correspondence dictated by the governor and his assistants. From the point of view of size, therefore, the basic staff suggested for the governor probably would run to at least four professional staff aides and three clerical employees. This recommendation was the outcome of a careful study of the governor's functions and is based on the staff needed to assist him in these functions rather than on any predetermined ideal size for the governor's staff. One implication which could be drawn from this recommendation is that any governor who now has a staff of less than seven persons is understaffed. The writer is not willing to draw this implication, since this would place the recommendation for a basic staff in the category of a formula for the determination of the proper size of gubernatorial staffs; and if there is one point above all others which has been brought out by this study of the governors' staffs, it is that rigid formulas have no place in gubernatorial staffing.

The difficulty of determining any sort of formula on which an intelligent recommendation for the proper size of the gubernatorial staff in a given state could be based is brought out by an analysis of the data presented in Table X. In this table, a comparison is made between the governors' staffs in 25 fairly representative states. The table records both the total number of employees and a further breakdown as to whether these employees were at the professional or clerical level.

TABLE X

*The Governors' Staffs in Twenty-Five Selected States**

State	Staff			State	Staff		
	Prof.	Cler.	Tot.		Prof.	Cler.	Tot.
New York	11	31	43	Virginia	3	4	7
California	12	30	42	Kentucky	2	5	7
Michigan	7	14	21	Arkansas	2	4	6
Georgia	5	14	19	Mississippi	1	5	6
Alabama	6	6	12	New Hampshire	3[d]	2	5
Oklahoma	5	7	12	Tennessee	2	3	5
South Carolina	3	9	12	Vermont	2[e]	1	3
Wisconsin	6[a]	5	11	Utah	2	1	3
Minnesota	6	4	10	Nevada	2	1	3
Florida	3[b]	6	9	Wyoming	1	2	3
Colorado	2	7	9	South Dakota	1	2	3
North Carolina	3[c]	5	8	New Mexico	1	2	3
Louisiana	2	6	8				

[a]Executive Counsel is a part-time position.
[b]Legislative Secretary is a part-time position.
[c]Legislative Assistant is a part-time position.
[d]Legislative Counsel is a part-time position filled during legislative session.
[e]Executive Clerk is a part-time position filled during legislative session.

*The figures in this table are based on information collected in interviews in these states, the source usually being the governor's executive secretary or a comparable member of the staff. Most of the data was collected in the summer of 1951 but the southern states were originally visited in 1949. The figures, therefore, are for two different years and must be interpreted with some caution on a comparative basis.

The terms "professional" and "clerical" are used in an attempt to give more content to the figure on the "total" staff. The professional staff is considered to be those persons who fill positions at the executive secretary or administrative level, while the clerical employees include stenographers, typists, messengers, switchboard operators, and the like, who make up the office force. While the figure representing the total number of persons on the staff is one of some significance, a more important comparison is between the number of employees at the professional level in the governor's office, for it is from this group that his major advice and assistance must be drawn.

The average size of the governor's staff in the 25 states visited is about eleven persons, of whom four are "professional" staff aides, such as the governor's executive secretary, press secretary, or legal counsel, and seven are clerical employees, such as stenographers, typists, or messengers. These averages, however, are not very useful in arriving at a formula for gubernatorial staffing because of the wide range of size which they conceal. For example, in New Mexico, one of the states with the smallest staff, the governor has only one professional aide and two clerical employees, while in New York, which is the state with the largest staff among those surveyed, the governor has eleven professional aides and 31 clerical employees. The table is useful in pointing up the range which does exist in the size of the gubernatorial staffs, and an analysis of the figures illustrates the fact that the establishment of any sort of a formula for gubernatorial staffing is a very risky proposition.

It is interesting, however, to note some of the contrasts which do emerge from this presentation and to attempt to find some over-all pattern. In general about the only pattern which emerges clearly is that all of the governors have at least one professional aide and one clerical employee and that there is a very rough correlation between the size of the state and the number of members on the governor's staff. In the upper and middle reaches of the population scale this correlation is close enough to be significant, but in the lower reaches it becomes less accurate. For example, in 1950 Nevada had a population of about 160,000 which made it the smallest state in the nation. Nevada in 1951 had a staff of only three persons, which placed it in that group of states in the sample with the smallest staffs. However, South Dakota, Wyoming, Vermont, New Mexico, and Utah also had staffs of only three persons, and all of these states had a population greater than that of Nevada. Therefore, in the group of states which had the smallest staffs, there is a considerable discrepancy in size as compared to staff, and there is no regular increase in the size of the staff as the population of the state increases.

The disparities in staff as compared to size and the variations which occur even in states in roughly the same population class may be brought out more clearly if they are compared on the basis of the ratio of total staff to total population. For example, the seven smallest states in the sample in terms of population are Nevada (160,083), Wyoming (290,529), Vermont (377,747), New Hampshire (533,242), South Dakota (652,740), New Mexico (681,-187), and Utah (688,862). It so happens that all of these states except New Hampshire have the same number of staff members, with each state having a total of three on the governor's staff. In New Hampshire there are five staff members, one of whom is a part-time employee. Vermont actually has the smallest staff of any state in the entire group, since it has only two full-time staff members and one part-time staff member. For purposes of comparison, however, it will be assumed that the governor's office in each state is at full strength and that, consequently, Vermont will be credited with a staff of three and New Hampshire with a staff of five. A comparison of the total staff to the total population shows that in Nevada there are roughly 53,000 persons in the state for each staff member. In Wyoming the ratio is 97,000 to one; in Vermont 126,000 to one; in New Hampshire 107,000 to one; in South Dakota 218,000 to one; in New Mexico 227,000 to one; and in Utah 230,000 to one. If it is assumed that there should be some positive correlation between the size of the state and its population, the question immediately arises as to which of these ratios, if any of them, should be accepted as a proper guide to gubernatorial staffing. Such a determination carries with it the implicit assumption that the state chosen now has an adequate staff. It also is obvious that the size of the governor's staff in each state will depend upon the ratio chosen and that quite different results may be obtained from using any given ratio. For example, if the Nevada ratio of one staff member for each 53,000 of the population is used, a random sampling shows that Wyoming would have five staff members under the new ratio as compared to its present staff of three, New Hampshire would have ten as compared to five at present, and Utah would have thirteen as compared with its present staff of only three. By these standards Wyoming, New Hampshire, and Utah are all understaffed, Wyoming needing two more staff members, while New Hampshire needs an additional five and Utah ten to bring the governor's staff in those states up to the Nevada standard. On this same basis, however, North Carolina and Louisiana, which are the median states in terms of the size of their staffs, would have 51 and 77 staff members each, as compared to their present staffs of eight members. At the other end of the scale, New York would have 280 staff members as compared to its present staff of 43. On the other hand, if the ratio of New Hampshire, which has the largest staff of any state in the first seven in population, is used, the results for the same states would be as follows: Nevada one (present staff three); Wyoming three (present staff three); Utah six (present staff three); Louisiana 25 (present staff eight); North Carolina 38 (present staff eight); and New York 138 (present staff 43).

If one starts at the other end of the scale, he will discover that New York has only one staff member for every 345,000 population. On this basis, the states at the lower end of the population scale would fare badly. Nevada and Wyoming would have no staff at all, while Vermont and New Hampshire would each have one staff member and South Dakota, New Mexico, and Utah would have only two staff members each. The median states, Louisiana and North Carolina, which now have eight members each would have eight and twelve staff members respectively. Judged by New York standards, California also is overstaffed, and its present staff of 42 would have to be cut to 31 to conform to the New York ratio.

Taking the 25 states as a group, the average staff to population ratio is one staff member for every 286,000 persons. The application of this ratio to random states reveals that it would leave Nevada without staff, Wyoming and Vermont with one each, New Hampshire with two, and Louisiana and North Carolina, the median states at present, would have nine and fourteen staff members respectively instead of their present eight each. On the same basis, California would lose four staff members to bring the staff in that state to 37, but New York would gain nine staff members to bring the governor's staff up to a strength of 52.

All of these calculations merely serve to emphasize the decided variations between states in terms of staff even when those states fall roughly in the same population class. Any formula for gubernatorial staffing which is set low enough in population terms to give the states with limited population a minimum staff of at least four professional and three clerical employees would have the effect of giving the largest states such a large staff that it might prove unwieldy for the purposes for which it was designed and probably would prove politically unacceptable as well. In the writer's opinion most of the smaller states in this group are understaffed. This evaluation is based primarily on an analysis of the functions of the governor in these states and on the degree to which his present staff can assist him in carrying out these functions rather than on any formula derived from a staff-population ratio. Above a minimum of four professional assistants, it would seem logical for the governor's need for additional staff aides to increase with the size of the state. However, there is nothing absolute about this progression, since the many variables involved, including such matters as the work habits of a particular governor and the ecology of government in a given state, make it extremely unwise to attempt to freeze such a progression into any kind of absolute formula.

It does appear, however, that an analysis of existing patterns furnishes valuable clues to the kinds of positions which might be included in a basic staffing pattern. A position which has proved practicable and useful in one state will not necessarily prove equally successful in another state, but some of the positions which have been developed have proved of sufficient value to be worth careful consideration. At first glance the over-all staffing patterns of the respective states do not present any more of a uniform pattern than do sizes of the staffs. The variety of titles used and the diversity of positions which are to be found tend to be rather confusing. For example, the governor's principal staff aide is usually called an executive secretary, as is the case in fifteen of the 25 states in the sample presented in Table XI. However, the principal aide is called the "secretary to the governor" in four states, the "private secretary" in two states, and the "executive assistant" in two additional states. In Colorado he has the title of Confidential Secretary, while in Vermont he has the even more imposing title of Secretary of Civil and Military Affairs. The same variation is found in the use of other titles, and the designations used do not always give a true picture of the duties of the position. For example, while the governor's legislative liaison man is called a Legislative Counsel in New Hampshire, which gives a fairly accurate picture of his major function, the position which embodies the same function in Vermont is called the Executive Clerk, while in Wisconsin it is called the Executive Counsel. In spite of such variations, there are a number of positions which have similar duties even though they may not have similar titles, so that there is in practice much more uniformity in the positions which make up the governors' staffs than in the size of these staffs.

A fairly meaningful picture of gubernatorial staffing patterns may be obtained from the more detailed breakdown of the gov-

TABLE XI

The Staff of the Governor's Office—Selected States, 1951

New Mexico		New Hampshire	
Executive Sec.	1	Sec. to the Governor	1
Clerical	2	Administrative Ass't.	1
		Legislative Counsel	1*
		Clerical	2
Total	3	Total	5
Wisconsin		**Oklahoma**	
Executive Sec.	1	Executive Sec.	1
Executive Counsel	1*	Press and Radio Sec.	1
Financial Sec.	1	Legal Counsel	2
Dir. Div. Dept. Research	1	Appointments Sec.	1
Admin. Analyst	2	Clerical	7
Clerical	5		
Total	11	Total	12
California		**New York**	
Executive Sec.	1	Sec. to the Governor	1
Governor's Personal Sec.	1	Ass't. Sec. to the Governor	1
Clemency and Appointments Sec.	1	Counsel to the Governor	1
Press and Public Rel. Sec.	1	Ass't. Counsel	1
Ass't. Press & P. R. Sec.	1	Confid. Law Ass'ts.	2
Research Sec.	1	Exec. Ass't. to the Governor	1
Legislative Sec.	1	Ass't. to the Governor	2
Departmental Sec.	1	Exec. Sec. to the Governor	1
Ass't. Dept. Sec.	1	Office Manager	1
Invitations and Travel Sec.	1	Clerical	32
Ass't. Invit. and Travel Sec.	1		
Office Supervisor	1		
Clerical	30		
Total	42	Total	43

*Part-time position; employed only during legislative sessions.

ernor's staff in six states which is presented in Table XI. These staffing patterns cannot be said to be typical, for each state is a case study of its own. However, the data presented do give several samples of staffing patterns which are currently being used in states of varying size and geographic location, and these samples cover most of the positions generally found in the governor's staff.

An analysis of the duties of the positions listed in Table XI brings to light some of the prototypes from which we derived the positions outlined in the suggested staffing pattern in the first section of this chapter. In some cases the similarity is readily apparent, while in others some explanation is necessary before the positions take on a degree of comparability.

To start with the most obvious model first, it might be pointed out that two of the states in Table XI have a position which is very similar to the public relations secretary suggested as one of the governor's key staff aides in the basic staffing pattern. In Oklahoma this position is called Press and Radio Secretary, while in California it is titled Press and Public Relations Secretary. In the latter state the work load of the position is such that the press and public relations secretary must have an assistant and a small clerical staff to assist him in the performance of his duties. The position of public relations or press secretary is not one which is encountered in the majority of states in this sample, since only two of the six states have a position whose title indicates that the occupant of the position is responsible for the kind of duties suggested for the public relations secretary. This does not mean, however, that these public relations duties are not performed by some member of the staff in the other states. It will be remembered that the duties suggested for the public relations secretary included acting as a buffer between the governor and the public in interviews and correspondence; the preparation of the governor's speeches, press releases, proclamations, and the like; and arranging for the governor's press conferences and speaking engagements. All of these duties are performed by one or more members of the governor's staff in all of the states, even though the title of the person performing the duties may not bear the label of press secretary or public relations secretary.

In a majority of the states duties of the kind suggested above are handled by the governor's executive secretary. In those states which have a public relations secretary, the duties are divided between that individual and the executive secretary. The press secretary's duties usually involve the preparation of the governor's speeches, press releases, and proclamations, the arrangements necessary for the governor's daily or semi-weekly press conferences, the determination of the governor's speaking schedule, which involves also the determination of which speaking engagements the governor should accept, and the arrangements necessary for the travel for speaking engagements. Frequently, the press secretary also handles the requests for funds from the governor for worthy causes or the endorsement by the governor of such activities. The press secretary may also handle some of the persons who come into the office for interviews with the governor and that part of the correspondence which relates to requests for information about the activities of the state government or which is concerned with the governor's views on topics of state or national importance. In general, the bulk of the interviews and the major part of the correspondence are handled by the executive secretary even in those states where there is a position of press secretary.

The discussion of the duties of the public relations secretary in the section on the basic staffing pattern included an additional duty which is not generally a formal part of the duties of either the press secretary or executive secretary in actual practice. This function was reporting to the governor on the public reaction to his program and, whenever possible, reporting on what the public relations secretary felt would be the public reaction to proposed programs. In practice the reporting of public opinion generally is handled on an informal basis by all of the members of the governor's staff and, frequently, is augmented by informal reports to the governor on the state of public opinion by a veteran legislator who is a friend of the administration or by a politician of known "savvy" in gauging public reaction. It is not likely that such informal contacts will be replaced by the proposed public relations secretary, but it does not seem too unrealistic to suggest that additional emphasis on this particular aspect of public relations might prove beneficial in some of the states. Frequently, the reporting aspect of public relations is neglected because of the concentration of the press secretaries' efforts on the problem of getting information to the press and the public. The writer believes that the gauging of public reaction to the governor's programs, present or proposed, is an important aspect of the public relations function and, hence, suggested this as a definite duty of the public relations secretary.

In the larger states, the duties suggested for the public relations secretary may be too great for one individual to handle. In this case the public relations secretary may be provided with an assistant or some of the duties may be shifted to other quarters. In California both of these approaches have been used. The press and public relations secretary has been given an assistant, and the duties relating to invitations and speaking arrangements are handled by the adjustments, invitations and travel secretary, who also has an assistant. In New York, there is no staff member who is officially called the public relations secretary, but the duties of this position are performed by the secretary to the governor.[14]

In the smaller states, represented in Table XI by New Mexico and New Hampshire, the governor's principal assistant must be jack of all trades and master of several, to twist the old expression a bit. Perhaps one of the hardest working but least publicized individuals in state government is the executive secretary to the governor. In a small state he is *the* staff of the governor and must function in a three-fold capacity as policy secretary, administrative secretary, and public relations secretary. This is too great a burden for any one person to carry with the hope of performing all of these functions with full effectiveness. The writer has the greatest sympathy and respect for persons in this position but feels that their effectiveness could be increased by shifting some of the duties which they now perform to other staff aides. Essentially, what is suggested here is that press relations and the major part of the interviewing and correspondence load borne by the executive secretary be shifted to the public relations secretary. This would relieve the executive secretary of the type of "public relations" which is at present his most time-consuming function. The management aspects of the executive secretary's duties, which are now generally neglected because of the lack of time, would be shifted to the administrative secretary. The shifting of public relations and management to other quarters would leave the executive secretary free to concentrate on policy matters and his position would be converted into the suggested one of policy secretary.

[14] The real nature of the duties of the secretary to the governor in New York becomes apparent when it is remembered that Mr. James C. Hagerty, who served for several years as Secretary to Governor Dewey, was selected by President Eisenhower to be his Press Secretary.

of which are meeting the public, handling correspondence, press and radio relations, and reporting public reaction, all seem to have a definite relationship to one another that makes it desirable that they be performed by the same individual. The designation of one individual on the governor's staff to handle these functions is simply a recognition of the importance of public relations as one of the governor's principal functions and an attempt to relieve him of some of the tremendous work load which he is now carrying in this field in most states. The public relations secretary cannot be expected to substitute for the governor at public functions or to deliver by proxy his major speeches. He can, however, be expected to sift the myriad of requests for public appearances and to do the spadework on the speeches which the governor decides are necessary. Similarly, the public relations secretary cannot see all the visitors who come into the governor's office or answer all the letters which the governor receives. He can, however, be expected to handle from 60 to 80 per cent of the visitors and probably 90 per cent of the correspondence. The duties outlined for this position are not, with the possible exception of the reporting of public sentiment, any great departure from present practices in the governors' offices. The grouping of these duties under one person and the separation of these duties from those involving major policy and management are, however, a departure from practice in those states where the staff is so small that one person now handles, if they are handled, all of these duties.

The position of policy secretary which was suggested as one of the governor's principal aides in the basic staffing pattern is perhaps more of a departure from current practice than is the position of public relations secretary. While this position has no exact prototype on the present staff of the governor in most states, it is not without antecedents to which it bears considerable resemblance. It will be remembered that the occupant of this position has the rather staggering task of trying to bring into some sort of focus the major policy proposals which the governor intends to put before the legislature and the people and of seeing those policy proposals through their legislative journey. The work of the policy secretary, therefore, involves the spadework necessary to translate the governor's general policy proposals into concrete proposals for legislation; the co-ordination, in so far as possible, of the programs of the respective departments with those proposals; the review of the budget from a policy point of view, since it is the single most important policy statement of the governor; and the very important function of legislative liaison.

To suggest that the policy secretary will be the sole source to whom the governor will turn for policy suggestions would be both unrealistic and not in keeping with the description of the duties of this position which were spelled out in more detail in the first section of this chapter. The governor has in the past received policy suggestions from his department heads, the party platform and party leaders, various interest groups, and many other sources. It is certainly unrealistic to assume that such advice will not continue to flow from all of these sources in the future or that the governor will not be guided to a greater or lesser extent by such advice. However, experience in several of the states demonstrates the value of a staff aide who can keep informed on this not inconsiderable flow of advice, who can maintain an over-all view of the various policy proposals, and who stands ready to give the governor an independent evaluation of these proposals.

In some states, the staff member who does most of the spadework in the preparation of the governor's program wields considerable personal influence on the shape of this program as it finally emerges. This is to be expected if the person in such a position has a strong personality, and something of this nature will occur even if the governor's policy secretary is not a particularly strong person. The governor will probably get not only assistance but advice from this quarter. This does not seem to be an undesirable development. It is high time that the governor had on his staff a source of informed advice on any program proposed by groups either within or without the government. The modern American governor is very successful in securing the enactment of his policies. What is needed in most states is not more effective legislative leadership but better program preparation. The position of policy secretary is seen as one device to secure this end. His functions in the field of legislative relations are important because the preparation of a better program is to no avail if it does not pass the legislature. The real area in which this position can be of considerable importance in the improvement of state government, however, is in the area of pre-legislative planning and program preparation.

The aspect of the duties of the policy secretary for which there are the most apparent prototypes is in the legislative liaison field. There are seven states in the sample of 25 which have an individual on the governor's staff responsible for what is euphemistically termed "legislative liaison." At one extreme this can mean keeping the governor informed on what is taking place in the legislature and at the other it can mean an active role in the influencing of legislation. One of the occupants of such a post described his functions as "getting the governor's program through the legislature and blocking any bills which seem to be opposed to that program." This is a rather pragmatic view of the function, but there is a considerable amount of truth in the observation. The governor's methods in attempting to influence the legislature were discussed at some length in a previous chapter and need not be repeated here. It might be well to point out, however, that the governor's influence in the legislature, once a bill is in the mill, depends in large part on his information as to how the legislative battle is going and a careful analysis of the need for gubernatorial intervention. In this area the legislative secretary performs a valuable function in keeping the governor briefed on legislative developments, the need, if any, for gubernatorial intervention, and the timing of that intervention.

Perhaps the closest approach to the kind of position that the writer suggests for the policy secretary is that of counsel to the governor in New York. The title of this position would lead one to suppose that the counsel would be the governor's legal adviser. In theory and to some extent in practice, this is true. The office was created by a statute in 1900 which gave the governor the authority to appoint and, at his pleasure, to remove a counsel. There was no appointment to this office until 1905, and in the interim all matters pertaining to legislation were referred to the attorney general's office. Beginning in 1905 and continuing to the present, each governor has taken advantage of the statutory permission and has appointed a counsel. The duties of the office are to advise the governor in regard to the constitutionality, consistency, and legal effects of the bills presented to the governor for his approval. As the office has developed, however, the counsel not only advises the governor on bills presented to him but actually draws up a great many of those which the governor wishes to have introduced into the legislature. In addition, the counsel clears all legislation from the departments prior to its submission to the legislature. Thus, the occupant of this office has become a powerful voice in policy determination, so far as the executive branch is concerned. The counsel also performs certain quasi-legal functions such as advising the governor on pardon and parole matters and rendering legal opinions on both legislation presented to the governor and on proposed courses of action. The key importance of the position, however, comes from its vital role in legislative policy formation. The counsel in New York ranks very close to the top of the staff hierarchy and is certainly one of the most influential of the governor's aides.

The legislative secretary in California is responsible for much the same functions as the counsel to the governor in New York but does not have the quasi-legal functions of that position. Like the counsel to the governor his position is a full time post. In the other five states in the sample having such a position, the individual responsible for legislative liaison is employed on a part time basis. In Wisconsin the executive counsel to the governor is responsible for assisting the governor in pardon matters, extradition, legal advice, and bill drafting. He also reviews the bills as they come down from the legislature. The executive counsel is not primarily responsible for legislative liaison, however, since this duty is shared by the other members of the governor's staff. In New Hampshire, Vermont, North Carolina, and Florida the governor's legislative secretary is a part time employee who is attached to the governor's office during the legislative session and who is primarily responsible for legislative liaison. The person appointed to this position is normally a lawyer and is frequently an ex-legislator. One of the occupants of this position pointed out that this latter qualification was particularly desirable because only an ex-legislator was likely to have the knowledge of the legislative process necessary to follow bills through the intricate procedures and thus be able to keep the governor informed of what was actually taking place.

There is no one position which embodies all of the duties of the proposed administrative secretary. However, the departmental secretary in California embodies at least one of the principal duties of the proposed position. The major function of the departmental secretary is to maintain liaison with a majority of the agencies and departments of government in order to keep the governor informed of the affairs of those agencies. The position, as it has developed in California, is closely tied in with the operation of the governor's council since the departmental secretary also serves as the secretary to the council. Consequently, it is difficult to separate the duties of these two positions. In his capacity of secretary to the council the departmental secretary receives monthly reports from the heads of the various agencies which are represented on the council and makes a digest of these reports for the governor and council members. These summaries are circulated prior to the council meetings and serve the dual purpose of keeping the governor informed of the activities of his departments and of keeping the various department heads informed of the activities of the other departments in the executive branch. The reporting system also serves the incidental purpose of keeping the departmental secretary informed on new developments in the various departments.

The duties of the departmental secretary, however, are not confined to reading agency reports and preparing summaries of current activities. He keeps in direct contact with the agencies involved through visits to these departments, telephone calls and interviews with department heads. In some instances the telephone calls or interviews may be the result of the request of the department head, while in other instances they are the result of action on the part of the secretary.

While the position of departmental secretary is not an intermediate level between the governor and the heads of the departments in the executive branch, the departmental secretary does attempt to assist the department heads in the solution of any problem which can be handled without being referred to the governor. His office also handles much of the correspondence which comes to the governor when it relates to departmental matters. The office of departmental secretary in California therefore, closely parallels the proposed position of administrative secretary insofar as the function of departmental liaison is concerned.

The duties of the departmental secretary in California, however, do not entirely encompass those proposed for the administrative secretary since the position apparently does not have the emphasis on budgetary and personnel matters which were suggested as a part of the duties of the administrative secretary. This lack of emphasis may in part be due to the fact that the operation in California is of such scope that the departmental secretary does not have time to concern himself with these matters but it in part is also probably due to a slightly different conception of the duties of the position.

A closer approximation on the side of relations with the budget and personnel functions is found in the position of financial secretary in Wisconsin or administrative secretary in Colorado. The occupants of these positions are primarily concerned with the budgeting, and to some extent, personnel functions of the governor rather than with department liaison. Two even more pertinent examples might be the heads of the division of personnel and the division of budget which are in the governor's executive office in Virginia. These two individuals and their staffs are an organic part of the governor's executive office. They not only keep the governor informed on budgeting and personnel matters, but also serve as heads of operating units concerned with the preparation of the budget and with personnel matters.

These two positions, however, while representing two of the functions suggested for the administrative secretary differ from the recommendations for that position in that the heads of these two agencies are operating both as members of the staff of the governor's office and also as the operating heads of service agencies. The recommendation for the administrative secretary does not envisage that individual as the head of an operating unit. On the contrary, his position is that of a staff man and he would not engage in day-to-day operating responsibility. In the larger states it might be necessary to have an entirely separate department for each of these two functions, whereas in some of the smaller or medium-sized states the situation which prevails in Virginia might be a satisfactory solution and both of these divisions might be in the governor's executive office. If this is the case, however, each unit would be under the supervision of its own head and the administrative secretary would be concerned with the budgeting and personnel functions primarily in a liaison capacity. The kind of work done by the financial secretary in Wisconsin and the administrative secretary in Colorado in keeping the governor informed on budgeting and personnel matters is perhaps more in keeping with the concept of the position of administrative secretary to the governor as set out in this section than are the positions in Virginia in which the heads of the budgeting and personnel units are serving in a dual capacity as both staff and operating officials.

The proper organization for the budgeting and personnel agencies in a given state is a matter which can be determined only after a careful study of the particular local situation. Therefore recommendations as to the type and location of such agencies cannot be made in a generalized way here with any hope of practical application in most states. It does seem important, however, for the governor to be adequately informed on personnel and budgetary matters, particularly on the latter. It is for this reason that the duties suggested for the administrative secretary include liaison with whatever personnel and budget agencies do exist. In a small state it may be entirely practicable for the administrative secretary to act in a dual capacity as an adviser to the governor on these matters and also as the general supervisor of these units. In most states it is probable that his other duties will be so time-consuming that he cannot be expected to do much more than keep himself informed in these two areas of operations and in turn to keep the governor informed of developments and problems. The administrative secretary would serve as a channel of communication from the agencies to the governor and vice versa. These functions also fit into his general function of maintaining liaison between the governor and the departments, since many of the matters on which liaison must be maintained will fall into one of these two categories.

The kind of position envisaged for the administrative secretary is not without its prototypes in actual staff organization. However, the position suggested would combine two functions which are sometimes assigned to separate members of the staff, namely the function of liaison with department heads and liaison on the budgeting and personnel functions.

As can be seen from the foregoing discussion, the positions

suggested for the governor's basic staff have considerable relation to those positions which are now used in many of the states on the governor's staff. The major difference in the positions suggested for the basic staff and those generally found in practice lies in the arrangement of duties.

Again it should be emphasized that the suggestions made for the basic staff are simply suggestions and that no one formula will fit the variety of situations found in the respective states. The element of flexibility should be the key element in the formulation of a staff for the governor's office. The suggestions made here should be taken only as considerations which might apply in a particular state under a particular governor if careful investigation shows one or more of the suggestions to be applicable to the local situation.

It should also be emphasized that the basic staff is subject to expansion or even to contraction as the local situation demands. It seems to the writer that the governor's office in the average American state at the present time tends to be understaffed rather than overstaffed. This does not mean, however, that every staff should necessarily be increased or that the same kind of staff can be used profitably by all governors in all states.

The number and kinds of persons which the governor needs depend on a variety of factors including the governor's personal work habits, his program, the traditions and customs of the office in a given state, the size of the state and its population, and a number of other not-easily-categorized factors. It is difficult therefore to suggest even a basic staffing pattern. However, the pattern suggested here is based on the governor's principal functions and has some basis in current experience. Those positions which have proved practicable in one state may, if the conditions are right, prove practicable in other states.

The key thing to remember in staffing is that the governor's staff should be designed to take care of as many details on management and public relations functions as possible and to assist but not to replace the governor in the realm of policy formation. The staff which has been suggested in this chapter is based upon the primary premise that the governor's principal function is that of policy formation—legislative, administrative, and party—but that he also has certain functions in the field of management and public relations. The staff suggested has been designed to fit the needs of this sort of formulation of the governor's duties.

Any steps toward more adequate staffing of the governor's office will probably come only over a considerable period of time, but there is apparently some realization among those who have studied the problem that the governor is understaffed in most states. Recently the commission to study state government in Illinois described a situation in that state which is probably typical of the staffing problem in most states and which points to the need for more adequate staffing. In part the commission said:

> We do, however, feel that the office of the governor is probably not adequately staffed to handle the necessary liaison with the legislature, the public, and administrative agencies. It is well known that over the years, governor after governor has had to borrow personnel from state administrative agencies in order to have the necessary staff of administrative assistance. We judge that the time has come to recognize that the practice exists and provide the governor with perhaps a half dozen persons who are responsible to him alone and who he can count upon for full-time service.[15]

This same criticism and suggestion might be repeated in most states and the time probably has come to recognize that the governor needs additional staff and to make adequate provision for staffing the governor's office. The procedure to be followed in a given state must be tailored to fit the local situation and the governor's ideas of his staff. However, through an enlarged staff and through better staff work the governor will be able to give better content to his program and to implement his already rather formidable legislative leadership with a better conceived program of public policy.

[15] Commission to Study State Government, *Organization and Functioning of the State Government* (Springfield, 1950), p. 28.

PART THREE

THE GOVERNOR AND DEMOCRATIC CONTROL

11. THE QUEST FOR ACCOUNTABILITY

ONE OF THE CENTRAL PROBLEMS of democratic government is to devise a system by which those who direct the government may be held accountable to the people for their actions. The problem is as pertinent to the state level as to any other level of government in this country. It is also as pertinent in discussing the legislature as in discussing the executive, and is as applicable to a discussion of the governor's role in policy formation as to his role in management. It is discussed at this particular juncture because the question of the governor's accountability was raised far more often by those interviewed in connection with the governor's powers in management than in connection with the governor's powers in legislative policy formation.

The question of the governor's accountability was raised in many different forms in connection with specific powers which either were being exercised by the governor in a particular state or which had been proposed as additions to his present powers. Most of these criticisms, however, had a common thesis; namely, that by increasing the powers of the governor over management the office had become, or was becoming, so powerful that the governorship could not be controlled by the people, the legislature, or the courts. In short, several groups of those interviewed were challenging in one way or another the basic concept that a governmental executive should be given power commensurate with his responsibility on the grounds that if he were given such power he would become too powerful to be subject to democratic control.

This proposition was attacked primarily by three groups. One of these was made up of the majority, but not all, of elected executive officers who saw in their positions a desirable balance wheel in state management which prevented the governor from becoming dictatorial. This group also argued that the management of state agencies is more democratic when the heads of these agencies are "kept close to the people" through frequent elections. A few of them also noted, in passing, that impeachment was a cumbersome device and was largely ineffective as a weapon of popular control.

While the concept of a strong governor was generally supported by the professional administrators interviewed, it was attacked by certain members of this group, particularly some of those administrators in the fields of public health, mental hygiene, social welfare, corrections, and education. Several of the department and division heads interviewed in these fields expressed the belief that these functions should be administered under an agency which was relatively free of gubernatorial control. The favorite device suggested to attain this end was a board or commission whose members would have long staggered terms so that any one governor usually would appoint only one member of the board. Most of the administrators, however, favored a single agency head selected by the board who would be in charge of the administration of the program. Thus, the board would be used to establish policy and the director would be used for administration. This sort of arrangement, it was argued, would take these departments out of politics. This group also argued that the administration of functions in these fields had been improved considerably in recent years because of the increasing "professionalism" of the staff of these departments. This professionalism was alleged to be the product of a career system fostered by continuity of policy and lack of political interference in the affairs of the departments. This continuity of policy and freedom from political interference was in turn the result of long tenure on the part of a department head who was not directly subject to the governor's removal power and, hence, continued his term of office through that of several governors.

The centralization of additional management functions and of additional fiscal controls in the hands of the governor was opposed also by some of the state legislators interviewed. These legislators felt that such an increase in the governor's powers would make him so powerful that it would destroy a desirable balance of power in favor of the legislature. It also was alleged that such an increase in power would place the governor in a favorable position to establish a "dictatorship."

Strangely enough, none of those interviewed directly mentioned the courts as an agency of control over the governor's actions or over the actions of his department heads. One attorney general did state that he felt that several of the governor's recent vetoes were unconstitutional and that he planned to institute a suit to test their constitutionality. He did not, however, comment on either the desirability or effectiveness of judicial review as a control mechanism. This lack of comment on one of the important avenues of democratic control may be interpreted in a number of different ways. One interpretation is that those interviewed were concerned primarily with policy controls and that they did not consider the courts as an agent for this type of control. It should be pointed out, however, that at least one attorney general in recent years has attempted to use the courts to settle policy differences with the governor and with his other colleagues in the executive branch. Tom Watson, who was the attorney general under two recent Florida governors, instituted a series of suits over such matters as the settlement of the estate of the late John Ringling, school bonds, oil leases on state lands, the state building program, the operation of the highway patrol, and the donation of state money and land for the Everglades Park which the state planned to turn over to the Federal Government.[1] The Attorney General's attempts to force policy changes via the legal route were markedly unsuccessful and lend support to what was apparently the underlying assumption by those interviewed, namely that the courts are unsatisfactory devices for policy control. Nevertheless, the failure of those who objected to the governor's increased powers to give any weight to the influence of the courts represents a serious weakness in their argument, since the courts are an important part of the pattern of democratic control.

These criticisms advanced by the department heads, legislators,

[1] See Coleman B. Ransone, Jr., *The Office of Governor in the South* (Bureau of Public Administration, University of Alabama, 1951), pp. 104-106 for a more detailed discussion of these suits.

and professional administrators do not represent all of those which could be made of the concept of the governor as the central figure in state management. However, they do represent those of persons actually engaged in state administration and, in the writer's opinion, are worthy of careful consideration. Certainly, they are some of the criticisms which must be met by those who advocate improvement of state management through the centralization of control over the executive branch in the governor. An attempt will be made to answer these objections in the following sections of this chapter. It should be pointed out, however, that the grounds for either completely proving or disproving the claims on both sides are not entirely sound, since the principle never actually has been put into effect in its ideal form at either the state or the national level. In spite of the rather extensive reorganizations of some state governments and of the national government, neither the state nor the national government has an executive branch which fully meets the criteria set out for the complete implementation of this principle. Consequently, in taking a position either for or against the centralization of management controls in the executive, we are arguing from only partial application of the principle in practice. The federal government, due to the foresight of the Congress which took care to see that the President appointed his major department heads, started out a step ahead of most of the states, where the governor did not have this power. However, Congress has not been consistent in its attitude and the proliferation of boards and commissions not subject to the President's control, so aptly characterized by the President's Committee on Administrative Management as a "headless fourth branch of government," has considerably weakened the application of this principle in practice. Even so, most governors have never reached the degree of control over state administration which the President now has over federal administration. The other major weapon of executive control, the executive budget and its accompanying fiscal controls, is far from perfectly developed at the national level. However, as was pointed out in a preceding section, it is nonexistent in several states and is fairly weak in many of those where it does exist. Consequently, in discussing this question, we are dependent to some degree on logical analysis to support either position.

IMPEACHMENT—JUDICIAL OR POLITICAL PROCESS?

In the opinion of those interviewed who mentioned impeachment as a control mechanism, it was regarded as a cumbersome device which was ineffective except in extreme circumstances. On the whole, the writer must agree with this evaluation, although impeachment has some usefulness as a preventive measure.

In all of the states except Oregon the governor may be removed from office by a procedure which is generally similar in form to that used in the Federal government. Charges of impeachment are brought by the lower house and the trial is conducted before the Senate. In some states an extraordinary majority, usually two-thirds, is required for conviction. The penalty for conviction is removal from office, usually with the provision that the offender subsequently may not hold any office of profit or trust in the state government. Other penalties such as fines and imprisonment may not be imposed by the legislature. However, if the action which led to impeachment is one which is punishable under criminal law, the governor is liable to criminal action after his removal.

Since impeachment proceedings are normally instituted only as a last resort, they are used very infrequently. Only four governor's in the United States have been convicted in impeachment proceedings since the Reconstruction.[2] Several others have been the object of impeachment proceedings but the attempts to impeach have failed. Many of these attempts no doubt have been inspired by the political opponents of the governor, and the use of impeachment in this manner has led one writer to call the process a "phase of the political warfare of factions and parties."

Whether impeachment is politically inspired or whether it is based on sounder grounds, it is a slow and cumbersome process. On the whole, it appears to be a judicial process whose full effect is potential rather than actual. The mere fact that the process is available and can be used as a last resort may have a salutary effect in preventing the more flagrant abuses of power and corruption on a grand scale. Hence, it should be retained if only

2 These were Sulzer of New York, 1913; Ferguson of Texas, 1917; Walton of Oklahoma, 1923; and Johnson of Oklahoma, 1927.

for its possible effect as a deterrent.[3] However, as a device for the popular control of government, it is sadly lacking. It can be used only in extreme cases of personal dishonesty or flagrant abuse of power and, therefore, is of little consequence in holding the governor responsible for the execution of policy. For this reason the process seems to have had very little effect on the exercise of many of the governors' most important functions.

In an attempt to render the removal process more effective and less cumbersome, eleven of the states have provided for the recall of the governor. The details of the system vary from state to state, but the essence of the system is that it allows the removal of the governor by an adverse popular vote. The first step in the process is the circulation of a petition for the governor's recall, stating the reasons for the action. This petition must be signed by a required percentage of the electorate. In a majority of the states about 25 per cent of the eligible voters is required. The petition is then filed with the secretary of state who determines whether or not it meets all the necessary requirements. If the petition is in order and the governor does not choose to resign, a recall election is ordered. Usually a special election is held but when a general election is imminent, the question of the governor's recall may be placed on the general election ballot. In some recall elections the question is simply whether or not the governor should be recalled; in others provision is made for the election of a successor. A majority is generally necessary for the recall to be valid.

While the proponents of this system claim for it many advantages over the impeachment process, it does not seem to have radically improved the removal process in those states where it has been adopted.[4] The only governor to be recalled was Lynn J. Frazier,

[3] For example, there is substantial reason to believe that the resignation of Richard W. Leche as Governor of Louisiana in 1940 was caused by fear of possible impeachment proceedings. If such is the case, the Governor had good grounds for his beliefs, for he was subsequently convicted in Federal court of graft charges involving $111,000 in connection with the sale of trucks to the State Highway Commission. Of this amount, he was supposed to have received $31,000 as his share. W. Brooke Graves, *American State Government,* 3rd Ed., (Boston, 1945), p. 373.

[4] See Cullen B. Gosnell and Lynwood M. Holland, *State and Local Government in the United States* (New York, 1951), p. 228 ff. for a discussion of the advantages and disadvantages of this system.

the Nonpartisan League Governor of North Dakota, in 1921. The system may, however, have some advantage in providing removal on grounds more closely approaching policy determination than generally is true under the impeachment process. It must be admitted, however, that both of these systems are in practice a last resort and that some other system must be used to provide for accountability on policy grounds. The chief value of impeachment or recall lies in the psychological effect on the governor. In practice, they are deterrents to major abuses of power and corruption on a grand scale rather than practical devices for the removal of the state's chief executive.

THE CITIZEN AND THE ADMINISTRATIVE PROCESS

While the citizen can influence administration in many ways other than by the election of administrative officials, including the governor, both those who oppose the centralization of additional power in the governorship and those who advocate such centralization use the argument of citizen participation through election to support their case. On one hand, the elected officials argue that the fact that they *were* elected made their offices subject to popular control and, hence, a desirable counterbalance against the governor. On the other hand, those who argue for a strong governor feel that his popular election is a primary device for democratic control, since the citizen exercises a control through his vote in the governor's initial nomination and election and can express his disapproval in the same manner at a subsequent election, if the governor seeks to succeed himself.

The argument of the elected officials that it is desirable to have a group in the executive branch which can act as a balance wheel to the governor has as its implicit assumption the idea that the elected official will be good and the governor will be bad and, therefore, that the good elected officials will protect the public interest against the actions of the bad governor who seeks to subvert the public interest to his own evil ends. This picture, of course, is exaggerated, but something of this line of reasoning was implicit in a good many interviews, particularly when the elected officials happened to be of one party and the governor of another. It is obvious that this argument can be used both ways. It can well be argued that there is no valid reason to assume that the elected officials will all be defenders of the public interest and that all governors will have evil intentions. Our experience does not show that this has been the case, and there is considerable ground for assuming that the governor, due to the publicity which is focused on his office, is likely to be less able to do evil than an obscure elected officer. It may be argued also that since the governor is elected on a statewide basis in a campaign, which even the elected officials admit usually is centered on the race for governor, the state's chief executive may be expected to be as representative of the public interests as any of the other elected officials. A careful selection of examples can be used to show that there have been occasions on which it appears that a bad governor was checked by good elected officials, or, on the other hand, where a bad official successfully opposed a good governor and destroyed the effectiveness of a part of his program. The burden of the evidence does not show, however, that the elected department heads are always on the side of the right and the governor is always in the wrong. Consequently, the assumption of these department heads is open to considerable question, and unless their basic assumption is accepted, their conclusion also is in doubt. If one is of the cynical turn of mind, he might point out that the department heads who use this argument were also those who stood to gain the most by the retention of these offices as elective positions. Even without questioning the sincerity of these officials, for many of them did indeed seem to hold this view as an important part of their philosophy of government, it is easy to see how their present positions might have unconsciously influenced their views on the desirability of the dispersion of executive authority.

Even among those elected officials who did not see their function primarily as serving as a check on the governor, there was a tendency to feel that the concentration of executive power in one office, even if the holder of that office originally had no evil designs, was inherently an undesirable concept. The idea that power begets a desire for more power and that this could lead to dictatorship seemed to be very prevalent. The counter philosophy offered by these gentlemen was that by dividing the executive power no one officer in the executive branch would have enough power to do very much evil. When it was pointed out that this assumption might easily lead to a stalemate and that also it implicitly limited the power of the governor to do very much good, the answer usually was that the possibility of dictatorship overbalanced any possible good that could come through the centralization of effective power in the hands of the governor.

In a democratic society one cannot lightly advocate a system which might lead to dictatorship. Nevertheless, the fears of those who opposed the centralization of management controls in the governor on this ground seemed to be overdrawn. It is certainly true that a governor who has the power to control the executive branch can use that power in a manner which may be contrary to the public interest. On the other hand, we have no examples from our past experience to show that governors who have been given substantial powers over administration have become dictators or even incipient dictators. The bogey man who was most often trotted out to show the possibilities of dictatorship was the late Huey Long. While there are many in Louisiana who will quarrel with the notion that "The Kingfish" was a dictator, nevertheless, this seemed to be a widely held concept. What the officials who cited Governor Long's career failed to take into consideration was the fact that he came into power in a state which at that time had very widely dispersed executive power. The Governor of Louisiana, when Huey Long was first elected to that office, did not have the centralization of executive controls over administration which is recommended by those who see the governor as a general manager. He did not come into power because there was a centralization of authority in the executive branch in Louisiana and he did not control the state through his power over administration. Huey Long controlled the State of Louisiana because he controlled the legislature and because he had a powerful political machine. A governor who is politically powerful and who wishes to control the operation of state government will not be stopped by a group of elected department heads. On the other hand, the centralization of effective control in the office of governor need not produce a dictator. There is always the danger that power given to any official may be used unwisely or even for his personal aggrandizement. This possibility should not be overlooked in our zeal to establish an effective executive. It does not necessarily follow, however, that power will usually or will necessarily be used for purposes contrary to the public interest. The alternative of divided executive power presented by these gentlemen frequently leads to a disorganized executive branch and may lead to a situation of stalemate and enforced inaction. This is not an attractive alternative since democratic government, like all government, must be able to operate effectively. In the present status of national, as well as international affairs, it seems unfortunate to base our philosophy of government on the concept of inaction. While it is very important that the increased powers of the governor be subject to democratic control, it is the contention here that giving the governor sufficient authority to carry out his responsibilities will result in more rather than less democratic control.

The same theme of possible dictatorship runs through the argument of some of the elected officials that state government is more democratic if kept "close to the people" through the popular election of department heads. The argument, however, goes further than the preceding contention since it claims not only the negative value of stifling incipient dictatorship but also the positive value of providing for the best possible type of democratic control. The merits or demerits of this argument are hard to illustrate in any practical way, since very few studies have been made at the state level to determine whether or not the voters who elect such officials actually know anything about the office or about the record of its incumbent as opposed to that of other candidates seeking the office. There has been, however, a recent study in Michigan which attempts to discover the degree to which the voter is familiar with elected and appointive offices in the executive branch in that state. The results of this study should be of considerable interest to those who are concerned with the democratic control of state administration via the ballot.[5]

The study was based on a sampling procedure in which a proportion of the voters of Bay County, Michigan were interviewed to determine their familiarity with the most important state officials. Bay County was selected as a "barometer county" on the basis of the fact that the vote in this county for state-wide elective

[5] *General Management of Michigan State Government,* A Staff Report to the Michigan Joint Legislative Committee on Reorganization of State Government, Report Number 30 (Lansing, November, 1951), Part III, Appendix XI, pp. 44-49.

offices in the last several elections had come within 3 per cent of the percentages for the state as a whole.

The first key question asked in the study was "Which of the state offices do you know most about?" The office was to be selected from an alphabetical list which was given to each person interviewed and included the offices of attorney general, auditor general, comptroller, health commissioner, highway commissioner, police commissioner, secretary of state, superintendent of public instruction, and treasurer. The replies to this question revealed that out of these nine major state offices the best known were that of highway commissioner, health commissioner, and secretary of state in that order. Fifteen per cent of those interviewed, however, answered "I don't know" or "I don't know about any of them." Each person was then asked to describe the office which he said that he knew the best. If no answers were forthcoming, specific questions were asked about the functions of the office, present office holder, whether the office holder was elected or appointed, the term of the office, and the time of the next election or appointment to the office. Even with the questioning confined to the one office which the voter said he knew the most about, only 59 per cent of those interviewed could answer as many as two questions about the office correctly and only 20 per cent could answer more than three questions. In answer to the questions concerning the method of selection and the name of the present incumbent the results showed that 66 per cent knew how the highway commissioner was selected but only 25 per cent knew who was the present incumbent of the office; 46 per cent knew how the health commissioner was selected but no one interviewed knew his name; and 61 per cent knew how the secretary of state was selected, while 27 per cent could name the incumbent. If these results were obtained in questioning those interviewed on the office they said *they knew best,* it is interesting to surmise what might have been the results if those interviewed had been asked to name the method of selection and the incumbents of the other offices!

Presumably, one of the goals of democratic government is that the people shall be able to control the policies of the government under which they live. In a representative democracy this control generally is exercised by the selection between competing individuals who represent different policies or who frequently merely claim that they will administer better and more honestly the policies already in existence. Faced with candidates making either of these claims, the average citizen cannot be expected to do much more than make a choice among these individuals. This choice will not always and perhaps not usually be made on an entirely rational basis. Nevertheless, it may be assumed with some justification that the better informed the citizen is on the issues and on the individuals the better choice he will make. In most political campaigns at the state level, as has been pointed out in our previous discussion of nominations and elections, the issues tend to be obscured to a considerable extent by the personalities of the candidates. Consequently, in a one-party situation, the average citizen is quite likely to be voting for the man rather than the issues, while in a two-party situation, such as that which exists in Michigan, he might be voting for the man or the party rather than the issues. Since this study was made some seventeen days before the 1950 election, it would seem that whatever grounds the citizens intended to use in the selection of a candidate, they could not have involved a very substantial knowledge of the office or of its present incumbent.

The Michigan study certainly does not give very much solace to those who believe that effective popular control over administration can be achieved by making the principal state administrative offices elective. Even when the questions were limited to the one elective office with which the voter said he was most familiar, 73 per cent could not name the incumbent secretary of state, 75 per cent could not name the highway commissioner, 77 per cent could not name the superintendent of public instruction, 81 per cent could not name the attorney general, and 96 per cent could not name the treasurer, who had been in office longer than any other official on the list.

The findings of this sample were substantiated by a similar study of 500 college students who presumably might be expected to be better informed on public affairs. In distinguishing between elective and appointive offices out of the same list submitted to the Bay County voters, the college students scored an over-all 60 per cent on all nine offices, hardly a figure to give much support to those who feel that the public is well enough informed to make a choice between candidates for these offices on the basis of the knowledge of their duties. Furthermore, on the six elective offices, which are those which have most significance for this inquiry, only 46 per cent of the students knew that these offices were elective, a figure which is less than the 50 per cent score which they could have obtained through guessing. Even more significant were the results on a question which asked the students to name the incumbents of the elective offices. At the time of the study, fifteen days before the hotly contested state election of 1950, only 15.4 per cent could name the incumbent office holders.

While these samples are small and might be challenged as to their validity for the state as a whole, they serve to reinforce the conclusions of careful students of state government elsewhere in the nation. Many of these students feel the average citizen is very poorly informed concerning the majority of offices and candidates who are running for state administrative positions. In Michigan some 40 per cent of the voters two weeks before a "hot" election were so uninformed about nine major state offices that they did not know whether they were elective or appointive and 83 per cent did not know the name of the incumbent. This would lead us to believe that there is considerable reason to doubt the proposition that making state administrative offices elective will keep the government close to and responsible to the public.

Since the voters in our first sample were not asked about the office of governor, we can draw no conclusion on this score from the data presented in that study. In the second study based on a sample of college students the office of governor was included in the list. It is significant to note that 99.2 per cent of the students were able to successfully identify the incumbent governor. It is quite probable that a much higher percentage of the voters of Bay County would be able to identify the governor than any other elective official. This would be a logical assumption, since most of the state campaigns are centered around the race for the governorship. The governor is by far the best known figure in state government, and while it might be too much to claim that a majority of the voters are familiar with his program, it is quite probable that two weeks before a state election a majority of the voters would at least know who the two major candidates for the governorship are and something about one or two issues of the campaign.

The conclusion that the governor is the focus of citizen attention in state government not only before but also after the campaign is borne out by the testimony of the governors interviewed. While the governors were at variance in their conclusions on many matters covered by this study, all of those interviewed were agreed that the people held the governor responsible for mistakes made in state administration. It may be obvious to the student of state government that the governor cannot logically be held responsible for the operation of agencies over which he has little control, as for example a board with long staggered terms, all of whose members had been appointed by previous governors. Nevertheless, the people on the whole do not make these fine distinctions.

If the governor is the focus of public attention and if he is held responsible for the actions of those who head the various administrative agencies, it would seem logical to place him in a position to control the agencies for which he is held responsible. This would seem to be a step in the direction of better popular control of administration. The governor would not only be strengthened in his internal control of the executive branch but also at the same time this control would enable him to take action which would insure the responsiveness of these agencies to popular control as expressed by their endorsement of the governor's program.

THE LEGISLATIVE OVERSIGHT OF ADMINISTRATION

This line of reasoning also seems to apply with considerable force to the complaints of some of the state legislators that the centralization of management functions under the governor would disturb a desirable legislative dominance over the executive branch. Certainly, it must be agreed that the legislature is one of the principal repositories of the people's delegated power in a democracy. It also must be agreed that it is desirable that the legislature approve the major policies of the government. However, it seems that the centralization of management controls in the governorship is a step toward greater rather than lesser legislative control over the executive branch. If the governor is given effective control over the departments which make up the executive branch and if he is given a strong set of fiscal controls including the executive budget, legislative oversight of administration will be strengthened rather than weakened. As the situation now stands in most states, the legislature has a very poor opportunity to judge the governor's major programs, particularly in fiscal terms, because the executive budget represents such a small part of the state's total expenditures that it gives only a very partial view of the total fiscal picture. By strengthening the governor's hand in the budget process, the budget can be made a real policy vehicle which covers the executive branch as a whole and not simply a few isolated agencies that happen to be under the governor's supervision. The executive budget would then serve the governor as an important means of internal control over his department heads and the legislature as an equally effective control over the governor, because that body could pass on the governor's total program. As has been suggested previously, this control can be made more effective by a reorganization of the committee system, more adequate staffing for committees, and by the installation of a thorough post audit under an agent of the legislature.

It is highly desirable that the legislative oversight of administration be improved and made as effective as possible. It is the contention here that giving the governor more effective control over his department heads both through making them appointees of the governor and through an effective executive budget and fiscal control system would be a major step in this direction. It would seem that a dual approach to the problem of more effective state government based on strengthening both the governor and the legislature would be the most profitable attack on the problem. This approach seems far superior to one based on the concept of two weak branches of government, neither of which could do much harm but neither of which could perform its proper role effectively. State government must be organized to perform its tasks effectively if it is not to lose many of its present functions to the national government on one hand and the rapidly developing metropolitan units on the other. Those who are sincerely desirous of seeing the state governments perform a useful and active role in the federal system cannot be content with impassioned appeals to the Tenth Amendment. To do so is to retreat into a dreamland which has never really existed since the Articles of Confederation. The problems of modern government demand effective administration. If that administration is not forthcoming by state action, or by joint federal-state, or state-local action, it will come by direct federal programs. A continuation of the advantages of the federal system is predicated on effective units of government at all three levels. The state governments must be alive to the implications of the situation and must strive for more effective administration at the state level.[6]

ORGANIZATION AND ACCOUNTABILITY

The objections of certain professional administrators, particularly in the fields of public health, mental hygiene, social welfare, education and corrections, to the concept of strengthening the governor in management are worth careful consideration. In the writer's view, these objections were the most cogent advanced by any of the groups interviewed. However, a thoughtful analysis of these objections does not prove them to be so compelling that the basic premises of this chapter should be revised.

The first objection of this group may be summarized by saying that, while the concept of the governor appointing his department heads generally is valid, there are some agencies in which continuity of policy is of such paramount importance that it is desirable for these agencies to be placed beyond the reach of gubernatorial controls. For example, some of the most outspoken critics of the extension of the governor's power to appoint and remove his department heads were several of the directors of departments of public welfare. These gentlemen were operating agencies which administered various programs designed to take care of the defective, delinquent, and dependent groups in the state's population.

[6] This discussion has not covered such important legislative checks over administration as the very important legislative investigative power through its ever-inquiring committees, the power of the legislature to establish and abolish agencies and prescribe by statute the broad outlines of their functions, and the power of the Senate to confirm gubernatorial appointees. These were omitted from the discussion in an attempt to answer the most frequently voiced criticisms of the legislators which were centered on the increase in the governor's appointing power and his power to prepare the executive budget and control the spending process. It might be pointed out, however, that the checks mentioned above add substantially to the legislature's effectiveness in the oversight of administration. If these controls are added to the central power of that body to control the purse strings, it certainly appears that the legislature is adequately equipped to furnish effective oversight of the administrative process. The major weakness of the legislature, as was suggested earlier, lies in its staff and organization. This weakness is an argument for improving the legislature rather than an argument for weakening the governor.

Some of the states divide these functions among several departments while others combine them into a single department. For the sake of illustrating the reasoning of these gentlemen, it will be assumed that the programs in the field of public welfare are all administered by one department. The typical organization for this department is that it is headed by a board, the members of which have long staggered terms. The board members are appointed by the governor but because of the staggered term arrangement, any one governor will normally appoint only one board member. The board in turn appoints a director who is responsible to the board and may be removed by the board. The director, however, is beyond the reach of the gubernatorial removal power. The governor normally has only limited removal power in connection with the board members, since they can be removed only for such unlikely offenses as moral turpitude or malfeasance in office. In short, the agency is designed so that it will be relatively free of gubernatorial control from the point of view of the governor's power to appoint and remove. This freedom frequently is reinforced by the fact that the agency's activities are financed in whole or in part from an earmarked fund so far as the state's share in its financing is concerned. Because of the nature of the programs there is also usually a substantial amount of federal funds which come to the state under the federal grant-in-aid programs.

The justification for such an arrangement which generally was advanced by those interviewed was that it "took the agency out of politics." This was alleged to be an advantage because these programs were too important to be tampered with by partisan politicians, the chief of whom was the governor. This argument seems to the writer to be based on the fallacious assumption that any agency can be taken out of politics. All the agencies of state government must operate under some policy. Consequently, they must all be "in politics," because it does not seem possible that policy direction can be non-political. The question is not whether the agency shall operate in a vacuum but whether it shall operate under the policy of the governor or the legislature as the elected representatives of the people or whether it shall operate under the policy of a board which is directly responsible neither to the people, the governor, nor the legislature. It is not a question of policy or no policy but a question of whose policy. If democratic government is to operate according to the usually recognized concepts, the policy in question should be either that of the elected representatives of the people directly or that of some body which is under the control of either the governor or the legislature. In this case, since these agencies are a part of the executive branch, the proper choice seems to be that they should operate under the supervision of the governor. The governor in turn, as it has been pointed out previously, operates under the scrutiny of the legislature.

The real objection of these administrators to gubernatorial control seems to be based on their desire to operate without policy direction. Many persons who are sincerely interested in improving state services in certain areas, such as in our mental institutions, prisons, aid to the needy, and the like, fall into the mistaken assumption that if these programs could only "be taken out of politics" they would operate more honestly and more effectively. On the surface this seems to be a reasonable argument, but it is highly destructive of democratic government if carried to its logical conclusions. Democratic government is possible only if it is controlled government. Establishing all of the services of the state government under a series of independent boards might produce some short run efficiencies, but it would produce long run irresponsibilities which would destroy the basic pattern of democratic government. "Politics" is a word which has come to have unfortunate connotations in the minds of most citizens and even of some students of government. However, politics is the process by which policy decisions are developed. All policy decisions are political decisions, and all the agencies of government must operate in a political atmosphere. We cannot improve government by atomizing it into a series of independent petty empires controlled by irresponsible boards and commissions. We can improve it by consolidating the executive branch into a relatively small number of single-headed departments subject to gubernatorial control. The governor in turn must be controlled by a revitalized legislative branch which will be in a position to make intelligent policy decisions and hold the governor responsible for the proper administration of the executive branch.

The experience with departments of welfare and other departments whose supporters wish to take them "out of politics" does not show that such departments can be administered effectively only under an independent board. The testimony of a number of state officials, both in and out of these departments, who were interviewed in the course of this study seems to indicate that there are many departments under directors appointed by the governor who have outstanding programs in these fields. Some bad appointments have been made by some governors, and some state departments in these fields do not come up to the general standard. The same can be said, however, for some directors appointed by independent boards and of the programs of the agencies which they supervise. The evidence is certainly not all on one side of the question. However, lacking any clear cut preponderance of evidence in favor of the board, the general dictates of democratic government suggest that there is no valid reason to regard these functions as a world apart in the question of gubernatorial control.

A subsidiary argument which was advanced in favor of the independence of agencies in these fields was that a professional staff could be selected only if these agencies were independent of political influence from the governor's office. There is much to this argument when it is made by those department heads who operate in spoils-system states. It is difficult for them to develop a competent professional staff if 30 to 50 per cent of their staff is dismissed for political reasons every two or four years. However, this seems to be primarily an argument for the extension of the merit system to cover all, rather than a part of, these departments. At the present time, some of the programs administered by these departments are under the merit system in all states because of the provisions attached to the grants under the Social Security Act. All of the employees of these departments, like those of the other departments of state government, should be under an effective merit system.

However, when this argument is broadened to advocate that the director should be under a merit system or at least removed from the governor's removal power, it becomes less justified. The argument here is that the director is essentially an administrator and that he should be appointed because of his professional competence and retained as long as he is performing satisfactorily. This argument, too, sounds persuasive, but again if it is broadly applied, it will destroy the governor's control over the executive branch. At the level of a department head, a point is reached where two principles come into conflict. One is that it is desirable to have a competent individual at the head of a department of government. The other is that in order to make a department head amenable to the governor's program he must be subject to gubernatorial appointment and removal. The experience of the states as a whole does not show that these two principles are necessarily mutually exclusive. Many able governors have been able to appoint department heads who are both competent and amenable to changes which the governor may consider necessary in the programs of their departments. Experience also shows that able department heads are quite likely to serve under successive governors even of different political parties. Nevertheless, the possibility that a department head may not be amenable to policy changes should not be overlooked. The governor should have the power to remove any of his department heads if this becomes necessary. In practice, it is fairly rare for the governor to go to this length to enforce his authority. This sanction, however, is a desirable backstop to the governor's other powers and no particular group of agencies should be singled out as being properly beyond the scope of the appointing and removal power.[7]

It seems quite true that the increasing professionalism of certain types of public servants has contributed considerably to the improvement of state administration. This professionalism should be encouraged by the provision of an adequate career service within the executive branch. This does not necessarily mean, however, that a professional group can develop only in agencies which are independent of the governor. It seems to the writer that the argument advanced by one department head that professional employees would not serve in an agency whose head was a political appointee is not borne out by the experience in many states. For example, in California the heads of the agencies concerned with such matters as public health and social welfare are appointed by the governor. These agencies have developed a competent staff and have programs which are widely copied in other states. The important point

[7] One possible exception might be those agencies which have primarily a regulatory function and which the courts regard as quasi-legislative or quasi-judicial in nature. Such agencies customarily have been regarded as arms of the legislature and might be placed in a special category in regard to the governor's appointing and removal power.

seems to be the caliber of the individual selected to head a particular department. Experience shows that capable individuals are selected in those states in which the governor makes the appointment as well as in those in which the appointment is made by an independent board. Given a competent department head and a reasonably effective merit system and pay scale, a professional staff can be developed in agencies whose head is a political appointee.

As was stated at the beginning of this section, the arguments for the concentration of authority as well as responsibility in the governor are based on only a partial application of this concept. Admitting the limitations which come from this partial application, the experience which has resulted and the logic of the concept both seem to point to its desirability. The fear that the concentration of considerable power in the executive may lead to dictatorship is a thread that runs through the arguments of most of those opposed to increased gubernatorial power. These fears do not seem to be based on essentially sound foundations. Woodrow Wilson, writing more than a half a century ago, pointed out that "there is no danger in power, if only it be not irresponsible. If it be divided, dealt out in shares to many, it is obscured; and if it be obscured, it is made irresponsible. But if it be centered in heads of the service and in heads of branches of the service, it is easily watched and brought to book."[8]

On the whole, our experience at the state level seems to bear out the truth of this proposition. Power in the executive branch of the government is indeed "divided," "obscured," and "irresponsible." It is divided in that it is parceled out among a multitude of boards and commissions, the elective state executive officers, and the governor; and it is obscured because the citizens do not know what the various agencies are supposed to do or who is in charge of those agencies. This results in an irresponsible executive branch which is not subject to the control of either the governor, the legislature, or the people. Strengthening the governor's control over administration undoubtedly will result in a more powerful governorship. This control, however, is vital for more responsible government and can become destructive of democratic government

[8] Quoted by George W. Spicer in "Gubernatorial Leadership in Virginia," *Public Administration Review,* I (Autumn, 1941), 455.

only if the power given to the governor is not subject to popular or legislative control.[9]

In this case it seems clear that increasing the governor's control over administration is not a delegation of uncontrolled power. Rather the increased power is being centered in an office which is more subject to public attention and, therefore, more subject to popular control than are the individual department heads from whom some of this power was taken. Similarly, by centralizing in the governor both authority as well as responsibility for administration, the control over administration by the legislature is made more meaningful. The executive budget now becomes a policy statement for all of the departments of government rather than for only a few, and if the governor appoints his principal department heads, he can now properly and effectively be held responsible for the action of his subordinates.

The role of the legislature in administration is primarily that of control over major policy. This control will be strengthened rather than weakened by increasing the governor's ability to control his own household and to present a meaningful executive budget. The legislature's ability to review major policy, as expressed in the budget and other administration measures, and their ultimate control over this policy through the power of the purse and their investigatory power, which may be used for detailed scrutiny of administrative actions when the occasion arises, are improved rather than hampered by the centralization of administrative control in the governor. These powers, buttressed by the very necessary power of an audit conducted by a legislative agent, are the principal

[9] The question of judicial control over administration has been omitted from this discussion largely in an attempt to meet the critics of the concentration of managerial controls in the governorship on their own grounds. Very few of those interviewed took any recognition of the fact that the judicial control of administration is an important aspect of democratic control. The courts at the state level can and do review the actions of the governor and those of the legislature delegating him discretionary power to determine the constitutionality of both actions. They also perform a similar function in relation to the activities of the administrative agencies which make up the executive branch. This control is an important part of the entire pattern of the democratic control of administration and is one which strengthens the argument that the governor is adequately checked in the performance of his functions in the field of management.

safeguards against the governor's abuse of his proposed powers in the field of management.

SETTING THE TONE OF ADMINISTRATION

It does not seem to be popular in writing about administration to discuss matters which might have a moral overtone, presumably because such a discussion might lead into the realm of value judgments. These are to be avoided apparently because they cannot be supported with any kind of statistical or other scientific data. Nevertheless, anyone writing about any area of government makes a multitude of such judgments, and anyone who is a practicing administrator makes them daily in the course of his operations. The governor makes many such judgments, and because of the importance of his position, his decisions, more than those of any other single state official, are responsible for what one governor called "setting the tone of the administration." As interpreted by this governor and by the writer, this function has distinctly moral overtones, since its exercise is concerned not only with the governor's good judgment but also with his standards of conduct. In various aspects of management the governor, because of the leeway given to him by the constitution or by statute, or simply because of the silence of the constitution or statutes on a particular area of operations, has rather wide discretionary powers. One fairly universal example is the fact that it lies within the governor's range of discretion whether to return or refuse to return a fugitive apprehended in his state to a sister state in which he is alleged to have committed a crime or from whose prison system he may have escaped. The governor, said the United States Supreme Court, has a moral obligation to return such a fugitive but not a legal obligation. In making such a decision, the governor may rely as much on his judgment of whether or not the Georgia chain gang is a humane form of punishment as on the legal aspect of the fugitive's position.

While the question of extradition may become a "cause célèbre" from time to time, it is not of great importance in contrast to the more unspectacular day-by-day exercise of the governor's discretion on other matters. The governor sets the tone of management directly through a multitude of decisions on such matters as pardon and parole, appointments, contracts to those who supply the state with goods and services, the application of the criteria for establishing the rate of taxation on corporations and businesses, the granting of licenses to do business or practice a profession, and the policies established in the recruitment, pay, and promotion of state employees. He also sets the tone of administration indirectly through the selection of his department heads. This is true in the nature of the original appointment and through the continuing effect of the actions of these department heads. Throughout the governor's administration each department head tends to set the tone of administration within his department and generally he takes his cue from the governor.

The governor in a given state may not have the power to appoint all of his department heads or may not control all of the matters suggested above. In so far as he does have such power, however, his decisions set the tone of his administration. Some governors come into office with a long background of public service and their actions as the state's chief executive can be predicted with some degree of assurance from their past actions. Others are something of an unknown quantity, since they have not been in important public posts and their actions as governor cannot be predicted with any degree of accuracy. In either case, however, the governor's actions on a series of both major and minor decisions quickly become known to the rank and file of state employees and soon are transmitted to the citizens of the state via the press and radio. If positions are being dispensed on a spoils basis, if pardons are being sold, if the cotton mill in which the governor owns stock gets a more favorable tax rate than has been its past lot, or if the governor places a contract for most of the state's insurance business with his brother-in-law, word gets around and the governor is judged accordingly. The cumulative effect of these decisions sets the tone of the governor's administration, and the tone of the administration has a vital effect on the management of the state's business. "Government by crony" and "mink coat deals" are as injurious to good management at the state level as they are at the national level. The governor owes to the people not only his good judgment but also a high level of personal integrity. There are clearly many decisions lying within the governor's discretion in which a keen sense of personal integrity will lead governors who have such an attribute to make similar decisions in widely differing states.

Perhaps nowhere in the state administration is the governor's influence in this regard more keenly felt than in personnel management. The arguments for a merit system of selecting state employees have been discussed thoroughly in other writings and it is not necessary to repeat these arguments here. In the writer's opinion, however, one of the most beneficial effects of such a system, if properly administered, is to provide an atmosphere in which the employee can feel free to do an honest and impartial job in the administration of the state's services. The provision of a merit system will not in itself give him this incentive but it will at least provide an atmosphere in which such an incentive is recognized as a legitimate goal of the state's career employees. The governor can do much to furnish such incentives by the establishment of policies in regard to initial appointment, pay, promotion, and retirement that will foster a career service dedicated to the honest and effective performance of the many vital functions carried on by the state for the benefit of its citizens. This career service may, in theory, operate effectively under any sort of governor; but, in practice, it is likely to take its cue from the state's chief executive. It is probably too much to ask that the state's civil servants give devoted and efficient service when they see that the governor is motivated by factors which at the best may be partisan and at the worst downright dishonest.

There are several states in which developments in personnel management might give pause to those who advocate a merit system as an ultimate goal in state management. It would seem that successive governors in a given state may be able to establish a fairly high level of administrative efficiency without a formal merit system, if the ecology of government in the state in question permits. Virginia is a case in point. While the state has no formal statewide merit system of the type generally recommended by the proponents of the merit idea, it has an informal merit system which has given it relatively scandal free administration over a long period of time. There are those, including the writer, who question the limited scope of some of the state's programs and who question the desirability of others. However, it should be noted that the programs which are established are carried out with considerable effectiveness by a group of public servants, most of whom have given long and faithful service. While the state has no mandatory merit system for selecting its employees and while there is no legal barrier to their dismissal for political reasons, the ecology of government in the Old Dominion is such that a tradition of employment on the basis of merit and fitness exists as does a tradition of the state service as a career service. Security of tenure is the rule rather than the exception even in the upper reaches of the service, and it rare that an incoming governor removes more than two or three of the department heads appointed by his predecessor. This tradition is reinforced by the continuity of policy which is the result of the Byrd organization's long control over the executive branch of the government. The incoming governor does not need to resort to wholesale removals to enforce his policies or reward the faithful, since he and his department heads as well as the rank and file of the civil service have been directly or indirectly elected or appointed by the Byrd organization and thus tend to "think alike," as one official put the matter.[10]

The Virginia pattern of a "traditional" merit system, minus the Byrd organization, is duplicated to some extent in Vermont, but it is not typical of most spoils-system states. The typical pattern in these states is that of a decided turnover in the state civil service following each election. This turnover is sometimes very extensive, with at least one governor placing the rate of turnover at "at least 50 per cent" after a hard fought election.[11] In these circumstances the positions in the executive branch are dispensed on the basis of rewarding those who supported the winning candidate for governor. This fact, in itself, tends to give employees little incentive to efficient or honest service. They know that their tenure is quite likely to be limited and that even if it does continue it will be continued on the basis of their efforts to support a winning candi-

[10] See Ransone, pp. 138-142 for a more detailed discussion of the operation of the Virginia system and the governor's role in personnel management in the Old Dominion.

[11] See H. O. Waldby, *The Patronage System in Oklahoma* (Norman, 1950) for a most revealing discussion of personnel management under a long established spoils system. The discussion of the procedures by which the governor's appointments are made, found on page 27 ff., and the problems produced by excessive turnover, discussed on page 67 ff., are both particularly in point here.

date and not on the basis of their efforts in their particular positions. The writer interviewed many officials in the spoils-system states who are trying to do an effective job of administration. Their efforts, however, are largely doomed to frustration because the rank and file of the employees with whom they must work do not have the motivation for efficient service.

This is not always true. It is sometimes possible for a department head to set the tone of administration in his department several levels higher than that of the administration in general. While this fact may do some violence to the concept advanced here in that it proves that the tone of at least some departments are not established by gubernatorial action, it reinforces the concept that the establishment of a congenial environment of administration is an important part of an executive's functions. The establishment of such an environment is the product of the actions of both the governor and his department heads. While the primary impetus probably will come from the governor, it will be reflected in his choice of department heads, and the governor and his appointees working together generally will set the tone of administration for the executive branch as a whole. From time to time, however, one runs across certain departments which stand out head and shoulders above the other departments in the executive branch. Sometimes this superiority lasts for only one administration and sometimes it becomes almost a tradition within the state. Generally, such a situation can be traced to the high caliber of the head of the particular department. For example, in Kentucky, where the spoils system flourishes in spite of a theoretical merit system, the Department of Revenue is staffed by an able group of public servants, most of whom are technically trained and very competent. The outstanding record of this department, both in terms of personnel and of its functional administration, is largely the result of the leadership of one Commissioner of Revenue who was retained in his position by succeeding governors for several administrations. The Commissioner "set the tone" of this department at a high level of technical competence, fostered a career service within the department, and demonstrated his capacity for decisions in a very important area of state operations which reflect his personal integrity as well as his good judgment.

It is examples of this sort which lead to the conclusion that while the governor may be responsible for the establishment of the general tone of administration, at least part of that tone is the result of the actions of his department heads. In this case, it might be said that the governors of Kentucky by retaining the commissioner have done their part in establishing the tone of administration as far as this particular department is concerned. At least, they placed no major obstacles in the path of the Commissioner in his attempts to organize and staff a superior organization.

Given our present system of nominations and elections, it is only by chance that an individual is elected governor who has a high level of competence as an administrator. If this is true, the element of personal integrity becomes of great importance. If the governor is committed to the concept of honest and effective administration and will use this criterion as at least part of his basis for the selection of department heads, he has taken a long step forward in securing honest and effective state administration. If the governor in making his day-to-day decisions evidences a high degree of personal integrity, then he will establish a climate of opinion in which good administration can flourish. On the contrary, if his selection of department heads is on a purely partisan basis and if his day-to-day decisions are motivated by a desire for personal gain or for increased political power, he will establish a climate of opinion in which good administration is made extremely difficult. This is a point of view which is not susceptible of statistical proof but its validity may be tested in any state by careful observation of succeeding administrations. It is felt that such observation will reveal that in many instances there is a distinct change in the tone of the executive branch from one administration to the next. Whether this change is for the better or for the worse depends in large measure on the governor. The internal control over administration which is established through the governor's actions in setting the tone of administration is, in the final analysis, a by-product of a wise choice by the voters at the polls.

THE QUEST CONTINUED

It was suggested at the beginning of this chapter that one of the central problems of democratic government is to devise a system by which those who direct the government may be held accountable to the people for their actions. This is not a static problem but one which grows more urgent as the functions of modern government increase and its power over the individual grows. At the state level many devices which sought to provide for popular control have been tried with varying degrees of success. While substantial progress has been made in the direction of more effective popular control, there is certainly no cause for complacency in the results thus far achieved and the quest for accountability should be continued on both the legislative and executive fronts.

In connection with the attempts to establish an executive branch which is more responsive to the popular will, there are three areas in particular on which attention should be concentrated. One of these is the system by which the executive may be made more accountable to the legislature and the other two are the closely related problem areas of elections and party responsibility.

The major approaches to executive responsibility include the popular election of the governor, popular control over the governor and the legislature via party responsibility, control through the courts, and the review of the governor's program by the legislature. Of these four, the area which seems to offer the hope of the easiest and most rapid improvement is in the area of executive-legislative relations. The legislature now provides one of the most effective controls over the executive of any of the four systems and has the potential of being an even more effective device for accountability. The road to improvement will not be easy, but it can be considerably less difficult and much more rapid than in the other areas, because the major changes necessary can be made by the legislature itself. The major function of the legislature in terms of executive accountability is that of the careful review of the governor's program in order to determine whether or not that program is in accord with the legislature's interpretation of the public interest. In order to arrive at such an interpretation, the legislature should act as a cross section of public opinion in making informed judgments on policy which the people presumably would make themselves in a simpler governmental unit. A legislature can present such a cross section of public opinion only if it is a truly representative body, and it can make an informed evaluation of the policy proposed by the governor or by one of its own members only if it has the proper organization, procedures, and staff. One of the principal defects of the state legislatures in most states at the present time is that they are not truly representative bodies because they are not apportioned on anything approaching a representative basis. Until most legislatures are reapportioned they cannot claim to adequately reflect the views of the citizens of the state as a whole. The reapportionment of most legislatures, therefore, is basic to any attempt to see that these bodies fulfill their vital part of the governmental process.

It is also clear that if the legislature is to perform adequately its difficult task of separating the wheat from the chaff in the multitude of proposals for governmental action coming before it during a legislative session, the present organization and staffing of the legislature must be improved. The concept that the legislature's function in reviewing the budget and other policy proposals is primarily a check on the governor is somewhat unfortunate, because it connotes an antagonism between these two. The fact that the governor's proposals are examined by the legislature is indeed a check, but it is more appropriately thought of as a review of the governor's proposals in the light of the legislature's interpretation of the public interest. In other words, it is a double consideration by two agents of the people of the proposals which the governor considers to be the major items of public business for the next fiscal period. This double consideration is basic to our particular system of democratic government. It may result in agreement on the part of the legislature that the governor has made a wise choice from among possible policy alternatives or it may result in a substantial modification of his program. In either case, it is desirable for the legislature to be adequately equipped to do the job in hand.

One of the principal changes which is needed is the overhaul of the legislative machinery used in reviewing the governor's budget. Several possible changes in this area have been suggested in a previous section, including the reorganization of the committee system in each house and the possibility of joint budget hearings. It also seems clear that the legislature needs more and better committee staff and that it certainly needs a post-audit agent in those states where it does not now have such an agent. In many of the states which now have a legislative auditor, his office needs more adequate staffing based on a broad concept of an administrative as well as a financial audit.

These are only suggestions and are not intended to exclude such devices as the legislative council, the legislative reference service or interim committees, all of which are now being used in a number of states. Another device which might prove useful is a department of legislative services. Such a department was recently proposed by the Minnesota Efficiency in Government Commission for that state. The proposed department would be established on a permanent, year-round basis to provide the legislature with a trained staff. Such a staff would assist the legislature in research, bill drafting, care of the the legislative archives, publishing the legislative manual, coding and publishing administrative rules and regulations, and operating the legislative reference library.[12]

Such procedural changes and the more basic change in legislative reapportionment will do much to improve the ability of the legislature to perform adequately its vital function of policy review. However, it also is necessary for the best operation of that body to improve the form in which the governor's policy proposals are presented to it. If the governor's budget is a document which covers only 30 per cent of the state's income and expenditures, it is not a very meaningful policy statement. It is fully as important to legislative control as to gubernatorial control of the executive branch to adopt the revisions in the budget process suggested earlier in this chapter. The legislature is handicapped in its consideration of policy because the major policy device of the executive budget does not live up to its potential usefulness in most states. Before the legislature can examine critically gubernatorial policy,

[12] *How to Achieve Greater Efficiency and Economy in Minnesota's Government,* the report of the Minnesota Efficiency in Government Commission, p. 16. The Commission was established primarily to make recommendations for the improvement of the executive branch. However, in the opening section of their report, they found it necessary to point out that "there is urgent need for strengthening the Legislative Branch of Minnesota's State government. The scope of legislation has increased many-fold in recent years. More than ever before, Legislators need competent assistance in bill drafting and obtaining reference library materials. Legislative committees need trained, year-round staff members. This is especially true in the fields of appropriation and tax legislation."

that policy must be presented to it in the form of a comprehensive and understandable policy statement by the governor. This should be provided by the executive budget. The quest for accountability must be continued in the area of legislation apportionment and of legislative procedure and organization. It also should be pushed in the parallel field of the executive budget so that the governor may present a more meaningful policy document to the legislature. Only if this is done can that body make really informed decisions on major policy.

Another time honored and important avenue of executive accountability is furnished by the popular election of the governor. As was pointed out in the first four chapters, this process stands in need of careful study and revision if it is to serve as an actual reflection of the popular will. However, one of the major defects in the electoral process as a control device is more basic than those resulting from any procedural defect. This defect is found in the fact that so few citizens in many states participate in the electoral process. This low level of participation is evident particularly in the South where usually not more than 30 per cent of the voters participate in the Democratic primary, the crucial stage of the electoral process in that area. This pitifully small percentage of popular participation is due primarily to the results of the one-party system and the isolation of the South from presidential politics. The only real possibility for an improvement of this situation seems to lie in the establishment of a two-party system in the South.

While the South is perhaps the chief offender in terms of neglecting state elections, the other states have no cause for complacency. All of the studies which have been made of the interrelation of state and national elections show that voter interest reaches its highest point in presidential years and its low points in off-year state elections. Furthermore, the percentage of voters who participate in state elections generally is far from warranting any cessation of effort on the part of those who hope that the election process will serve as a real expression of the popular will. It seems unrealistic to the writer to hope that state elections usually will have the drawing power of a presidential race. To the average citizen the latter is not only more colorful but also more important and rightly so. Consequently, it is difficult to prescribe any devices which will draw the reluctant voter from his den in non-presidential years. However, it seems desirable to set gubernatorial and other state elections in non-presidential years in order to center the voter's attention on state affairs. This change probably will not result in as large a turnout as the system used at the present time in some of the states. It does seem to have the advantage, however, of making the election one based on state issues or at least on state personalities. To the extent that this is true, it would be a desirable development, since the more popular attention is centered on this level of government the more popular control is obtained.

Closely related to the question of accountability via the ballot is the possibility that more responsible government can be obtained through the party system. There are many advantages which are claimed by the proponents of the cabinet system for that particular form of party accountability. Nevertheless, it seems more fruitful to consider this problem within the present context of the American party system at the state level than to consider the advantages which might result from the introduction of the concept of party government as it exists in other countries.

If the party system is to provide a means of popular control over government, it must meet at least two minimum criteria. Certainly a fundamental requirement for party accountability is "a two-party system in which the opposition party acts as the critic of the party in power, developing, defining, and presenting the policy alternatives which are necessary for a true choice in reaching public decisions."[13] A second requirement for an accountable party system is that each of the parties have an announced program to which it commits itself and that each party have the internal cohesion necessary to carry out these programs. In addition, it might be suggested that the two-party system can be of maximum effectiveness only if the party in power is able to show sufficient strength to capture control of both the executive and legislative branches of the government. Otherwise, a deadlock may result and the party will be unable to carry out its announced program.

[13] "Toward a More Responsible Two-Party System," A Report of the Committee on Political Parties of the American Political Science Association, *American Political Science Review,* XLIV, Supplement (September, 1950), 18.

When these criteria for a responsible party system are applied at the state level, the party system is found to be sadly lacking. If the first four chapters revealed anything about the nature of political parties at the state level, they showed that an active two-party system exists only in a relatively limited number of states. Certainly it cannot be said to exist in the eleven southern states and in Oklahoma. It also cannot be said to be very robust in Vermont and New Hampshire. Further, it seems to exist only in a very attenuated form in the twenty states which were classified as being normally Democratic or Republican. Even in the remaining fourteen two-party states there is some doubt about the actual health of the two-party system. Each party in these states is strong enough to capture the governorship or one or both houses of the legislature from time to time, but not strong enough to capture both the governorship and both branches of the legislature as well. This raises a question as to whether the parties can produce programs which they can see enacted, since effective policy control is predicated upon the control of both the executive and legislative branches.

Even if we assume that a true two-party situation pevails in fourteen of the 48 states, what of the other 34 states? Is there an effective opposition party in these states to provide the kind of criticism and policy definition which the Committee on Political Parties of the American Political Science Association saw as "the fundamental requirement of accountability"? The answer seems to be no. The same answer must be given to the question of internal cohesion. The single dominant party in the fourteen one-party states does have the degree of internal cohesion which permits responsible party government. This is clearly shown in the analysis in Chapter 7 in which it was discovered that the governor in dealing with the legislature is, in fact, dealing with a series of factions within the major party and sometimes with one or more factions of the minor party. There can be no responsible party government in a one-party state since the party is simply a "holding company" for the various factions which operate within its framework. These factions do not have a permanence or internal cohesion of their own which enables them to serve as a substitute for parties. The party has no program and, hence, cannot be held responsible at the polls for its failure to live up to that program.

It cannot be turned out of office because there is no opposition party which can replace it. It is not subject to opposition criticism because there is no organized opposition. The actions of the governor or of individual legislators or of a legislative faction are subject to criticism and certainly receive as much of it as do their counterparts in the two-party states. But the criticism comes from individuals, from other factions, from would-be gubernatorial candidates, not from a responsible organized opposition which is ready and willing to take over the government if the people will only co-operate by "throwing the rascals out" in the next election. One of the serious effects of the factionalism found in so many of the states is the weakening of party responsibility and the impossibility of popular control through factions.

These comments apply with less force to the normally Democratic and Republican states since in those states there is at least a token opposition party. In so far as this opposition is actual and in so far as the opposition party has any real opportunity to replace the dominant party in power via an election, the normally Democratic and Republican states more closely approach the pattern suggested by the Committee. Unfortunately, the opposition in these states is more apparent than real, and it cannot be said with any degree of accuracy that the two-party system performs its necessary functions in terms of accountability in these states.

The lack of a real two-party system in the majority of the states is a vital flaw in the whole pattern of democratic control. Consequently, it is an area in which the quest for accountability should be pushed with increased vigor. While it has been considered here mainly in the light of executive accountability, it is obvious that it applies with equal force to legislative accountability. In fact, these are simply two aspects of the same problem. An effective two-party system gives the voter real policy alternatives based on the programs of the two major parties. Either of these parties is prepared to take over both branches of the government if given the sanction of the voters through an election and, hence, is a force for improved accountability in both branches of government.

The writer regards the quest for accountability through the development of the two-party system as a very long and hard struggle. The impetus must come from the national level in the form of a two-party national system which will be based on a real presidential campaign in all of the states, not just in doubtful areas. If the 1952 presidential campaign succeeded in making the South a doubtful area and if future presidential campaigns are pushed with vigor in that section, it may be that the year 1952 saw the beginning of an effective two-party system in the South. However, the writer does not share the confidence expressed by some Republican leaders that a new era is now at hand in Dixie. The Republican success in the South in the 1952 presidential election was extremely impressive but may have been more the result of a southern reaction to "Trumanism" and to the popular appeal of General Eisenhower than to any mass shift to the Republican camp. State and local elections in the South in 1952 did not reveal any startling shifts to the Republican banner in state or local allegiance. Apparently, there is still a long road ahead for the Republicans in an attempt to establish the two-party system at the state level in the South. It is the writer's hope that he may be shortly proven wrong in this prediction. It is highly desirable that a two-party system be developed in the South, since it will only be as a result of such a system that more meaningful party government can be established and a higher percentage of the state's citizens lured into participating in state elections. One change which would greatly improve the chances of the success of reconstructing the two-party system would be the revision of the present antiquated electoral college system of presidential elections. If the electoral votes in the southern states could be split under a system such as that outlined in the Lodge-Gossett proposal, it would be a very important step in the increase in the Republican vote in the South. Under this system, a Republican vote for President would count even in a state which the party could not carry outright. Hence, there is the possibility of building up the Republican vote, election by election, since even a rather limited turnout in a small state might be worth at least one electoral vote. Under such a system, attention would continue to be focused on the large states which have the greatest concentration of voters. But some of the attention would spread to the smaller southern states in the hope of picking up a few electoral votes in each state so that the total might overbalance the vote of the larger states. The fact that the votes of the larger states also would be split would encourage this shift of attention.

Even if the two-party system were more firmly established at the national level and if more active campaigning in all of the states were carried out, there would still be a considerable period of lag in the development of a two-party system at the state level. However, the proper atmosphere for the development of such a system would have been created and the gradual development of two active parties in the South seems highly probable.

The foregoing picture of the present systems of responsibility stresses the need for a continuing quest for accountability. The impression may have been created that the states are operating under governments which are irresponsible, but such an impression would be false. Present state governments are far from being unmindful of their dependence upon public consent. Instead, the writer intended to suggest that the present systems of accountability are far from perfect and that the quest for improved systems should be pursued with vigor.

This does not mean that other necessary improvements in state management should be delayed until the system of accountability is perfected. Such changes can proceed hand in hand with those designed to make both the governor and the legislature more readily accountable to the popular will. The excuse that our present system of accountability is imperfect should not be used to block the improvement of the governor's position in the executive branch.

In spite of the defects of the present electoral system, it seems clear that what attention is given to state elections by the citizen is concentrated largely on the gubernatorial race. This means that in so far as popular election now serves as a control device, that device is more effective in relation to the governor than to any other single elected officer. The fact that the governor is elected on a state-wide basis as compared to the single-member district system used in electing most legislators adds to the effectiveness of this control. While the turnout of voters in some states is small, the governor has considerable justification for considering his program a mandate from the people. At least, it is a mandate from those who bothered to vote and under our system of democracy this is the group whose voice is heard. The fact that the state legislators are on the whole not truly representative bodies also reinforces the governor's claim to some preference for his program. It certainly is not desirable that so few of the state's citizens vote, nor is it desirable that the legislature is not a representative body. Nevertheless, these facts are a part of the present political pattern, and until they are changed, the governor must operate within the framework which has been established. Within that framework, the concentration of attention on the gubernatorial race and the state-wide nature of that race make the governor's election a reasonably effective control mechanism.

The concentration of attention on the governorship and the occupant of that office after the governor has been elected is also an important check on his actions. The governors were unanimous in their opinion that the people looked to the governor for the proper conduct of the whole executive branch in spite of the fact that the governor may not, in practice, be able to control all the departments in that branch. This centering of public attention and the publicity which surrounds the governor's every move are certainly deterrents to actions which might be called into question by informed members of the press or radio staffs which cover the capitol beat.

If the popular election of the governor and the constant scrutiny of his actions are to be really meaningful control devices, the governorship must be an office with sufficient power to be an important factor in state government. If the governor is to be a factor for popular control, then he must be able in turn to control the departments which he is supposed to manage. The executive branch must be so organized that the governor can take remedial action if he discovers that a particular department is at fault. If the governor is not given such power, then the check over the executive which is provided by his election and by the publicity which is focused on his office is only an illusion. There is no popular check over the executive branch if a good governor is elected but is powerless to take action to correct the conditions which may have prompted his election or for which he is now being criticized. Responsible government means more than elected government. It means a government which can be held responsible for its actions because it has the power to take action. A government of inaction is not a responsible government. A governor without power is not a responsible governor. Responsible government implies a government which can act and which can be removed if it fails to act or if it acts contrary to the public interest as that interest is interpreted by the majority of the citizens. If this is true, it seems appropriate for the citizens to pass upon the program of the governor in an election held after he has served one term in office. Strangely enough, several four-year states prohibit such expression of citizen opinion by preventing the governor from running for a second term at the close of his first term in office. The people should be given the opportunity to express their approval or disapproval of the governor's program and of the way in which he administered that program. On occasion, the people may not choose wisely, at least in the view of some political scientists. Nevertheless, our system is based on the theory that they will choose wisely over the long run. A careful study of the present day American governorship shows no evidence that this faith has been misplaced or that effective government with democratic control is not possible at the state level.

INDEX